Race and Higher Education

Rethinking Pedagogy in Diverse College Classrooms

Race and Higher Education

Rethinking Pedagogy in Diverse College Classrooms

ANNIE HOWELL

and

FRANK TUITT

Editors

Harvard Educational Review
Reprint Series No. 36

Library of Congress Control Number 2003101240
ISBN 0-916690-38-5

Published by Harvard Educational Review,
an imprint of the Harvard Education Publishing Group

Harvard Education Publishing Group
8 Story Street, 5th Floor
Cambridge, MA 02138

Cover art by John G. Harris
Cover design by Anne Carter

The typefaces used in this book are Kuenstler 480 for the text and Tiepolo for display. Kuenstler 480 is the Bitstream version of Trump Mediaeval, an Old Style font developed by Georg Trump between 1954 and 1962. Tiepolo was designed at AlphaOmega Typography for the International Typeface Corporation in 1987.

CONTENTS

Introduction

Since the late 1960s, colleges and universities have attempted to transform predominantly White institutions into multicultural organizations. With varying degrees of success, some institutions have been able to take advantage of the increasingly racially diverse college population (Hodgkinson, 1995; Mow & Nettles, 1996) and place themselves in an advantageous position over their rivals by making a stronger commitment to diversity. In addition to bringing diverse students to campus, higher education institutions have made modest gains in the area of developing multicultural college curricula, as evident in the existence of ethnic studies departments throughout the United States (Butler, 1996; Sullivan, 1995).

Unfortunately, even though higher education institutions have become more racially diverse over the last forty years, not much has changed in their overall approach to teaching students (Gándara & Maxwell-Jolly, 1999). One consequence of this is a growing concern that traditional pedagogical practices do not serve today's racially diverse student body (Adams, 1992; Banks, 1991). Faculty members, operating on the notion that one pedagogy fits all students, continue to use traditional modes of instruction that create hostile and potentially harmful learning environments (Feagin & Imani, 1993). While the failure to effectively teach racially diverse classrooms affects all students, we are concerned that the consequences may be more costly for students of color than they are for White students.

The College Board Report, "Priming the Pump: Strategies for Increasing the Achievement of Underrepresented Minority Undergraduates" (Gándara & Maxwell-Jolly, 1999), found that students of color at traditionally White institutions perform lower than their White classmates who enter with comparable test scores. Since traditional pedagogical practices tend to be in cultural alignment with White students' experiences, these results are not surprising to us (Tuitt, 2000). Baker (1998) indicates that the "lack of research regarding the classroom behavior of faculty has a negative impact for students of color. The teaching strategies that may be most successful with these students are often different from the traditional strategies most often used. In fact, more appealing teaching-learning strategies for students of color have not been identified" (p. 5).

Race and Higher Education, a collection of articles originally published in the *Harvard Educational Review,* addresses this dilemma from various angles. The book aims to help educators understand how the changing demographics of the college and university students in this country have complicated the manner in which higher education institutions think about what it means to teach in racially diverse classrooms. The chapters herein represent theories and practices in education that at times overlap or even conflict with one another. Although they can be read independently, we believe that these intersections provide powerful insights into the complexity of the topic. For example, the reader may find that one teacher's pedagogical strategy may implicitly challenge the reflections of another teacher's practice, or that the theories of academic researchers included in the third section of this book bring new light to the aforementioned classroom experiences. We believe that this circle of theory informing practice and practice informing theory is crucial to building a strong foundation for today's diverse higher education institutions.

We believe that this topic is particularly relevant at this moment, when some higher education institutions find themselves in the middle of a heated battle to maintain their rights to build and sustain racially diverse campuses. Submerged in a hostile climate of legal challenges to affirmative action and race-based considerations in college admissions, recent court decisions (Sparks, 1994) have challenged educators to articulate clearly the educational purposes and benefits of diversity. Fortunately, several institutions have responded to the call by producing empirical evidence that supports what many have long known experientially — that diversity enhances learning. The first chapter in this book provides a compelling argument in support of this claim.

In "Diversity in Higher Education: Theory and Impact on Educational Outcomes," Patricia Gurin, Eric Dey, Sylvia Hurtado, and Gerald Gurin use both single- and multi-institutional data to examine the effects of classroom diversity and informal interaction among African American, Asian American, Latino/a, and White students on learning and democracy outcomes. Their results emphasize the educational and democratic imperative of maintaining racially diverse college campuses by providing evidence of the continuing importance of affirmative action and diversity efforts as a means of fostering students' academic and social growth. Beyond its compelling conclusion that diversity matters, this chapter reminds us that it is not simply enough to bring diverse students to campus. Higher education institutions also have the responsibility to create conditions under which diversity can flourish. In *Race and Higher Education* we speak to this concern by featuring chapters that focus on classroom pedagogy through the lenses of practice and theory.

In Part Two, Voices Inside Classrooms, the authors provide a critical exploration of their personal and professional experiences in diverse college classrooms. Some of the authors share their vulnerability with the reader by reflecting on startling experiences in which they are challenged to face their hidden assumptions about race and racism. Others focus their attention on specific strategies that have helped them create a safe space for open dialogue and critical self-reflection. Together they represent the struggles and the benefits of establishing new modes of instruction in diverse classrooms.

We open this section with "Against Repetition: Addressing Resistance to Anti-Oppressive Change in the Practices of Learning," by teacher-researcher Kevin Kumashiro. Kumashiro examines how teachers, students, researchers, and supervisors often subscribe to anti-oppressive practices, yet unintentionally resist change that challenges their existing framework. Due to an interest in popular notions of authenticity, tradition, and nature that offer a sense of belonging, adults are often drawn to repetitive behaviors that do little to disrupt oppression. Kumashiro offers a new framework to consider how the other authors in this section challenge, and at times maintain, their notions of repetition in teaching and learning.

For example, in chapter three, "Learning in the Dark: How Assumptions of Whiteness Shape Classroom Knowledge," Frances Maher and Mary Kay Thompson Tetreault reexamine the data from their previously published book, *The Feminist Classroom*. In their original work, these researchers analyzed the classroom from a feminist perspective, but did not address how issues of race affect educational dynamics. In particular, they did not initially include the position of their own Whiteness and its interpersonal and intrapersonal relation to their study. By reanalyzing the data from three classrooms, Maher and Thompson Tetreault focus on the question, "How firmly are assumptions of Whiteness lodged in the academy's ideological frameworks, in its exercise of intellectual domination, and how do they work to shape classroom knowledge?"

While Maher and Thompson Tetreault struggle to understand the impact their own White identity had on their research, the next two authors offer insight into teachers' personal challenges with race and racism in their classrooms. Marilyn Cochran-Smith begins chapter four, "Blind Vision: Unlearning Racism in Teacher Education," with a narrative about an experience in which she was faced with a student of color's honest and critical appraisal of her strategies for antiracist teaching. This startling experience creates an opportunity for Cochran-Smith, a White woman, to reexamine deeply embedded assumptions in her own curriculum and pedagogy. Through a process of "unlearning racism," she comes to see teaching as a "racialized text" with both explicit and implicit subtexts. By illuminating some of these texts, Cochran-Smith invites the reader to examine the subtleties of exclusivity and power in teacher education.

Barbara Vacarr, in "Moving Beyond Polite Correctness: Practicing Mindfulness in the Diverse Classroom," provides a similar perspective through the story of a tension-filled encounter that erupts in her classroom. After the only student of color in a class of twenty-four questions a White student's use of the word "tolerance," Vacarr struggles with the immediate challenge of how to remain present in the classroom as an authority figure. Wanting neither to abandon the situation through silence nor to become the "Super Teacher" who tries to rescue the feelings of her students, Vacarr confronts her own fears and vulnerability. Through the practice of Buddhist mindfulness, Vacarr proposes a way to consider entering the conversation about race and racism with students that goes beyond the typical multicultural training.

Following these reflections on teaching are two chapters that provide pedagogical strategies for exploring race and diversity in a theoretical and personally challenging way. In chapter six, "Talking about Race, Learning about Racism: The Application of Racial Identity Development Theory in the Classroom," Beverly Daniel Tatum writes that "when students are given the opportunity to explore race-related material in a classroom where both their affective and intellectual responses are acknowledged and addressed, their level of understanding is greatly enhanced." In her graduate course on the psychology of racism, students explore the racial development theories of

Helms (1990) and Cross (1991). These theories build a foundation for students to understand the social and psychological reality of racism and the forms of resistance they engage in as they go through the process of learning about race.

Another pedagogical tool is offered by Sondra Perl in the final chapter in this section, "Teaching and Practice: Composing Texts, Composing Lives." Perl uses composition to help students explore their ideas about the structural limits that have been imposed on them by our society. By writing personal responses to the literature introduced in her curriculum, adult students are encouraged to "go to the edge" of their understanding. One assignment, a written dialogue between the multiple characters in these works, pushes students to critically examine their disparate voices and how they relate to the students' own theories of power. Through the investigation of personal experiences, the teacher and students in this course create a space where they are free to consider the possibilities for challenge and change.

Building on the experiences of teachers featured in Part Two, the authors in Part Three provide a variety of lenses through which we may find some ideas as to how educators might reconceptualize their practice to teach in racially diverse college classrooms. For example, chapter eight lets us in on a dialogue about race, culture, and language between Donaldo Macedo and Paulo Freire. In this conversation, Macedo and Freire address criticisms of Freire's work along the lines of gender and race. This dialogue not only challenges the frequent misinterpretations of his leading philosophical ideas by conservative and some liberal educators, but also embraces contemporary educational issues by discussing what it means to educate for critical citizenry in the increasingly multiracial and multicultural world of the twenty-first century. In chapter nine, "Freire and a Feminist Pedagogy of Difference," Kathleen Weiler continues the conversation on Freire's profound work by framing her critical analysis through a feminist epistemology. In this essay, Weiler illustrates how a feminist pedagogy offers a more complex vision of liberatory pedagogy by concentrating on the role of authority, the value of personal experience, and the impact of having a diverse background. In his afterword, "Realizing a More Inclusive Pedagogy," Frank Tuitt draws on the work of several scholars — including several featured in this book — to conceptualize transformative ways of teaching in racially diverse college classrooms. Searching for a more inclusive practice, Tuitt outlines a variety of pedagogical models that have the potential to make the classroom more accessible to all students, regardless of their racial background.

All of the authors featured in *Race and Higher Education* speak to the challenge of educating an ever more racially diverse society. While there is no simple or easy answer for addressing the many challenges diversity presents educators today, the authors offer several ideas and strategies for maximizing the educational benefits existing in racially diverse classrooms. As our nation becomes more and more segregated (Orfield, 2002), college classrooms may be our last hope for producing citizens who are prepared to work without scapegoating, live without fear, and flourish in a democratic society.

Annie Howell
Frank Tuitt

REFERENCES

Adams, M. (1992). Cultural inclusion in the American college classroom. In N. V. N. Chism & L. L. B. Border (Eds.), *New directions for teaching and learning: Teaching for diversity* (vol. 49, pp. 5–17). San Francisco: Jossey-Bass.

Baker, P. (1998). Students' perception of classroom factors that impact success for African-American students in higher education settings. Doctoral dissertation, Northern Illinois University, 1998. *DAI-A, 59*, 1434.

Banks, J. (1991). Multicultural literacy and curriculum reform. *Education Horizons Quarterly, 69*, 135–140.

Butler, J. E. (1996). Complicating the question: Black studies and women's studies. In C. Turner, M. Garcia, A. Nora, & L. I. Rendon (Eds.), *Racial and ethnic diversity in higher education* (pp. 108–114). Needham Heights, MA: Simon & Schuster.

Cross, W. E., Jr. (1991). *Shades of Black: Diversity in African-American identity*. Philadelphia: Temple University Press.

Feagin, J. R., & Imani, N. (1993). Black in a White world. In J. R. Feagin & M. P. Sikes, *Living with racism: The Black middle-class experience*. Boston: Beacon Press.

Gándara, P., & Maxwell-Jolly, J. (1999). *Priming the pump: Strategies for increasing the achievement of underrepresented minority undergraduates*. New York: College Board.

Helms, J. E. (Ed.). (1990). *Black and White racial identity: Theory, research, and practice*. Westport, CT: Greenwood Press.

Hodgkinson, H. L. (1995). Demographic imperatives for the future. In B. P. Bowser, T. Jones, & G. A. Young (Eds.), *Toward the multicultural university* (pp. 1–19). Westport, CT: Praeger.

Mow, S. L., & Nettles, M. T. (1996). Minority student access to, and persistence and performance in college: A review of the trends and research in literature. In C. Turner, M. Garcia, A. Nora, & L. I. Rendon (Eds.), *Racial and ethnic diversity in higher education* (pp. 594–617). Needham Heights, MA: Simon & Schuster.

Orfield, G., (2001). *School segregation on the rise despite growing diversity among school-aged children: A new study from The Civil Rights Project*. Available at http://www.gse.harvard.edu/news/features/orfield07172001.html

Sparks, S. (1994). Hopwood v. State of Tex., 861 F.Supp. (W.D. Texas).

Sullivan, A. V. S. (1995). Realizing the vision: Transforming the curriculum through women's studies. *Journal of General Education, 44*(1), 45–57.

Tuitt, F. A. (2000). *Towards a more inclusive pedagogy: Rethinking how we teach racially diverse college classrooms*. Unpublished manuscript, Harvard Graduate School of Education, Cambridge, MA.

PART ONE

Racial and Ethnic Diversity
in Higher Education

Diversity and Higher Education:
Theory and Impact
on Educational Outcomes

PATRICIA GURIN
ERIC L. DEY
SYLVIA HURTADO
GERALD GURIN

Educators in U.S. higher education have long argued that affirmative action policies are justified because they ensure the creation of the racially and ethnically diverse student bodies essential to providing the best possible educational environment for students, white and minority alike. Yet until recently these arguments have lacked empirical evidence and a strong theoretical rationale to support the link between diversity and educational outcomes. As Jonathan Alger, former counsel for the American Association of University Professors, argues: "The unfinished homework in the affirmative action debate concerns the development of an articulated vision — supported by a strong evidentiary basis — of the educational benefits of racial diversity in higher education" (1998, p. 74). This suggests not only that educators must clarify the conceptual link between diversity and learning in educational practice, but also that educational researchers play a key role in providing evidence on whether diversity contributes to achieving the central goals of higher education. The purpose of this article is both to provide a theory of how diversity can be linked to educational outcomes in higher education and to test this theory using national data and data from students at the University of Michigan — an institution that has faced affirmative action legal challenges.

In the 1978 case *Regents of the University of California v. Bakke*, U.S. Supreme Court Justice Lewis Powell wrote the pivotal opinion, arguing that the "atmosphere of 'speculation, experiment and creation' — so essential to the quality of higher education — is widely believed to be promoted by a diverse student body. . . . It is not too much to say that the nation's future depends upon leaders trained through wide exposure to the ideas and mores of students as diverse as this Nation of many peoples"

Harvard Educational Review Vol. 72 No. 3 Fall 2002, 330–366

(p. 2760).[1] Since the *Bakke* decision, the educational benefits of diversity as a compelling governmental interest have provided the primary justification for affirmative action at selective institutions across the country.[2] However, the diversity argument has not been supported in all lower court cases since the original *Bakke* decision. For example, in *Hopwood v. University of Texas*, the Fifth Circuit Court of Appeals denied that diversity has any impact on educational experience: "The use of race, in and of itself, to choose students simply achieves a student body that looks different. Such a criterion is no more rational on its own terms than would be choices based upon the physical size or blood type of applicants" (*Hopwood*, 1996, p. 950). If this statement were true, there would be no basis for arguing that there was a compelling interest in a racially/ethnically diverse student body. However, such a conclusion flies in the face of the role that race and ethnicity have played in our polity and society. As Victor Bolden, David Goldberg, and Dennis Parker point out, "No constitutional compromise was required over blood type; no civil war was fought and no Southern Manifesto signed over physical size" (1999, p. 27).

Since the *Hopwood* decision, courts across the country have produced conflicting rulings on diversity as a compelling governmental interest. In *Smith v. University of Washington Law School* (2001), the Ninth Circuit Court of Appeals affirmed the district court's ruling that *Bakke* is still good law and stands for the proposition that educational diversity can be a compelling governmental interest that justifies race-sensitive admissions programs. In *Johnson v. Board of Regents of the University of Georgia* (2001), the Eleventh Circuit Court of Appeals declined to rule on the question of whether diversity is a compelling governmental interest but struck down the University of Georgia's admissions policy on the grounds that it was not "narrowly tailored" to that interest. In two cases involving the University of Michigan, one challenging its undergraduate admissions and the other its law school admissions, two different rulings on diversity as a compelling governmental interest were given at the district court level. In *Gratz v. Bollinger, et al.* (2000), the court ruled on summary judgment in favor of the University of Michigan, upholding its current undergraduate admissions policy and finding that diversity was a compelling governmental interest that justified the policy. In *Grutter v. Bollinger, et al.* (2002), the court held that the educational benefits of diversity were not a compelling state interest, and even if they were, the law school's policy was not "narrowly tailored" to the interest of diversity. Both cases were appealed to the Sixth Circuit Court of Appeals, which heard arguments in December 2001. This court overturned the lower court decision in *Grutter*, deciding in favor of the university and setting the stage for an appeal to the U.S. Supreme Court.[3] It is clear from these now-famous higher education cases that the question of whether *Bakke* is still good law and whether diversity is a compelling state interest justifying the use of race-sensitive admissions policies remains controversial. It is also clear that diversity is the primary basis for arguing the constitutionality of using race as one of many factors in college admission, and thus research on *whether* and *how* diversity might affect education is of crucial legal and practical importance.

It is important to explain how higher education might expose students to racial and ethnic diversity, since they may experience it in several ways. First, students attend colleges with different levels of racial/ethnic diversity in their student bodies. This has been termed *structural diversity*, or the numerical representation of diverse groups (Hurtado, Milem, Clayton-Peterson, & Allen, 1999). Although structural diversity increases the probability that students will encounter others of diverse backgrounds, given the U.S. history of race relations, simply attending an ethnically diverse college does not guarantee that students will have the meaningful intergroup interactions that social psychologist Gordon Allport (1954) suggested in his classic book, *The Nature of Prejudice*, are important for the reduction of racial prejudice. For this reason, a second definition of racial/ethnic diversity is important, one that involves both the *frequency* and the *quality* of intergroup interaction as keys to meaningful diversity experiences during college, or what we term *informal interactional diversity*. Although these informal interactions with racially diverse peers can occur in many campus contexts, the majority of them occur outside of the classroom. Such interactions may include informal discussions, daily interactions in residence halls, campus events, and social activities (Antonio, 1998; Chang, 1996). Finally, a third form of diversity experience includes learning about diverse people (content knowledge) and gaining experience with diverse peers in the classroom, or what we term *classroom diversity*. We contend that the impact of racial/ethnic diversity on educational outcomes comes primarily from engagement with diverse peers in the informal campus environment and in college classrooms. Structural diversity is a necessary but insufficient condition for maximal educational benefits; therefore, the theory that guides our study is based on students' actual engagement with diverse peers.

Recent reviews of educational research, as well as summaries of new studies, present an emerging body of scholarship that speaks directly to the benefits of a racially/ethnically diverse postsecondary educational experience (Hurtado et al., 1999; Milem & Hakuta, 2000; Orfield, 2001; Smith, 1997). The evidence for the diversity rationale for affirmative action has come from four approaches to research:

1. students' subjective assessments of the benefits they receive from interacting with diverse peers (e.g., Orfield & Whitla, 1999);
2. faculty assessments about the impact of diversity on student learning or on other outcomes related to the missions of their universities (e.g., Maruyama, Moreno, Gudeman, & Marin, 2000);
3. analyses of monetary and nonmonetary returns to students and the larger community in terms of graduation rates, attainment of advanced and professional degrees that prepare students to become leaders in underserved communities, personal income or other postcollege attainment that results from attending highly selective institutions where affirmative action is critical to achieving diversity (e.g., Bowen & Bok, 1998; Bowen, Bok, & Burkhart, 1999; Komaromy et al., 1997);
4. analyses tying diversity experience during the college years to a wide variety of educational outcomes (Astin, 1993a, 1993b; Chang, 1996; Chang, Witt-Sandis, & Hakuta, 1999; Hurtado, 2001; Pascarella, Edison, Nora, Hagedorn, & Terenzini, 1996; Terenzini, Rendon et al., 1994; Terenzini, Springer, Pascarella, & Nora, 1994).

It is important to note that, across these different approaches and different samples of students and faculty, researchers have found similar results showing that a wide variety of individual, institutional, and societal benefits are linked with diversity experiences.

The research reported here is an example of the fourth approach in which we compare how different types of diversity experiences are associated with differences in educational outcomes among students from different racial and ethnic backgrounds. We first present the theoretical foundation for the educational value of racial/ethnic diversity, and then we examine the effects of two kinds of diversity experiences — diversity in the formal classroom and in the informal campus environment — on different educational outcomes.

THEORETICAL FOUNDATIONS FOR THE EFFECT OF DIVERSITY

Racial and ethnic diversity may promote a broad range of educational outcomes, but we focus on two general categories. Learning outcomes include active thinking skills, intellectual engagement and motivation, and a variety of academic skills. Democracy outcomes include perspective-taking, citizenship engagement, racial and cultural understanding, and judgment of the compatibility among different groups in a democracy. The impact of diversity on learning and democracy outcomes is believed to be especially important during the college years because students are at a critical developmental stage, which takes place in institutions explicitly constituted to promote late adolescent development.

The Critical Importance of Higher Education

In essays that profoundly affected our understanding of social development, psychologist Erik Erikson (1946, 1956) introduced the concept of identity and argued that late adolescence and early adulthood are the unique times when a sense of personal and social identity is formed. Identity involves two important elements: a persistent sameness within oneself and a persistent sharing with others. Erikson theorized that identity develops best when young people are given a psychosocial moratorium — a time and a place in which they can experiment with different social roles before making permanent commitments to an occupation, to intimate relationships, to social and political groups and ideas, and to a philosophy of life. We argue that such a moratorium should ideally involve a confrontation with diversity and complexity, lest young people passively make commitments based on their past experiences, rather than actively think and make decisions informed by new and more complex perspectives and relationships.

Institutions of higher education can provide an opportunity for such a psychosocial moratorium, thus supporting young adults through this identity development stage. Residential colleges and universities provide many students with an opportunity to experiment with new ideas, new relationships, and new roles. Peer influences play a normative role in this development, and students are able to explore options and possibilities before making permanent adult commitments. Yet not all institutions of higher education serve this developmental function equally well (Pascarella & Terenzini, 1991). Higher education is especially influential when its social milieu is different from students' home and community background and when it is diverse and complex enough to encourage intellectual experimentation and recognition of varied future possibilities. We maintain that attending college in one's home environment or replicating the home community's social life and expectations in a homogeneous college that is simply an extension of the home community impedes the personal struggle and conscious thought that are so important for identity development.

Sociologist Theodore Newcomb's classic study of students at Bennington College (1943) supported Erikson's assertion that late adolescence is a time to determine one's relationship to the sociopolitical world and affirmed the developmental impact of the college experience. Newcomb's study demonstrated that political and social attitudes — what Erikson would call one aspect of social identity — are quite malleable in late adolescence and that change occurred particularly in those students to whom Bennington presented new and different ideas and attitudes. Peer influence was critical in shaping the attitudinal changes that Newcomb documented. Follow-ups with these students showed that the attitudes formed during the college experience were quite stable, even twenty-five (Newcomb, Koenig, Flacks, & Warwick, 1967) and fifty years later (Alwin, Cohen, & Newcomb, 1991).

Developmental theorists emphasize that discontinuity and discrepancy spur cognitive growth. Jean Piaget (1971, 1975/1985) termed this process *disequilibrium*. Drawing on these theories, psychologist Diane Ruble (1994) offers a model that ties developmental change to life transitions such as going to college. Transitions are significant because they present new situations about which individuals know little and in which they will experience uncertainty. The early phase of a transition, what Ruble calls construction, is especially important, since people have to seek information in order to make sense of the new situation. Under these conditions individuals are likely to undergo cognitive growth unless they are able to retreat to a familiar world. Ruble's model gives special importance to the first year of college, since it is during this time that classroom and social relationships discrepant from students' home environments become especially important in fostering cognitive growth.

Writing long before the controversies about diversity and affirmative action became politically important or were studied academically, Erikson, Newcomb, and Piaget were not making an explicit case for racial/ethnic diversity. Nonetheless, their arguments about the significance of discontinuity and the power of a late adolescence/early adulthood moratorium provide a strong theoretical rationale for the importance of bringing students from varied backgrounds together to create a diverse and complex learning environment.

Campus environments and policies that foster interaction among diverse students are discontinuous from the home environments of many American students. Because of the racial separation that persists in this country, most students have lived in segregated communities before coming to college. The work of Gary Orfield and associates documents a deepening segregation in U.S. public schools (Orfield, 2001; Orfield, Bachmeier, James, & Eitle, 1997; Orfield & Kurlaender, 1999; Orfield & Miller, 1998). This segregated precollege educational background means that many students, White and minority alike, enter college without experience with diverse peers. Colleges that diversify their student bodies and institute policies that foster genuine interaction across race and ethnicity provide the first opportunity for many students to learn from peers with different cultures, values, and experiences. Genuine interaction goes far beyond mere contact and includes learning about difference in background, experience, and perspectives, as well as getting to know one another individually in an intimate enough way to discern common goals and personal qualities. In this kind of interaction — in and out of the classroom — diverse peers will learn from each other. This can be viewed as extending the traditional conception of a liberal education as one "intended to break down the narrow certainties and provincial vision with which we are born" (Association of American Colleges and Universities, 1985, p. 22).

Learning Outcomes

As educators, we might expect that a curriculum that deals explicitly with social and cultural diversity and a learning environment in which diverse students interact frequently with one another would affect the content of what is learned. However, based on the recent social psychological research that we discuss below, we consider the less obvious notion that features of the learning environment affect students' modes of thought. In this study we hypothesize that a curriculum that exposes students to knowledge about race and ethnicity acquired through the curriculum and classroom environment and to interactions with peers from diverse racial and ethnic backgrounds in the informal college environment will foster a learning environment that supports active thinking and intellectual engagement.

Research in social psychology over the past twenty years has shown that active engagement in learning and thinking cannot be assumed (Bargh, 1997). This research confirms that much apparent thinking and thoughtful action are actually automatic, or what psychologist Ellen Langer (1978) calls mindless. To some extent, mindlessness is the result of previous learning that has become so routine that thinking is unnecessary. Instead, scripts or schemas that are activated and operate automatically guide these learned routines. Some argue that mindlessness is necessary because there are too many stimuli in the world to which to pay attention. It is more efficient for us to select only a few stimuli or, better still, to go on automatic pilot — to be what some people call cognitive misers (Fiske, 1993; Hilton & von Hippel, 1996).

Psychologist John Bargh (1997) reviews both historical and recent research evidence showing that automatic psychological processes play a pervasive role in all aspects of everyday thinking. He concludes that automatic thinking is evident not only in perceptual processes (such as categorization) and in the execution of perceptional and motor skills (such as driving and typing), but that it is also pervasive in evaluation, emotional reactions, determination of goals, and social behavior itself. Bargh uses the term *preconscious* to describe processes that act as mental servants to take over from conscious, effortful thinking. One of our tasks as educators is to interrupt these automatic processes and facilitate active thinking in our students.

In one early study indicating the pervasiveness of automatic thinking, Langer (1978) described the many positive psychological benefits that people derive from using active, effortful, conscious modes of thought. She also argued that such thinking helps people develop new ideas and ways of processing information that may have been available to them but were simply not often used. In several experimental studies, she showed that such thinking increases alertness and greater mental activity, which fosters better learning and supports the developmental goals of higher education.

What are the conditions that encourage effortful, mindful, and conscious modes of thought? Langer (1978) contends that people will engage in such modes of thought when they encounter a situation for which they have no script or when the environment demands more than their current scripts provide, such as an encounter discrepant with their past experience. These conditions are similar to what sociologist Rose Coser (1975) calls complex social structures — situations where we encounter people who are unfamiliar to us, when these people challenge us to think or act in new ways, when people and relationships change and thus produce unpredictability, and when people we encounter hold different expectations of us. Coser shows that people who function within complex social structures develop a clearer and stronger sense of individuality and a deeper understanding of the social world.[4]

The specific environmental features that Langer and Coser suggest will promote mental activity are compatible with cognitive-developmental theories. In general, those theories posit that cognitive growth is fostered by discontinuity and discrepancy (as in Piaget's notion of disequilibrium). To learn or grow cognitively, individuals need to recognize cognitive conflicts or contradictions, situations that, as psychologist Diane Ruble (1994) argues, then lead to a state of uncertainty, instability, and possibly anxiety (see also Acredolo & O'Connor, 1991; Berlyne, 1970; Doise & Palmonaari, 1984). Ruble states:

> Such a state may occur for a number of reasons. . . . It may be generated either internally via the recognition of incompatible cognitions or externally during social interaction. The latter is particularly relevant to many types of life transitions, because such transitions are likely to alter the probability of encountering people whose viewpoints differ from one's own. (1994, p. 171)

Racial and ethnic diversity in the student body and university efforts to foster opportunities for diverse students to interact and learn from each other in and out of the classroom offer college students who have grown up in the racially segregated United States the very features that these theories suggest will foster active thinking and personal development. These features include:

- novelty and unfamiliarity that occurs upon the transition to college
- opportunities to identify discrepancies between students with distinct pre-college social experiences
- diversity as a source of multiple and different perspectives[5]

A White student, evaluating a course on intergroup relations that one of the authors taught at the University of Michigan, conveys the importance of these facets of diversity:

> I come from a town in Michigan where everyone was white, middle-class and generally pretty closed-down to the rest of the world, although we didn't think so. It never touched us, so I never questioned the fact that we were "normal" and everyone else was "different." Listening to other students in the class, especially the African American students from Detroit and other urban areas just blew me away. We only live a few hours away and yet we live in completely separate worlds. Even more shocking was the fact that they knew about "my world" and I knew nothing about theirs. Nor did I think that this was even a problem at first. I realize now that many people like me can go through life and not have to see another point of view, that somehow we are protected from it. The beginning for me was when I realized that not everyone shares the same views as I, and that our different experiences have a lot to do with that.

One of our primary goals was to discover whether such encounters with diversity contribute to learning outcomes, not only among students at the University of Michigan but also among those attending a variety of four-year institutions across the country. A second key goal was to understand the extent to which these same diversity experiences contribute to the development of the skills and dispositions that students will need to be leaders in a pluralistic democracy.

Democracy Outcomes

From the time the founding fathers debated what form U.S. democracy should take — representational or directly participatory — education has been seen as the key to achieving an informed citizenry. In the compromise they reached involving both representation and broad participation, education was the mechanism that was to make broad participation possible. Benjamin Barber (1998) argues that it was Jefferson, certainly no advocate of diversity, who most forcefully argued that broad civic participation required education: "It remained clear to Jefferson to the end of his life that a theory of democracy that is rooted in active participation and continuing consent by each generation of citizens demands a civic pedagogy rooted in the obligation to educate all who would be citizens" (p. 169). To be sure, Jefferson was talking about education for those he defined as the body of citizens and not for the many who were not citizens at that time.

If education is the very foundation of democracy, how do experiences with racial/ethnic diversity affect the process of learning to become citizens? We contend that students educated in diverse institutions will be more motivated and better able to participate in an increasingly heterogeneous and complex society. In *Democratic Education in an Age of Difference*, Richard Guarasci and Grant Cornwell (1997) concur, claiming that "community and democratic citizenship are strengthened when undergraduates understand and experience social connections with those outside of their often parochial 'autobiographies,' and when they experience the way their lives are necessarily shaped by others" (p. xiii).

However, the compatibility of diversity and democracy is not self-evident. Current critics of multicultural education worry that identities based on race, ethnicity, gender, class, and other categorizations are inimical to the unity needed for democracy. Yet the tension between unity and diversity, however politically charged, is not new in the United States.

In *Fear of Diversity*, Arlene Saxonhouse (1992) describes how the pre-Socratic playwrights as well as Plato and Aristotle dealt with the fear that "differences bring on chaos and thus demand that the world be put into an orderly pattern" (p. x). While Plato envisioned a city in which unity and harmony would be based on the shared characteristics of a homogeneous citizenry, Aristotle recognized the value of heterogeneity and welcomed the diverse. Saxonhouse writes: "Aristotle embraces diversity as the others had not. . . . The typologies that fill almost every page of Aristotle's *Politics* show him uniting and separating, finding underlying unity and significant differences" (p. 235). Aristotle advanced a political theory in which unity could be achieved through differences and contended that democracy based on such a unity would be more likely to thrive than one based on homogeneity. What makes democracy work, according to Aristotle, is equality among citizens (admittedly, in his time only free men, not women or slaves) who hold diverse perspectives and whose relationships are governed by freedom and rules of civil discourse. It is a multiplicity of perspectives and discourses in response to the inevitable conflicts that arise when citizens have differing points of view, not unanimity, that help democracy thrive (Pitkin & Shumer, 1982).

Diversity, plurality, equality, and freedom are also implied in Piaget's theory of intellectual and moral development. He argues that children and adolescents can best develop a capacity to understand the ideas and feelings of others — what he calls perspective-taking — and move to a more advanced stage of moral reasoning when they interact with peers who have different points of view. Both differing perspectives and equality in relationships are important for intellectual and moral development (Piaget, 1965). In a homogeneous environment in which young people are not forced to confront the relativity or limitations of their point of view, they are likely to conform to a single perspective defined by an authority. In a hierarchical environment in which young people are not obliged to discuss and argue with others on an equal basis, they are not likely to do the cognitive and emotional work that is required to understand how other people think and feel. These cognitive and emotional processes promote the moral development needed to make a pluralistic democracy work.

In the United States, however, common conceptions of democracy do not treat difference as being compatible with unity. In general, popular understandings of democracy and citizenship take one of two forms: 1) a liberal individualist conception in which citizens participate by voting for public servants to represent them and by other individual acts, and 2) a direct participatory conception in which people from similar backgrounds who are familiar with each other come together to debate the common good, as in the New England town meeting. Both of these conceptions privilege individuals and similarities rather than groups and differences.

The increasingly heterogeneous U.S. population challenges these popular conceptions of democracy. Consequently, we are now facing cultural, academic, and political debates over the extent to which American democracy can survive increasing heterogeneity and group-based social and political claims. Yet, it is clear that an ethnic hierarchy or one-way assimilation, both of which call for muting differences and cultural identities, is much less likely to prevail than in the past (Fredrickson, 1999).

The theories of Aristotle and Piaget both suggest that difference and democracy can be compatible. The conditions deemed important for this compatibility include the presence of diverse others and diverse perspectives, equality among peers, and discussion according to rules of civil discourse. We hypothesize that these conditions foster the orientations that students will need to be citizens and leaders in the postcollege world: perspective-taking, mutuality and reciprocity, acceptance of conflict as a normal part of life, capacity to perceive differences and commonalties both within and between social groups, interest in the wider social world, and citizen participation.

METHOD

Samples

We tested our theory using two longitudinal databases — one from the University of Michigan and one from a national sample of college students — that would allow us to parallel our analysis as closely as possible. The Michigan Student Survey (MSS) was initiated to monitor students' response to the University of Michigan's diversity focus. This focus was the result of the Michigan Mandate, a major initiative designed both to reaffirm the centrality of diversity to the university's institutional mission and to directly address racial concerns that arose on campus during the late 1980s. The MSS database is a single-institution survey of students who entered the University of Michigan in 1990 and a follow-up survey four years later. The Michigan sample examined here included 1,129 White students, 187 African American students, and 266 Asian American students. (Native American and Latino/a students were not included due to their small sample sizes.) The MSS concluded its data collection three years before the affirmative action lawsuits were filed against the University of Michigan.

The Michigan data were particularly useful in examining the effects of experiences with racial/ethnic diversity on student outcomes. For most of its students the University of Michigan's racial and ethnic diversity create the discrepancy, discontinuity, and disequilibrium that may produce the active thinking and intellectual engagement that educators demand. At the time the MSS was conducted, 92 percent of White students and 52 percent of African American students came to the University of Michigan from segregated communities. As groups, only Asian American and Latino/a students came to the University having lived and gone to school in environments where they were not in the majority. Thus, the university's conscious effort to help students experience diversity in and out of the classroom provide the very features that foster active, conscious, and effortful thinking.

The second dataset came from the Cooperative Institutional Research Program (CIRP), a national survey conducted by the Higher Educational Research Institute at

UCLA. The CIRP included 11, 383 students from 184 institutions who were surveyed upon entering college in 1985 and again four years later (see Astin, 1993b, for administration details). The national sample included 216 African American, 496 Asian American, 206 Latino/a, and 10,465 White students attending predominantly White, four-year institutions. (Native Americans were not included due to their small sample size.) In order to parallel important controls and analyses of the CIRP with those of the Michigan dataset, we selected only students in their fourth year (1989) who participated in the four-year follow-up and in a subsequent nine-year follow-up survey. This was done to control for the level of segregation of the students' neighborhood before they entered college (a key retrospective question included only in the nine-year follow-up). The CIRP is the largest national dataset that incorporates questions about diversity that can be used to study students' educational outcomes longitudinally. The survey was conducted during an era when there were numerous racial incidents on college campuses and racial climates were highly variable according to student reports (Hurtado, 1992).

Although developed for a wide range of educational purposes, the CIRP longitudinal study was the closest national parallel to data collected locally at the University of Michigan. By examining these two datasets, we were able to identify broad patterns of educational benefits both within a single institution and across varying institutional contexts. These patterns suggest that our findings at the University of Michigan were not an anomaly but generalizable to many types of campuses. In both the national and institutional studies we used parallel controls for student demographic characteristics that could influence involvement in diversity experiences and the learning and democracy outcomes, as well as controls for pretest measures of most of the educational outcomes. Therefore, we focus here on the effects of diversity experiences on student outcomes, controlling for relevant student background characteristics and institutional characteristics, which are pertinent in the national, multi-institutional analyses.

Measures

Tables 1 and 2 show the independent and dependent measures employed in both the multi- and single-institution analyses. These are described as control variables, institutional characteristics (for the multi-institutional sample), diversity experiences, and educational outcomes. Many of the measures were constructed as indices, with alpha reliabilities shown in these tables.

Control Variables   Table 1 shows that the two studies included comparable measures of control variables: ethnic/racial composition of the high school and of the precollege neighborhood, gender, high school cumulative grade point average, total SAT scores, and parental education as a measure of the student's socioeconomic background.[6] While these are not of primary substantive interest, they are important considerations in the analyses because they represent the previous choices, preferences, and experiences of students that, unless taken into account, could have influenced the outcomes and caused an overestimation of the effects of experiences with diversity. In instances where the measures of the expected outcomes were also available on the entrance questionnaire, the entrance measures were included as control variables.

In the national study we also controlled for institutional features that might foster classroom and informal diversity experiences and/or the educational outcomes of interest in this study. In all multi-institutional analyses, we controlled for the percentage of minority enrollments in order to distinguish the effects of classroom and informal diversity interactions from the mere presence of diverse students on campus. We also controlled for two additional diversity-related institutional features obtained from faculty responses. One is an index of academic emphasis on diversity, obtained by asking faculty to assess how much they emphasize diversity in their teaching, research, and writing. The second index represents institutional emphasis on diversity, measured by faculty perceptions of the priority the institution placed on diversity. These measures have been used in previous studies (for reliability indices see Astin, 1993b; Dey, 1991; Hurtado, 1992). Finally, in *all* analyses of the national data we controlled for characteristics of institutions that are typically controlled for in multi-institutional studies such as the CIRP: whether the school is private or public, a university or a four-year college, and the selectivity of the institution (Pascarella & Terenzini, 1991).[7]

Diversity Experiences   Although different questions were asked in the two studies, each provided measures of both classroom and informal interactional diversity. In the Michigan Student Study, classroom diversity was measured in the 1994 fourth-year survey using two questions. One question asked students to assess the extent to which they had been exposed in classes to "information/activities devoted to understanding other racial/ethnic groups and inter-racial ethnic relationships." The other asked students if they had taken a course during college that had an important impact on their "views of racial/ethnic diversity and multiculturalism."

Classroom diversity involves more than just exposure to content about racial and ethnic groups. In the MSS, students' answers likely referred to classes that exposed them to racially/ethnically diverse students as well as to curriculum content. In 1994, when these students were seniors, they had to have taken a course that met the Race and Ethnicity Requirement (R&E) for which the Literature, Sciences, and Arts College had approved 111 courses. We obtained the racial/ethnic distribution of students in those courses for 1993–1994, the year that the MSS gathered senior data. Two-thirds of these courses had enrolled between 20 percent and 80 percent students of color. Consequently, there is a strong probability that the majority of classes White students were referring to in the MSS measure of classroom diversity included at least 20 percent students of color.

The CIRP asked fourth-year students if they had taken an ethnic studies course in college. Enrollment data for these courses were not available; however, there is no reason to believe that the ethnic studies courses attracted fewer students of color than the R&E courses did at the University of Michigan, unless one of the institutions fell into the group of colleges with very little diversity — a factor that we controlled for using institutional enrollment data.

TABLE 1   *Measures of Independent Variables in the Analysis*

Control Variables	*CIRP Data*	*Michigan Student Study (MSS)*
Student Background:		
Gender (female)	Dichotomous measure	Dichotomous measure
SAT scores	Obtained on entrance survey	Obtained from Michigan Registrar
Cumulative high school GPA	Obtained on entrance survey	Obtained from Michigan Registrar
Parents' education level	Obtained on entrance survey	Measured on entrance/senior survey
Racial composition of the high school	Not available at entrance, but similar items captured on the 9-year follow-up survey	Measured on entrance survey
Racial composition of the neighborhood	Not available at entrance, but similar items captured on the 9-year follow-up survey	Measured on entrance survey
Pretests on selected measures*	Measured on entrance survey	Measured on entrance survey
Institutional Characteristics:		
Selectivity of the college	Average SAT of entering freshmen	Not applicable—institutional characteristics are a constant for all students
Private/public control	Dichotomous measure	
University/four-year college	Dichotomous measure	
Percentage students of color (African Americans, Latino/as, Native Americans, and Asian Americans)	Derived from IPEDS data on student enrollment for each institution	
Faculty diversity emphasis	Aggregate measure of faculty incorporation of information on women and racial/ethnic groups into research, readings for courses, and writing **	No faculty level data were collected
Institutional emphasis on diversity	Aggregate measure of faculty responses to institutional diversity priorities **	No faculty level data were collected
Diversity Experiences:		
Informal interaction	Index of items (α = .561): attended cultural awareness workshop, discussed racial issues, and socialized with a person of a different race	Index of four items (α = .780): amount of contact with students from other racial groups, proportion of six best friends from other racial groups, positive interaction with diverse peers
Classroom diversity	Enrollment in an ethnic studies course	Index of two items (α = .507): exposure in classes to information/ activities devoted to understanding other racial groups, and enrollment in a course that had an impact on views on racial/ethnic diversity
Diversity events/dialogues	Not available	Index of six items (α = .612): number of multicultural events attended and participation in a dialogue group

* Dependent measures with pretests at entrance shown in Table 2

** Derived from faculty survey at participating institutions, reported in Astin (1993b)

Exposure to diverse peers, however, does not only occur in college classrooms. For this reason, experiences with informal interactional diversity were measured in both studies. In the CIRP, this experience was measured by an index summarizing responses to three questions asked in 1989 about the extent to which students, over their college years, had socialized with someone from a different racial/ethnic group, had discussed racial issues, and had attended a racial/cultural awareness workshop. In the MSS, an index summarizing responses to several questions asked in 1994 was used to measure informal interaction. Two questions probed the positive quality of interracial/interethnic interactions in college, asking students how much such interactions had involved "meaningful and honest discussions about race and ethnic relations" and "sharing of personal feelings and problems." Another asked students to describe the gender, geographical home residency, and race/ethnicity of their "six closest friends at Michigan." For this measure we coded for the number of friends who were not of the students' own racial/ethnic group. The last question focused on quantity rather than quality, asking how much contact they had at Michigan with racial/ethnic groups other than their own. For White students we included contact with African American, Asian American, and Latino/a students, and for African American and Asian American students we included contact with White students in this measure of informal interactional diversity.[8]

In the Michigan Student Study, we also assessed experience with diversity through the number of multicultural campus events students had attended and whether they had participated in intergroup dialogues during college. The multicultural campus events were Hispanic Heritage Month, Native American Month, the annual Pow Wow, Asian American Awareness Week, a Martin Luther King Jr. Symposium, and Black History Month. Intergroup dialogues are also offered on the Michigan campus within various courses. These dialogues involve weekly sessions of structured discussion between an equal number of members (usually seven or eight) from each of two identity groups (Arab/Jewish, Anglo/Latino/a, men/women, African American/White, Native American/Latino/a, and others). The students discuss contentious issues that are relevant to their particular groups. The goals of the dialogues are four-fold: 1) to discern differences and commonalties in perspectives between and within the groups; 2) to incorporate readings on intergroup relations in their discussions; 3) to learn how to deal with conflict; and 4) to define one action that the two groups can take in coalition with each other. Participation in these multicultural events and intergroup dialogues comprise an index that includes both knowledge content and interaction with diverse others.

Learning Outcome   Table 2 shows the outcome measures in the study. The theory linking diversity to learning outcomes led us to focus on measures of active thinking and engagement in learning. In the CIRP, intellectual engagement included self-rated aspirations for postgraduate education, the drive to achieve, intellectual self-confidence, and the importance placed on original writing and creating artistic works. The other learning outcome in the CIRP, academic skills, included self-rated academic ability, writing ability, and listening ability, as well as self-reported change in general knowledge, analytic and problem-solving skills, ability to think critically, writing skills, and foreign language skills.

Gurin, Dey, Hurtado, and Gurin   23

TABLE 2   *Measures of Dependent Variables*

	CIRP Data	Michigan Student Study (MSS)
Learning Outcomes:		
Active thinking	Not available	Index (α = .797) of four complex thinking items and three socio-historical thinking items based on Fletcher's measure of Attributional Complexity (1986, 1990), correlated with total scale .81. *
Intellectual engagement and motivation	Index of items (α = .613): self-ratings of drive to achieve and self-ratings of intellectual self-confidence; degree aspirations in 1989; interest in attending graduate school; importance of writing original works and creating artistic works *	Index of two items (α = .650): gained a broad, intellectually exciting education at Michigan, and satisfaction with intellectual quality and challenge of classes.
Academic skills	Index of items (α = .657): self-change assessments in general knowledge, analytical/problem-solving skills, ability to think critically, writing skills, foreign language skills, and self-ratings of academic ability, writing, and listening ability *	Not available
Democracy Outcomes:		
Citizenship engagement	Index of items (α = .752): importance of influencing the political structure, influencing social values, helping others in difficulty, involvement in cleaning up the environment, and participation in community action programs *	Not available
Compatibility of difference and democracy	Not available	Index of five items (α = .583): belief that diversity is non-divisive; perceived commonality in life values with groups other than one's own *
Perspective-taking	Not available	Index (α = .684) of four items of Davis's scale (1983), correlated with total scale .85 *
Racial/cultural engagement	Index of items: self-change in cultural awareness and appreciation, and acceptance of persons from different races (α = .700)	Single item: learned about other racial/ethnic groups during college

* Pretest also available used as control at entrance to college

In the MSS, we had available a measure that directly represented the active thinking that we hypothesize is promoted by experiences with diversity. This measure includes seven items from a longer scale, which is correlated with this seven-item measure at .81 (Fletcher, Danilovics, Fernandez, Peterson, & Reeder, 1986). They define their scale as the motivation to understand human behavior, a preference for complex rather than simple explanations, and the tendency to think about underlying processes involved in causal analysis. It has both discriminant and convergent validity and is not related to the tendency to answer questions in a socially desirable way. It is related, as it should be, to a measure of a similar construct developed by John Cacioppo and Richard Petty (1982) of an individual need for cognition, defined as the need to understand and explain the world and the enjoyment of thinking. Examples of the items in our seven-item measure are: "I take people's behavior at face value" (reverse coding), "I enjoy analyzing reasons for behavior," and "I prefer simple rather than complex explanations" (reverse coding). Because the same questions were included in the entrance questionnaire and used as controls in our regression analyses, diversity effects can be construed as affecting active thinking. The other learning outcome measure in the MSS, intellectual engagement and motivation, asked students to assess the extent to which they had "gained a broad, intellectually exciting education at Michigan" and how satisfied they were with "the intellectual quality and challenge of classes."

Democracy Outcomes   According to the theory outlined here, students who had the most experience with diversity during college would be more motivated and better able to participate in an increasingly heterogeneous democracy. To participate effectively, students need to understand and consider multiple perspectives that are likely to exist when people of different backgrounds interact, to appreciate the common values and integrative forces that incorporate differences in the pursuit of the broader common good, and to understand and accept cultural differences that arise in a racially/ethnically diverse society.

In the CIRP data, citizenship engagement is a measure of students' motivation to participate in activities that affect society and the political structure. These activities include "influencing the political structure," "influencing social values," "helping others in difficulty," "being involved in programs to clean up the environment," and "participating in a community action program." Racial and cultural understanding is assessed by students' self-ratings of how much they had changed in "cultural awareness and appreciation" and "acceptance of persons from different races/cultures" since entering college.

The MSS included three measures of democracy outcomes. One outcome, perspective-taking, refers directly to the tendency to consider other people's points of view. This four-item index comes from a longer scale of empathy that was developed by Mark Davis (1983), with which the MSS index is correlated at .85. An example is "I sometimes find it difficult to see things from the other person's point of view" (reversed). The Davis scale is internally reliable and has both discriminant and convergent validity. The second MSS measure, racial/cultural engagement, is a one-item question asking students how much they have learned during college "about the contributions to American society of other racial/ethnic groups."

A third MSS democracy measure was developed to ascertain student views about the compatibility of difference and democracy. Critics of diversity and multicultural education assert that an emphasis on groups rather than individuals and on differences between groups creates division on college campuses and threatens the very fabric of democracy. If that were true, students who had experienced the most classroom and informal interactional diversity would perceive only differences rather than commonalties and would believe that difference is inimical to democracy. Our questions directly challenged these beliefs. Commonality in values was assessed at the time of entrance to the University of Michigan and again four years later by asking students how much difference in "values in life — like values about work and family" they perceived between their own racial/ethnic group and other groups. Perception of nondivisiveness was measured by asking how much students agreed/disagreed with four statements (also used in Gurin, Peng, Lopez, & Nagda, 1999). Examples are: "The University's commitment to diversity fosters more intergroup division than understanding" and "The University's emphasis on diversity means I can't talk honestly about ethnic, racial, and gender issues." These items were scored so that high scores indicate that difference is nondivisive. The commonality in values and perception of nondivisiveness measures were combined into a compatibility of difference and democracy index (see Table 2 for construction of measures for different groups).

Self-Assessments All of these measures required students to assess themselves. Self-assessments are credible and widely accepted methods of measuring educational outcomes. For example, in a review of the research on a variety of possible indicators of college outcomes, the National Center for Higher Education Management Systems concluded that self-reported data on academic development and experiences have moderate to high potential as proxies for a national test and as possible indicators for decisionmaking in higher education (Ewell & Jones, 1993). In addition, in their major review of over 2,600 studies on the impact of college on students, Ernest Pascarella and Patrick Terenzini (1991) found that self-assessments are positively correlated with standard tests of achievement and serve quite well as indicators of college outcomes.[9]

GRE scores were not used as a measure of learning outcomes for two reasons: 1) student performance on the SAT (already in the analysis as a control variable) was correlated at .85 with the GRE, and 2) including only students who had taken the GRE in their fourth year of college would have substantially reduced the sample of students within each of the racial/ethnic groups and skewed the analytical sample with extremely high-ability students. College grades were not selected as a measure of learning primarily because grades inadequately capture the active thinking and intellectual engagement we were attempting to test. The meaning of grades also varies substantially from institution to institution, major to major, and course to course. This was particularly evident in the institution with which we were most familiar, where some departments grade on a curve and other departments have no standard method.

ANALYSES

Multiple regression analyses were performed using the two datasets. We conducted regression analyses on the multi-institutional CIRP data to explore the relationships between two types of diversity (classroom and informal interactional diversity) and the four dependent variables (intellectual engagement, academic skills, citizenship engagement, and racial/cultural engagement). Separate regressions were fit for African American, Asian American, Latino/a, and White students in the national study. Regressions were also conducted on the MSS data to explore the relationships between three types of diversity experiences (interactional diversity, classroom diversity, and events/dialogues) and the five dependent variables (active thinking, intellectual engagement, compatibility of differences, perspective-taking, and racial/cultural engagement). Again, separate regressions were run for three student groups in the MSS: African American, Asian American, and White.

Given our primary interest in the effects of informal interaction and classroom diversity measures on the outcomes described above, the regressions were structured in a blocked hierarchical regression to provide information on how these variables relate to the outcome measures after first controlling for student background characteristics (including entrance pretest measures where available) and institutional characteristics found in the CIRP data. After these statistical controls were applied, the effect of each diversity experience variable was first considered as the sole diversity predictor and then simultaneously with other diversity experiences in the entire predictive model.[10] We conducted both kinds of analyses because students who have the most experience with diversity also tend to have the most informal interaction with peers from different backgrounds. We were interested in *both* the total and net effects of each type of diversity experience. Finally, variation in sample size of each of the groups necessitated reporting a wide range of significance tests — using the traditional significance levels (.05, .01, and .001) to evaluate results for the very large sample of White students, and adding the significance level of .10 for the much smaller samples of students of color.

RESULTS

As noted in the methods section, we examined the effects of each type of diversity experience in two ways — its individual impact, ignoring the other kinds of diversity experiences, and its net impact, controlling for the other kinds of diversity experiences. In the national study and the Michigan study, both sets of analyses show that diversity experiences had robust effects on educational outcomes for all groups of students, although to varying degrees.

Learning Outcomes

Table 3 summarizes the results for both the Michigan and the national study of the effects of diversity experiences on learning outcomes. The first set of columns (Model

1) provides the zero-order correlations showing the size of the maximal possible effect of diversity experiences. Model 1 also shows the standardized betas for each diversity experience when it is entered as the sole diversity predictor, along with the various control variables. The second set of columns (Model 2) gives the standardized betas for each diversity experience when it is entered simultaneously with the other diversity experience(s), again, after statistically removing the effects of the various control variables. Finally, the third set of columns gives the amount of variance that is explained by the entire model, including the control variables and the amount of variance that is attributable specifically to all the diversity experiences.

We predicted that diversity experiences would have a positive relationship with the learning outcomes. In both the national study and the MSS, this prediction was consistently supported. As shown in Table 3 and described in more detail below, one kind of diversity experience or another was significantly related to each of the learning outcomes, even after adjusting for individual students' differences upon entering college that might have predisposed them to participate, or not, in diversity experiences on their campuses. Moreover, with all but one exception, when there was a statistically significant relationship between diversity experience and learning outcomes, the observed effect was universally positive for each of the groups of students we studied.

In the national study, informal interactional diversity was especially influential in accounting for higher levels of intellectual engagement and self-assessed academic skills for all four groups of students (Table 3). The impact of classroom diversity was also statistically significant and positive for White students and for Latinos/as. The effects of classroom diversity disappeared for Asian American students when we examined the net effect, controlling for the simultaneous effect of informal interaction. One statistically significant negative result emerged for African American students in the analyses that tested the net effect of classroom diversity on self-assessed academic skills.

It is important to note in Table 3 that, when both types of diversity were simultaneously used as predictors with the national data, the effect of informal interactional diversity was nearly always maintained and was considerably larger than the effect of classroom diversity. This was true for all four groups of students, except in the comparative effects of the two kinds of diversity on intellectual engagement among Latino/a students.

A reason for the relatively greater effects of informal interactional diversity in the national data might come in part from the fact that it was measured by three indicators, while classroom diversity was represented by only one question that asked about enrollment in an ethnic studies course. Conclusions about relative importance are affected by properties of particular measures of various concepts. Still, at the very least, these analyses show that actual interaction with diverse others was an influential aspect of the educational experiences of the students in the national sample.

The Michigan study provided both a broader measure of classroom diversity and two types of informal interactional diversity measures. One measure, the amount and quality of interaction with diverse peers, was conceptually comparable to the informal interactional measure in the national study. It is important to point out, however,

TABLE 3   Effect of Diversity Experiences on Learning Outcomes

A. CIRP National Study

	Model 1				Model 2		Percent variance explained	
	As sole diversity predictor							
	Informal interaction		Classroom diversity		Informal interaction controlling for classroom diversity	Classroom diversity controlling for informal interaction		Attributable to both diversity measures
	Zero-order correlation	Beta	Zero-order correlation	Beta	Beta	Beta	Whole model	
Whites								
Intellectual engagement	.230	.130***	.095	.057***	.123***	.026**	26.2%	1.5%
Academic skills	.243	.168***	.115	.075***	.159***	.035***	14.7%	2.5%
African American								
Intellectual engagement	.149	.146**	.014	–.040	.166**	–.083	24.0%	2.4%
Academic skills	.196	.175**	–.021	–.072	.206**	–.126 *	16.1%	3.9%
Asian American								
Intellectual engagement	.218	.170***	.044	.078*	.161***	.038	28.9%	2.6%
Academic skills	.199	.134**	.078	.072*	.124**	.042	15.4%	1.7%
Latino								
Intellectual engagement	.147	.138*	.116	.157*	.096	.126*	31.7%	2.8%
Academic skills	.241	.258***	.178	.205**	.212**	.135*	21.5%	7.0%

Model 1

Model 2

B. Michigan Student Study

| | As sole diversity predictor | | | | | | Informal interaction controlling for classroom diversity and Events/Dialogues | Classroom diversity controlling for informal interaction and Events/Dialogues | Events/dialogues controlling for informal interaction and classroom diversity | Percent variance explained | |
| | Interactional diversity | | Classroom diversity | | Events/Dialogues | | | | | | |
	Zero-order correlation	Beta	Zero-order correlation	Beta	Zero-order correlation	Beta	Beta	Beta	Beta	Whole model	Attributable to the three diversity measures
White students											
Active thinking	.174	.100***	.348	.196***	.321	.176***	.054*	.158***	.130***	43.2%	5.3%
Intellectual engagement	.053	.084	.121	.112***	.119	.108***	.018	.090**	.086***	3.2%	1.9%
African American students											
Active thinking	.064	.019	.258	.211*	.086	−.052	.022	.227**	.227**	42.3%	5.1%
Intellectual engagement	.157	.117	.151	.169*	.121	.126**	.166*	.168*	.168*	9.3%	6.6%
Asian American students											
Active thinking	.179	.077	.374	.256***	.207	.060	.102*	.291***	.291***	48.9%	8.1%
Intellectual engagement	.093	.086	.158	.156**	.002	.001	.087	.361**	.161**	4.3%	3.0%

Note: In the MSS, Betas shown control for student characteristics; in the CIRP, the Betas shown control for student characteristics, institutional characteristics, and (where available) for measures of the outcomes taken at time of entrance to college. $p < .10 = \sim$, $p < .05 = *$, $p < .01 = **$, and $p < .001 = ***$

that the Michigan measure is unique in that it assesses both the quality and the quantity of interaction with diverse peers. It includes students' assessments of how many positive personal interactions they had with peers from racial/ethnic backgrounds different from their own. The other, a measure of participation in multicultural events and intergroup dialogues, takes advantage of our knowledge of diversity experiences within the student environment at the University of Michigan.

In the Michigan study, all three kinds of diversity experiences were influential for at least one of the groups, and for at least one measure of learning outcomes. This may simply indicate that students of color respond differently to opportunities for diversity experiences and have distinct interaction patterns that affect different outcomes. The most consistent effects were found for White students. All three kinds of diversity experiences were significantly related to higher levels of active thinking scores in the senior year, controlling for levels of active thinking in the freshman year among White students. In addition, both classroom diversity and events/dialogues were significantly related to intellectual engagement for this group. The results show clearly that the largest effects came from campus-facilitated diversity activities, namely classroom diversity and multicultural events, and intergroup dialogues held on campus (the dialogues facilitate interaction among an equal number of diverse peers). For Asian American students, classroom diversity also fostered both of the learning outcomes.

For African American students in the Michigan study, classroom diversity was the only predictor that had a statistically significant effect on both learning outcomes. The other two diversity experiences were related to one of each of these learning outcomes: events/dialogues participation was statistically related to intellectual engagement in the Model 1 regression; informal interaction was statistically related to intellectual engagement in Model 2.

Democracy Outcomes

We also predicted that diversity experiences would help students develop the skills to participate and lead in a diverse democracy. The results of both studies support this prediction for all groups of students. Some kind of diversity experience was related to each of the democracy outcomes, even after adjusting for individual differences on measures of most of these outcomes at the time students entered college. (See Table 4 and the description of results that follows.)

In the national study, informal interactional diversity was significantly related to both citizenship engagement and racial/cultural engagement for all four groups. This was also true of the effect of classroom diversity on democracy outcomes for White students. In contrast, the effects of classroom diversity were more group-specific for students of color and, on the whole, classroom diversity had less consistent effects for these students. The major finding, however, is that informal interaction was the key for fostering democracy outcomes for all groups in the national study.

In the Michigan study all three types of diversity experiences had significant positive effects on the compatibility of difference and the racial/cultural engagement outcomes for White students. White students who had the greatest amount of informal interactional diversity and experience with diversity in the classroom most frequently believed that difference is compatible with democracy and were the most engaged with racial/cultural issues. These two diversity experiences also significantly affected White students' perspective-taking.

For African American and Asian American students in the Michigan study, the impact of the three diversity experiences was less consistent. Among both groups, informal interaction with diverse peers was associated with an understanding that difference and democracy can be compatible. Further, classroom diversity had a positive effect on racial and cultural engagement for both groups. Participation in multicultural events and intergroup dialogues only had a significant effect on perspective-taking among African Americans. Among Asian Americans these activities were related to two of the democracy outcomes (Model 1), although the net effect of this kind of diversity was no longer statistically significant when the other kinds of diversity were taken into account (Model 2).

Summary

Several conclusions can be drawn from these results. First, an important feature of our analyses is the consistency of results across both the national and Michigan studies. Second, in the national study informal interactional diversity was influential for all groups and more influential than classroom diversity. Third, of the many analyses we conducted, all but one that had a significant effect confirmed our prediction of a positive relationship between diversity experiences and educational outcomes as posited in our theory. Fourth, with few exceptions, the separate diversity effects remained statistically significant after controlling for the other diversity experiences in Model 2.[11]

Finally, Tables 3 and 4 show that the whole models (including the precollege background controls, initial measures of senior-year outcomes, where available, diversity experience measures, and, in the national study, measures of institutional characteristics) explain between 3 percent and 49 percent of the variance across both studies, across the various groups of students, and across the various outcome measures. More important, however, is the amount of variance that is attributable to diversity experiences. In the national study, the two diversity experiences explained between 1.5 percent and 12.6 percent of the variance in the different educational outcomes for the four groups. In the Michigan study, the three diversity experiences explained between 1.9 percent and 13.8 percent of the variance across the educational outcomes of the three groups.

The size of these effects is commonly viewed in social science as highly consequential for policy, especially when outcomes and predictors are likely to be measured with substantial random error, as they typically are in studies of college impact. It is widely known that the kinds of processes and outcomes of interest here are difficult to measure with high precision and that measurement error diminishes effect size. Given that the dependent variables in the CIRP analyses were multiple-item scales with calculated reliability estimates, we replicated the analyses for each of the racial/ethnic groups in the national study after applying the standard attenuation correction. In

TABLE 4 *Effect of Diversity Experiences on Democracy Outcomes*

A. CIRP National Study	Model 1				Model 2		Percent variance explained	
	As sole diversity predictor				Informal interaction controlling for classroom diversity	Classroom diversity controlling for informal interaction		
	Informal interaction		Classroom diversity					Attributable to both diversity measures
	Zero-order correlation	Beta	Zero-order correlation	Beta	Beta	Beta	Whole model	
Whites								
Citizenship engagement	.372	.301***	.211	.138***	.282***	.070***	20.2%	7.8%
Racial/cultural engagement	.350	.337***	.200	.164***	.314***	.083***	4.3%	10.2%
African American								
Citizenship engagement	.335	.328***	.138	.121**	.319***	.035	25.1%	9.3%
Racial/cultural engagement	.269	.251***	.097	.040	.258***	–.027	5.4%	5.6%
Asian American								
Citizenship engagement	.342	.272***	.138	.066	.271***	.001	18.8%	6.3%
Racial/cultural engagement	.375	.365***	.211	.185***	.341**	.100*	8.5%	12.6%
Latino								
Citizenship engagement	.383	.311***	.334	.214***	.270***	.134*	28.1%	9.1%
Racial/cultural engagement	.330	.313***	.175	.142*	.298***	.044	5.3%	8.5%

B. Michigan Student Study

	Model 1						Model 2				
	As sole diversity predictor									Percent variance explained	
	Interactional diversity		Classroom diversity		Events/ Dialogues		Informal interaction controlling for classroom diversity and Events/ Dialogues	Classroom diversity controlling for informal interaction and Events/ Dialogues	Events/ dialogues controlling for informal interaction and classroom diversity		
	Zero-order correlation	Beta	Zero-order correlation	Beta	Zero-order correlation	Beta	Beta	Beta	Beta	Whole model	Attributable to the three diversity measures
White Students											
Compatibility of differences	.178	.156***	.142	.129***	.259	.233***	.105**	.082*	.195***	10.6%	7.4%
Perspective-taking	.167	.090**	.185	.123***	.143	.048	.077**	.117**	.003	28.7%	2.0%
Racial/cultural engagement	.172	.172***	.316	.300***	.197	.186***	.120***	.261***	.096***	16.0%	11.1%
African American Students											
Compatibility of differences	.230	.270*	.279	.251**	-.113	-.079	.262*	.233*	-.098	20.5%	11.2%
Perspective-taking	.158	.138	.088	-.052	.236	.207*	.150	-.072	.212*	30.4%	6.1%
Racial/cultural engagement	.049	.107	.338	.352***	.048	.042	.098	.365***	-.026	16.9%	13.8%
Asian American Students											
Compatibility of differences	.198	.193*	.087	.088	.161	.163*	.197*	.056	.142	11.1%	6.2%
Perspective-taking	.061	.056	.040	.069	.048	.006	.048	.085	-.024	33.6%	0.8%
Racial/cultural engagement	-.009	-.047	.359	.350***	.178	.170**	-.045	.320***	.071	15.0%	11.8%

Note: In the MSS, Betas shown control for student characteristics; in the CIRP, the Betas shown control for student characteristics, institutional characteristics, and (where available) for measures of the outcomes taken at time of entrance to college. $p < .10 = \sim$, $p < .05 = *$, $p < .01 = **$, and $p < .001 = ***$

each instance, the results were consistent with those presented here, but with larger regression coefficients and an enhanced level of explained variance. For example, the coefficients and degree of predictability associated with the White student analyses were roughly one-third larger in the attenuation-corrected analyses.

DISCUSSION

The results of these longitudinal analyses show, as our theory predicts, that the actual experiences students have with diversity consistently and meaningfully affect important learning and democracy outcomes of a college education. Diversity experiences explain an important amount of variance in these outcomes. These effects are quite consistent across the various outcomes, across the national and single institutional studies, and across the different groups of students.

Is Curriculum Enough?

Some opponents of affirmative action advance the view that the educational benefits of diversity can be achieved without the presence of racially/ethnically diverse peers (*Hopwood*, 1996). Since content about race/ethnicity can be introduced into courses even at institutions with minimal student diversity, it was especially important for our research to explore whether informal interaction with diverse peers had significant effects independent of the effects of classroom diversity. In the national study, informal interaction remained statistically significant in all but one test when classroom diversity was added as a control. We also found that informal interaction with diverse peers was consistently influential on all educational outcomes for all four groups of students and, with one exception, that the effect of informal interaction was larger than that of classroom diversity.

In the Michigan study, the unique contribution of significant informal interaction effects remained on democracy outcomes when the other diversity experiences were added as controls, and were actually more consistent on learning outcomes in Model 2 than in Model 1. The results for White students show that the effects of the three different kinds of diversity experiences are more comparable to each other than was true in the national study, and the results for African American and Asian American students show a fairly differentiated picture of effects. While classroom diversity carried greater weight in some cases and informal interactional diversity or events/dialogues in others, we could not conclude that the presence of racially/ethnically diverse peers is irrelevant to the diversity benefits for any of these groups of students. Moreover, as pointed out earlier, classroom diversity at the University of Michigan nearly always involves the presence of diverse students as well as exposure to curriculum content addressing diversity. The success of these curricular initiatives is facilitated by the presence of diverse students and a pedagogy that facilitates learning in a diverse environment. In conclusion, we find that education is enhanced by extensive and meaningful informal interracial interaction, which depends on the presence of significantly diverse student bodies.

In the introduction to this article, we laid out a theoretical rationale for why actual experience with diversity provides the process through which the presence of diverse peers affects the education of all students. The results of our research support this rationale across both studies and for all groups of students. Still, in the months immediately following the *Gratz v. Bollinger* and *Grutter v. Bollinger* trials in district court, opponents of affirmative action began to argue that diversity experience is irrelevant legally and that the only evidence relevant to these cases would have to show that the percentage of minority students on a campus has a direct effect on educational outcomes. An *amicus* brief filed on behalf of the plaintiffs in these Michigan lawsuits claims that Justice Powell defined diversity in his opinion in the *Bakke* case simply as the percentage of minority students on a campus. While the interpretation of what Justice Powell said is, of course, up to the courts, his statement includes a long passage quoting William Bowen, then president of Princeton University, on how "a great deal of learning occurs informally . . . through interactions among students" (*Regents*, 1978, p. 312). Justice Powell's use of Bowen's statement indicates that Powell understood that actual interaction with diverse peers is a major component of the effects of diversity.

The conclusion that the racial diversity of a campus operates *through* students' experiences is powerfully supported by the research reported here. It is also supported by a developing body of research on diversity that demonstrates the significant impact of interactions with diverse peers (Chang, 1999; Hurtado, 2001; Pascarella et al., 1996). At a more general level, higher education researchers have noted the critical importance of students' college experiences in their personal development. In a review of the impact of college on students, Pascarella and Terenzini (1991) note that structural features of institutions (size, control, selectivity, percentage of minority students, etc.) generally have only an indirect influence on students — their effects being mediated through the experiences students have in the institution's general environment. If it were true that increasing the number of minority students on a campus must *by itself be sufficient* for achieving desired educational outcomes, then having good buildings, high faculty salaries, and good libraries would all be sufficient to ensure a good education. No one with the responsibility for educating students would make such an argument, precisely because the nature of educational activities and the extent to which the students make use of these resources are crucial for achieving an excellent education. Thus, a diverse student body is clearly a resource and a necessary condition for engagement with diverse peers that permits higher education to achieve its educational goals.

Diversity enables students to perceive differences both within groups and between groups and is the primary reason why significant numbers of students of various groups are needed in the classroom. The worst consequence of the lack of diversity arises when a minority student is a token in a classroom. In such situations, the solo or token minority individual is often given undue attention, visibility, and distinctiveness, which can lead to greater stereotyping by majority group members (Kanter, 1977). These effects of the solo or token situation are well-documented in the research literature (Lord & Saenz, 1985; Mellor, 1996; Sekaquaptewa & Thompson, 2002; Spangler, Gordon, & Pipkin, 1978; Thompson & Sekaquaptewa, 2002; Yoder,

1994). Research shows that individuals become more aware of within-group variability when the minority group is not too small relative to the majority group (Mullen & Hu, 1989; Mullen & Johnson, 1993), and that individuals have more complex views of members of other groups when relative group size is not greatly imbalanced (Mullen, Rozell, & Johnson, 2000).

The results of our research also support the conclusion of an *amicus* brief filed on behalf of the University of Michigan by General Motors:

> Diversity in academic institutions is essential to teaching students the human relations and analytic skills they need to thrive and lead in the work environments of the twenty-first century. These skills include the abilities to work well with colleagues and subordinates from diverse backgrounds; to view issues from multiple perspectives; and to anticipate and respond with sensitivity to the needs and cultural differences of highly diverse customers, colleagues, employees, and global business partners. (Brief of General Motors, 2000, p. 2)

Significant Features of the Research

Four features of this research give it particular importance in the continuing debate about education and diversity. First, we have offered a theoretical rationale for the impact of diversity, whereas much of the testimony offered in previous court cases in higher education has been largely anecdotal. Second, the consistency of the results across both a national study of multiple institutions and a single institution provides significant support for our theoretical rationale. This kind of cross-validation is not always possible and in this instance increases confidence in our conclusions. Third, having both a national and a single institutional study protects against inappropriate generalizations that might have been made had only one study been available for this research. For example, we might have generalized from the national study that informal interactional diversity is always more important than classroom diversity, whereas the Michigan study calls for a more nuanced conclusion. Fourth, the longitudinal nature of both studies, in which many of the same measures were taken at entrance to college and four years later, made it possible to talk about an effect of diversity with some assuredness. In most of the analyses reported here it was possible to control for students' scores on the outcome measures when they entered college. This is a traditional method of assessing effects in studies of college students and allows us to conclude that diversity experiences had an impact on active thinking and intellectual engagement and on the orientations and sentiments that students will need to become leaders in a diverse democracy.

Other control variables that we employed in all analyses also address, at least partially, the selectivity problem — that certain kinds of students might be predisposed to take courses that deal with race and ethnicity and to interact with students from varied backgrounds. For example, it is plausible that students who entered college with greater exposure to diverse peers because they lived in racially heterogeneous neighborhoods and attended heterogeneous high schools might seek diversity experiences in college. We were able to control for this because we had measures of neighborhood and high school racial composition in both studies. The control for initial position on the outcome measures also minimizes selectivity to some extent. It adjusts for the possibility that students already intellectually engaged and motivated to be active thinkers — or students already committed to participate in citizenship activities and to understand the perspectives of other people when they enter college — might choose to take diversity courses and to seek relationships with diverse students. A careful reader will know, however, that the controls for these predisposing influences do not remove all sources of selection bias. Our approach does not control for correlated error in the predisposing and outcome measures, and correlated error may bring about selection bias. This is a limitation in the study, although in the Michigan data we have attempted to further reduce selection bias in another way. We were able to demonstrate an effect of classroom diversity for students who did not choose to take race and ethnicity courses but were required to do so for college graduation. As we have already noted, undergraduates in the College of Literature, Sciences, and the Arts, who comprise 70 percent of the Michigan study sample, are required to take at least one course that addresses issues of race/ethnicity. This requirement significantly decreases the likelihood that selection bias could explain the effects of experience with classroom diversity in the Michigan study results.

Implications for Practice

In the post–civil rights era and beyond, higher education leaders set the vision to create in their institutions a microcosm of the equitable and democratic society we aspire to become. The admission of a more racially/ethnically diverse student body is an important starting point in realizing this vision. Classroom diversity, diversity programming, opportunities for interaction, and learning across diverse groups of students in the college environment now constitute important initiatives to enhance the education of all students.[12] The results of this research not only support the curricular initiatives that introduce diversity into college courses, but also suggest that more attention should be given to the types of experiences students have with diverse peers inside and outside the classroom. Both the theory and findings indicate that individual students benefit when they are engaged with diverse peers; however, as a society we have provided no template for interaction across racial/ethnic groups and such interaction cannot be taken for granted in the college environment. Helping faculty develop a pedagogy that makes the most of the diverse perspectives and student backgrounds in their classrooms can foster active thinking, intellectual engagement, and democratic participation. In addition, colleges and universities should provide a supportive environment in which disequilibrium and experimentation can occur by increasing interaction among diverse peers and help faculty and students manage conflict when individuals share different points of views. (See Gurin, Nagda, and Lopez, in press; Lopez, Gurin, and Nagda, 1998; and Nagda, Gurin, and Lopez, in press, for analyses of the effects of the Intergroup Relations, Community and Conflict Program, a program at the University of Michigan explicitly designed to accomplish these pedagogical and learning goals.) Given the evidence from higher education research on the impact of peer groups (Astin, 1993b; Kuh, 1993; Pasacarella & Terenzini, 1991), student affairs administrators may understand best the power of peer group interaction for student learning and development. However, in order to foster citizenship for a diverse democracy, educators must intentionally structure opportunities for students to leave the comfort of their homogeneous peer group and build relationships across racially/ethnically diverse student communities on campus.

NOTES

1. Justice Lewis Powell is quoting, in part, the U.S. Supreme Court's decision in Keyshian v. Board of Regents (1967).
2. The Supreme Court has not acted on affirmative action in higher education admissions since the Bakke case in 1978. In that case, Justice Powell wrote the defining opinion. Controversy exists with respect to how many justices joined him in arguing that race could be used as one of many factors in admissions provided that the institution could show that it was being used to achieve racial/ethnic diversity, that diversity was a compelling governmental interest, and that the method of achieving diversity was "narrowly tailored" to meet that interest. Narrow tailoring means that race is used no more than is necessary to achieve diversity and that it is only one of many factors being used. Justice Powell argued that diversity is a compelling interest, though of course there are debates about what he meant by diversity. These arguments are part of the legal dispute now being heard in the courts in two cases involving the University of Michigan (Gratz v. Bollinger, et al., 2002; Grutter v. Bollinger, et al., 2002).
3. As of this writing, the Court has not ruled in Gratz. The Center for Individual Rights, representing the plaintiff, Barbara Grutter, has appealed the Sixth Circuit Court decision in the law school case to the U.S. Supreme Court.
4. Similar ideas have been offered by sociologists Melvin Kohn and Carmi Schooler (1978) in a series of classic papers delineating features of work environments that produce "intellectual flexibility." They found that work that involves tasks requiring workers to think and make judgments is an important determinant of intellectual flexibility. Workers who are less closely supervised and thus have to think about what they are doing demonstrate more thoughtful response patterns.
5. Connecting racial and ethnic diversity to multiple perspectives does not mean that students from a particular group have identical perspectives. Our point is not to argue that all members of a particular racial/ethnic group are the same due to some inherent, essential, and probably biological quality. Our argument is the exact opposite of such a group-based and stereotypical assumption. As Jonathan Alger (1998) stresses, the import of diversity comes from the range of similarities and differences within and among racial groups.
6. Parental education level was the only socioeconomic status (SES) proxy common to both the national and Michigan datasets. It is important to note that measures of parental education have been used in previous CIRP studies as part of a latent SES construct in confirmatory factor analyses using samples of diverse students, with father's education loading at .79 and mother's education loading at .86 (Hurtado, Dey, & Trevino, 1994).
7. We ran preliminary analyses using a Hierarchical Linear Modeling (HLM) approach, but the results obtained were not substantially different from those produced by models based on a traditional linear model approach. Moreover, an analysis of diagnostic statistics (such as the intraclass correlation coefficient) did not suggest that it would be productive to consistently employ the HLM approach. Therefore, we proceeded with the multiple regression analysis.
8. The MSS queried students of color about their interactions with other groups of color, but in this article we emphasize the major racial divide in the United States between Whites and groups of color. The complexities of interactions among different groups of color require separate treatment because they cannot be given the depth of analysis they deserve within this one paper.
9. Further evidence for the validity of using self-reports comes from a study (Anaya, 1999) that analyzed data from a subsample of the students who had taken the GRE, drawn from the CIRP co-

hort analyzed here. Anaya's results show that similar substantive conclusions can be made using GRE scores and using students' self-assessments of their learning.

10. Analyses testing for statistical interaction effects among the diversity experiences and outcomes did not produce a significant increase in the variance explained in the additive regression model. Therefore, we focus here on the main effects of the diversity experiences.

11. In the national study, 82 percent of the separate diversity effects were still statistically reliable when the two diversity experiences were considered simultaneously. When the three diversity experiences were considered simultaneously in the Michigan Student Study data, three of the separate diversity effects were no longer statistically reliable, and two additional net effects were statistically significant.

12. Over 60 percent of institutions have added some type of diversity course requirement to their general education program.

REFERENCES

Acredolo, C., & O'Connor, J. (1991). On the difficulty of detecting cognitive uncertainty. *Human Development, 34*, 204–223.

Alger, J. R. (1998). Unfinished homework for universities: Making the case for affirmative action. *Washington University Journal of Urban and Contemporary Law, 54*, 73–92.

Allport, G. (1954). *The nature of prejudice.* Cambridge, MA: Addison-Wesley.

Alwin, D. F., Cohen, R. I., & Newcomb, T. L. (1991). *Political attitudes over the life span.* Madison: University of Wisconsin Press.

Anaya, G. (1999). College impact on student learning: Comparing the use of self-reported gains, standardized test scores, and college grades. *Research in Higher Education, 40*, 499–526.

Antonio, A. (1998). *The impact of friendship groups in a multicultural university.* Unpublished doctoral dissertation, University of California, Los Angeles.

Association of American Colleges and Universities. (1985). Integrity in the college curriculum. Washington, DC: Author.

Astin, A. W. (1993a). Diversity and multiculturalism on campus: How are students affected? *Change, 25*(2), 44–49.

Astin, A. W. (1993b). *What matters in college?* San Francisco: Jossey-Bass.

Barber, B. R. (1998). *A passion for democracy.* Princeton, NJ: Princeton University Press.

Bargh, J. A. (1997). The automaticity of everyday life. *Advances in Social Cognition, 10*, 2–48.

Berlyne, D. E. (1970). Children's reasoning and thinking. In P. H. Mussen (Ed.), *Carmichael's manual of child psychology* (vol. 1, pp. 939–981). New York: Wiley.

Bolden, V. A., Goldberg, D. T., & Parker, D. D. (1999). Affirmative action in court: The case for optimism. *Equity and Excellence in Education, 3*(2), 24–30.

Bowen, W. G., & Bok, D. (1998). *The shape of the river: Long-term consequences of considering race in college and university admissions.* Princeton, NJ: Princeton University Press.

Bowen, W. G., Bok, D., & Burkhart, G. (1999). A report card on diversity: Lessons for business from higher education. *Harvard Business Review, 77*, 138–149.

Brief of General Motors Corporation as amicus curiae in support of defendants, Gratz v. Bollinger, et al., 122 F.Supp.2d 811 (2000).

Cacioppo, J. T., & Petty, R. E. (1982). The need for cognition. *Journal of Personality and Social Psychology, 42*, 116–131.

Chang, M. J. (1996). *Racial diversity in higher education: Does a racially mixed student population affect educational outcomes?* Unpublished doctoral dissertation, University of California, Los Angeles.

Chang, M. J. (1999). Does diversity matter? The educational impact of a racially diverse undergraduate population. *Journal of College Student Development, 40*, 377–395.

Chang, M. J., Witt-Sandis, D., Hakuta, K. (1999). The dynamics of race in higher education: An examination of the evidence. *Equity and Excellence in Education, 32*(2), 12–16.

Coser, R. (1975). The complexity of roles as a seedbed of individual autonomy. In L. A. Coser (Ed.), *The idea of social structure: Papers in honor of Robert K. Merton* (pp. 85–102). New York: Harcourt Brace Jovanovich.

Davis, M. H. (1983). Measuring individual differences in empathy: Evidence for a multidimensional approach. *Journal of Personality and Social Psychology, 44,* 113–126.

Dey, E. L. (1991). *Perceptions of the college environment: An analysis of organizational, interpersonal, and behavioral influences.* Unpublished dissertation, University of California, Los Angeles.

Doise, W., & Palmonari, A. (Eds.). (1984). *Social interaction in individual development.* New York: Cambridge University Press.

Erikson, E. (1946). Ego development and historical change. *Psychoanalytic Study of the Child, 2,* 359–396.

Erikson, E. (1956). The problem of ego identity. *Journal of American Psychoanalytic Association, 4,* 56–121.

Ewell, P. T., & Jones, D. P. (1993). Actions matter: The case for indirect measures in assessing higher education's progress on the national education goals. *Journal of General Education, 42,* 123–148.

Fiske, S. T. (1993). Social cognition and social perception. *Annual Review of Psychology, 44,* 155–194.

Fletcher, G. J. O., Danilovics, P., Fernandez, G., Peterson, D., & Reeder, G. D. (1986). Attributional complexity: An individual differences measure. *Journal of Personality and Social Psychology, 51,* 875–884.

Fredrickson, G. M. (1999). Models of American ethnic relations: An historical perspective. In D. Prentice & D. Miller (Eds.), *Cultural divides: The social psychology of intergroup contact* (pp. 23–45). New York: Russell Sage.

Gratz v. Bollinger, et al., 122 F.Supp.2d 811 (2000).

Grutter v. Bollinger, et al., 137 F. Supp.2d 821 (E.D. Mich. 2001), rev'd, 288 F.3d 732 (6th Cir. 2002).

Gurin, P., Nagda, R., & Lopez, G. (in press). Preparation for citizenship. *Journal of Social Issues.*

Gurin, P., Peng, T., Lopez, G., & Nagda, B. R. (1999). Context, identity, and intergroup relations. In D. Prentice & D. Miller (Eds.), *Cultural divides: The social psychology of intergroup contact* (pp. 133–172). New York: Russell Sage.

Guarasci, R., & Cornwell, G. H. (Eds.). (1997). *Democratic education in an age of difference: Redefining citizenship in higher education.* San Francisco: Jossey-Bass.

Hilton, J. L., & von Hippel, W. (1996). Stereotypes. In J. T. Spence, J. M. Darley, & D. J. Foss (Eds.), *Annual review of psychology* (vol. 47, pp. 237–271). Palo Alto, CA: Annual Reviews.

Hopwood v. University of Texas, 78 F.3d 932 (5th Cir., 1996), cert. Denied, 518 U.S. 1033.

Hurtado, S. (1992). Campus racial climates: Contexts for conflict. *Journal of Higher Education, 63,* 539–569.

Hurtado, S. (2001) Linking diversity and educational purpose: How diversity affects the classroom environment and student development. In G. Orfield (Ed.), *Diversity challenged: Evidence on the impact of affirmative action* (pp. 187–203). Cambridge, MA: Harvard Education Publishing Group and The Civil Rights Project at Harvard University.

Hurtado, S., Dey, E. L., & Trevino, J. G. (1994, April). *Exclusion or self-segregation? Interaction across racial/ethnic groups on campus.* Paper presented at the annual meeting of the American Educational Research Association, New Orleans.

Hurtado, S., Milem, J., Clayton-Pederson, A., & Allen, W. (1999). *Enacting diverse learning environments: Improving the climate for racial/ethnic diversity in higher education.* San Francisco: Jossey-Bass.

Johnson v. Board of Regents of the University of Georgia, 263 F.3d. 1234 (11th Cir. 2001).

Kanter, R. M. (1977). Some effects of proportions on group life: Skewed sex ratios and responses to token women. *American Journal of Sociology, 82,* 965–990.

Keyshian v. Board of Regents, 385 U.S. 589 (1967).

Kohn, M. L., & Schooler, C. (1978). The reciprocal effects of the substantive complexity of work and intellectual flexibility: A longitudinal assessment. *American Journal of Sociology, 84*(1), 24–52.

Komaromy, M., Grumbach, K., Drake, M., Vranizan, K., Lurie, N., Keane, D., & Bindman, A. B. (1997). The role of Black and Hispanic physicians in providing health care for underserved populations. *New England Journal of Medicine, 334,* 1305–1310.

Kuh, G. D. (1993). In their own words: What students learn outside the classroom. *American Educational Review Journal, 30,* 277–304.

Langer, E. J. (1978). Rethinking the role of thought in social interaction. In J. Harvey, W. Ickes, & R. Kiss (Eds.), *New directions in attribution research* (vol. 3, pp. 35–38). Hillsdale, NJ: Erlbaum.

Lopez, G. E., Gurin, P., & Nagda, B. A. (1998). Education and understanding structural causes for group inequalities. *Political Psychology, 19,* 305–329.

Lord, C. G., & Saenz, D. S. (1985). Memory deficits and memory surfeits: Differential cognitive consequences of tokenism for tokens and observers. *Journal of Personality and Social Psychology, 49,* 918–926.

Maruyama, G., Moreno, J. F., Gudeman, R. W., & Marin, P. (2000). *Does diversity make a difference? Three research studies on diversity in college classrooms.* Washington, DC: American Council on Education.

Mellor, S. (1996). Gender composition and gender representation in local unions: Relationships between women's participation in local office and women's participation in local activities. *Journal of Applied Psychology, 80,* 706–720.

Milem, J., & Hakuta, K. (2000). The benefits of racial and ethnic diversity in higher education. In D. J. Wilds (Ed.), *Minorities in higher education, 1999–2000, seventeenth annual status report* (pp. 39–67). Washington, DC: American Council on Education.

Mullen, B., & Hu, L. (1989). Perceptions of ingroup and outgroup variability: A meta-analytic integration. *Basic Applied Social Psychology, 25,* 525–559.

Mullen, B., & Johnson C. (1993). The determinants of differential group evaluations in distinctiveness-based illusory correlations in stereotyping. *British Journal of Social Psychology, 32,* 253–304.

Mullen, B., Rozell, D., & Johnson, C. (2000). Ethnophaulisms for ethnic immigrant groups: Cognitive representation of the minority and the foreigner. *Group Processes and Intergroup Relations, 3,* 5–24.

Nagda, R., Gurin, P., & Lopez, G. (in press). Transformative pedagogy for democracy and social justice. *Race, Ethnicity, and Education.*

Newcomb, T. L. (1943). *Personality and social change: Attitude formation in a student community.* New York: Dryden Press.

Newcomb, T. L., Koenig, K. E., Flacks, R., & Warwick, D. P. (1967). *Persistence and change: Bennington College and its students after 25 years.* New York: John Wiley & Sons.

Orfield, G. (Ed.). (2001). *Diversity challenged: Evidence on the impact of affirmative action.* Cambridge, MA: Harvard Education Publishing Group.

Orfield, G., Bachmeier, M., James, D. R., & Eitle, T. (1997). Deepening segregation in American public schools: A special report from the Harvard Project on School Desegregation. *Equity and Excellence in Education, 30*(2), 5–24.

Orfield, G., & Miller, E. (Eds.). (1998). *Chilling admissions: The affirmative action crisis and the search for alternatives.* Cambridge, MA: Harvard Education Publishing Group and Civil Rights Project at Harvard University.

Orfield, G., & Kurlaender, M. (1999). In defense of diversity: New research and evidence from the University of Michigan. *Equity and Excellence in Education, 32*(2), 31–35.

Orfield, G., & Whitla, D. (1999). *Diversity and legal education: Student experiences in leading law schools.* Cambridge, MA: Civil Rights Project at Harvard University.

Pascarella, E. T., Edison, M., Nora, A., Hagedorn, L. S., & Terenzini, P. T. (1996). Influences on student's openness to diversity and challenge in the first year of college. *Journal of Higher Education, 67,* 174–195.

Pascarella, E. T., & Terenzini, P. T. (1991). *How college affects students.* San Francisco: Jossey-Bass.

Piaget, J. (1965). *The moral judgement of the child.* New York: Free Press.

Piaget, J. (1971). The theory of stages in cognitive development. In D. R. Green, M. P. Ford, & G. B. Flamer (Eds.), *Measurement and Piaget* (pp. 1–111). New York: McGraw-Hill.

Piaget, J. (1985). *The equilibration of cognitive structures: The central problem of intellectual development*. Chicago: University of Chicago Press. (Original work published 1975)

Pitkin, H. F., & Shumer, S. M. (1982). On participation. *Democracy, 2*, 43–54.

Regents of the University of California v. Bakke, 438 U.S. 312, 98 S. Ct. 2760 (1978).

Ruble, D. (1994). Developmental changes in achievement evaluation: motivational implications of self-other differences. *Child Development, 65*, 1095–1110.

Saxonhouse, A. (1992). *Fear of diversity: The birth of political science in ancient Greek thought*, Chicago: University of Chicago Press.

Sekaquaptewa, D., & Thompson, M. (2002). The differential effects of solo status on members of high and low status groups. *Personality and Social Psychology Bulletin, 28*, 694–707.

Smith, D. G. (1997). *Diversity works: The emerging picture of how students benefit*. Washington, DC: Association of American Colleges and Universities.

Smith v. University of Washington Law School, 233 F.3d 1188 (9th Cir. 2000) cert. Denied 532 U.S. 1051 (2001)

Spangler, E., Gordon, M. A., & Pipkin, R. M. (1978). Token women: An empirical test of Kanter's hypothesis. *American Journal of Sociology, 84, 160–170.*

Terenzini, P. T., Rendon. L. I., Upcraft, M. L., Millar, S. B., Allison, K. W., Gregg, P. L., & Jalomo, R. (1994). The transition to college: Diverse students, diverse stories. *Research in Higher Education, 35*(1), 57–73.

Terenzini, P. T., Springer, L., Pascarella, E. T., & Nora, A. (1994*). The multiple influences of college on students' critical thinking skills.* Paper presented at the annual meeting of the Association for the Study of Higher Education, Tucson, AZ.

Thompson, M., & Sekaquaptewa, D. (2002). When being different is detrimental: Solo status and the performance of women and racial minorities. *Analyses of Social Issues and Public Policy, 2*, 183–203.

Yoder, J. D. (1994). Looking beyond numbers: The effects of gender status, job prestige, and occupational gender-typing on tokenism processes. *Social Psychology Quarterly, 57*, 150–159.

We wish to acknowledge the invaluable assistance of Karina Wade-Golden in conducting the analyses of the Michigan Student Study data, and Elizabeth Barry and Jonathan Alger in commenting on the legal aspects of this article.

PART TWO

Voices Inside Classrooms

Against Repetition:
Addressing Resistance to Anti–Oppressive Change in the Practices of Learning, Teaching, Supervising, and Researching

KEVIN K. KUMASHIRO

Recently, education researchers have articulated many theories about and provided many illustrations of ways that racism, classism, sexism, heterosexism, and other forms of oppression play out in schools (Apple, 1995; Delpit, 1995; Kenway & Willis, 1998; Lipkin, 2000). Their varying conceptualizations of the nature and dynamics of oppression have suggested to educators a range of approaches to challenging and changing oppression in schools (for a summary of these approaches, see Kumashiro, 2000b). By critiquing what has become accepted by many in society as conventional wisdom, or common sense, in classrooms, teacher-education programs, and research communities, and by offering alternatives that explicitly aim to work against the ways that oppression is already playing out in schools and society, such anti-oppressive efforts in research and practice do much to change the status quo of education.

However, in my experience, these efforts to challenge oppression are not free of contradictions. Anti-oppressive approaches to teaching and researching operate in ways that challenge some forms of oppression while complying with others (Kumashiro, 2001). This complicity is not always intentional or visible. Students, educators, and researchers, including those committed to social justice, often want certain forms of social change but resist others, sometimes knowingly, sometimes not (Kumashiro, 1999, 2000a). One reason that a desire for social change can coincide with a resistance to social change is that some educational practices, perspectives, social relations, and identities remain unquestioned. In fact, people often consider some practices and relations to be part of what schools and society are supposed to be, and fail to recognize how the repetition of such practices and relations — how having to experience them again and again — can help to maintain the oppressive status quo of schools and society.

Harvard Educational Review   Vol. 72   No. 1   Spring 2002, 67–92

Butler (1997) tells us that oppression can often be characterized by the repetition in society of regulatory identities, knowledge, and practices. In particular, what is oppressive is having to experience, again and again, the privileging of only certain ways of identifying, thinking, or relating to others. The privileging of certain identities and the marginalizing of others happens when members of and institutions in society learn to associate these identities and groups with differentiating markers. Examples include associating Whiteness with Americanness, Asianness with foreignness; maleness with strength, femaleness with weakness; or heterosexuality with normalcy, homo- or bisexuality with queerness. When social interactions, legal protections, and religious teaching continuously perpetuate these associations (as when stereotyping Asian Americans, failing to prohibit discrimination on the basis of sexual orientation, or teaching that men are leaders of the household), what can result are the systematic inclusion and exclusion of different groups, valuing and denigrating of different identities, and normalizing and dismissing of different practices. Often, these forms of repetition are masked by popular notions of the "authentic" American, the "traditional" gender roles, and the "natural" sexual orientation, and, therefore, are hard to recognize. In fact, because these popular notions of authenticity, tradition, and nature offer a sense of identity, belonging, and normalcy, people often unknowingly desire what is oppressive. People often desire repetition and resist anti-oppressive change.

Such desire for repetition does not disappear when people, including educators engaging in anti-oppressive research and teaching, commit to working for social justice. Even while interrupting some forms of repetition, they often continue to desire and partake in other forms, primarily because the oppressiveness of such repetition remains invisible. In this article, I examine some ways that educational practices, particularly anti-oppressive ones, both confront and participate in potentially harmful repetition. Specifically, I focus on ways that desire among students, educators, and researchers to repeat certain practices often translates into resistance to anti-oppressive change. I organize my arguments around four practices in the field of education — learning, teaching, supervising student teachers, and conducting educational research — as I explore what it could mean to work against the repetition that hinders anti-oppressive change. I argue that addressing resistance to anti-oppressive change requires addressing our desire for certain harmful practices to be repeated.

I recognize that not all forms of repetition are harmful; some forms can be helpful in movements for social justice. Nor is the goal to find learning, teaching, supervising, or research practices that are fully anti-oppressive. All practices are helpful in some ways, but not in others. They are partial in both senses of the word: they are incomplete, addressing only certain problems; and they are biased, informed by what is known and limited by what is not. Nonetheless, I argue that many efforts made toward social justice are encumbered by harmful repetitions, and that engaging in anti-oppressive education requires constantly working against these oppressive tendencies. Much takes place in classrooms, teacher-education programs, and research communities and processes that, despite our good intentions, actually contributes to oppression.

My own experiences are illustrative. Over the past few years, I have researched anti-oppressive education and attempted to put theory into practice as both a classroom teacher and teacher educator. During this time, I have repeatedly confronted resistance to anti-oppressive change, even among people, including myself, who have made explicit their commitment to social justice. Throughout this article, I draw on my experiences working in the field of education to describe some of the barriers I have encountered to anti-oppressive change. I argue that certain ideas about what it means to learn, to teach, to supervise student teachers, and to conduct educational research have become so entrenched in schools and universities that my students and colleagues and I often accept anti-oppressive change only insofar as it conforms to those ideas. In particular, I argue that our desire to work for social justice often contradicts and is superceded by our desire to repeat only certain ideas of what educational work is "supposed" to be.

LEARNING AGAINST REPETITION

Anti-oppressive educators have long recognized the problematic nature of biased, non-inclusive curricula that are Eurocentric (Asante, 1991), male centered (Kenway & Willis, 1998), heterosexist (Lipkin, 2000), or class biased (Apple, 1995). By focusing on only certain stories and perspectives, such curricula normalize and privilege certain groups in society while marginalizing others. For students who gain such partial knowledge, the impact can be far reaching, influencing not only how they think about and relate to others, but also how they think and feel about themselves. Students enter school with a range of identities and life experiences, only some of which may be represented favorably in the curriculum. Inclusive curricula, therefore, are important not only for learning to embrace various social differences, but also for affirming oneself.

Britzman (1998a) tells us that students, at least subconsciously, want learning that affirms their identities, experiences, perspectives, and values. However, she also tells us that, to learn in anti-oppressive ways, students need to do much more than learn that which affirms how they already understand themselves and what they already believe. Simultaneously and contradictorily, students also need to interrupt their desire to see their identifications, perspectives, and values repeated. They need to interrupt their resistance to disruptive, disaffirming knowledge. Reflecting on my own classroom experiences, I can think of at least three situations in which my students' desire to see their identifications and knowledge repeated seemed to hinder their learning and change. All three situations occurred when I taught in teacher-education and educational studies programs at small, undergraduate liberal arts colleges in the eastern United States.

The first situation involved students' resistance to thinking differently about themselves. In an advanced course on the relationship between schools and society, I had assigned an essay early in the semester in which my students were to draw on course readings as they analyzed how their identities and life experiences influenced their K–12 schooling experiences. I also required them to examine some of the ways they were both privileged and marginalized in school.[1] The purpose of the assignment was for them to explore how the readings might help them to think differently about their experiences in school. I wanted the students to explore what new insights are possible when they use different theoretical lenses to make sense of who they are and what they have experienced. As I collected their essays, I asked for feedback on the assignment. Some students complained that they had difficulty connecting their lives to the course readings because they did not see themselves in the readings.

For example, some students wanted to talk about their religious identities, but the course readings focused primarily on identifications of race, social class, gender, and sexual orientation. Other students wanted to talk about race, about their experiences as Latina or Black or White American students, but such identities were not central in the primary course reading on race relations and racial identities. I had assigned Lee's (1996) ethnography of Asian American students in an urban high school for its theories on the relationship between identity and academic achievement, for its concrete data on intra- and interracial relations, and for its critique of the Black-White framework that dominates discussions of race in the United States. I had explained to students that their task was not to find places in the readings that simply mirrored their own lives but to examine how the readings suggested new frameworks for understanding how their racial identities mattered in school. I pointed out that finding instances where the text confirmed their sense of self would not necessarily result in their learning anything they did not already know.

The second situation involved students' resistance to thinking differently about "good" teaching. Toward the end of the semester, student groups were responsible for leading portions of class sessions. One session focused on how educators can make more connections between schools and the communities and lives of their students; the primary course reading was Ladson-Billings's (1994) study of culturally relevant pedagogy. The students leading the session wanted to bring our discussion from the abstract to the concrete, so they ended class by asking students to spend a few minutes writing about whether they thought our course was "culturally relevant," and why or why not. Students then passed around their responses and read aloud one another's writings, anonymously. Some students felt the course was culturally relevant: it addressed a range of issues related to cultural differences and the marginalization of certain groups of students; it invited students to connect the theories in the readings to their own life experiences; and it required students to address issues of social inequity through research projects with local schools and educators.

Other students felt the course was not culturally relevant to them because they did not see themselves in the curriculum: it focused much more on marginalized groups in society than on the White American, middle-class, heterosexual mainstream that presumably comprised the majority of the students in the course; and it emphasized "liberal" and "politically correct" views that left little room to explore more traditional perspectives on and approaches to teaching, approaches that did not center on working against oppression. I had hoped the students would learn to think about "good" teaching differently, that they would shift their understanding of "cultural relevancy" from a curriculum that merely includes their own experiences and perspectives to a pedagogy that challenges the privilege of certain cultural groups and ideas. While this may have happened for some students, others seemed to resist interrupting their desire to see their own vision of "good" teaching modeled in the classroom.

The third situation involved students' resistance to thinking differently about what it means to learn. In a survey course that introduced students to a range of perspectives on and issues in U.S. schools, students were required to spend several hours each week observing and participating in a local K–12 classroom or educational setting. After each visit, students were to write a journal entry in which they described their observations and then analyzed them through various lenses suggested by course readings. I explained that the purpose of the journal was not merely to offer personal reactions to what they experienced. Such a process of journaling does have educational benefits, but my goals were different: I wanted students to explore different ways of making sense of their observations and, in particular, to explore how the course readings provided analytic lenses that differed from and even contradicted commonsense interpretations of schooling processes.

Throughout the semester, students expressed discomfort with the journal assignment. At first they were unsure how to analyze observations that were not mirrored in the course readings, so we discussed ways that "analysis" did not mean pointing out the similarities between observational data and anecdotes in course readings. We developed examples of how the readings critiqued the events observed, or how the events observed suggested gaps in educational practices mentioned by the readings. We also analyzed how the events both confirmed and challenged the theories in the readings, or how the different authors might suggest addressing problems observed by the students. We discussed ways to juxtapose observations with readings that seemed to be completely unrelated, and how that juxtaposition could lead to insights neither the author of the reading nor the observer of the classroom could have foreseen. We even practiced looking for hidden curricula as we explored processes of observation and analysis that centered on what is visible only after time. However, even when students agreed that it was possible to constantly measure their observations against the course readings, they did not always feel such a practice was helpful. They seemed to resist an assignment that required them constantly to question their desire to analyze in personalized, familiar ways. In other words, they seemed to resist uncomfortable changes in what it meant for them to learn.

In each of the three situations, I tried to make it clear that I was not saying that my curriculum materials, pedagogies, and assignments were the "best" ones possible for learning in anti-oppressive ways. Any choice could only be helpful in some ways, and I agreed that my choices were limited in the issues they raised, the questions they asked, and the learning they made possible for my students. However, in each of the three situations it seems that the limitations of my choices were not the main problem. Rather, what seemed to hinder my students' learning was their desire to see repeated in our classrooms only certain ideas about what it means to learn. Wanting to see themselves in the curriculum prevented some students from using readings on different groups in society to learn to think differently about their own lives or even to learn to use their lives to complicate theory. Wanting to experience what they already believed to be good teaching prevented some students from learning how cultural relevance could function as much to challenge their identities and beliefs as to affirm them. Wanting to do assignments in ways they already believed to be educational prevented some students from understanding the processes of schools in ways that differed from what they were used to. My students' desire for repetition prevented them from learning and changing in ways that would have drawn on anti-oppressive research and theory.

Psychoanalytic theorists (e.g., Britzman, 1998a; Felman, 1995; Luhmann, 1998) argue that such barriers to learning should be expected; students' unconscious desire for repetition and psychic resistance to change often hinder anti-oppressive education. Students come to school not as blank slates, but as individuals who are already invested in their thoughts, beliefs, and desires. Thus, the problem that educators need to address is not merely a lack of knowledge, but a resistance to knowledge (Luhmann, 1998), and in particular a resistance to any knowledge that disrupts what the students already know. Britzman (1998a) suggests that, unconsciously, students often want learning that affirms their knowledge and self-identifications. In particular, students often desire learning that affirms their belief that they are good people and resist learning anything that reveals their complicity with oppression. For example, as I have argued elsewhere (Kumashiro, 2000a), some students often express discomfort with the term *queer* as a self-identification of people who are gay, lesbian, bisexual, transgender, intersexual (GLBTI), or in other ways different because of their sexual identity or orientation. Even after learning that many GLBTIs use the term politically to reject "normal" sexualities and genders, some students ask that the silence generally surrounding that term in academia and in politically correct communities be repeated. Instead, they prefer the less confrontational terms *gay* and *lesbian*, which, unlike *queer*, do not invoke a history of bigotry, hatred, and violence, and do not contest the very meaning of normal (Tierney & Dilley, 1998). Learning about the term *queer* requires confronting their relationship with heterosexism, which is not something many students feel comfortable doing.

Learning in anti-oppressive ways involves un-learning or questioning what students already know. By implication, desiring to learn involves resisting repetition, especially the repetition of what students believe they are supposed to be learning. Were I to reenact the three situations described above, I would attempt to address their resistance to anti-oppressive learning by asking students to analyze ways in which the repetitions they desire both facilitate and hinder learning something new. For example, in the first situation, I might revise the autobiographical essay assignment to ask students to sketch out two parallel analyses, one that draws on readings in which they see themselves mirrored, and one that draws on readings that they believe differ from their own experiences. I might then assign an appendix to the essay in which students reflect on what different insights were made possible by each of the two routes of analysis, whether some of these insights are more desirable or comforting than others, and why. In the second situation, I might ask students to role-play several different visions of a culturally relevant classroom, and then ask what type of learning is made possible, or not, in each scenario. I might then ask why we desire some kinds of learning more than others. In the third situation, I might assign several different types of journal entries, some of which require analyses of readings and some that do not. I might then ask students to reflect on whether the different types of journal entries led to different kinds of insights, whether they preferred one type over another, and why that might be the case. Such lessons might help students at least to recognize their resistance, though I acknowledge that overcoming resistance is a much larger task.

Repeating what is already learned can be comforting and therefore desirable; students' learning things that question their knowledge and identities can be emotionally upsetting. For example, suppose students think society is meritocratic but learn that it is racist, or think that they themselves are not contributing to homophobia but learn that in fact they are. In such situations, students learn that the ways they think and act are not only limited but also oppressive. Learning about oppression and about the ways they often unknowingly comply with oppression can lead students to feel paralyzed with anger, sadness, anxiety, and guilt; it can lead to a form of emotional crisis. I know that I do not typically choose to do something with the expectation that it would make me upset, or at least do not do so without good reason.

Not surprisingly, some educators choose not to teach such information or to lead students to uncomfortable places. In fact, in response to my presentations on anti-oppressive education in conferences and classrooms, university educators and students have questioned whether it is even ethical to knowingly lead students into possible crisis by teaching things that we expect will make them upset. Felman (1995) suggests that learning through crisis is not only ethical, but also necessary when working against oppression. What is unethical, she suggests, is leaving students in such harmful repetition. Entering crisis, then, is a required and desired part of learning in anti-oppressive ways.

Of course, not all students will respond to a lesson by entering some form of crisis, nor will all students benefit from a crisis. Once in a crisis, a student can go in many directions, some that may lead to anti-oppressive change, others that may lead to more entrenched resistance. Therefore, educators have a responsibility not only to draw students into a possible crisis, but also to structure experiences that can help them work through their crises productively.

As I describe elsewhere (Kumashiro, 1999), one example of students entering and working through crisis occurred in a workshop on stereotypes that I taught to high school students. Many of my students expressed feelings of sadness or guilt when they learned about the harmfulness of stereotypes and about some of the ways they have unintentionally and unknowingly perpetuated them. They seemed more concerned with talking about and working through their feelings than proceeding with the more academic part of the workshop. In an attempt to address their emotional discomfort, they decided to write and perform a skit for fellow students about the harmfulness and pervasiveness of stereotypes. I believe the process of writing and performing the skit helped the students work through their crisis in two ways: they experienced the difference between being the stereotyper (with the intent to harm) and playing the stereotyper (with the intent to critique), and they came to associate many stereotypes with critical perspectives on stereotypes. In other words, they were working through crisis by changing the ways they understood and related to the process of stereotyping. My students' experiences do suggest some of the issues educators might consider when creating spaces in their curriculum for students to work through the crises inherent in learning and unlearning.

TEACHING AGAINST REPETITION

Students are not the only ones who desire repetition. Consciously and unconsciously, educators do the same when they plan what they want students to learn. Traditionally, educators have conceived of education as akin to banking (Freire, 1995) and have practiced teaching as if they were depositing knowledge into the minds of students. Although many educators today agree with Freire's critique of the "banking" approach when it concerns teaching a list of facts, many still use the banking approach when teaching thinking skills and ideologies. Educators often want students to learn theories and interpretive frameworks and be able to repeat them back "correctly" or apply them "appropriately"; educators often want students to learn to read and write in particular, identifiable, and repeatable ways, as when interpreting texts "justifiably" or writing essays "properly." Even anti-oppressive educators often value the repetition of certain knowledge and skills; we structure courses around anti-oppressive educational theories that we believe are important for aspiring teachers to learn and put into practice if they are to challenge oppression through their teaching.

I do not wish to imply that such goals are not worthwhile, since the ability to demonstrate accepted knowledge and marketable skills is cultural capital in today's society. However, it is problematic when educators presume to know exactly what the student is to learn, foretell this learning with a list of "standards," and structure education accordingly. Presuming to know and control what students are to learn makes possible only certain kinds of changes and closes off the infinite changes yet to be imagined. This presumption is especially problematic when recognizing that all knowledge is partial (Haraway, 1988). Even so-called anti-oppressive educational knowledge and practices are necessarily limited.

The problematic nature of my own incomplete knowledge is apparent when I reflect on my experiences teaching middle school English, when I emphasized learning to write "good" academic essays and analyze "themes" in literature, yet failed to teach how different forms of writing can accomplish different goals and how different readings of literature can reveal different insights on social issues. It is also apparent when I reflect on my experiences teaching high school mathematics, when I emphasized learning concepts and applications of algebra and geometry and failed to teach how different approaches to thinking mathematically can make possible different responses to social problems, and how only certain math is currently privileged in society. The problematic nature of my partial knowledge is apparent even in my attempts to teach about anti-oppressive education. When teaching an advanced seminar on anti-oppressive education at a small liberal arts college, I focused so much on teaching about my favored theories of anti-oppressive education that I neglected to provide students with the skills needed to look beyond these theories and to begin to explore possibilities for challenging oppression that the field of research has yet to articulate. This gap in my curriculum became apparent to me only when reading their final essays and realizing that their commitment to engage in anti-oppressive education often centered on implementing the types of theories we studied in class, not on challenging and expanding the very field of study.

Educators' desire to repeatedly implement what they believe is the effective approach to challenging oppression hinders many articulations of anti-oppressive pedagogy. Such is the case with some critical, feminist, multicultural, and queer pedagogies that privilege rationality when raising awareness and challenging oppression. As Ellsworth (1992) tells us, the rationalist approach to consciousness-raising assumes that reason — detached from and uninfluenced by other aspects of who we are — can lead to understanding and change. But rational detachment is impossible: students' identities, experiences, privileges, investments, and so forth always influence how they think and perceive, and what they know and choose not to know. What many people consider to be detached rationalism is really the perspective of groups in society whose identities and experiences are considered the *mythical norm*. For example, many people consider male, White, middle-class, heterosexual perspectives to be rational or normal, and other perspectives to be "influenced" by gender, race, etc., and, therefore, not rational. Thus, even while attempting to challenge oppression, pedagogies using such a rationalist approach can engage in harmful repetitions. This is not to say that the use of rationality is unhelpful in challenging oppression; like any other educational process, it makes some changes possible, others impossible. What is problematic is when educators continue to privilege rationality without questioning ways that it can perpetuate oppressive social relations.

In my own attempts to teach in anti-oppressive ways, I have found that repeating this privileging of rationalist approaches to teaching often caused me to miss my students in harmful ways. For example, in the seminar on anti-oppressive education mentioned above, I usually planned a range of activities to help students learn about various approaches to challenging oppression in schools. My lessons had often proceeded rationally from reading various theories to discussing central concepts to experiencing some aspect of the theories to imagining implications for classroom practice. Midway through the course, a group of students was leading a lesson on ways in which anti-oppressive practices often challenge one form of oppression while complying with others, and to conclude their lesson they asked the other students to discuss whether they personally felt oppressed in our class. We commonly ended class sessions by discussing how students felt that day's lesson both invited and hindered different kinds of learning and change. This time, however, they were reflecting on the overall course, and their responses stunned me.

Not all students focused on issues of oppression; some redefined the question from feeling "oppressed" to being "turned off." Nonetheless, they had much to say about how the repetition of certain aspects of the course was hindering their learning about anti-oppressive education. Some felt the structure of the course did not give enough opportunity to examine ways in which their identities as raced, gendered, classed, and sexualized people might mean that they read, respond to, and implement these theories in differing ways. The course instead seemed to suggest that there was an objective way to think about the theories. Some felt the other students in the course were not doing enough to practice what we preached and were behaving in ways that silenced others. For example, some students dismissed others' ideas as ignorant or politically incorrect. Some felt the course content did not invite hopeful feelings because many readings revealed more about oppression and about the difficulties of challenging oppression than any one educator could possibly expect to address. Clearly, their identities, experiences, and emotions influenced how they were learning. Had we not discussed these concerns, my rationalist lesson plans would have continued to miss my students in harmful ways.

The failure of teachers' lessons to reach their students does not necessarily lead to harmful consequences. Ellsworth (1997) suggests that teachers' lessons miss their students all the time. Such is the nature of teaching. She tells us that teachers address their students like a film addresses its audience:

> No matter how much the film's mode of address tries to construct a fixed and coher-
> ent position within knowledge, gender, race, sexuality, from which the film "should"
> be read, actual viewers have always read films against their modes of address, and
> "answered" films from places different from the ones that the films speak to. (p. 31)

What is problematic, however, is not that teachers' messages miss their students. The "problem" is that teachers often address their students in ways that try to fix who they are supposed to be, as when teachers assume that students begin at a place of ig-norance, that they want to be enlightened, that they need to have certain knowledge, or that they will benefit from certain experiences. The solution is not somehow to align who the teacher thinks the students are with who they actually are. Such a match is never possible because no student is ever unitary or stable. In fact, when teachers address a fixed position and students come to assume that position, both teachers and students are merely repeating a social relationship that is not moving to-ward anti-oppressive change; such a "match" is a relationship stuck in repetition.

In contrast, Ellsworth (1997) suggests that an anti-oppressive mode of address misses students in ways that invite multiple and fluid ways of learning. I can imagine several ways to change how I addressed my students in my anti-oppressive education seminar. Rather than expect that they were moving developmentally from a state of ignorance to enlightenment, I might design a lesson that expected students to have various types of knowledge, and expected them to both learn and unlearn various per-spectives on oppression and on anti-oppressive change. Rather than expect that they were committed to anti-oppressive education, I might design a lesson that expected students to want to learn some things, resist learning other things, and simply miss opportunities to learn yet other things. Rather than expect that they were becoming anti-oppressive educators, I might design a lesson that expected students to be anti-oppressive in some ways and oppressive in others. In other words, my revised lessons would refuse to expect that students would merely repeat my ideas of who they were and were supposed to become. For example, in addition to what they are learning, I might ask students to discuss, reflect on, and write about what they are unlearning, what they feel resistance to learning, and how the implementation of what they are learning can lead to contradictory results.

This is not to say that teachers should reject a traditional format for lesson plan-ning, which is necessary when educators are required to meet standards. However, teaching does not consist solely of a rational, predictable, controllable process. In many ways, teaching is unknowable and uncontrollable. Ellsworth (1997) points out that there is always a "space between" the teacher/teaching and learner/learning; for instance, between who the teacher thinks the students are and who they actually are, or between what the teacher teaches and what the students learn. Educators often respond to this uncertain space by focusing on what is known and knowable, and do whatever they can to maintain a sense of control over whom they want their students to be, what they want students to learn, and how they want students to behave (Lather, 1998). Working in a state of uncertainty, after all, often causes discomfort.

However, Ellsworth (1997) goes on to suggest that the space between is actually a very liberating space. When educators refuse to foretell who students are supposed to be and become, students are invited to explore many possible ways of learning and being. Students are not forced to merely repeat the teachers' expectations for them, which is a process that denies students their agency and limits the possibilities of change to what is imaginable within the partial knowledge of the teacher. Rather, students are invited to take responsibility for their own learning and to do the labor necessary to find and create identities and relationships with a teacher who expects only multiple, shifting ways of learning and being. In other words, teaching is not about repeating the status quo or utopian visions that are themselves partial. Rather, teaching can be about constantly working against harmful and partial repetitions; about working constantly to become a part of social relations that challenge oppression but that can never be fully anti-oppressive. To teach in this way, educators cannot presume to know who their students are, what they need, and whether they have changed in desired ways as a result of their lesson.

Such a process will likely require teachers to unlearn their ideas of "good" teaching. Anti-oppressive teaching involves educators constantly complicating their identities, knowledge, and practices. It is not unlike anti-oppressive learning. Just as students are likely to enter and work through crises as they learn and unlearn, so too are educators likely to enter and work through a crisis as they learn to engage in uncomfortable ways of teaching. Both students and educators need to challenge what and how they are learning and teaching.

What might this look like? Educators might ask students not merely to learn the theories and repeat the educator's knowledge, but also to juxtapose the theories with other texts to see what different insights are made possible — insights that the educator perhaps had not foreseen (Kumashiro, 2001). Educators might ask students not only to articulate what it is they desire to learn, but also to reflect constantly on their desire *not* to "learn," which means that educators might center their curriculum not only on what many call the core academic disciplines, nor only on uncomfortable knowledge about differences and oppression, but also on the desires and resistance that hinder anti-oppressive learning (Britzman, 1998b). In other words, educators might plan lessons with the expectation that both educator and student constantly look beyond what is being taught, and think critically about what they are expecting to constitute the processes of teaching and learning (Miller, 1998).

SUPERVISING AGAINST REPETITION

The notion that educators need to alter their teaching practices significantly in order to address issues of social justice contradicts many popular views of what it means to teach and to learn to teach. Often defined as "commonsense" are views of teaching and teacher education that do not include anti-oppressive goals and do not even value anti-oppressive perspectives. In my own experiences working with student teachers, I have repeatedly confronted at least three commonsense or "folkloric" (McWilliam, 1992) discourses of teacher education that have hindered my efforts to prepare them to teach in anti-oppressive ways.

One such discourse focuses on "academics." When teaching student teachers and even when interacting with their cooperating teachers in schools, I have encountered several interrelated reasons for resisting learning about and implementing anti-oppressive education. Some student teachers have insisted that their job and, as one put it, the "true intention of schools" is to teach the "core" academic subjects of math, science, social studies, English, and so forth. They did not agree with me that academics and oppression are connected, and argued that teachers can teach the academic subjects in ways that are neither oppressive nor anti-oppressive. In their future role as teachers, they asserted, they can and should be morally neutral and the responsibility of challenging oppression should not fall on schools. This resistance manifests even among student teachers who have read about how U.S. schools have historically focused as much if not more on moral development than on academic instruction, including Kaestle's (1983) study of the common-school movement in the antebellum era of the United States. Like proponents of the "back to basics" movement, my student teachers often seemed to embrace the discourse of schooling that has become common sense in contemporary U.S. society, namely, that the purpose of schools is to teach the "three Rs" of reading, writing, and arithmetic. Learning to teach, according to this discourse, does not need to involve learning about anti-oppressive education, moral education, or any form of education that is not commonly deemed "academic."

A second popular discourse on teacher education focuses on "experience." When discussing the degree to which their coursework helped in their development as teachers, my student teachers have often expressed a disregard for the theories and research learned in class. They complained that the theories were too abstract and idealistic in the face of day-to-day demands in "real" classrooms. Even when students found the theories and research interesting and meaningful, they had often been advised by their cooperating teachers that they would learn the important things about teaching when they got in the classroom and tried teaching firsthand. This popular notion that classroom experience is how teachers "really" learn to teach is what Britzman (1991) calls the "discourse of the real," or the cultural myth that "experience makes the teacher" (p. 7). According to this discourse, there is little reason to study educational research, including anti-oppressive educational research, since such study is not what will prepare the student to teach. I should note that teacher educators are not much different in their own professional development and efforts at anti-oppressive reform. As Zeichner (1999) tells us, teacher educators often rely on experience and cultural myths more than on educational research when learning what it means to prepare teachers to teach and when reforming teacher-education programs.

A third popular discourse on teacher education focuses on "intention." Many teacher educators with whom I have interacted often place primary emphasis in their student-teaching seminars on developing in their student teachers the skills needed to plan and implement lessons and to manage classrooms. As supervisors, they often continue to prioritize classroom instruction and management by focusing on those issues during their observations and evaluative conferences. I often am no different. When I was trained to supervise student teachers, much importance was placed on using the lesson plan to guide my observations and the student teacher's reflections. Sample questions included, "What was the objective of this activity?" and "Did the students learn or experience what was intended?" Such an approach to teacher education seems to assume that learning to teach involves learning to match what we want and do in our lessons with the results of the lessons. In other words, such an approach assumes that our "teaching" is constituted by our actions, and that the "effectiveness" of our teaching can be measured by the degree to which our intentions were realized in our students' progress.

Of course, much that is taught and learned in schools happens unintentionally and unknowingly, and constitutes what researchers have called the "hidden curriculum" of schools (Jackson, Boostrom, & Hanson, 1993). I will return to the notion of the hidden curriculum later in this article. My point here is that despite this recognition much of teacher education only focuses on the "formal" curriculum and the ways that teaching happens intentionally and visibly. Indeed, research reveals that teacher-education programs often emphasize the formal curriculum, such as when emphasizing "the acquisition of disciplinary knowledge" or "helping teachers gain deep knowledge of students' patterns of learning and growth" (Zeichner, 1999, p. 10). This is not to say that such knowledge and skills are not anti-oppressive; they can be. However, according to the formal curriculum discourse, educators often seem to believe that they are already engaging in anti-oppressive or at least non-oppressive education if they are not intentionally or visibly harming students; therefore, they express no desire to learn more about anti-oppressive perspectives (Kumashiro, 2000a).

The recognition that these commonsense discourses of what it means to learn to teach can function as barriers to anti-oppressive education is not surprising. As Apple (1995) tells us, what society defines as common sense may appear to be just the way things are, but they actually are social constructs that function to "confirm and reinforce . . . structurally generated relations of domination" (p. 12). What society defines as common sense justifies the oppressive status quo of society by sustaining "the appearance of the world as given and received, and of reality as existing on its own" (Britzman, 1991, p. 55). Commonsense discourses, then, not only socialize us to accept oppressive conditions as "normal" and the way things are, but also to make these conditions normative and the way things ought to be. In the process, such discourses suppress alternative perspectives and the possibilities for changed social relations.

I am not arguing that there is no social value to teaching the core academic disciplines, learning firsthand from classroom teaching experience, and planning objectives-based curricula. I do argue, however, that much more is needed in teacher education. Educators who presume that academic subject matter is and can be divorced from the dynamics of oppression cannot help but teach in ways that repeat the oppression already in play in these necessarily partial disciplines (Kumashiro, 2001). Educators who presume that "experience makes the teacher" cannot help but teach in ways that repeat the oppression already masked as common sense (Britzman, 1991). Educators who presume that their teaching consists solely of the formal curriculum cannot help but teach in ways that repeat the often oppressive hidden curricula that pervade U.S. classrooms. In particular, they cannot help but continue to ignore that what educators do *not* do is as instructive as what they do, which is problematic since what educators communicate indirectly and often unintentionally through silence, inaction, gestures, casual conversation, and so forth is arguably more educationally significant than what they intend to and try to teach (Jackson et al., 1993).

One way to address the commonsense assumptions that hinder student teachers' openness to anti-oppressive teacher education is to have them engage in self-analysis, as is commonly done through journaling. Zeichner (1999) reminds us that it is often very difficult to change student teachers' "tacit beliefs, understandings, and world-views" (p. 11). Simply exposing student teachers to new perspectives does not always bring about change, since the ways they have already learned to think about teaching often filter this new knowledge. The result is that student teachers often "transform the messages given in teacher education programs to fit their preconceptions, sometimes in ways that conflict with the intentions and hopes of teacher educators" (p. 11). Therefore, it is important for teacher educators to teach student teachers to look within themselves and make explicit their assumptions and preconceptions. Learning to teach involves unlearning what they have already learned about teaching, and exposing and challenging the discourses that already frame how they think about and approach teaching and learning to teach.

Self-reflection, however, is not enough. In addition, it is important for teacher educators to help student teachers recognize that their teaching exceeds their intentions. Since teaching does not consist solely of what we intend to teach, the "problem" is not merely the failure to teach what we want to teach. The "problem" is also educators' reluctance to recognize that we often teach what we do not intend to teach and do not realize we are teaching. Changing our teaching practices involves learning to examine and change ways that we unintentionally teach through what we say and do not say, do and do not do, repeat and do not repeat.

I remember supervising student teachers in math classrooms who were organized and creative lesson planners, skillful and affable classroom managers, and knowledgeable mathematicians. They were convinced that their classrooms were not oppressive since they saw and did nothing that they considered oppressive. The questions I asked during our post-observation conferences did not help to change their minds, since my questions focused primarily on whether their students seemed to be achieving the objectives set out for them, and on whether any difficulties emerged in their attempts at classroom management. In fact, by focusing on the effectiveness of their intended lesson, my questions likely reinforced the notion that they did not need to learn more about anti-oppressive education.

If I were to revise those post-observation conferences, I would likely ask questions that might prompt student teachers to recognize hidden ways that oppression could be playing out in their classroom. For example, I might ask them to reflect on their silences, on their inaction, on the hidden messages that permeate classrooms, and not just on a given day, but cumulatively throughout the year. What might students have been learning when the student teacher was silent on a particular topic? How might different groups of students have felt when the student teacher failed to act in a given crisis? How might the repetition of a particular practice daily throughout the term impact students' perception of fairness in this class? Has the student teacher learned about ways that different forms of oppression play out repeatedly in society? Are variations of these oppressive repetitions playing out in this classroom, albeit unintentionally? And what might these repetitions be teaching the students? Do any hidden messages contradict what the student teacher is intentionally trying to teach?

As another example, I might ask the student teachers to reflect on what their students were desiring, what was being repeated in the classroom, and whether they were interrupting comforting forms of repetition. Did their students want to learn only some of the information and perspectives being taught and resist learning others? Why might this have been the case? Was the student teacher addressing students in ways that required them to repeatedly identify and relate to others only in particular ways? If so, what might the student teacher have wanted? Was the student teacher inviting students into crises by interrupting certain resistance and repetitions, and then helping the students work through those crises in productive ways? And, was the student teacher teaching through crisis as the students learned through crisis? How was the student teacher helping students look beyond what was being taught and learned?

Anti-oppressive teacher education involves learning to teach the disciplines while learning to critique the ways that the disciplines and the teaching of the disciplines have historically been oppressive. It involves experiencing the realities of classroom teaching while learning anti-oppressive perspectives that can complicate the commonsense lenses often used to frame those experiences. It involves learning to teach intentionally while learning to recognize the hidden ways we often teach unintentionally. Anti-oppressive teacher education involves interrupting the repetition of commonsense discourses of what it means to teach and to learn to teach.

RESEARCHING AGAINST REPETITION

Like learning, teaching, and supervising, researching can often be characterized by harmful repetition. Certain notions of what it means to "do research" or "be a researcher" are being repeated in academia, and this repetition is proving to be a formidable barrier to anti-oppressive change, even among researchers committed to social justice. In my own interactions with other educational researchers, I have confronted at least three harmful forms of repetition.

The first form of repetition consists of researchers responding to "new" knowledge in ways that affirm what they already know. At professional meetings, such as those of the American Educational Research Association, researchers commonly present their research on panels, to which "discussants" offer responses. I have seen discussants respond to presentations in a variety of ways, some of which I have found helpful for interpreting the presentations through lenses that explore insights that neither the presenter nor the discussant could have developed before juxtaposing their knowledge. However, the discussants often seem to focus less on the possible insights and changes opened up by the presented research, and more on reasserting the knowledge they brought to the presentations.

For example, I once heard a discussant begin her response with the assertion that the presenter's use of a particular theoretical framework did not lead to conclusions that the discussant felt research has already proven. Rather than examine ways that the presentation indirectly critiqued the discussant's own research, the discussant spent her time explaining what she felt the presenter missed. In another session, a discussant began his response by asserting that his background in the field of study allowed him to ascertain that the presentation was at times insightful and at times problematic. Rather than discuss how the presentation might take the field of research in new directions, the discussant spent his time evaluating the presentation, explaining what parts of the analysis he found accurate and why, and what parts of the analysis he found inadequately supported and why.

It should not be surprising that researchers often want confirmation. Confirmation is central to how students are often taught to research and solve problems, namely, through the scientific method (Dewey, 1938). At its most basic level, the scientific method is a way of knowing that ends in repetition. A hypothesis is presented, data is collected and analyzed against that hypothesis, and if the hypothesis is confirmed by the data, the confirmation is presented. If data exist that disconfirms the hypothesis, the hypothesis is reworked and the process repeated, but the goal is eventually to find a hypothesis that is confirmed by the data. Repetition is the desired end product of such research.

Researchers often desire repetition, especially the repetition of theories that they believe have been developed and proven by the scientific method. Simultaneously, researchers often resist disruptive knowledge that requires them to unlearn what they had come to believe to be proven. Just as students often want to learn what is being taught in ways that repeat their knowledge and identities, so too do researchers often desire to respond to "new" research in ways that do not disrupt what they have already come to know. I am no different — I often feel comforted when I encounter research that confirms my assumptions or ideas, and feel distressed when I encounter research that reveals problems and even oppressive tendencies of my own knowledge and practices. After all, the process of unlearning can be emotionally upsetting. Encountering disruptive new knowledge can lead researchers into crisis. For this reason, researchers such as those described above often respond to disruptive concepts with dismissiveness, insisting instead on the repetition of what they already know to be proven.

Yet anti-oppressive research does not involve developing proven knowledge on education, nor does it involve insisting on that knowledge. Like anti-oppressive learning, anti-oppressive research involves constantly questioning and expanding what is already known. Such a disruptive move is necessary when recognizing that research and knowledge cannot help but be partial. All research is framed by the researcher's ideologies, epistemologies, theoretical frameworks, and methodologies. As Smith (1997) argues, when researchers research, they are at least subconsciously subscribing to particular "stories" or discourses of what it means to do research and be a researcher. The stories to which we subscribe frame the ways we do research. Similarly, Richardson (1997) tells us that researchers are "restrained and limited by the kinds of cultural stories available to us" (p. 2), not unlike the folkloric stories of teacher education, or the "three R's" stories of learning and teaching. Some research methodology stories, such as the scientific model, are more commonsense; others, such as narrative inquiry or feminist methodologies, are more marginalized. But all are being repeated in academia in ways that both help and hinder our abilities to research in anti-oppressive ways.

Apple (1999) tells us that subscribing to different stories or discourses can lead to significantly different ways of reviewing literature and analyzing data. He contrasted analyses of the same material by researchers from two different theoretical perspectives, and found that

> "what the data said" was a construction, subtly yet deeply connected to the social and epistemological commitments and conventions of the "discourse community" in which one is situated. This provided a compelling example of how "fields" are constructed, how discourses both construct and are constructed by, political/ epistemological moves, even when as in this case the authors shared a broad agreement on "progressive" readings of material. (p. 344)

Because different "stories" can lead to different insights about oppression and challenging oppression, and because all stories are limited, anti-oppressive research cannot simply repeat only certain stories. Anti-oppressive research involves exploring what changes are made possible and impossible by the use of different stories. No one story or set of stories can be the panacea. Ellsworth (1997) argues that anti-oppressive educational research has been conducted primarily within the social science and critical theory frameworks. In contrast, her research has drawn on film studies to offer radically different and liberating ways to conceptualize and bring about change. She reminds us that the "problem" in research is not our inability to subscribe to the "best" stories, but our desire to subscribe only to certain stories that close off other possibilities for anti-oppressive change.

By not learning constantly to explore different stories than the ones we are used to using, researchers are not being trained to do research in ways that constantly look for difference and challenge their own knowledge. And by not learning constantly to disrupt their desire to see only certain stories repeated, researchers are not being prepared to research through crisis. Yet, anti-oppressive research happens only through crisis. Anti-oppressive research does not merely repeat already proven knowledge; rather, it explores the insights and changes made possible with disruptive ways of knowing. Unless researchers are prepared to research through crisis, they will not be prepared to engage with "new" knowledge.

The second repetition I encounter consists of researchers responding to new knowledge in ways that affirm their own sense of self. I have often attended professional meetings where I presented my research on either anti-oppressive education or queer Asian American identities. Both strands of my research have emphasized the importance of addressing multiple oppression and identities, and I have often centered my presentations on the argument that challenging oppression or addressing differences among students requires examining the intersections of race, gender, class, sexuality, and other social markers. I have found it ironic, therefore, when students, educators, and researchers alike categorized my research as either multicultural/Asian American studies or gender/queer studies, but not both.

This tendency to categorize exclusively is perhaps not surprising. Like students and educators, researchers often want the confirmation not only of their knowledge, but also of their identities. I have argued elsewhere (Kumashiro, 2000a) that people often resist seeing me as *queer* and prefer the terms *gay* or *homosexual*, since such terms do not carry the in-your-face, oppressive history that queer often invokes, nor do they imply that the norm/non-queer is problematic. I also argued that people — straight and queer — often resist seeing me as bisexual and prefer to say "gay" because bisexual identities make explicit the possibility that sexual orientation is not either/or, and that sexual differences do not consist solely of polar opposites. The identifications of queer and bisexual can be discomforting because they disrupt the normalized, essentialized, commonsense ways that people often think about their own sexual identities.

I believe that I confront a similar resistance when I insist that race and sexuality are not always separable. For example, when researchers categorize my work as queer studies they are able to push to the margins the ways that I try to critique multicultural, critical, feminist, and other anti-oppressive pedagogies. This happens both informally, as when conversing with colleagues, and formally, as when respondents comment on my presentations. The insistence that multicultural/critical/feminist studies look at intersections of race, class, gender, and sexuality is easier to dismiss if voiced from a queer outsider than from someone at the presumed heteronormal center of these movements. The ongoing debate on what should be included in multicultural education is illustrative. Some say the focus should be only racism, others add classism and sexism, and still others add heterosexism and other "isms" but are told that such a move places too much of a burden on multicultural educators and diverts attention away from their primary focus, race.

I argue elsewhere (Kumashiro, 2001) that the desire to separate issues of race from issues of sexuality ignores ways that racial identifications have always been sexualized, and sexual orientation has always been racialized. It ignores ways in which anti-racist movements already reinforce heterosexism and anti-heterosexist movements already reinforce Eurocentrism. And it ignores ways in which racism and heterosexism often play out in ways that are not merely simultaneous, but intertwined and codependent. Addressing one is often impossible without addressing the other, and trying to do so can perpetuate the ways this oppression is already playing out in schools and society. This is not to say that educators and researchers must always address all forms of oppression, since the multiplicity and ever-shifting nature of oppression make any attempt to be fully inclusive impossible. However, they do need to address ways that their efforts to address some forms of oppression might be complying with others. Education researchers cannot engage in anti-oppressive research if they are only willing to engage with knowledge that allows them to repeat their social identities (based on race, gender, etc.) in comforting ways.

Anti-oppressive research involves disrupting our resistance to critiques of our own practices. Research should not be done in ways that merely repeat the researcher's desire to affirm their identity as an anti-oppressive educator. I concede that it is often difficult for researchers to acknowledge their own complicity with other forms of oppression, especially when they are trying to challenge multiple forms of oppression. Yet, since educational practices cannot help but be limited, they also cannot help but be problematic, which means that complicity is always and necessarily in play. The solution, then, is not to say, "I do my job and you do yours," as if change can be brought about additively. The solution is not to repeat our practices as if our practices were not themselves oppressive. Rather, the solution is for all of us to rethink our practices constantly. Anti-oppressive research involves responding to other researchers and their research in ways that interrupt our complicity with multiple forms of oppression.

The third repetition consists of researchers doing research in ways that reinforce their desire for detachment. Educators and students in K–12 schools have often told me that they feel that professors of education do little to try to improve schools. They complain that many professors have lost touch with reality, and that their distanced existence in the ivory tower gives them little credibility as teacher educators and reformers. They suspect that schools of education are potentially rich in resources but that these resources are barely tapped by schools. For their part, education professors do not always dispute these perceptions. Some assert that their job is to do research, not to try to improve schools; they are scholars, not educators, and certainly not reformers. Others insist that they do try to improve schools but do so indirectly by providing, through their publications, new knowledge for schools and teacher-education programs to use. Even researchers committed to anti-oppressive education do not always try to do much more to change schools than publish articles in journals read primarily by other researchers. Some professors of education have told me that they do not engage in school advocacy and reform because they are trying to produce research uninfluenced by such activism. As an outsider, they expect to be able to produce research from a more objective perspective.

This desire for detachment is problematic. Feminist researchers have long critiqued the masculinist desire for objectivity and detachment, the researcher's desire to refrain from disclosing personal opinions and feelings and from developing personalized relationships with the participants (e.g., Fine, 1994; Oakley, 1981; Richardson, 1997). In fact, some have argued that full detachment is impossible, since what the interviewees say is highly influenced by how they read, feel about, respond to, and relate to the interviewer at any given moment (Foster, 1994; Scheurich, 1995). The impossibility of detachment extends beyond the researcher's interpersonal interaction with the participants. Activist researchers have argued that research and the construction of knowledge cannot take place without the researcher's presence, involvement in, and attachment to their research. Since the researcher will always have an impact on the lives and communities of the researched, the researcher should try to have an impact that works against oppression. As Delgado-Gaitan (1993) explains, research should construct knowledge "through the social interaction between researcher and researched, with the fundamental purpose of improving the living conditions of the communities being researched" (pp. 391–392). To do otherwise is to expect the participants to participate and labor in a study that benefits only the researchers.

Similarly, when presenting the results of research, the goal cannot be to produce objective knowledge. Because knowledge is always partial (Haraway, 1988) and can always be used in multiple and contradictory ways (Lather, 1991), researchers cannot continue to assume that their production of knowledge is neutral with regard to oppression. Engaging in anti-oppressive research involves more than researching the topic of oppression, and even more than researching in ways that challenge oppression in the lives of the participants.

It also involves researching in ways that result in products and reports that can be used by others to work against oppression in larger society. Richardson (1997) tells us that the process of choosing how to write about and textually re-present research findings

> involves many major and minor ethical and rhetorical decisions. . . . But because there is no such thing as "a thing" speaking of "itself," because "things" are always constructed and interpreted . . . there is no getting it right about who or what another is; there is no essence defining what "right" is. . . . We are always viewing something from somewhere, from some embodied position. Consequently, the problem becomes a practical-ethical one: How can we use our skills and privileges to advance the case of the nonprivileged? (p. 58)

Because any "story" we use or tell makes possible and impossible different knowledge and practices, the value of research derives not from its purported truth, but from our ability to use the research in anti-oppressive ways. Doing anti-oppressive research requires that researchers look at "how the stories we tell do and do not reinscribe tyrannies, large and small — do and do not improve the material, symbolic, and aesthetic conditions of our lives" (p. 77). The question researchers need to ask themselves is, "What are we doing with the knowledge we produce to challenge oppression in schools and society?" Research cannot be anti-oppressive if it continues to repeat the desire among researchers to be detached.

I do not often see education professors doing much to get involved in changing oppression in schools near their university or college, in schools that they research, or in schools where they supervise. I do not often see education professors doing much to get involved in education reform more broadly, such as through advocacy in local districts for marginalized groups, testimonies during statewide policy debates, or publications that reach schoolteachers nationwide. Nor do I see education professors place on activism the type of value placed on scholarship, and while this problem may result from the pressure on departments to ensure that their faculty are doing what is necessary to get tenure, it seems that the field of researchers as a whole are not doing enough to change the ivory tower.

This is not to imply that there is a best or even agreed-upon way to engage in activism. I do not believe that research translates directly into specific classroom practices or policies, nor do I believe that large organizations of educators and educational researchers like the American Educational Research Association will be able to reach consensus on which anti-oppressive practices or policies should be implemented. However, I do agree with Berliner (1997) that educational researchers have an ethical obligation to work against oppression through the kinds of activities and efforts mentioned above: "We need educational activism with regard to our research and educational activism in conjunction with other agencies to promote social justice" (p. 15). We need to disrupt the repetition of commonsense discourses that define a researcher as an individual who is detached from real schools and the problems in schools. Researchers can never be detached, and to think that we are is to fall prey to the hegemonic discourses that mask our own complicity with oppression.

CONCLUSION

There is not one right way to be anti-oppressive educational activists. Even the framework of repetition that I have developed in this article to understand the problem has its limitations. There are multiple ways of conceptualizing oppression, including ways that researchers have yet to imagine. The notion of repetition makes some critiques possible but leaves others silenced; it makes some changes foreseeable and closes off others. However, the notion of repetition does provide those committed to anti-oppressive changes with a framework that complicates many commonsense approaches to learning, teaching, supervising, and researching. I urge researchers to continue to explore ways to disrupt these and other harmful repetitions in our practices, as well as to explore insights on challenging oppression that have yet to be explored by many educational researchers in the United States. I urge educators to explore the changes made possible when they juxtapose the insights in this article with their own current practices. Of course, such work is not easy. As I have argued throughout this article, anti-oppressive education involves entering and working through crisis. However, I believe more and more support is out there to help us in these processes. Clearly, increasing numbers of educators are committed to engaging in anti-oppressive practices in education, and I hope that this article helps advance our efforts.

NOTES

1. My description in the course syllabus stated that the class examined, among other things, ways that schools perpetuate social inequities. Therefore, I assumed that, by taking this course, students demonstrated their interest in learning such perspectives, and perhaps in challenging these inequities as well.

REFERENCES

Apple, M. W. (1995). *Education and power* (2nd ed.). New York: Routledge.

Apple, M. W. (1999). What counts as legitimate knowledge? The social production and use of reviews. *Review of Educational Research, 69*, 343–346.

Asante, M. K. (1991). The Afrocentric idea in education. *Journal of Negro Education, 60*, 170–180.

Berliner, D. C. (1997). "The vision thing": Educational research and AERA in the 21st century: Part 2. Competing visions for enhancing the impact of educational research. *Educational Researcher, 26*(5), 12, 14–15.

Britzman, D. P. (1991). *Practice makes practice: A critical study of learning to teach.* Albany: State University of New York Press.

Britzman, D. P. (1998a). *Lost subjects, contested objects: Toward a psychoanalytic inquiry of learning.* Albany: State University of New York Press.

Britzman, D. P. (1998b). On some psychical consequences of AIDS education. In W. F. Pinar (Ed.), *Queer theory in education* (pp. 321–335). Mahwah, NJ: Lawrence Erlbaum Associates.

Butler, J. (1997). *Excitable speech: A politics of the performative.* New York: Routledge.

Delgado-Gaitan, C. (1993). Researching change and changing the researcher. *Harvard Educational Review, 63*, 389–411.

Delpit, L. (1995). *Other people's children: Cultural conflict in the classroom.* New York: New Press.

Dewey, J. (1938). *Experience and education.* New York: Touchstone.

Ellsworth, E. (1992). Why doesn't this feel empowering? Working through the repressive myths of critical pedagogy. In C. Luke & J. Gore (Eds.), *Feminisms and critical pedagogies* (pp. 90–119). New York: Routledge.

Ellsworth, E. (1997). *Teaching positions: Difference, pedagogy, and the power of address.* New York: Teachers College Press.

Felman, S. (1995). Education and crisis, or the vicissitudes of teaching. In C. Caruth (Ed.), *Trauma: Explorations in memory* (pp. 13–66). Baltimore, MD: Johns Hopkins University Press.

Fine, M. (1994). Dis-stance and other stances: Negotiations of power inside feminist research. In A. Gitlin (Ed.), *Power and method: Political activism and educational research* (pp. 13–35). New York: Routledge.

Foster, M. (1994). The power to know one thing is never the power to know all things: Methodological notes on two studies of Black American teachers. In A. Gitlin (Ed.), *Power and method: Political activism and educational research* (pp. 129–146). New York: Routledge.

Freire, P. (1995). *Pedagogy of the oppressed* (M. B. Ramos, Trans.). New York: Continuum.

Haraway, D. (1988). Situated knowledges: The science question in feminism and the privilege of partial perspective. *Feminist Studies, 14*, 575–599.

Jackson, P. W., Boostrom, R., & Hanson, D. (1993). *The moral life of schools.* San Francisco: Jossey-Bass.

Kaestle, C. (1983). *Pillars of the republic.* New York: Hill &Wang.

Kenway, J., & Willis, S. (1998). *Answering back: Girls, boys and feminism in school.* New York: Routledge.

Kumashiro, K. K. (1999). "Barbie," "big dicks," and "faggots": Paradox, performativity, and anti-oppressive pedagogy. *Journal of Curriculum Theorizing, 15*(1), 27–42.

Kumashiro, K. K. (2000a). Teaching and learning through desire, crisis, and difference: Perverted reflections on anti-oppressive education. *Radical Teacher, 58*, 6–11.

Kumashiro, K. K. (2000b). Toward a theory of anti-oppressive education. *Review of Educational Research, 70*, 25–53.

Kumashiro, K. K. (2001). "Posts" perspectives on anti-oppressive education in social studies, English, mathematics, and science classrooms. *Educational Researcher, 30*(3), 3–12.

Ladson-Billings, G. (1994). *The dreamkeepers: Successful teachers of African American children.* San Francisco: Jossey-Bass.

Lather, P. (1991). *Getting smart: Feminist research and pedagogy with/in the postmodern.* New York: Routledge.

Lather, P. (1998). Critical pedagogy and its complicities: A praxis of stuck places. *Educational Theory, 48*, 487–497.

Lee, S. J. (1996). *Unraveling the "model minority" stereotype: Listening to Asian American youth.* New York: Teachers College Press.

Lipkin, A. (2000). *Understanding homosexuality, changing schools.* Boulder, CO: Westview Press.

Luhmann, S. (1998). Queering/querying pedagogy? Or, pedagogy is a pretty queer thing. In W. F. Pinar (Ed.), *Queer theory in education* (pp. 141–155). Mahwah, NJ: Lawrence Erlbaum Associates.

McWilliam, E. (1992). Towards advocacy: Post-positivist directions for progressive teacher educators. *British Journal of the Sociology of Education, 13*(1), 3–17.

Miller, J. L. (1998). Autobiography as queer curriculum practice. In W. F. Pinar (Ed.), *Queer theory in education* (pp. 365–373). Mahwah, NJ: Lawrence Erlbaum Associates.

Oakley, A. (1981). Interviewing women: A contradiction in terms. In H. Roberts (Ed.), *Doing feminist research* (pp. 30–61). New York: Routledge.

Richardson, L. (1997). *Fields of play: Constructing an academic life.* New Brunswick, NJ: Rutgers University Press.

Scheurich, J. J. (1995). A postmodernist critique of research interviewing. *Qualitative Studies in Education, 8*, 239–252.

Smith, J. K. (1997). The stories educational researchers tell about themselves. *Educational Researcher, 26*(5), 4–11.

Tierney, W. G., & Dilley, P. (1998). Constructing knowledge: Educational research and gay and lesbian studies. In W. F. Pinar (Ed.), *Queer theory in education* (pp. 49–71). Mahwah, NJ: Lawrence Erlbaum Associates.

Zeichner, K. (1999). The new scholarship in teacher education. *Educational Researcher, 28*(9), 4–15.

I wish to thank Diane Anderson for bouncing around ideas that eventually gelled into this piece, and Lisa Smulyan for her thorough and helpful feedback on an earlier draft.

Learning in the Dark:
How Assumptions of Whiteness Shape
Classroom Knowledge

FRANCES A. MAHER
MARY KAY THOMPSON TETREAULT

So when they met, first in those chocolate halls (of Garfield Primary School) and next through the ropes of the swing, they felt the ease and comfort of old friends. Because each had discovered years before that they were neither White nor male, and that all freedom and triumph was forbidden to them, they had set about creating something else to be.[1]

This quotation from Toni Morrison's novel *Sula* opened one of the chapters in our recent book, *The Feminist Classroom*, a study of learning and teaching in six colleges and universities across the country.[2] We chose this quote because it captured one of the central interpretive frames of our research, which explored how feminist professors and their students "set about creating something else to be" by choosing to study the histories, experiences, and aspirations of women, people of color, and other groups previously ignored or trivialized by the academy. As we gathered our observations, audiotaped classes, conducted in-depth interviews with selected students and seventeen of the teachers, and constructed a portrait of each professor's teaching, we engaged in a process of bringing their perspectives to light and explored the implications of these perspectives for the social construction of classroom knowledge.

In our self-defined role as champions of suppressed voices, we missed Morrison's invitation to Whites to examine what it means to be "White." Instead, we considered ourselves feminist researchers sharing a common perspective with the women of color that we studied, all of us being feminists resisting a male-centered academy. While we sought to acknowledge and understand our own position as White researchers, we did not fully interrogate our social position of privilege, which made us, vis à vis our subjects, oppressors as well as feminist allies.

Harvard Educational Review   Vol. 67   No. 2   Summer 1997, 321–349

Our original analysis of this data resulted in our book, *The Feminist Classroom*, which was organized around four themes: mastery, voice, authority, and positionality. In our subsequent reanalysis of our *Feminist Classroom* data, we found that exploring the theme of positionality became the most salient theme in understanding our own Whiteness. Positionality is the concept advanced by postmodern and other feminist thinkers that validates knowledge only when it includes attention to the knower's position in any specific context.[3] While position is always defined by gender, race, class, and other significant dimensions of societal domination and oppression, it is also always evolving, context dependent, and relational, in the sense that constructs of "female" create and depend on constructs of "male"; "Black" and the term "of color" are articulated against ideas of "White." Thus peoples' locations within these networks are susceptible to critique and change when they are explored rather than ignored, individualized, or universalized.

We ended *The Feminist Classroom* with a call for "pedagogies of positionality," for approaches to teaching in which these complex dynamics of difference and inequality could be named and examined. What we ignored, however, were the persisting powers of the *dominant* voices that continue to "call the tune" — that is, to maintain the conceptual and ideological frameworks through which suppressed voices were distorted or not fully heard. We did not see the ways in which a thorough "pedagogy of positionality" must entail an excavation of Whiteness in its many dimensions and complexities.

One reason for our omission is that we lacked the interpretive frameworks to examine Whiteness, which the proliferation of recent literature on the topic has since given us.[4] Much feminist theory has come from examining certain types of marginality; we, like other White feminists, focused on the situations and experiences of women as victims of gender oppression, leaving the positions of racial domination unexplored.[5] To explore Whiteness would have meant examining and reframing our own positions vis à vis our informants, particularly our informants of color.

In Toni Morrison's *Playing in the Dark: Whiteness and the Literary Imagination*, she invites us to go beyond looking at racism in terms of its effects on the victim and to consider, through works of American literature, "the impact of racism on those who perpetuate it. It seems both poignant and striking how avoided and unanalyzed is the effect of racist inflection on the subject."[6] Morrison's proposal drew us back to a quote we used in our book to show the complex ways in which students from the dominant White culture began to learn about themselves from these newly emerging voices:

> Never in my life have I ever been ashamed of being an upper-class white male. . . . I don't have anything to gain by having Black and White equal. I feel like if it happens, I'll still have a good life, a profitable life. And if women stay home or not, you know like men want them to . . . I can gain, like mankind gains, or womankind, but personally I don't have to deal with that. I'm an upper-class White male; I'm the boss. . . . If you're born and you could have your choice of what you wanted to be, White male would probably be the choice, because that's the best thing to be.[7]

This student's construction of his identity was bound up with, and expressive of, a deep-rooted sense of entitlement based on gender and class, as well as race. Reflecting on the importance of taking a course that addressed both sexism and racism, he went into great detail about being a minority in a class composed of a majority of African Americans, both female and male, and a small group of White women.[8]

This student, Mark, was from a privileged Atlanta family and had attended high school at both an exclusive private day school and a local magnet school for the performing arts, which was 60 percent African American.[9] In both places he had friendly acquaintances with Black students. His father owned an art gallery specializing in African art, and he had taken several African American history classes, which he had loved, at his historically White research university. Characterizing himself in an interview as not being brought up "typically Southern," he placed great store in learning about Black culture and history as an antidote to racism. Mark was in a class on "Women and Literature" taught by an African American woman, which emphasized texts by women of color. When we saw that learning about the lives and works of African American women left Mark's own racial and gender positions intact and unexplored, we were initially taken aback. We did not examine our assumption that by learning about African American lives, Mark and others would be more aware of the pernicious effects of racism on everyone, and thus more conscious of the standpoint from which he, and many other Whites, look at the world. Could a different emphasis in this class have made Mark more conscious and reflective about his position of privilege in a network of relations of dominance?

We began to wonder how to address the implications of ingrained assumptions of White privilege amid the persistence of racial oppression and the growing racial alienation of our society. Among the most powerful mechanisms maintaining the superiority of dominant voices is the failure to acknowledge and understand how assumptions of Whiteness shape and even dictate the limits of discourse, in the classroom as elsewhere.[10] Assumptions of Whiteness gain much of their power by passing as "normal," "an invisible package of unearned assets" that Whites "can count on cashing in on each day, but about which they were meant to remain oblivious."[11]

As we became increasingly aware of these issues in our own professional and personal lives, and as we decided to return to our classroom data, we were drawn to new literature on the ideology and practices of Whiteness. Writers and scholars such as Toni Morrison, David Roediger, Elizabeth Ellsworth, Andrew Hacker, and Karen Sacks have recently focused on the cultural construction of the categories "White" and "Black," or "White" and "of color," attacking the assumption that racial differences are "natural states" deducible from physical characteristics. These writers assert, as the concept of positionality implies, that these categories of race depend on each other for their elaboration as meaningful entities, as well as for the multiple (and changing) significance attached to them.[12] Whiteness, like maleness, becomes the norm for "human"; it is the often silent and invisible basis against which other racial and cultural identities are named as "other," and are measured and marginalized.

Whiteness operates at different levels simultaneously. Authors such as Becky Thompson and her colleagues have distinguished among "Whiteness as description," referring to the assignment of racial categories to physical features, "Whiteness as experience," referring to the daily benefits of being White in our society, and finally, "Whiteness as ideology," referring to the beliefs, policies, and practices that enable

Whites to maintain social power and control.[13] By the institutionalization of physical appearance as social status, all Whites gain special advantage over those marked "Black" or "people of color." Whiteness thus becomes a marker for location of social privilege, as well as individual identity. To understand Whiteness as a social position is to assign everyone, not only people of color, differentiated places in complex and shifting relations of racialized and gendered hierarchies.

Whiteness may be further defined, in Elizabeth Ellsworth's recent work, as "instead of a fixed, locatable identity, or even social positioning, . . . a dynamic of cultural production and interrelation."[14] In the college classrooms we studied, as in other settings, Whiteness was both assumed and continually in need of assertion, always being constituted as it was simultaneously being challenged and resisted.

David Roediger, Karen Sacks, and Andrew Hacker all show how notions of Whiteness change over time. To become White has often been constructed as synonymous with becoming truly American. Roediger explores ways in which nineteenth-century White workers learned to depend for their self-definition on their sense of themselves as White by defining themselves against Black slaves and freedmen.[15] The concept of who was White also changed to include successive groups of European immigrants, just as immigrants themselves changed to fit into some concept of Whiteness. America's larger systems of racial formation often confounded religion and race as well. For example, Hacker observes that Irish-Catholic immigrants took longer to shed an alien identity because Catholics were not regarded as altogether White, and Jews were kept at the margin of White America because they were not Christians.[16] Further, Sacks shows how this concept of Whiteness evolved as Jews "became White folks" following World War II. Roediger says that "the central implication of the insight that race is socially constructed is the specific need to attack *Whiteness* as a destructive ideology rather than to attack the concept of race abstractly."[17]

What new questions, therefore, do we need to ask as teachers and classroom researchers in order to expose Mark's and others' classroom experiences as complex reflections of and reactions to the racialized power relations of our society? How firmly, for example, are assumptions of Whiteness lodged in the academy's ideological frameworks, in its exercise of intellectual domination, and how do they work to shape classroom knowledge? How is Whiteness produced and resisted as a function of the ongoing production of classroom meanings, and what role does it play in the students' construction of their own places within racial, as well as class and gender, hierarchies? Given the practice of understanding racialism only in terms of its effect on people of color, how do people of color construct the role of Whiteness as they go about "imagining something else to be?"

A necessary part of perceiving how the assumption of Whiteness shapes the construction of classroom knowledge is understanding its centrality to the academy's practices of intellectual domination, namely, the imposition of certain ways of constructing the world through the lenses of traditional disciplines. Such domination is often couched in the language of detachment and universality, wherein the class, race, and gender position of the "knower" is ignored or presumed irrelevant. By evoking the academic mirror's assumptions of Whiteness as well as maleness, Adrienne Rich named two major attributes of the universalized perspective that scholarly pursuits both depart from and aim for:

> When those who have the power to name and to socially construct reality choose not to see you or hear you, whether you are dark-skinned, old, disabled, female, or speak with a different accent or dialect than theirs, when someone with the authority of a teacher, say, describes the world and you are not in it, there is a moment of psychic disequilibrium, as if you looked into a mirror and saw nothing.[18]

Our use throughout *The Feminist Classroom* of a "methodology of positionality," one in which we continually revisited our work and our own position with perspectives gained from new experiences and insights, allows us now to write a new "last chapter" as both an extension and a reversal of how we initially looked at race in our book. We can now use theories of Whiteness as lenses to reexamine some of our classroom portraits, to see how Whiteness was constructed, and how that construction shaped the discourse. By comparing our original analysis with this new perspective, we can also see our own positions as researchers anew.[19]

In undertaking this reanalysis of our data, now from the acknowledged position of our own Whiteness, we have to ask ourselves why we are revisiting these classrooms. As Ellsworth points out, academic writing on Whiteness, by Whites, often makes us again into "experts" on race, reifying the same relations of oppression that we wish to contest.[20] With these warnings in mind, we want to reexamine several classroom vignettes, not to produce the White experts' last word on them, but to illuminate some ways of rereading the students' production of "White," "Black," and other racialized positions and identities. We stress the particularity of these rereadings, not only as being contingent on our present take on our own positions, but as presentations of unique situations, "not the one but the one among many," and as "responses to historically specific encounters with particular racisms." We want to portray some of "the context-specific responses made possible when Whiteness is related to the other social positioning that people live out and live through" — in these cases, not only gender and class, but the specific dynamics produced by the teacher and student composition of these different classrooms as well.[21]

Our first few examples will reflect class discussions in which Whiteness is assumed as a normal condition of life rather than a privileged position within networks of power. It appears to be a safe, well-marked path, powerful because it is an invisible one to Whites, which allows discussions of race to slide effortlessly forward as notations of features of "the other." Specifically, we look at the dynamics of White racial formations in enactments of gender and class.

Next we turn to a situation where Whiteness began to come into focus as a position. The path of discussion becomes bumpy and painful, but the critique of the relationships of oppression necessary to a positional understanding of Whiteness becomes possible through these interactions. Finally, we look at one class, in which the teacher and the majority of participants were people of color. In this class, Whiteness had to be named and actively resisted in order for participants to proceed with the construction of knowledge on their own terms.

CONSTRUCTING SOCIAL CLASS AS WHITE AND MALE

We look first at the ways White males construct their masculinity and class positions, using the assumption of Whiteness as part of their guiding ideological framework. The first case we look at is a senior seminar in literary theory at a small liberal arts college. Nine students were enrolled, five males and four females, all White, several of whom were in their late twenties to mid-thirties. One of us was always present in the classroom as an observer, in this case, Mary Kay Tetreault. All discussions were taped and later transcribed and edited. This discussion, from which the following excerpt is drawn, concerned the ideas of a prominent French feminist, Julia Kristeva, as analyzed in Toril Moi's book *Sexual/Textual Politics*.[22] The initial focus on Kristeva was "derailed" when the professor, who is White, used "class" to show how the same term can have different meanings.

Her comment led to an extended argument about whether women could be seen as a class; two males fought vigorously against the idea, and one female defended it. Ralph, who referred to himself as a "former SDSer,"[23] began this debate by saying, "I'm rejecting sexes as defined as classes; I think classes are defined by economics." Jane replied, "Right, and economics are defined by gender." Ralph's next remarks — that "gender is defined by economics," that "it has less to do with . . . sexual oppression in itself as it does [with] power, or acquisition, or ownership" — made Jane bristle. She responded, "That seems so irrelevant to this — you argue that it's power and acquisition, but the fact of the matter is a high majority of women are making less money [than men]." Ned came to Ralph's defense, asserting at one point that "if you look at gender, you will see all women as being oppressed," implying that not all women are oppressed in economic terms.

These students did not mention race at all as being part of their discussion of class analysis, but we can examine how assumptions about race and gender drove the discussion. Ralph, for example, drew class divisions along both gender and racial lines, unconsciously constructing class as both White and male while simultaneously claiming class as the primary oppression. In this discussion, sex belonged only to women; males' gender was not named. Therefore, Jane's introduction of gender into the analysis was treated by Ralph and Ned as an introduction of women. When Ralph said, "it has less to do with sexual oppression than power or ownership," he was resisting the introduction of women's oppression into the equation because it muddied the water and because class oppression has no gender (i.e., it is assumed to be male against male). Jane's earlier comment about working-class women's lower wages (when compared to working-class men's wages) led only to a stalemate about whether gender or class is the primary type of oppression. That stalemate continually reinforces and normalizes the idea that the working class (and the ruling class, too, presumably) is male.

But were these students constructing the working class as White, as well as male? After a while the teacher introduced the concept of positionality to move the discussion forward:

> What we need is a description that is not based on categories but on positionality, on relations. No group is in and of itself oppressed or marginal. It's only in relation to

something else. So that women, we can say, are marginal compared to men. But Black women are marginal compared to White, middle-class women.

What is perceived as marginal at any given time depends on the position one occupies. You have to see centrality and marginality, oppression, oppressor and oppressed as relational concepts. That is, they are marked by difference, not by any positive kind of thing. [So] you have to keep the whole thing moving.

Feminism posits itself as a counter to patriarchy. It argues that patriarchy is central and women are marginal. The working class has been fairly ignored in the feminist movement. . . . Black women's struggles have been marginal to the feminist movement. The feminist movement in this country, by and large, has been White and middle class. So, already they have reinscribed that same center-margin dichotomy within itself.

Ralph then asked his teacher, "What determines White and middle class? I still have problems with this." The teacher responded, "Well, again you have to see it as relational, not a positive kind of term." Ralph then replied, "Well, that is different, then. It is negative, you know."

In our original analysis of this class, we worried that women's oppression could be ignored in the relativism of such an approach. We observed gender oppression being given a back seat to the males' assertion that economic class was the main oppression, which we thought enabled them to ignore the issue of male privilege. We saw male dominance enacted, not only in their vocal domination of the discussion, but also in the way Ned and Ralph collaborated in opposing Jane. Even though we noted that their own position was not critiqued or made visible by either the professor or the students, we also inadvertently equated gender primarily with women.

What we did not see were the powerful ways in which the students and teacher were constructing maleness and Whiteness as the norm, both for economic classes and for people in general. While the teacher's use of positionality challenged the students to break out of the categories they were debating and to see them all in relation to each other, race and gender were still presented as sets of complementary opposites and exclusions (women compared to men, Black women compared to White women). While the professor called centrality and marginality into question as shifting and relational concepts "marked by difference, not by any positive kind of thing," she failed to articulate (nor did we pick up) the power relationships that produce these forms of centrality and marginality in the first place, namely Whiteness and maleness.

Ralph's class analysis may have been his way of expressing a covert identity politics, one whose central figure is not working people in general, but the working-class White male. If Ralph were to include the perspectives of women and Blacks in his construction of working class, this might challenge the primacy of class oppression, and make the interrelations of class, gender, and race oppression more complex. In a subsequent interview, Ralph reaffirmed his view of the importance of class while continuing to construct it as White and male. He wondered if it would ever be possible to "quantify human needs," and thought that paying attention to gender detracted from human needs. "Once you consider gender issues, you're immediately led to the sword of economic theory . . . and I haven't seen any fundamental change in the level of suffering among women." Again, "gender" is "women." Ned told us he preferred

Kristeva's call to deconstruct the hierarchies over "feminism's idea of a feminist self," which he viewed as "a limitation on the human self." Better to erase all differences than risk the reversal of the hierarchies that a feminist self implied. Both men wished that the whole notion of gender would go away, because White males, in their formulation, have no gender (and perhaps no race) themselves.

Despite the professor's assertion that "what we need is a description that is not based on categories," this discussion of race presupposed the categories Black and White as a binary opposition, rather than exploring the ways in which these categories (as well as the categories "woman" and "man") actively produce each other. Race only entered the discussion when the professor began speaking about positionality. But Whiteness, like maleness, had been central to the identity of the working class in the discussion all along. In short, this whole discussion, in which the students resisted the inclusion of race and gender, was profoundly "racialized" and "genderized."

CONSTRUCTING WHITENESS IN INDIVIDUALIZED TERMS

In reexamining much of our original research data, we found that the students in other classes tended to construct social class in implicitly White and male terms as well. Moreover, in one case where Whiteness was acknowledged, its treatment as an aspect of individual identity masked its operations on deeper social and ideological levels.

Our next example comes from an honors freshman writing class of five male and five female White students at a large comprehensive university, which, as a state institution, draws upon a less affluent, predominantly White student body.[24] This discussion treated issues of social class in much more concrete terms than the previous example, perhaps due to the participants' location nearer the bottom of the class hierarchy. In our book, we described the discussion as reflecting many White students' typical attitudes towards social class, where middle-class status is assumed for all White people, leaving the category "poor" as a marker for Blacks and avoiding exploration of the wide class differences among White people themselves.

As an introduction to *The Women of Brewster Place,* Gloria Naylor's novel about working-class Black women in an urban setting, the professor, a middle-class White female, wanted the students to look at the structural elements of class, race, and gender oppression, and see how they are interrelated. In response to her question, "Have any of you read any books that talked about social class?" the male students (no females spoke) described class in anecdotal terms, telling stories of financial upward mobility. One student contrasted rich people who "can afford to do what they want . . ." with those who have only a moderate amount of money, who "cannot just go crazy; they are saving up and investing."

While agreeing with the students that "income is a major determinant of class," the instructor pushed them towards more structural issues, asking, "Is there class mobility?" Most students answered, "Sure," but several males noted underlying class rigidities. For example, one said,

A lot of snobbery exists between old money and new money. I could become rich tomorrow, but because I don't come from a rich family I couldn't be in that upper class. Class isn't what I determine myself to be, but what someone else makes it. That's the problem.

A few minutes after the above remarks, she asked, "What about racism?" and a few minutes later, "What about Affirmative Action? Does that help [to fight racism]?" Based on an equation of Blacks with the underclass, and extending to other minorities as well, the students assumed that those who get ahead are a priori lacking the proper qualifications:

It's really like a slap in the face. You've got the jobs just because you're Black or Asian, they're not saying you got the job because you're better or more qualified, [but that] we need your minority groups because our supervisor is going to come down on us.

When the teacher later sought to turn the discussion back to race, we saw one of the rare instances in our data where the construct of race included the idea of Whiteness:

The consciousness level in the United States has been raised, where we're much more highly aware of gender issues. Whereas race, White people don't often think of racial identity in terms of their own identity, what it means to be a White person. . . . The minority races are much more conscious of who they are. That's not true for Whites in America, that the first thing you identify with as "Who are you?" is White.

Our original analysis in *The Feminist Classroom* characterized this comment as showing how the teacher "helped her students confront racial issues," and we still associated "race" with African Americans, not Whites. Upon further reflection, we see this remark, and indeed this whole discussion, as a vivid example of the extreme individualism in mainstream culture. While the students assert that class position is determined by individual upward mobility, the students also seem to be unconsciously noting structural factors, such as snobbery: "class is what someone else makes it." However, these factors are always experienced in individual terms, "I could not be upper class." This perspective is carried over to their dismissal of Affirmative Action policies as unfair acts of favoritism, a personalized "slap in the face." But again, this "slap" is read as coming from "your minority groups"; Blacks are seen not as individuals, but as a group. Yet, because of the White student's construction of Affirmative Action as a threat to his individual mobility rather than a response to a group history of discrimination, he spouted the worst stereotypes about unqualified people getting jobs.

These students tell a familiar narrative of discrimination in which they feel simultaneously victimized as individuals by groups from above and below. However, only the latter group is racialized and seen as "the other." Whiteness is unconsciously constructed and relied upon here as the social glue normalizing their connection to other, "higher-up" Whites, thus stabilizing an inherently unstable situation. The professor could not get her White students to understand the position of Blacks because they didn't understand their own position as Whites. Although they understood something of class privilege, through their lack of it, they could not see themselves as privileged within the social relations of race.

We now see that even the teacher's insightful last remark about White racial identity, while ahead of our own thinking at the time, still casts Whiteness in individualized rather than structural terms — as an issue of "what it means to be a White person." Indeed, this excerpt illustrates that the acknowledgment of Whiteness as an individual attribute does not automatically lead to an expanded understanding of its social structural relations, or of its ideological power; rather, people may acknowledge their Whiteness simply as a self-justifying or self-excusing marker of relative personal privilege, and no more. That Whiteness is a social construction organizing people into social relations of dominance and oppression, through which some individuals benefit, eluded us at the time as well. Moreover, we now wonder if, among the students who spoke, their exploration of their class and race resentments assumed maleness as another unmarked attribute of their identity, an assumption that would have accounted for the female students' silence in that discussion. Assumptions of Whiteness took another form in our next example, however, as women students explored issues of femininity and beauty from different, but no less complex, racial positions.

WHITENESS, SEXUALITY, AND FEMININITY

In her novel *The Bluest Eye,* Toni Morrison offers an illustration of the ways in which dichotomizing White as the norm and Black as different shapes notions of beauty in the African American world. In the relationships among Pecola, a powerless girl, and the other characters in the novel, Morrison shows how the others construct themselves through demonizing her:

> All of us felt so wholesome after we cleaned ourselves on her. We were so beautiful when we stood astride her ugliness. Her simplicity decorated us, her guilt sanctified us, her pain made us glow with health. . . . Her inarticulateness made us believe we were eloquent. Her poverty kept us generous. Even her waking dreams we used, to silence our own nightmares.[25]

Remembering this insight prompted us to examine the racialization of femininity and sexual attractiveness in classes in *The Feminist Classroom.* One of the most telling examples of this theme took place in a course entitled "Women Writers since 1800." The class was composed of seventeen women and five men, ranging from freshmen to seniors, and was taught at the same liberal arts college as our first excerpt. The teacher began one class by asking if anyone had written in their journal about Emily Dickinson in response to the discussion of her poetry in the previous class. Nancy, a Japanese American woman who sat at the edge of the room and had not spoken during our previous observations, nodded, and began to read from her journal entry. She based part of her entry on a poem that begins, "I'm Nobody! Who are you?"

I'm Nobody! Who are you?
Are you — Nobody — Too?
Then there's a pair of us?
Don't tell! They'd advertise —
you know!

How dreary — to be — Somebody!
How public — like a frog —
To tell one's name — the live-
long June
to an admiring Bog![26]

I couldn't help thinking of the idea of a mute culture within a dominant culture. A "nobody" knowing she's different from the dominant culture keeps silent and is surprised to find out there are others who share this feeling. But they speak only to each other and hide otherwise. This is what it must have been like being a woman and thinking against the grain. But don't tell! At least if you are silent and no one knows, you can continue to live your inner life as you wish, your thoughts at least still belong to you. If "they," the somebodies, find out, they'll advertise and you'll have to become one of them.

Nancy then turned to some comments about Poem 327:

Before I got my eye put out
I liked as well to see —
As other Creatures, that have
Eyes
And know no other way —

But were it told to me — Today —
That I might have the sky
For mine — I tell you that my
heart
Would split, for size of me —

The Meadows — mine —
The Mountains — mine —
All Forests — Stintless Stars —
As much of Noon as I could
take
Between my finite eyes —

The Motions of the Dipping
Birds
The Morning's Amber Road —
for mine — to look at when I
liked —
The News would strike me dead —

So safer — guess — with must my
soul
Upon the Window pane —
Where other Creatures put their eyes —
Incautious — of the Sun —[27]

But looking at poem 327 it's problematic, there is a price to pay, and it isn't always voluntary. Infinite vision seems to come from suffering through enforced pain. "Before I got my eyes put out I liked as well to see — As other Creatures, that have Eyes and know no other way." You can run around in ignorant bliss until something breaks through this level of illusion, takes out the "eye" that makes it possible for you to view the world this way and once you see through it, you can't go back, trying to face yourself backwards would "strike you dead." I'm not articulating this well but it's like growing awareness.

A silly example: It's like watching a Walt Disney movie as a child where Hayley Mills and these other girls dance and primp before a party singing "Femininity" how being a woman is all about looking pretty and smiling pretty and acting stupid to attract men. As a child I ate it up, at least it seemed benign, at the most I eagerly studied it. But once your eye gets put out and you realize how this vision has warped you, it would split your heart to try and believe that again, it would strike you dead.

In our interpretation of this class, we concluded that Nancy was rejecting her earlier attempt to model herself on Hayley Mills, a prototypical White teenager of the 1960s, and embarking on a second rite of passage in which she recognized the harm of modeling herself on such a trite stereotype of American femininity. In the invocations of both Emily Dickinson's poetry and of Hayley Mills, who is young and blond, Nancy's images of femininity and of womanhood are not only images of superficial physical characteristics associated with Whiteness, but of female sexuality as well. Neither in the class discussion nor in our original interpretation was this point taken up. By concentrating on her evocation of gender oppression, we allowed Nancy's recognition of the harm of modeling herself on a stereotype of White femininity to pass us by. We also did not see that Hayley Mills's "beauty" depended on Nancy's "otherness" for its intensity. This oversight reveals the extent to which we too had internalized the complex interplay of physical beauty and sexuality that on the one hand primarily constructs femininity as White, and on the other hand fails to understand the extent to which women of color also carry around a White norm of beauty.

Nancy's musings underscore the physical and visual power of race as part of imagining one's appearance to others, and therefore one's effect on others. How does one read and internalize messages of beauty and ugliness, visibility and invisibility, as inscribed on one's body? Feminist theorists have long since taught us the importance of understanding the ways in which women internalize "the male gaze," learning how to see themselves as objects of others' viewpoints rather than subjects of their own construction. We have learned from Nancy the extent to which physical racial identification confers instant ascribed identity, and with it, social status. However, since we as White women are not often conscious of our race, we do not experience our bodies as "raced" as many women of color do.

A subsequent interview with Nancy, who grew up in a Japanese American family in a small Finnish community in the Northwest, "where there were three Japanese families that lived down our little road," leads us to wonder now about how much Nancy had in fact internalized White images. As a young Asian American, did she after all identify as "White" most of the time?

> We were the only Japanese family that went to school in a Finnish community. [If] you look at my yearbook, everyone is blond and tall and then there is us. We grew up in this community where we're obviously very different physically, but since we grew up there we didn't really perceive ourselves as very different. Whenever we were among a lot of other Japanese, we would notice that and feel, "Oh, look, everybody's Japanese!"

We are now also struck by the complexity of Nancy's racial identification — "We're obviously very different physically, but we didn't really perceive ourselves as very different." Writers on Whiteness like Andrew Hacker, Neil Gotanda, and others have pointed out that one of the most pernicious aspects of American racism has been its rigid construction of anything "non-White" as Black. The confusion caused by these dichotomies has left some Asian Americans, for example, identifying as White and others as junior versions of Blacks.[28]

The impact of the ideal of "pretty and blond" on Nancy's sense of herself as a woman, and the cost of "living in the roles" of the dominant culture, meant that Nancy had to see herself in terms of Hayley Mills, or *not* Hayley Mills, before she could construct an alternative vision of who she was. But who "was" she, in terms of "Black" and "White"? What are the fault lines and discontinuities that emerge when the category of "Whiteness" as description offers up only mixed messages to an Asian American woman? The vivid, visual nature of the lesson Nancy learned about Whiteness is shown in the language she used to name the end of innocence — "how this vision has warped you."

Mirrors are also metaphors for showing us how others see us, and therefore for the imposition of ideology and culture onto our multilayered consciousness of self. The earlier quote from Adrienne Rich describes the pain of looking into a mirror, and the impossibility of merging the way you see yourself with the ways the outer world experiences you. By contrast, a professor we worked with at a historically Black women's college told her African American students how to use a mirror to reclaim their bodies against the Whiteness of the "beauty myth":

> So I tell my students, the way I look at the "beauty myth" is about trying to look into a mirror and trying to see yourself. In a very systematic way thinking about those sociocultural corporate entities that keep you from seeing and appreciating who you are — your face, your breasts, everything. And then we move on from there to how to wipe the mirror clean. Not with Windex, which involves buying something already packaged, but with vinegar and water, which is something that your mother told you will cut through the dirt in a real special way.[29]

When Toni Morrison made "our" beauty contingent on Pecola's ugliness, she too was emphasizing the ideological and cultural freight carried by White standards of beauty, its association with virtue and truth, the "normal" against which the "other" is demonized, or disappears. To reconceptualize the assumptions that construct beauty, as did Nancy, is to claim the possibility and necessity of conscious resistance. As Nancy wrote: "Once you see through it, you can't go back, trying to face yourself backwards would `strike you dead.'"

WHITENESS AND THE RESISTANCE TO INTELLECTUAL DOMINATION

The professor who helped us to see most clearly how intellectual domination is tied to Whiteness, as well as to issues of classroom processes and power relations, taught history and gender studies at the liberal arts college Nancy attended.[30] Worrying about a gender studies class, Feminism in Historical Perspective/Feminist Theory, in which thirty students were enrolled (including three people of color — a man and two women) the professor found that about half the students were silent. The professor, a White woman, assumed at first that the quieter students just needed time to become equal participants. She did not realize that they felt unprepared to join a discussion that presumed so much prior knowledge and experience of feminist theory and practice. She viewed part of the problem as her own emphasis on the academic discipline: "My engagement with the subject matter interfered with my performance as a teacher."

But her use of democratic classroom processes, in enabling some students to become authorities for each other, also meant that a few students who were more outspoken were dominating the others. She observed that it was common for the student majority from the dominant White culture, in exploring their own experiences, to end up avoiding and resisting the experiences of others. She reported in a paper:

> The culture of our gender studies program validates personal experiences and suppresses the expression of differences that challenge other peoples' perspectives. People feel empowered to speak of their own experiences, and construct theory on that basis, and that is good. But they do not feel impelled to include other peoples' experience in their explanatory frameworks, . . . and when the other people insist that their experiences too must be taken into account, they respond with barely concealed hostility.[31]

To illustrate these problems, and their relation to Whiteness, we turn to the professor's course, in which a small number of theoretically minded seniors were taking over class discussions. Their distinctive discourse, which drew heavily on the poststructural language they had learned in literary theory courses, was incomprehensible to the rest of the students.[32] This pattern was broken by Amy Santos, a quiet student who described herself as "mixed Latina and Native American." Her frustration with these seniors led her to a critique of the "academic realm" as one of domination and subordination, one in which "you can be in the `not knowing' position or you can be in the `knowing.'" Academic discourse constricts "what we really mean and puts a real limitation on how we communicate." She said, "Sometimes I go to class thinking, that was a bunch of theory, and feeling like the more abstract people are looking down on me, which I think is a product of their own insecurity and insensitivity."

While the students themselves came up with a solution together about their own responsibility for the class,[33] we now believe that this earlier revolt against a few seniors created a climate for some of the formerly quieter students to bring issues of racial and gender oppression and invisibility into the classroom. The discussion we take up next, led by the three students of color, concerned the absence of a discussion of race in feminist theory and their own need for the creation of explicit racial and ethnic identities. While part of it was in the book, we missed the continuing assumptions of Whiteness that framed the discourse.

We now want to reconsider this class by looking at how the White students' construction of gender and racial oppression worked to mask the naming of Whiteness as a social position and as an oppressive aspect of feminist theory. We also want to illustrate the ways the students of color challenged the White students by insisting on exploring the need to name themselves, to give themselves identities, and how the pervasiveness of Whiteness as a dominating conceptual apparatus frustrated their efforts. We can see here how Whiteness is actively constructed and maintained even as it is resisted.

The discussion began with some observations by Sharon, a Filipino American, about the absence of women of color in Sheila Rowbotham's book, *Woman's Consciousness, Man's World,* because discussions of the Black movement focus on men and discussions of women focus on White women. "Most of the feminist literature that I've come across doesn't say a lot about racism," she commented.

Ned, a White male student who also took the literary theory course discussed earlier, responded by pointing out that the problem lay in the connections between experience and theory; specifically Rowbotham's "extolling of individual experience" and "looking for too generalized similarities between us . . . which overlooks problems like race." He then added, "If she never had to entertain race and it never crossed her mind once, I would indict her methodology, her starting from personal experience," implying that Rowbotham went wrong because she started from personal experience, which does not include her race because she is White. To his mind, to take up race would be to consider women of color.

The frequent reaction of the White female students who spoke to these points was to push for a general theory of gender that would unite all women across their different experiences, without having to pay attention to particular forms of oppression and dominance, namely Whiteness and White racism, that would disrupt that unity and cast them into oppressor roles. One White female student, for example, wanted to know "how you can maintain the diversity but still get some kind of unity." Another resisted the loss of women as a "distinct" group, saying, "[When] women's issues are intermixed with racial issues and oppression . . . women (i.e., White women) get lost in the shuffle."

But Ned continued to worry about both the necessities and the perils of beginning with individual experiences. He believed that theory ought to broaden out by connecting "personal experiences" of oppression by giving groups a "common battle to fight," or "linking up with someone who is similarly oppressed and slog through the bog."

He worried that "increasingly narrow experiences" would result, as if combining all the different oppressions cancels out each one:

> I think my question about women's consciousness earlier was, is this an attempt to erode class [unity]? I think you can just assume it was answered yes and was also an attempt to erode racial barriers — but what comes out of [talking about gender and race] is an increasingly narrow experience.

Ned seemed to understand that individual experiences in and of themselves are at best a starting point of analysis, and he was reaching for a more structural analysis. However, he overlooked the complex relations of oppression and dominance hidden by Whiteness and maleness that are not being marked as social positions; only the "oppressed" position is marked.

Thus the feminism of all these White students, based on assumptions of Whiteness, did not include any consciousness of being White. Race was seen as an exclusive (and obstructive) property of Black women only. Indeed, for Ned and Ralph, gender, belonging only to women, is also an obstruction to unity. Moreover, while they were able to construct Black women as members of a social group, not as individuals, the White students could not see that White people, too, were not simply individuals with common personal experiences, but differentially placed members of an unequal social order. But there was another discussion going on, led particularly by Sharon and Ron, an African American male, where the prevailing assumptions of Whiteness operated not only as unacknowledged social location, but also as active ideology — where Whiteness was a key feature of a normalized and unmarked "center" of intellectual discourse. In later interviews, both Sharon and Ron acknowledged that they were very aware of working to raise the White students' consciousness around issues of race. In response to comments like those from Ned and the White female students earlier in the discussion, Sharon tried to show how looking at people of color exposed the intellectual dominance of the White academy, and its distance from the real world:

> It makes me wonder if we're not being too theoretical and abstract when we don't consider those things. It makes me wonder if this isn't just a bunch of you know intellectual masturbation and what action is going to come out of it, if we're not going to be diverse about what we're going to be concerned about and be realistic about it.

She went on:

> Ya, but if I weren't here to voice these concerns — we are not Black people in this class and I keep thinking to myself I'm a surburban kid, I'm not an urban kid. And I think, this is all great but how do we apply it?

Sharon attributed the lack of attention to racism to the culture of the campus. She said in an interview, "I've been at this college for a long time and it's predominantly White. People aren't really dealing with the issue of racism." Her comment that "we are not Black people in this class" was perhaps about the impossibility of encountering layers of "Blackness" in a context where the complexities and varieties of other cultures are erased by the Black/White duality imposed by the dominant discourse.

"Black" could only be apprehended as "not White," where both White and Black are defined on White terms.

Later, Ron tried another tack, addressing the need to construct identities outside the margin:

> In a way, to get at the center you have rings of light to bring to light what is marginal and spread [it]. And the only way to do that being a woman or being a Black person whose experience is marginalized, you've got to talk about that experience, you have to establish some kind of identity.

He was trying to push gently at the limits of the White students' understandings, to help them look at identities relationally, as situated positions implicating both Whites and people of color in the social construction of gender and race. But his quote illustrates the silent workings of Whiteness, in that "the center" is not named. The White students continued to insist on marking race as a concern only for Blacks, so that unity could only occur either through transcending race, or "doing it for them," as one White female student remarked:

> *Ned:* Or we never have a common battle to fight? If we're not all suburbanites together then we can't fight the same battle?

> *Laurie:* If a White person defines Black struggles, that's not an answer, so somehow we have to, if we're White or if we're privileged or if we're male or whatever . . . people have to somehow empower others to do it instead of doing it for them.

As the discussion proceeded, Sharon and Ron, joined by Amy, made comments that suggest that they were also continuing to struggle specifically against Whiteness as a form of intellectual domination. Because they could not identify the center of knowledge production as White, they could not fully articulate a language of their own to produce a different knowledge:

> *Sharon:* But [oppressed groups] all have to form an identity first . . . in a lot of ways it doesn't exist, in that it is so *threatened* given — (italics are authors')

> *Ron:* I think it's *dangerous* to form, the question of whether we have the wherewithal to form groups without first knowing who you are.

> *Sharon:* You know just part of it is the individual knowing his or her cultural experience, historical experience.

> . . .

> *Amy:* I think one thing interesting about learning *political language that the mainstream culture understands* [is] so that you can, as an oppressed group, be validized [sic]. But once you learn how to communicate then I think it is necessary to go back to your own language, your own identity, your own culture and I guess they, we, the marginal people face sort of a problem on the one hand to be autonomous and form an identity and reevaluate it, on the other hand, be able to communicate to —

> *Ron:* So there will always be a double consciousness, sisters under the veil.

Sharon then made the point that most feminist theory is written by White women, "with their ideologies and values," to which Ron replied,

> But that's the whole point, that's how language is used to oppress people. People close the doors and talk about all this stuff, and I'm saying that theory provides a key to that door — it also presents a way of changing meaning, changing the way things are.

As a muted challenge to the fixed path of assumed Whiteness, this conversation was halting, rocky, uncomfortable, representing a "`teeth-gritting' and often contradictory intersection of voices constituted by gender, race, class, ability, ethnicity, sexual orientation, [and] ideology," in Elizabeth Ellsworth's words.[34] In the face of unspoken assumptions about Whiteness as the norm, the students of color struggled to "get at the center." If the center could be named and positioned as White, then the processes of "forming groups," of knowing one's "cultural and historical experience," would be shared by all groups and would not be only the task of the marginalized. A language exposing the positional operations of power relations could be developed, by which all "cultures" could be constructed and deconstructed relationally. The key is undertaking a conscious discourse of Whiteness, theorizing Whiteness, and thus "changing language" in order to change meaning, and "changing the way things are."

It was not that the students of color did not understand what they were up against. Ron clearly understood that the oppressor has a position. He said in an interview:

> The position of the oppressor is the most inflexible. A person who is in an oppressed position will idealize what is above him. [The oppressor] objectifies everything. I just think that oppressed people . . . are better at ripping apart the disguises than creating them. The oppressors are greater at creating them.

Amy and Sharon also saw the problem as tied to Whiteness. The numerical and intellectual dominance of White students on campus contributed to Sharon's wish that "we would try to imagine ourselves to be something other than White, upper-class people." Amy too felt "cultural alienation on campus because the majority of students in the class are White and . . . over-looking a lot, a lot of things that are conscious but can't be formed into academic lingo and come out in weird ways or don't come out."

In the book we noted that, according to the professor, "the White students [avoided] confronting their own position as Whites, [as] they repeatedly objectified, generalized about, and posited the unknowability of the `other.'" We pointed out that "White students' resistance to theorizing their `Whiteness' — to being caught in the racial matrix — hampered the students of color in their aim of articulating their ethnic identities."[35] We were helped to these insights by the professor herself, who saw her class as reflecting deep societal inequalities because of assumptions of Whiteness as the norm, on the one hand, and individuals' unawareness of that on the other. She left the college in 1988 in part because she could not accept these limitations to her teaching, limits "rooted in the fundamental nature, social location, and ideology of this institution."[36] While the emphasis on student perspectives in the gender studies program "passed as feminist because it seemed to be supportive and sisterly, in practice it reinforced the exclusion and subordination of people of color." After our initial positive analysis of her class, this teacher wrote:

> I may have done better around authority than around race, but sharing authority with students who are predominantly White and who are unwilling to recognize their position and the different positions of other, or unable to develop a systemic analysis of racial inequality, leaves crucial problems unsolved.[37]

In our tentative grasp of these issues, however, we underestimated the power of Whiteness as ideology, as the assumed basis of a governing intellectual framework, in part precisely because it was not confronted or named directly; we have returned to read between the lines. Indeed, it was only in situations where people of color were a majority, as in the class below, that issues of Whiteness were explicitly taken up in class discussions.

RESISTING INTELLECTUAL DOMINATION: A WHITE AUTHOR AND A BLACK AUDIENCE

What problems are caused for people of color because the crucial problem of Whiteness is left unnamed and unresolved? To answer this question, we turn to a class where the majority of students, and the teacher, were people of color. In classes like these we can more fully see the effects of unanalyzed Whiteness on the ways in which people of color framed their own views, in resistance to, and outside of, the worldviews accorded them by the dominant White culture. African American students at the historically Black college mentioned above, for example, affirmed the value of constructing knowledge from their own standpoint, against "truths" of White social scientists who claimed they were "deviant" and "pathological." They complained about being prevented by White stereotypes from living the normal, complex lives of "ordinary" middle-class people. One said:

> I always hear people talk about NBC as the Negro Broadcasting Company, (laughter) because they always tend to try, well this is a stereotype, they try to cater to Black struggles, but it's not necessarily that realistic, because we go from "Good Times" to "Cosby," and there is no middle.

When the teacher at this college urged her students to understand the culture's "beauty myth," it was the ideology of Whiteness that kept them from seeing and appreciating who they were. Until they saw the loaded meaning and value behind those categories, they could not reconstruct the world and their place in it.

When we wrote about her classroom in our book, we emphasized the participants' struggles to forge their own knowledge. But, in emphasizing this new knowledge, we minimized the role of Whiteness. These teachers and students, in essence, had to come to terms with Whiteness, almost before they could go about "creating something else to be."

The following classroom discussion explored the ways in which a White author used an African American figure for his own critique of White society. This was a class at a large, elite, predominantly White southern university in which the teacher, a visiting African American female literature professor, was teaching "Images of Women in Literature" to a group mixed by both race and gender. The twenty-six students included thirteen African American women, seven African American men, four White women, and two White men. The teacher made a point of consciously exposing the racial and gender stereotypes embedded in the dominant culture's views of Black and White women. One day she gave a summary of the learning process she wanted them to go through, stressing the importance of revealing what is on one's mind so that stereotypical assumptions can be named and confronted:

> The problem is that the culture tells you these things again and again and you internalize them, and you make an effort to find the cases that support [what you've been programmed to believe. Liberation is liberation of the mind. You liberate your mind. Then you change society. But you can't liberate your mind until you examine honestly what has been put in your mind.[38]

In *The Feminist Classroom* we noted that this setting, in looking at White privilege, may have simply made the few White students in the class, like Mark, who was quoted in the introduction, appreciate their positions more.[39] The following discussion, centering on Dilsey, the mammy figure in William Faulkner's *The Sound and the Fury*, shows the students beginning with an analysis of an African American central character, a victim of racial oppression, and then shifting to a focus on the perpetuators, in this case Faulkner himself. In the course of uncovering the meanings in the book, the students discovered that Faulkner, while critiquing White society, was not writing for or to African Americans, but for White people. Paradoxically, they found, in a literary treatment that explores White racism, African American readers are shut out.

The way into Faulkner's view of Dilsey had been paved by lengthy observations, directed by the teacher, into the many ways that Faulkner emphasizes, subverts, and ultimately exposes the toxic effects of racism on a decaying White southern culture. For example, in an echo of Toni Morrison's point from *The Bluest Eye* about beauty and ugliness offsetting each other, she had a student read aloud a passage where the family son, Quentin, goes north to Harvard, and reflects on his changed views of African Americans:

> When I first came East I kept thinking You've got to remember to think of them as colored people, not niggers. . . . And if it hadn't happened that I wasn't thrown with many of them, I'd have wasted a lot of time before I learned that the best way to take all people, Black or White, is to take them for what they think they are, then leave them alone. That was when I realized that a nigger is not a person so much as a form of behavior; a sort of obverse reflection of the White people he lives among.

The professor initiated the following discussion by soliciting the students' reactions to the stereotype of the mammy figure. She asked them, "What do you want to say to Dilsey?" Immediately Stacy, a Black female, spoke up, expressing the point of view of a Black child whose mother had to take care of Whites: "It doesn't seem she cares about her own children as much as she does about Quentin [the White family's son]." The next students to speak were Edgar, Kathy, Michael, and James, African Americans whose "explanations" for Dilsey's failure to nurture her own children ranged from fear that Whites might take them away to the idea that her role as nanny meant she had to ignore her children in favor of the White children:

> *Kathy:* Maybe she doesn't want to get too attached, maybe they'll get rid of her kids. She still has this mindset not very different from slavery. . . .

> *Edgar:* I agree — even though it was the 1920s, she did have that mindset that . . . goes from generation to generation, so the time we are dealing with is something like slavery. Look at what it did to African American lives! You really can't put a time limit on that. But she totally forgot about the nurturing of her children.

> *Michael:* I felt that she didn't love her children, in fact I would go as far as to say that she more or less did not give them a stable beginning whatsoever, she criticized everything they did. . . .

> *Kathy:* It's not her fault that she has to take care of those other children!

> *Edgar:* Regardless of what the social constraints are or whatever, she's a Mom, and she could nurture them in some way. It is obvious that she has the capability to nurture. Why couldn't she do it with her own children!?

> *Mark (White male):* It seems like it's more of a job though, isn't it? Wouldn't it be her job to do that? It would be like any other job, when the job's over you're not like what you were on the job.

> *James:* But that's the thing — it's not just a job!

More discussion of Dilsey's relationship with Quentin's family ensued, during which the professor pointed out that Faulkner made Dilsey "the moral conscience of the novel," and that "she is also a stereotype":

> *Edgar:* I think that Faulkner thinks Dilsey's positive, but she's positive for White people. And that really upsets me, that I get the impression that Faulkner thinks he's doing us a favor by showing a positive image — when she's not really being positive for us! I wish she could be positive for us, not for them, because they have their own family — their mother and their daddy.

> *Professor:* She's positive — I mean, be honest. The negative images are the images of the White people! I mean give Faulkner credit. . . . She's the moral conscience of this novel, and we, the readers, are supposed to say this is positive.

In our analysis of this class in our book, we focused on the African American students' identification with Dilsey's children and concluded that Dilsey was so objectionable to them:

> Not so much because her portrayal in the novel seemed to them to contradict stereotypic notions of women as nurturing; rather, it was because of the whole history of the merging of femaleness and racial identification in slavery.[40]

Could the Black students' anger have also been focused on the unspoken racialized assumptions of the White students — namely, their unproblematic location of Dilsey in the servant role, leaving "normal" mothers as White women taking care of their own children?

However, despite the attempts by the White students to locate Dilsey unproblematically in her servant role, the students of color were able to uncover "literary Whiteness" — to position Faulkner as a writer not for a universal, normative, and unnamed audience, but specifically for White readers. We now see also that these students were resisting the connection of a certain kind of motherhood with Black racial identity, namely that Blacks "mother" Whites, not their own children. More broadly, they were displaying the resentment they felt that once again, both in the way Dilsey acted and in the way Faulkner appropriated the figure of a Black woman to be the conscience of a White family, Blacks were being made to live for Whites and not on their own terms. As Edgar put it, Faulkner made Dilsey positive for White people, "who already have their own family — their mother and their daddy." The African American students' discussion of Dilsey reveals their struggle to perceive themselves as "normal," as children with all the expectations of American children in middle-class nuclear families in the late twentieth century. It was important to confront Faulkner's "universal appeal," his hiding assumptions of Whiteness as the center of his normative universe, in order to reconsider these issues in their own lives.

CONCLUSION

In this reanalysis of some of the classroom vignettes we used in writing *The Feminist Classroom,* we have returned to our themes of "pedagogies" and "methodologies" of positionality, using the construct of "Whiteness" to examine positions of dominance, rather than marginalities as we did in our book. We have focused here on largely unacknowledged assumptions of Whiteness as a key aspect of the dominant culture, and how these assumptions interact with constructions of gender, class, ethnicity, and race to shape the construction of classroom knowledge. We have seen Whiteness operate both differentially and simultaneously, as "always more than one thing"; it has been physical description, individual identity, social position, ideology, and, throughout, a "dynamic of cultural production and interrelation" operating "within a particular time period and place, and within particular relations of power."[41]

Thus for Nancy, "breaking through illusion" was necessary to confront Whiteness both as physical description and feminine ideal. To her, as to the students in the Images of Women in Literature class, the ideology of appropriate gender roles, all the way from "looking stupid to attract men" to being a good mother, was derived from White stereotypes that needed to be named and deconstructed. For the students in the literary theory course and the honors freshman writing course, it was maleness as well as Whiteness that was assumed in their discussions of working-class unity and middle-class mobility. From the unacknowledged perspective of the dominant position, both "race" and "gender" were properties of the "other."

While in the honors freshman writing class, Whiteness was constructed primarily as a matter of individual identity, in the literary theory class the White students fretted about the ways in which "race," and to a lesser extent "gender," interrupted the theoretical unity of the oppressed that they were seeking within feminist theory. Based on physical description as marker for social location, both groups of students assigned "race" to minorities, especially to Blacks, while staying oblivious to their own position as Whites.

Thinking about Whiteness as ideology as well, we can see how the conceptualization of race as a bipolar construct, with Black and White as the two poles, operated to make all "difference" oppositional in nature, so that Black lives could not be normal, but only the obverse or the exception to those of Whites — whether in *The Bluest Eye*, Faulkner, a Hayley Mills movie, or *The Cosby Show*. Also caught in this dualism, the Asian, Filipina, and Hispanic students lacked any appropriate "mirror" for their identities. Finally, the pervasive power of Whiteness as a feature of the intellectual dominance of the academy, wherein the universalized knower and known are always assumed to be White, can probably be seen everywhere in these discussions; however, only in the Images of Women in Literature class, and to some extent in Feminism in Historical Perspective, was it actively named and resisted. Each discussion probably reveals Whiteness operating at many more levels than we have captured here, through layers of personal, political, and ideological constructions and assumptions, and through discourses of gender and class as well as race.

We have also to come to terms with the fact that we now "see" dynamics in our data hidden from us before. Yet to "recognize" (or "re-see") those dynamics positions us partly as expert-detectives who want to "get it right" this time around. We see more clearly the importance of continuing to learn about ourselves, to interrogate our own social positions of privilege and to use that knowledge to inform our research, our teaching, and our professional practice. As White scholar-activists committed to anti-racist work, we are always, to quote Ellsworth again, "simultaneously ignorant and knowledgeable, resistant and implicated, committed and forgetful, ambivalent, tired, enjoying the pleasures and safety of privilege; effective in one arena and ineffective in another."[42]

We also see again the value of the community of feminist scholars that we and others have created. It was in a final interview with Angela Davis that we first learned about the whole field of scholarship on Whiteness, in the form of Ruth Frankenberg's work examining the constructions of race in White women's life narratives.[43] Grey Osterud's observations that we had treated positionality only as it arises from marginality, thus concealing the dominant position, became another nagging issue that would not go away.[44] The last-minute arrival of articles, some pre-publication, by Neil Gotanda, Elizabeth Ellsworth, and Sandra Lawrence gave us new insights into this work.[45]

Finally, beginning to be able to understand and "track" Whiteness in these ways, as constructed socially and historically, allows us to think about the possibilities of revealing its various operations so as to challenge and renegotiate its meanings — "to change language, change meaning, and change the way things are," as Roy put it above. Because we, having lived through and participated in the civil rights and women's movements, know that some of our generation have begun to examine their dominant positions, we believe that many more Whites now can do the same. We also know from our students and our own children that one aspect of our positionality is generational; that our children, growing up in a much more diverse society than we did, have different relations and constructions of gender and race than we. We have seen how, for example, several Latinos and Asian American students have begun to push up against the bipolar construction of Black and White that we ourselves experienced.

While classrooms often not only reflect, but also impose, the dominant culture's ideological frameworks, they may also function as somewhat sheltered laboratories where those frameworks may be exposed and interrogated. One hope thus lies in students (and professors) becoming authorities for each other as they are explicit about themselves as positioned subjects with respect to an issue or a text. As this article has shown, however, many of the steps towards these kinds of awareness are tentative. They are often undertaken, at some risk, by people occupying the subordinate positions. Students of color in the Feminist in Historical Perspective class speak of danger and threat in looking at their own identities.

In relation to Whiteness in particular, however, increasing numbers of teachers have begun to use the literature on Whiteness with students, both Whites and students of color, to help them see themselves and each other differently: not as individuals, whose relations to racism must be either "innocent" or "guilty," but as participants in social and ideological networks. While these networks are not of their own making, they can nevertheless come to understand and challenge them. Indeed, some writers have described Whiteness as not only a social position, but also as a set of ways of thinking and acting in the world. Whiteness, in this sense, can be about making choices.[46] Teachers such as Ellsworth, Beverly Tatum, and Sandra Lawrence, among others, have written about work with students in this regard.[47] In the course of working on this article over the 1995–1996 academic year, Maher has used the work on Whiteness by Tatum, McIntosh, Roediger, and Morrison described in this article with various groups of students to help them understand the workings of Whiteness in their own lives, as well as "cultural mapping exercises" to help students find themselves in a variety of different and simultaneously overlapping social positions. In so doing, she has not "solved" the problem, but has continually located, dislocated and relocated herself in terms of the students' sometimes uncomfortable, sometimes resentful, but always interested growth in awareness of these issues. As one of our professor-informants once told us, "They don't live their Whiteness, I don't live my Whiteness. I'm working hard to see how to do that."

A glimmer of hope in the direction we would like to proceed may lie in a final comment by Mark, the White male student we quoted at the beginning of this article. Mentioning that an older African American woman student in the class had become an authority for him, he told us that:

> [the professor] seems like she's teaching on more than one level. She's teaching me just to open my eyes, but with Blanche it's totally different because she has open eyes. Blanche is ten steps ahead of me in understanding all this. . . .

This class could easily have ended up all Black women, but it's important for me to be in there because I have to understand it. I can't understand it when I am in a nice little fraternity house, predominantly White men from North and South. It's good for me and maybe if I take something from this and go home and sit with my room-mates and talk about it and open it up there, rather than keep it in the classroom . . . it seems like we need it for us. We need it and [other] White males and females probably need it just as much.

One teacher in our study, an African American woman, left us with a message, one that we now see exhorts Whites to understand our Whiteness and to work from that position: "Black women need to understand how special they are. For Whites, you need to understand what you can do working as a White American, one who can make a difference."

NOTES

1. Toni Morrison, *Sula* (New York: Alfred A. Knopf, 1974), p. 52.
2. Frances A. Maher and Mary Kay Tetreault, *The Feminist Classroom: An Inside Look at How Professors and Students Are Transforming Higher Education for a Diverse Society* (New York: Basic Books, 1994). In this article, we include excerpts from five classes at three different institutions. The first one is from a seminar in literary theory at Lewis and Clark College. The second is from an honors freshman writing course at Towson State University. The third is from a course on women writers since 1800, and the fourth is from a course entitled "Feminism in Historical Per-spective/Feminist Theory"; both of these courses were also at Lewis and Clark College. The fifth is from a class, "Images of Women in Literature," taught at Emory University.
3. Maher and Tetreault, *The Feminist Classroom*, chapter one.
4. See, among other works, the following: Ruth Frankenberg, *White Women, Race Matters: The Social Construction of Whiteness* (Minneapolis: University of Minnesota Press, 1993), and Ruth Frankenberg, "Whiteness and Americanness: Examining Constructions of Race, Culture and Nation in White Women's Life Narratives," in *Race*, ed. Steven Gregory and Roger Sanjek (New Brunswick, NJ: Rutgers University Press, 1994), pp. 62–77; Peggy McIntosh, "White Privilege and Male Privilege: A Personal Account of Coming to See Correspondences Through Work in Women's Studies," in *Race, Class and Gender: An Anthology*, ed. Margaret Andersen and Patricia Hill Collins (Belmont, CA: Wadsworth, 1992); Toni Morrison, *Playing in the Dark: Whiteness and the Literary Imagination* (New York: Vintage, 1993); David Roediger, *The Wages of Whiteness: Race and the Making of the American Working Class* (New York: Verso, 1991), and David Roediger, *Towards the Abolition of Whiteness: Essays on Race, Politics and Working Class History* (New York: Verso, 1994); Karen Brodkin Sacks, "How Did Jews Become White Folks?" in Gregory and Sanjek, *Race*, pp. 78–102; Beverly Daniel Tatum, "Talking about Race, Learning about Racism: The Application of Racial Identity Development Theory in the Classroom," *Harvard Educational Review, 62* (1992), 1–24.
5. Grey Osterud made this point to us in a telephone conversation with Mary Kay Tetreault on October 22, 1993.
6. Morrison, *Playing in the Dark*, p. 11.
7. Maher and Tetreault, *The Feminist Classroom*, p. 196.
8. There was only one other White male in the class; he rarely attended.
9. We use pseudonyms for all the students in this article.
10. Privileges accorded people because they are middle or upper class, male, and heterosexual are also often unacknowledged, and operate in similar ways. In this essay we focus on Whiteness, while noting ways that Whiteness intersects with other forms of privilege in the different vignettes that we explore.

11. McIntosh, "White Privilege," p. 71.

12. Morrison, *Playing in the Dark*; Roediger, *Towards the Abolition of Whiteness*; Elizabeth Ellsworth, "Double Binds of Whiteness," in *Off-White, Readings on Society, Race and Culture*, ed. Michelle Fine, Lois Weis, Linda C. Powell, and Mun Wong (New York: Routledge, 1997), pp. 259–269; and Elizabeth Ellsworth, "Working Difference in Education," *Curriculum Inquiry*, forthcoming; Andrew Hacker, *Two Nations, Black and White, Separate, Hostile, Unequal* (New York: Ballantine Books, 1995); Sacks, "How Did Jews Become White Folks?"

13. Becky Thompson and White Women Challenging Racism, "Home Work: Anti-Racism Activism and the Meaning of Whiteness," in Fine et al., *Off-White*, pp. 354–366.

14. See Ellsworth, "Double Binds of Whiteness," p. 260.

15. Sacks, "How Did Jews Become White Folks?"; Roediger, *Towards the Abolition of Whiteness*, pp. 13–14.

16. Hacker, *Two Nations*, p. 8.

17. Roediger, *Towards the Abolition of Whiteness*, p. 3.

18. We first saw this quote from Adrienne Rich in a paper by Renato Rosaldo, entitled "Symbolic Violence: A Battle Raging in Academe," presented at the American Anthropological Association Annual Meeting, Phoenix, Arizona, 1988.

19. Maher and Tetreault, *The Feminist Classroom*, chapter seven.

20. Ellsworth, "Double Binds of Whiteness," p. 265.

21. All quotes in this paragraph from Ellsworth, "Double Binds of Whiteness."

22. Toril Moi, *Sexual/Textual Politics: Feminist Literary Theory* (London: Methuen, 1985). See Maher and Tetreault, *The Feminist Classroom*, pp. 72–76, for a discussion of this class. The quotes in this essay are not always fully quoted in the book; we returned to the data to reexamine it for other issues. The data for the classroom vignettes and analyses in *The Feminist Classroom* were gathered over a period of at least three weeks through classroom visits and taping of class discussions. Class discussion data were supplemented by interviews with the professor and four or five selected students. Based on this material, we wrote detailed case studies of each professor's teaching, and shared them with our informants. Based on informants' comments and our own further research, we revised these case studies, and finally used them as the basis for the vignettes and analyses in the book, which were organized around four themes: "Mastery," "Voice," "Authority," and "Positionality."

23. SDS, Students for a Democratic Society, was a student movement in the 1960s that opposed the war in Vietnam and worked for civil rights.

24. Maher and Tetreault, *The Feminist Classroom*, pp.178–185.

25. Toni Morrison, *The Bluest Eye* (New York: Pocket Books, 1972), p. 159.

26. Thomas H. Johnson, ed., *Complete Poems of Emily Dickinson* (New York: Macmillan, 1967), Poem 288, p. 133.

27. Johnson, *Complete Poems*, Poem 327, p. 155.

28. Hacker, *Two Nations*, pp. 18–19. Neil Gotanda spoke of these issues at a presentation, "Reconstructing Whiteness: Color Blindness, Asian Americans, and the New Ethnicity," at California State University, Fullerton, April 16, 1996.

29. Interview with a teacher at Spelman College, April 1993.

30. The college is known for its strong Gender Studies program and an institutional pedagogy focused on student perspectives as learners. A hallmark of their pedagogy is the practice of beginning with the students' questions rather than the common approach of beginning with the teachers' questions.

31. Nancy Grey Osterud, "Teaching and Learning about Race at Lewis and Clark College," Unpublished manuscript, 1987.

32. There were other issues present that beset many feminist classrooms: how to attend to theory by getting students to think theoretically without separating it from the their personal experience and feminist practice; how to enable the students to set their own agenda; and how to deal with the disparate discourses in a class that arise from, in the professor's words, "that real separation, the gap between inside the classroom and the real world of personal experience out there . . ."

33. The students agreed that they had to take collective responsibility for the class as a whole and changed some of their classroom processes. Students met in small groups for part of the class and then as the full group of thirty students. They agreed to select report topics for the small groups and the subsequent agenda for the large one, and to choose a student to chair the large-group discussion each day.

34. Elizabeth Ellsworth, "Why Doesn't This Feel Empowering? Working through the Repressive Myths of Critical Pedagogy," *Harvard Educational Review, 59* (1989), 297–324.

35. Maher and Tetreault, *The Feminist Classroom,* pp. 112–113.

36. Maher and Tetreault, *The Feminist Classroom,* p. 39.

37. Maher and Tetreault, *The Feminist Classroom,* p. 160.

38. Maher and Tetreault, *The Feminist Classroom,* p. 178.

39. Maher and Tetreault, *The Feminist Classroom,* pp. 172–178; 191–197.

40. Maher and Tetreault, *The Feminist Classroom,* p. 194.

41. Ellsworth, "Double Binds of Whiteness," pp. 260–261.

42. Ellsworth, "Working Difference," p. 14.

43. Frankenberg, *White Women.*

44. Maher and Tetreault, *The Feminist Classroom,* p. 112.

45. Ellsworth, "Working Difference"; Lawrence, "White Educators"; Gotanda, "Reconstructing Whiteness."

46. Anoop Nayak, "Tales from the Dark Side: Negotiating Whiteness in School Arenas," Unpublished manuscript, University of Newcastle, UK.

47. Ellsworth, "Working Difference"; Lawrence, "White Educators"; Tatum, "Talking about Race."

Thanks to all our participants, especially those included in this article, whose contributions in the form of classroom dialogues in some cases go back ten years. Thanks also to Gloria Wade-Gayles, K. Edgington, Joyce Canaan, and Ellen Junn for commenting on this article.

Blind Vision: Unlearning Racism
in Teacher Education

MARILYN COCHRAN-SMITH

Literary theorist Barbara Hardy (1978) once asserted that narrative ought not be regarded as an "aesthetic invention used by artists to control, manipulate, and order experience, but as a primary act of mind transferred to art from life" (p. 12). Elaborating on the primacy of narrative in both our interior and exterior lives, Hardy suggests that

> storytelling plays a major role in our sleeping and waking lives. We dream in narrative, daydream in narrative, remember, anticipate, hope, despair, believe, doubt, plan, revise, criticize, construct, gossip, learn, hate and love by narrative. (p. 13)

From this perspective, narrative can be regarded as locally illuminating, a central way we organize and understand experience (Mishler, 1986; VanManen, 1990). It is also a primary way we construct our multiple identities as human beings for whom race, gender, class, culture, ethnicity, language, ability, sexual orientation, role, and position make a profound difference in the nature and interpretation of experience (Tatum, 1997; Thompson & Tyagi, 1996).

In this article, I explore and write about *un*learning racism in teaching and teacher education. I do not begin in the scholarly tradition of crisply framing an educational problem by connecting it to current policy and practice and/or to the relevant research literature. Instead, I begin with a lengthy narrative based on my experiences as a teacher educator at a moment in time when issues of race and racism were brought into unexpectedly sharp relief. I do so with the assumption that narrative is not only locally illuminating, as Hardy's work suggests, but also that it has the capacity to contain and entertain within it contradictions, nuances, tensions, and complexities that traditional academic discourse with its expository stance and more distanced impersonal voice cannot (Fine, 1994; Gitlin, 1994; Metzger, 1986).

The idea that racism is something that all of us have inevitably learned simply by living in a racist society is profoundly provocative (King, Hollins, & Hayman, 1997; McIntosh, 1989; Tatum, 1992). For many of us, it challenges not only our most precious democratic ideals about equitable access to opportunity, but also our most per-

Harvard Educational Review Vol. 70 No. 2 Summer 2000, 157–190

sistent beliefs in the possibilities of school and social change through enlightened human agency (Apple, 1996; Giroux, 1988; Leistyna, Woodrum, & Sherblom, 1996; Noffke, 1997). Perhaps even more provocative is the position that part of our responsibility as teachers and teacher educators is to struggle along with others in order to *un*learn racism (Britzman, 1991; Cochran-Smith, 1995a; Sleeter, 1992), or to interrogate the racist assumptions that may be deeply embedded in our own courses and curricula, to own our own complicity in maintaining existing systems of privilege and oppression, and to grapple with our own failures to produce the kinds of changes we advocate. Attempting to make the unending process of *un*learning racism explicit and public is challenging and somewhat risky. Easily susceptible to misinterpretation and misrepresentation, going public involves complex nuances of interpretation, multiple layers of contradiction, competing perspectives, and personal exposure (Cochran-Smith, 1995b; Cole & Knowles, 1998; Rosenberg, 1997). I go public with the stories in this article not because they offer explicit directions for unlearning racism, but because they pointedly suggest some of the most complex questions we need to wrestle with in teacher education: In our everyday lives as teachers and teacher educators, how are we complicit — intentionally or otherwise — in maintaining the cycles of oppression (Lawrence & Tatum, 1997) that operate daily in our courses, our universities, our schools, and our society? Under what conditions is it possible to examine, expand, and alter long-standing (and often implicit) assumptions, attitudes, beliefs, and practices about schools, teaching, students, and communities? What roles do collaboration, inquiry, self-examination, and story play in learning of this kind? As teacher educators, what should we say about race and racism, what should we have our students read and write? What should we tell them about who can teach whom, who can speak for whom, and who has the right to speak at all about racism and teaching?

BLIND VISION: A STORY FROM A TEACHER EDUCATOR

A White European American woman, I taught for many years at the University of Pennsylvania, a large research university in urban Philadelphia whose population was predominantly White, but whose next-door neighbors in west Philadelphia were schools and communities populated by African Americans and Asian immigrants. Seventy-five to 80 percent of the students I taught were White European Americans, but they worked as student teachers primarily in the public schools of Philadelphia where the population was often mostly African American or — in parts of north and northeast Philadelphia — mostly Latino. In those schools that appeared on the surface to be more ideally integrated, the racial tension was sometimes intense, with individual groups insulated from or even hostile toward one another.

The teacher education program I directed had for years included in the curriculum an examination of race, class, and culture and the ways these structure both the U.S. educational system and the experiences of individuals in that system.[1] For years my students read Comer (1989), Delpit (1986, 1988), Giroux (1984), Heath (1982 a, 1982b), Ogbu (1978), as well as Asante (1991), McIntosh (1989), Moll, Amanti, Neff, and Gonzalez (1992), Rose (1989), Sleeter and Grant (1987), Tatum (1992), and others who explore issues of race, class, culture, and language from critical and other perspectives. I thought that the commitment of my program to urban student-teaching placements and to devoting a significant portion of the curriculum to issues of race and racism gave me a certain right to speak about these issues as a teacher educator. I thought this with some degree of confidence until an event occurred that was to change forever the way I thought about racism and teacher education. This event was to influence the work I did with colleagues in the Penn program over the next six years, as well as the work in which I am presently engaged as a teacher educator at Boston College, where I collaborate with other teacher educators, teachers, and student teachers in the Boston area.

The event that is described in the following narrative occurred at the end of a two-hour student teaching seminar that was held biweekly for the thirty-some students in the Penn program at the time.[2]

*   *   *   *   *

We had come to the end of a powerful presentation about the speaker's personal experiences with racism, both as a young Native boy in an all-White class and later as the single minority teacher in a small rural school. The presentation had visibly moved many of us. The guest speaker — a Native American who worked in a teacher education program at another university — asked my student teachers about their program at Penn. I had no qualms. Our program was well known and well received. Students often raved about it to visitors from outside. Knowing and sharing the commitment of my program to exploring issues of race, my guest asked in the last few minutes of our two-hour seminar, "And what does this program do to help you examine questions about race and racism in teaching and schooling?" Without hesitation, one student teacher, a Puerto Rican woman, raised her hand and said with passion and an anger that bordered on rage, "Nothing! This program does *nothing* to address issues of race!" After a few seconds of silence that felt to me like hours, two other students — one African American and one Black South African — agreed with her, adding their frustration and criticism to the first comment and indicating that we read nothing and said nothing that addressed these questions. I was stunned. With another class waiting to enter the room, students — and I — quickly exited the room.

My first responses to this event included every personally defensive strategy I could muster. In the same way that my students sometimes did, I identified and equated myself with "the program." And in certain important ways, I suppose I *was* the program in that I had been the major architect of its social and organizational structures, and I was ultimately responsible for its decisions. I relived the final moments of the seminar, turning the same thoughts over and over in my head: How could she say that? How could others agree? After all, the compelling presentation we had all just heard was in and of itself evidence that we addressed issues of race in our program. And besides, just a few days earlier, she and a group of five other women students had presented a paper at a teacher research conference at Penn. They had chosen to be part of an inquiry group that was to write a paper about race and their student-teaching experiences because I had invited them to, I had suggested the topic.

They had used the data of their writing and teacher research projects from my class to examine the impact of race and racism on their student-teaching experiences. How could she say that?

I counted up the ongoing efforts I had made to increase the diversity in our supervisory staff and in our pool of cooperating teachers. I had insisted that we send student teachers to schools where the population was nearly 100 percent African American and Latino, schools that some colleagues cautioned me were too tough for student teachers, that some student teachers complained were too dangerous, and one had once threatened to sue me if I made her go there even for a brief field visit. I talked about issues of race openly and, I thought, authentically in my classes — all of them, no matter what the course title or the topic. I thought about the individual and personal efforts I had made on behalf of some of those students — helping them get scholarships, intervening with cooperating teachers or supervisors, working for hours with them on papers, lending books and articles. I constructed a long and convincing mental argument that I was one of the people on the right side of this issue. Nobody can do everything, and I was sure that I already paid more attention to questions of racism and teaching than did many teacher educators. How could she say that? I was stunned by what had happened, and deeply hurt — surprised as much as angry.

During the first few days after that seminar session, many students — most of them White — stopped by my office to tell me that they thought we were indeed doing a great deal to address issues of race and racism in the program, but they had clearly heard the outrage and dissatisfaction of their fellow students and they wanted to learn more, to figure out what we should do differently. Some students — both White students and students of color — stopped by or wrote notes saying that they thought we were currently doing exactly what we should be doing to address issues of race in the program. And a few students — all White — stopped by to say that all we ever talked about in the program and in my classes was race and racism and what they really wanted to know was when we were going to learn how to teach reading.

I knew that the next meeting of the seminar group would be a turning point for me and for the program. I struggled with what to say, how to proceed, what kind of stance I needed to take and would be able to take. I knew that I needed to open (not foreclose) the discussion, to acknowledge the frustration and anger (even the rage) that had been expressed, and, above all, I knew that I needed not to be defensive. I felt very heavy — it was clear to me that I was about to teach my student teachers one of the most important lessons I would ever teach them. I was about to teach them how a White teacher, who — notwithstanding the rhetoric in my classes about collaboration, shared learning, and co-construction of knowledge — had a great deal of power over their futures in the program and in the job market, how that White teacher, who fancied herself pretty liberal and enlightened, responded when confronted directly and angrily about some of the issues of race that were right in front of her in her own teaching and her own work as a teacher educator.

The very different responses of my students and my own shock and hurt at some of those responses pointed out to me on a visceral level the truth that many of the articles we were reading in class argued on a more intellectual level: how we are positioned in terms of race and power vis-à-vis others has a great deal to do with how we see, what we see or want to see, and what we are able not to see. I thought of Clifford Geertz's discussion of the difficulties involved in representing insider knowledge and meaning perspectives. He suggests that, ultimately, anthropologists cannot really represent "local knowledge" — what native inhabitants see — but only what they see through; that is, their interpretive perspectives on their own experiences. This situation laid bare the enormous differences between what I — and people differently situated from me — saw and saw through as we constructed our lives as teachers and students.

I didn't decide until right before the seminar exactly what I would say. I had thought of little else during the week. I felt exposed, failed, trapped, and completely inadequate to the task. In the end, I commented briefly then opened up the two hours for students to say whatever they wished. I tried to sort out and say back as clearly as I could both what I had heard people say at the seminar and the quite disparate responses I had heard in the ensuing week. It was clear from these, I said, that nobody speaks for anybody or everybody else. As I spoke, I tried not to gloss over the scathing critique or make the discrepancies appear to be less discrepant than they were. Especially for many of the students of color in the program, I said that I had clearly heard that there was a feeling of isolation, of being silenced, a feeling that we had not dealt with issues of race and racism in a "real" way — briefly perhaps, but in ways that were too intellectualized and theoretical rather than personal and honest. Notwithstanding the view expressed by some students that all we ever talked about was race, I reported a strong consensus that an important conversation had been opened up and needed to continue, although I also noted that it was clear some conversations about race and racism, maybe the most important ones, could not be led by me, a White teacher.

I concluded by saying that despite my deep commitments to an antiracist curriculum for all students, whether children or adults, and despite my intentions to promote constructive discourse about the issues in teacher education, I realized I didn't "get it" some (or much) of the time. This seemed to be one of those times. I admitted that these things were hard, uncomfortable, and sometimes even devastating to hear, but we needed to hear, to listen hard, and to stay with it.

What I remember most vividly about that seminar are the tension and the long silence that followed my comments and my open invitation to others to speak. My seminar co-leader (and friend) told me later that she was sure we all sat in silence for at least twenty minutes (my watch indicated that about three minutes had passed). The same woman who had responded so angrily the week before spoke first, thanking us for hearing and for providing time for people to name the issues. Others followed. All of the women of color in the program spoke, most of them many times. A small portion of the White students participated actively. Students critiqued their inner-city school placements, describing the inability or unwillingness of some of the experienced teachers at their schools to talk about issues of race and racism, to be mentors to them about these issues. They said we needed more cooperating teachers and more student teachers of color. They spoke of middle-class, mostly White teachers treating poor children, mostly children of color, in ways that were abrupt and disrespectful at best, reprehensible and racist at worst. Some spoke passionately about the disparities they had observed between their home schools and the schools they had cross-visited — disparities in resources and facilities, but even more in the fundamental ways teachers treated children in poor urban schools on the one hand, and in middle-class urban or suburban schools on the other. They complained that our Penn faculty and administrators were all White, naming and counting up each of us and assuming I had the power and authority, but not the will, to change things. They said that the lack of faculty of color and the small number of students of color in the program gave little validation to the issues they wished to raise as women and prospective teachers of color. Many of them were angry, bitter. They spoke with a certain sense of unity as if their scattered, restrained voices had been conjoined, unleashed.

The coleader and I avoided eye contact with one another, our faces serious and intense but carefully trying not to signal approval or disapproval, agreement or disagreement. Many White students were silent, some almost ashen. Some seemed afraid to speak. One said people were at different levels with issues of race and racism, implying that others in the room might not understand but that she herself was beyond that. Another commented that she too had experienced racism, especially because her boyfriend was African American. One said that when she looked around her student-teaching classroom, she saw only children, not color. Another complained that she didn't see why somebody couldn't just tell her what she didn't get so she could just get it and get on with teaching. I cringed inside at some of these comments, while several of the women of color rolled their eyes, whispered among themselves. One who was older than most of the students in the program eventually stopped making any attempt to hide her hostility and exasperation. She was openly disdainful in her side comments. Finally, a young White woman, with clear eyes and steady voice, turned to the older woman and said she was willing to hear any criticism, any truth about herself, but she wanted it said in front of her, to her face. The only man of color in the program, who sat apart from the other students, said all he wanted to do was to be an effective teacher. He did not want to be seen as a Black male teacher and a role model for Black children, but as a good teacher. Others immediately challenged him on the impossibility and irresponsibility of that stance.

For nearly two hours, the tension in the room was palpable, raw. As leaders we said little, partly because we had little idea what to say, partly because we had agreed to open up the time to the students. We nodded, listened, took notes. Toward the end, we asked for suggestions — how the group wanted to spend the two or three seminar sessions remaining in the year that had any flexibility in terms of topic, schedule, or speakers. We asked for recommendations. There were many suggestions but only a few that we could actually do something about in the six weeks or so that remained before the students graduated, given the already full schedule and the final press of certification and graduation details. (Many of the suggestions that we took up in the following year are described in the remainder of this article. For the current year, we opened up discussion time and included student teachers in planning and evaluation groups.)

Two students wrote me letters shortly after this seminar. One was appreciative, one was disgusted. Both, I believe, were heartfelt. A White woman wrote: "When you began to speak at the last seminar, I held my breath. The atmosphere in the room was so loaded, so brooding. It felt very unsafe. What would you say? What could you say? It would have been so very easy at this point to retreat into academe — to play The Professor, The Program Director, and not respond or address the fact that there were painful unresolved issues to be acknowledged, if not confronted. . . . Instead you responded honestly and openly, telling us how you were thinking about things, how you felt and the dilemmas you encountered as you too struggled to 'get it.' . . . Your words were carefully considered . . . and seemed spoken not without some cost to you." In contrast, a White man wrote:

> After this evening's seminar, I thought I would drop you this note to let you know how I react to the issues that were (and were not) confronted. . . . To be honest, I feel that the critical issues of race and racism have been made apparent and important in my studies . . . since I began [the program]. That they should have been made the fulcrum point of the curriculum and each course is problematic. I would say no; others (more vehemently) would insist on it. . . . I really have no idea how to most effectively proceed. I do know one thing. I am committed to bringing issues of race into my classroom, wherever I may teach. However, being nonconfrontational by nature, and with sincere respect for the opinions of my fellow students, I will probably not attend another session about this. Frankly, I, my students, and my career in education will benefit a lot more by staying at home and spending a few hours trying to integrate multicultural issues into my lesson plans than they will by talking one more time about race.

*   *   *   *   *

It would be an understatement to say that these events were galvanizing as well as destabilizing for me, for the people I worked closely with, and for the students who graduated just six weeks later. Everything was called into question — what we thought we were about as a program, who we were as a community, what learning opportunities were available in our curriculum, whose interests were served, whose needs were met, and whose were not. But it would be inaccurate to say that these events *caused* changes in the program over the next six years or that we proceeded from this point in a linear way, learning from our "mistakes" and then correcting them. Although the story of "so then what happened?" is of course chronological in one sense, it is decidedly *not* a story of year-by-year, closer and closer approximations of "the right way" to open and sustain a discourse about race and racism in teacher education programs aimed at preparing both students of color and White students to be teachers in both urban and other schools. Rather, the story is an evolving, recursive, and current one about what it means to grapple with the issues of racism and teaching in deeper and more uncertain ways.

It is also important to say, I think, that the above account of what happened is a fiction, not reality or truth, but my interpretation of my own and other people's experience in a way that makes sense to me and speaks for me. Although part of my intention in telling this story is to uncover my failure and unravel my complicity in maintaining the existing system of privilege and oppression, it is impossible for me to do so without sympathy for my own predicament. My experience as a first-generation-to-college, working-class girl who pushed into a middle-class, highly educated male profession has helped give me some vision about the personal and institutional impact of class and gender differences on work, status, and ways of knowing. But my lifelong membership in the privileged racial group has helped keep me blind about much of the impact of race. In fact, I have come to think of the story related above as a story of "blind vision" — a White female teacher educator with a vision about the importance of making issues of race and diversity explicit parts of the preservice curriculum and, in the process, grappling (sometimes blindly) with the tension, contradiction, difficulty, pain, and failure inherent in unlearning racism.

Of course, it is what we do after we tell stories like this one that matters most, or, more correctly, it is what we do afterwards that makes these stories matter at all. In the remainder of this article, I examine what I tried to do as a teacher educator and what we tried to do in our teacher education community after this story was told. We wanted to do nothing short of total transformation, nothing short of inventing a curriculum that was once and for all free of racism. What we *did* do over time was much more modest. Over time we struggled to unlearn racism by learning to read teacher education as racial text,[3] a process that involved analyzing and altering the learning opportunities available in our program along the lines of their implicit and explicit messages about race, racism, and teaching, as well as — and as important as — acknowledging to each other and to our students that this process would never be finished, would never be "once and for all." In the pages that follow, I analyze and illustrate this process, drawing on the following experiences and data sources: the evolution of three courses I regularly taught during the years that followed these events; the changes we made over time in the intellectual, social, and organizational contexts of the program; and the persistent doubts, questions, and failures we experienced as recorded in notes, reflections, conversations, and other correspondence.[4] In the final section of the article, I consider lessons learned and unlearned. I address the implications of reading teacher education as racial text for my own continuing efforts as a teacher educator now working with student teachers and teacher educators in a different urban context (Cochran-Smith et al., 1999; Cochran-Smith & Lytle, 1998).

READING TEACHER EDUCATION AS RACIAL TEXT

Reading teacher education as racial text is an analytical approach that draws from three interrelated and somewhat overlapping ideas. First is the idea that teaching and teacher education — in terms of both curriculum and pedagogy — can be regarded and read as "text." Second is the idea that preservice teacher education has both an explicit text (a sequence of required courses and fieldwork experiences, as well as the public documents that advertise or represent the goals of a given program) and a subtext (implicit messages, subtle aspects of formal and informal program arrangements, and the underlying perspectives conveyed in discourse, materials, and consistency/inconsistency between ideals and realities). Third is the notion that any curriculum, teacher education or otherwise, can and — given the racialized society in which we live — ought to be read not simply as text but as racial text.

Teaching as Text

A number of recent writers have advanced the idea that the work of teaching can be regarded as "text" that can — like any other text — be read, reread, analyzed, critiqued, revised, and made public by the teacher and his or her local community. This assumes that teaching, like all human experience, is constructed primarily out of the social and language interactions of participants. To make teaching into readable "text," it is necessary to establish space between teachers and their everyday work in order to find what McDonald (1992) calls "apartness." He suggests:

> This is the gist of reading teaching, its minimal core: to step outside the room, figu-ratively speaking, and to search for perspective on the events inside. It is simple work on its face, private and comparatively safe, the consequence perhaps of deliber-ately noticing one's own practice in the eyes of a student teacher, of undertaking some classroom research, even — as in my case — of keeping a simple journal and doing a little theoretical browsing. By such means, teachers may spot the uncer-tainty in their own practice. They may spot it, as I did, in unexpected tangles of con-flicting values, in stubborn ambivalence, in a surprising prevalence of half-steps. (p. 11)

McDonald suggests that reading teaching collaboratively is difficult and complex, re-quiring group members to set aside the pretensions and fears born of isolation, but also allowing, eventually, for the discovery of voice and a certain sense of unity.

Along related but different lines, I have been suggesting in work with Susan Lytle (Cochran-Smith & Lytle, 1992, 1993, 1999) that communities of teachers use multi-ple forms of inquiry to help make visible and accessible everyday events and practices and the ways they are differently understood by different stakeholders in the educa-tional process. Oral and written inquiry that is systematic and intentional, we have argued, "transforms what is ordinarily regarded as 'just teaching' . . . into multi-layered portraits of school life" (Cochran-Smith & Lytle, 1992, p. 310). These por-traits and the ways teachers shape and interpret them draw on, but also make prob-lematic, the knowledge about teaching and learning that has been generated by oth-ers. At the same time, they help to build bodies of evidence, provide analytic frameworks, and suggest cross-references for comparison. Part of the point in Mc-Donald's work, and in ours, is that "reading teaching as text" means representing teaching through oral and written language as well as other means of documentation that can be revisited, "REsearched" — to use Ann Berthoff's language (Berthoff, 1987) — connected to other "texts" of teaching, and made accessible and public beyond the immediate local context. Using the metaphor "teaching as text" makes it possible to see that connecting the various texts of teaching in the context of local inquiry com-munities (Cochran-Smith & Lytle, 1999) can be understood as a kind of social and collective construction of intertextuality or dialogue among texts. This leads to the second aspect of conceptualizing teacher education as text — examining not only what is explicit (the major text), but also what is not easily visible or openly public (the subtext).

Texts and Subtexts in Teacher Education

As text, teacher education is dynamic and complex — much more than a sequence of courses, a set of fieldwork experiences, or the readings and written assignments that are required for certification or credentialing purposes. Although these are part of what it means to take teacher education as text, they are not all of it. This also means examining its subtexts, hidden texts, and intertexts — reading between the lines as well as reading under, behind, through, and beyond them. This includes scrutinizing what is absent from the main texts and what themes are central to them, what happens to the formal texts, how differently positioned people read and write these texts differently, what they do and do not do with them, and what happens that is not planned or public. Ginsburg and Clift's (1990) concept of the hidden curriculum in teacher education is illuminating here, as is Rosenberg's (1997) discussion of the underground discourses of teacher education. Both of these call attention to the missing, obscured, or subverted texts — what is left out, implied, veiled, or subtly signaled as the norm by virtue of being unmarked or marked with modifying language. Ginsburg and Clift suggest that

> [the] sources of hidden curricular messages include the institutional and broader social contexts in which teacher education operates and the structure and processes of the teacher education program, including pedagogical techniques and texts and materials within the program. Messages are also sent by the . . . interpersonal relationships that exist between the numerous groups who might be considered to be educators of teachers. (p. 451)

Along more specific lines, Rosenberg (1997) describes the underground discourse about race in a small teacher education program in a rural area of New England. Rosenberg refers to "the presence of an absence," or the figurative presence of racism even in the actual absence of people of color at an overwhelmingly White institution. Rosenberg's characterization of an underground discourse about race connects to the third idea I have drawn upon in this discussion: the necessity of reading teacher education not just as complicated and dynamic text, but as racial text.

Teacher Education as Racial Text

Castenell and Pinar (1993) argue that curriculum can and ought to be regarded as racial text. Their introduction to a collection of essays by that name, *Understanding Curriculum as Racial Text*, develops this argument by locating current curriculum issues within the context of public debates about the canon and about the racial issues that are embedded within curriculum controversies. To understand curriculum as racial text, they suggest, is to understand that

> all Americans are racialized beings; knowledge of who we have been, who we are, and who we will become is a story or text we construct. In this sense curriculum — our construction and reconstruction of this knowledge for dissemination to the young — is racial text. (p. 8)

In forwarding this view of curriculum, Castenell and Pinar imply that it is critical to analyze any curriculum to see what kind of message or story about race and racism is being told, what assumptions are being made, what identity perspectives and points of view are implicit, and what is valued or devalued. They acknowledge, of course, that curriculum is not only racial text, but is also a text that is political, aesthetic, and gendered. They argue, however, that it is, "to a degree that European Americans have been unlikely to acknowledge, racial text" (p. 4). In conceptualizing curriculum as racial text, then, they link knowledge and identity, focusing particularly on issues of representation and difference. They argue that, although it is true that "We are what we know. We are, however, also what we do not know" (p. 4).

Taken together, the three ideas just outlined — that all teaching (including teacher education) can be regarded as text, that teacher education has both public and implicit or hidden texts, and that the text of teacher education is (in large part) racial text — lay the groundwork for the two sections that follow. In these sections I suggest that my colleagues and I — as participants in one teacher education community — struggled to unlearn racism by learning to read teacher education as racial text. In the first section I discuss both the possibilities and the pitfalls of making race and racism central to the curriculum by using "up close and personal" narratives, as well as distanced and more intellectualized theories and accounts. Next I show that it is necessary to "read between the lines," or to scrutinize closely the implicit messages about perspective, identity, and difference in a curriculum even after race and racism have been made central. Finally I turn to more general issues in teacher education offering brief lessons learned and unlearned when teacher education is regarded as racial text and when narrative is used to interrogate race and racism.

GETTING PERSONAL: USING STORIES ABOUT RACE AND RACISM IN THE CURRICULUM

For the teacher education community referred to in the opening narrative of this article, reading teacher education as racial text came to mean making issues of diversity (particularly of race and racism) central and integral, rather than marginal and piecemeal, to what we as student teachers, cooperating teachers, and teacher educators read, wrote, and talked about. Consciously deciding to privilege these issues meant rewriting course syllabi and program materials, reinventing the ways we evaluated student teachers, changing the composition of faculty and staff, drawing on the expertise and experience of people beyond ourselves, and altering the content of teacher research groups, student seminars, and whole-community sessions. For example, in response to the events described above, we worked the following year with a group of outside consultants to plan and participate in a series of "cultural diversity workshops" jointly attended by students, cooperating teachers, supervisors, and program directors. In the next year, we focused monthly seminars for the same groups on race and culture through the medium of story, led by Charlotte Blake Alston, a nationally known African American storyteller and staff-development leader. In the years to follow, we participated in sessions on Afrocentric curriculum led by Molefi Asante; on Black family socialization patterns and school culture led by Michele Foster; on multicultural teaching and Asian American issues in urban schools led by Deborah Wei; on constructing curriculum based on Hispanic children's literature, particularly using books with Puerto Rican themes and characters, led by Sonia Nieto; and on learning to talk about racial identity and racism led by Beverly Tatum. In addition, we offered sessions on using children's cultural and linguistic resources in the classroom and on constructing antiracist pedagogy led by our program's most experienced cooperating teachers — both teachers of color and White teachers — from urban and suburban, public and private, poor and privileged schools in the Philadelphia area.

Telling Stories

A central part of these activities was "getting personal" about race and racism — putting more emphasis on reading, writing, and sharing personal experiences of racism and digging at the roots of our own attitudes at the same time that we continued to read the more intellectualized, and thus somewhat safer, discourse of the academy. This meant making individual insider accounts (even though not as well known as the writing of the academy) a larger part of the required reading. Along with the usual reading of Comer, Delpit, Ogbu, Heath, and Tatum we began to read more of Parham, Foreman, Eastman, Cohen, and Creighton — all of whom were student teachers, cooperating teachers, and supervisors in our program.[5]

All of us in the community wrote and read personal accounts about race and class that were published in-house in an annual collection we called, "A Sense of Who We Are." These were used as the starting point for many class discussions, school-site meetings, and monthly seminars. For example, Daryl Foreman, an experienced cooperating teacher, wrote about her experiences as a child whose mother took her north to Pennsylvania for a summer visit. She wrote about the sights and scenes of 1960s Harrisburg and then turned to one unforgettable experience:

> It had been four days since my mother left Harrisburg. . . . She left us in the warm and capable hands of my aunt. We'd been behaving as tourists. But now, my younger sister and I had to accompany my aunt to work. For years, she'd been employed by a well-to-do White family whom I'd never met. . . .
>
> At four o'clock, I was starving and my aunt informed me that it was "normal" for us to eat in the kitchen while [the family] dined elsewhere.
>
> Before dinner, the woman of the house entered the kitchen offering to set the tables — one in the kitchen and the other in the dining room. She grabbed two sets of dishes from the cupboard. She delivered a pretty set of yellow plastic plates to the kitchen dining area and a set of blue china to the dining room. After dinner she came back and thanked my aunt for the delicious meal, then prepared to feed the dog. She walked toward the cupboard and opened it. Her eyes and hands traveled past the pretty set of plastic dishes and landed on the blue china plates. After she pulled a blue china plate from the cupboard, she filled it with moist dog food and placed it on the floor. He ran for the plate. I shrieked! . . .

To this day, I'm not sure if I shrieked at the shock of [people] sharing dinnerware with a dog or because the dog got a piece of blue china while I ate from yellow plastic.

David Creighton, a student teacher, wrote about working in an Italian restaurant in South Philadelphia in the 1990s:

"Yo, Dave, what *are* you anyway?" said Tony Meoli, a waiter in LaTrattoria in South Philadelphia.

"Whaddaya mean?" I, the new busboy, said.

"Like, uh, what's your nationality? You know, where are you from? I mean, you're obviously not Italian."

"Oh. Well, I'm Russian with some German mixed in," I said.

"Well, just as long as you're not Jewish," said Tony. "We don't like Jews around here."

"Actually, I am Jewish," I said.

"Oh, sorry, I was just kiddin' you know."

"Don't worry about it," I said . . .

Creighton went on to describe the culture of South Philadelphia, pointing out the racial and ethnic insulation and the considerable hostility between and among various groups. Then he continued:

I had only worked there about four months when at the end of my Sunday night shift I was told with no warning, "We won't be needing you anymore."

"What?" I said. I felt I had done a good job. No one ever complained about my work. I was always on time, and I was developing a good rapport with the waiters who often commended me on my efforts. Also, I really needed the money. "Why?" I said.

"I don't know," said the bartender.

"You know, Dave, Hitler had the right idea for you people, with the gas chambers and all," said Joe Piselli only half jokingly. "One day I'm gonna gas you down there in the kitchen."

"You know, Joe, Hitler wasn't all that crazy about Catholics either. You woulda been next," I said.

"Yeah, well at least I ain't no Jew," he said.

"Thank God," I said.

Reading and writing first-person accounts like these as starting points for interrogating unexamined assumptions and practices can evoke a shared vulnerability that helps a group of loosely connected individuals gel into a community committed to dealing with issues of race more openly. Accounts like these can move a preservice curriculum beyond the level of celebrating diversity, enhancing human relations, or incorporating ethnic studies into the curriculum, positions that are rightly criticized for their focus on ethnicity as individual choice and their limited goal of attitudinal change (McCarthy, 1990, 1993; Nieto, 1999; Sleeter & Grant, 1987) rather than analysis of systemic and institutional structures and practices that perpetuate racism and oppression. As I pointed out above, narratives also have the capacity to contain many of the contradictions, nuances, and complexities that are necessary for understanding the roots and twists of racism and the many ways these interact with the social life of schools and classrooms. But the considerable power of accounts that "get personal" about race is also their pitfall. They can use some people's pain in the service of others' understanding, as I suggest below, and they can also imply that we all share similar experiences with racism, experiences that beneath the surface of their details and contexts are the same. Over the years, I have come to realize that this lesson in unlearning racism, which is an especially difficult one to hold onto, helps to explain some of the depth of anger expressed by the student teachers in the story with which this article began.

Stories about Whom? Stories for Whom?

Several of the students of color in the blind vision story related above claimed we had done nothing in the program to help students understand issues of race, that we did not talk about it in "real" ways. Factually, this was not the case. We had read a large number of articles by both White scholars and scholars of color, and we had shared some personal incidents in class and had intellectualized discussions. It is clear to me now, though, that these discussions were framed primarily for the benefit of White students who were invited to learn more about racism through stories of other people's oppression. The stories were not sufficiently linked to larger issues or framed in ways that pushed everybody to learn not *regardless of* but *with full regard for* differences in race, culture, and ethnicity.

I should have learned this lesson a long time ago. I had known it in certain ways even at the time of the incident described in my narrative — my detailed notes indicate that it was one of the points I tried to make to the students after the incident occurred. But for me, as a White teacher educator, it is a lesson that needs to be learned over and over again. Although I thought I had learned this lesson then, I learned it again several years later from Tuesday Vanstory, an African American woman who was a supervisor in the program that year but had been a student in the program years before. We had had a difficult discussion about race in our supervisors' inquiry group where we had considered ways to respond to a particularly troubling journal entry written by a White student teacher. In it she had complained about the students of color in the program sometimes separating themselves from the others, sitting together on the perimeter of the classroom and/or not participating in certain discussions. The journal writer used the phrase "reverse discrimination" and questioned how we could ever move forward if everybody would not even talk to each other. Several White members of the supervisors' group voiced somewhat similar concerns. They were genuinely distressed, wanting open conversations and resentful of the figurative as well as literal separation along racial lines of some members from the larger group when certain topics arose.

Vanstory had sat silent for a long time during this discussion, then finally burst out and demanded, "But *who* are those discussions *for*? *Who* do they really serve?" There was silence for a while and then confusion. She wrote to me that same day about the discussion:

I must say that I was very upset after today's supervisors' meeting. There's nothing like a discussion on race, class, and culture to get my blood boiling, especially when I am one of a few who is in the "minority." Believe me, it is not at all comfortable. I really wanted to say nothing. I didn't want to blow my cool. I wanted to remain silent, tranquil. Instead I spouted off in what felt like a very emotional and, at times, a nonsensical response. . . .

I ran across a sociological term a few years ago: "master status." It is the thing you can never get away from, the label that others give you that they won't ever release and they won't let you forget. Can you imagine the constant confrontation of the issue of race permeating every day of your life for one reason or another? (Over representation or under representation of people who look like you do in whatever arena, the blatant inequities in quality of life for the masses — educational opportunities, housing, ability to pass down wealth or privilege, the stinging humiliations that come from the mouths or pens of others who may or may not be well-intentioned, IQ scores being thrown in your face, etc.). It is reality for us. It is not a discussion, not a theory. It is flesh and blood. . . .

And to come to school and have to play "educator" to the others who want to discuss race or understand, or release some guilt, or even in a very few cases, people who want to see a real change . . . It gets tired . . .

Marilyn, I think that you are very brave and genuine to ask the tough questions that you ask yourself and your White students. But the truth is, your perspective, your reality does not necessarily reflect ours.

In *Teaching to Transgress* (1994), bell hooks makes a point remarkably similar to Vanstory's. Although hooks is discussing White feminist writers rather than teachers or teacher educators as Vanstory was, her comments contribute to a larger argument about the necessity of rethinking pedagogy in the current age of multiculturalism:

Now Black women are placed in the position of serving White female desire to know more about race and racism, to "master" the subject. Drawing on the work of Black women, work that they once dismissed as irrelevant, they now reproduce the servant-served paradigms in their scholarship. Armed with new knowledge of race, their willingness to say that their work is coming from a White perspective (usually without explaining what that means), they forget that the very focus on racism emerged from the concrete political effort to forge meaningful ties between women of different race and class groups. This struggle is often completely ignored. (pp. 103–104)

I am convinced that reading and writing accounts about race and racism that get personal, as well as reading more intellectualized arguments about these issues, is vital to preservice teacher education. As I have tried to suggest, however, reading teacher education as racial text reveals that this is also a complex activity that is fraught with problems. Compelling personal stories often evoke a strong sense of empathy for others (Rosenberg, 1997), a false sense that all of us have experienced hurt and frustration varying in degree but not in kind, that all of us underneath have the same issues, that all of us can understand racism as personal struggle, as individual instance of cruelty, discrete moment of shame, outrage, or fear. In addition to using some people's experience in the service of others' education, then, personal narratives can also obscure more direct confrontation of the ways that individual instances of prejudice are *not* all the same — that some are deeply embedded in and entangled with institutional and historical systems of racism based on power and privilege, and some are not. Reading teacher education as racial text means trying to make issues of racism central, not marginal, and close and personal, not distant and academic. But it also means helping all of the readers and writers of such stories understand that schools and other organizational contexts are always sites for institutional and collective struggles of power and oppression (Villegas, 1991), not neutral backdrops for individual achievement and failure (McCarthy, 1993). And it means being very careful about what is said after stories are told and considering carefully whose stories are used in whose interest.

The foregoing discussion is not meant to suggest that racism was or should be the only topic in the teacher education curriculum or that everything else is secondary. I am not suggesting here that student teachers and their more experienced mentors should talk only about racism or that if we learn to talk about race and racism constructively, we do not need to learn anything else in the teacher education curriculum. It is a problem, for example, if there is no time in courses on language and literacy in the elementary school to explore and critique process writing, basal reading programs, whole language, phonics instruction, and standardized and nonstandardized means of assessing verbal aptitude and achievement. But issues of language, race, and cultural diversity are implicated in and by all of these topics, as I discuss in the next section of this article, and it is a fallacy to assume that there is a forced and mutually exclusive choice in preservice education — emphasizing *either* pedagogical and subject matter knowledge *or* knowledge about culture, racism, and schools as reflections of societal conflicts and sites for power struggle.

READING BETWEEN THE LINES: PERSPECTIVES, IDENTITY, AND DIFFERENCE

Understanding curriculum as racial text requires thorough scrutiny of implicit perspectives about race and careful attention to issues of identity and difference (Castenell & Pinar, 1993). In teacher education this means not looking simply at a synopsis of the "plot" of a preservice program (to carry the text metaphor further). It also means examining the roles of starring and supporting characters and analyzing the plot line by line, as well as between the lines, for underlying themes and for the twists and turns of the stories told or implied about race, racism, and teaching.

Following the events recounted in the "blind vision" story, our teacher education community attempted not only to make issues of race up close and personal, but also to "read between the lines" of the curriculum. As director of the program and instructor of core courses on language, learning, and literacy, I had earlier examined class discussions that explicitly dealt with racism and teaching, as well as the essays and projects my students completed (see Cochran-Smith, 1995a, 1995b). In these analyses, I had tried to understand how student teachers constructed issues related to race and racism and how they linked these to their roles as prospective teachers. I had also looked at how I constructed the issues and how I linked them to my role as teacher educator and mentor. But at this point, as part of our group's larger, more intensive efforts, I wanted to look further — between and underneath the explicit lines that narrated my courses. I wanted to get at the implicit, more subtle perspectives by scrutinizing what was included and omitted from readings and discussions, how issues were sequenced and juxtaposed with one another, which messages were consistent and fundamental, and — inevitably — which were not. To do so, I used as data the evolution of course syllabi, assignments, and activities, as well as students' responses, class discussions, and my own detailed notes and reflections on three required courses I taught (a two-course sequence on reading and language arts in the elementary school and a course on children's literature). All three were designed to explore the relationships of literacy, learning, and culture and their implications for the teaching of reading, writing, literature, and oral language development.

What I found was in one sense exactly what I expected to find. Over the years we had increased the amount of time and attention we gave to questions of culture, race, and racism. In fact, these issues had become a central theme of my courses and of the program in general. But what I found when I read between and under the lines of the curriculum as racial text was a contradiction. On the one hand, the first part of the course presented heavy critique of the inequities embedded in the status quo and of the ways these were perpetuated by the current arrangements of schooling. On the other hand, the latter part of the course privileged pedagogical perspectives drawn from theories and practices developed primarily by White teachers and scholars of child development, language learning, and progressive education. There was as well an underlying White European American construction of self-identity and other, of "we" and "they."

White Theory, White Practice

My courses were intended to help students think through the relationships of theory and practice, learn how to learn from children, and construct principled perspectives about teaching and assessing language and literacy learning. Two themes ran throughout that were not about literacy and literature per se but were intended to be fundamental to these courses and to the entire program: 1) understanding teaching as an intellectual and political activity and the teacher as active constructor (not simply receiver) of meaning, knowledge, and curriculum; and 2) developing critical perspectives about the relationships of race, class, culture, and schooling.

A between-the-lines analysis revealed a sharp contrast in the subtle messages my courses projected about these two themes. The notion of teacher as a constructor of meaning and active decisionmaker was consistent. Readings and class discussions conceptualized the teacher as knowledge generator, as well as critical consumer of others' knowledge, as active constructor of interpretive frameworks as well as poser and ponderer of questions, and as agent for school and social change within local communities and larger social movements. Student teachers were required to construct (rather than simply implement) literature and literacy curriculum, critique teachers' manuals and reading textbooks according to their assumptions about teacher and student agency, and function as researchers by treating their ongoing work with children as sites for inquiry about language learning access and opportunity. Research and writing by experienced teachers from the local and larger inquiry communities were part of the required reading for every topic on the syllabi.

In addition, the knowledge and interpretive frameworks generated by teachers were regarded as part of the knowledge base for language and literacy teaching. They were *not* mentioned only when the topic was teacher research itself or when the point was to provide examples of classroom practice or of the application of others' ideas. Guest speakers included teachers as often as university-based experts. Teachers' ways of analyzing and interpreting data, creating theories, assessing children's progress, and constructing and critiquing practice (Lytle & Cochran-Smith, 1992) were foregrounded and valued as much as those generated by researchers based outside classrooms and schools. In addition, in multiple assignments in my courses, students were required to alter and analyze conventional curriculum and pedagogy based on systematic data collection about teaching and learning. They were prompted to challenge conventional labeling and grouping practices, and they were invited to be part of teacher-initiated alternative professional development groups struggling to "teach against the grain" (Cochran-Smith, 1991). Reading between and under the lines exposed little discrepancy, with regard to teachers' roles as knowledge generators and change agents, between the texts and subtexts of the curriculum.

By contrast, the same kind of close reading with regard to critical perspectives on race and racism led to different and more troubling insights. In my two-semester language and literacy course, a major segment early in the syllabus had to do with race, class, and culture. For this segment students read selections by the well-known scholars mentioned earlier, as well as personal narratives written by members of the local and larger teacher education communities. Spread over three to four weeks, this portion of the course emphasized the following: both schooling systems and individuals' school experiences are deeply embedded within social, cultural, and historical contexts, including institutional and historical racism; European perspectives are not universal standards of the evolution of higher order thought, but culturally and historically constructed habits of mind; and the standard "neutral" U.S. school and its curriculum have been generated out of, and help to sustain, unearned advantages and disadvantages for particular groups of students based on race, class, culture, gender, linguistic background, and ability/disability. Described in detail elsewhere (Cochran-Smith, 1995b), this part of the course gave students the opportunity to "rewrite their autobiographies" or reinterpret some of their own life stories and experiences based on new insights about power, privilege, and oppression. This part of the course also prompted students to "construct uncertainty" — that is, to pose and investigate questions of curriculum and instructional strategies informed by their experiences as raced, classed, and gendered beings and contingent upon the varying school contexts and student populations with whom they worked.

The remainder of the course was organized around major topics in elementary school language and literacy: controversies about learning to read and write (including child language acquisition, whole language as a theory of practice, basal reading approaches, reading groups, and phonics instruction); teaching reading and writing in elementary classrooms (including emergent literacy and extending literacy through reading aloud, language experience, literature study, process writing, journals, and other activities and strategies); and interpretation and use of assessments in language and literacy (including standardized tests and alternative assessments such as portfolios, informal reading inventories, and holistic assessments). For each topic, underlying assumptions about the nature of language, children as learners, teaching and learning as constructive processes, and classrooms/schools as social and cultural contexts were identified and critiqued.

The pedagogy that was advocated was more or less "progressive," "whole language," "developmental," and "meaning-centered," with emphasis on children as readers and writers of authentic texts and the classroom as a social context within which children and teachers together construct knowledge. There was a distinct bias against skills-centered approaches that taught reading and writing in isolated bits and pieces using texts and exercises constructed specifically for that purpose. Instead it was emphasized that language skills emerged from authentic language use and from instruction within the context of language use.

Reading between the lines forced other realizations. The pedagogy I advocated was drawn from theories and practices developed primarily by White teachers and scholars. The prominent names on this part of the syllabus were revealing — Dewey (1916), Britton (1987), Berthoff (1987), Graves (1983), Calkins (1991, 1994), Edelsky, Altwerger, and Flores (1991), Dyson (1987), Paley (1979), Rosenblatt (1976), and Goodman (1988), as well as teachers and teacher groups at the North Dakota Study Group (Strieb, 1985), the Prospect School (Carini, 1986), the National Writing Project (Pincus, 1993; Waff, 1994), the Breadloaf School of English (Goswami & Stillman, 1987), the Philadelphia Teachers Learning Cooperative (1984), and other local teacher and practitioner groups.[6] Absent from these segments of the syllabus and from our discussions were contrasting cultural perspectives on child language and learning and child socialization. Also absent were rich accounts of successful pedagogies, particularly with poor children and children of color, that were not necessarily "progressive" or "whole language" oriented.

Notwithstanding the fact that students read Lisa Delpit, Shirley Brice Heath, and others earlier in the course, it became clear to me by reading between the lines that there was a powerful contradictory subtext in the course about pedagogy for language and literacy. The subtle message was that pedagogy developed primarily from research and writing by and about White mainstream persons was the pedagogy that was best for everybody — Dewey's argument, more or less, that what the "wisest and best" parent wants for his or her child is what we should want for all children, or what we should want for "other people's children" (Delpit, 1988, 1995; Kozol, 1991). This subtle message implied that "progressive" language pedagogy was culture neutral, although just weeks earlier the course had emphasized that all aspects of schooling were socially and culturally constructed and needed to be understood within particular historical and cultural contexts. Because progressive language pedagogy was unmarked as cultural theory, culturally embedded practice, and/or cultural perspective, however, the subtle message was that it was an a-cultural position about how best to teach language and literacy that applied across contexts, historical moments, and school populations.

Part of what this meant was that my courses offered student teachers no theoretical framework for understanding the successful teachers they observed in their field-work schools who used traditional, skills-based reading and writing pedagogies with their students, particularly in urban schools where there were large numbers of poor children and children of color. Although my courses explicitly emphasized the importance of teachers' knowledge, there was a contradictory and perhaps more powerful implicit message: the knowledge of some teachers was more valuable than others, the knowledge of teachers who worked (successfully) from a more or less skills-based, direct-instruction perspective was perhaps not so important, and the pedagogy of these teachers was somewhat misguided and out of date. Reading between the lines of my students' discussions and writings revealed that they were confused about what to make of the successes they observed in urban classrooms when the pedagogy we read about and valued in class was not apparent. On the other hand, my student teachers knew precisely what to make of the unsuccessful teachers they observed in those same contexts. My students had a powerful framework for critique and could easily conclude that many urban teachers were unsuccessful because they were too traditional, too focused on skills, not progressive enough.

What was missing from the sections of my courses that dealt specifically with reading and language pedagogy were theories of practice developed by and about people of color, as well as rich and detailed analyses of successful teachers of urban children, particularly poor children of color, who used a variety of pedagogies including, but not necessarily limited to, those pedagogies that could be called "progressive." Gloria Ladson-Billings's work (1994, 1995) had just been published at the time I was struggling to read deeply between the lines of my courses and our larger curriculum. Hers and related analyses of culturally appropriate, culturally relevant, and/or culturally sensitive pedagogies (Au & Kawakami, 1994; Ballenger, 1992; Foster, 1993, 1994; Hollins, King, & Hayman, 1994; Irvine, 1990; Irvine & York, 1995; King, 1994) were extremely useful in my efforts to rethink the ways I taught my courses and structured the program. In fact, Ladson-Billings's book, *The Dreamkeepers: Successful Teachers of African American Children* (1994), speaks directly to the issue of skills- and whole language–based approaches to language instruction by contrasting two very different but highly successful teachers of reading to African American children. One of these taught from a (more or less) whole language perspective, focusing on student-teacher interactions, skills in the context of meaning, and use of literature and other authentic texts, while the other taught from a (more or less) traditional skills perspective, focusing on direct instruction, phonics and word identification skills, and basal texts written for the explicit purpose of instruction. Ladson-Billings points out what is wrong with framing the debate about how to teach African American children in terms of whole language versus a purely skill-based approach:

> In some ways their differences represent the larger debate about literacy teaching, that of whole-language versus basal-text techniques. However, beneath the surface, at the personal ideological level, the differences between these instructional strategies lose meaning. Both teachers want their students to become literate. Both believe that their students are capable of high levels of literacy. (p. 116)

Ladson-Billings's commentary lifts the debates about literacy instruction out of the realm of language theory and practice *only* and into the realm of ideology and politics as well — that is, into the realm of teachers' commitments to communities, to parents, and to activism.[7] Her analysis of successful and culturally relevant pedagogy for African American children repeatedly emphasizes teachers' ties to the school community, teachers' belief in the learning ability of all children (not just an exceptional few who, through education, can make their way "out" of the lives common to their parents and community members), and teachers' strategies for establishing personal connections with students and helping them connect new knowledge to previous experiences and ideas.

When I revised my language and reading courses, Ladson-Billings's *The Dreamkeepers* was one of the central texts, and I included in discussions about reading/writing pedagogy many other readings about culturally relevant language pedagogy (e.g., Au & Kawakami, 1994; Ballenger, 1992; Foster, 1993). In addition to readings about language and literacy theory, debates about pedagogy, and so on, new additions were intended in part to alter the curriculum as racial text. Particularly, they were intended to provide frameworks for understanding successful and unsuccessful teaching of poor and privileged White children and children of color — frameworks that were not dichotomous and that included but were more complex than whole language versus basals. These were also intended to prompt more attention to issues of community, as well as richer and more diverse perspectives on pedagogy, skills, and explicit versus implicit instruction (Delpit, 1988). I also wanted to diminish the implicit subtext of criticism of teachers who worked successfully, particularly with children of color, using methods other than those that might be termed "progressive" or "whole." Including these new readings also made the course more complicated and made its underlying conception of teaching as an uncertain activity (Dudley-Marling, 1997; McDonald, 1992) even more pronounced than it had been. Always eschewing the possibility of "best practices" that cut across the contexts and conditions of local settings, I had for years told students that the answer to most questions about "the best" ways to teach something was "it depends" (Cochran-Smith, 1995b). Having uncovered unintended contradictions in the lessons I taught my students made me realize that pedagogical decisions "depend" on an even wider, richer, and more nuanced array of variables and conditions than I had implied.[8]

Identity and Difference: We and They

Understanding the racial narrative that underlies a curriculum is a process that requires intense self-critical reflection and analysis, as Castenell and Pinar (1993) have made clear:

> Debates over what we teach the young are also — in addition to being debates over what knowledge is of most worth — debates over who we perceive ourselves to be, and how we will represent that identity, including what remains as "left over," as "difference." (p. 2)

Reading between the lines of my own courses and of the larger teacher education curriculum revealed a White European American construction of self-identity and "other." "We," I came to realize, often referred not to "we who are committed to teaching elementary school differently and improving the life chances of all children," but to "we White people (especially we White women) who are trying to learn how to teach people who are different from us." On the one hand, it could be argued that this perspective is exactly what is needed, given the demographic disparities, now well documented (National Education Goals Panel, 1997; Quality Education for Minorities Project, 1990), between the racial composition of the group entering the nation's teaching force (more than 90% White European American) and the nation's schoolchildren (increasingly a wide array of racial, cultural, and language groups). In elementary education, in addition to being White and European American, the group entering the teaching force is also overwhelmingly female. In a certain sense, then, one could make a persuasive case that a White European American and female construction of self and other is just what the preservice teacher education curriculum ought to have. On the other hand, the program I directed had 20–25 percent students of color and 15–20 percent male students. A curriculum for "White girls" was surely not the answer. Rather, we were committed to constructing a curriculum that helped all student teachers — with full acknowledgement of differences in race, culture, and gender — interrogate their experiences, understand schools and schooling as sites for struggles over power, and become prepared to teach in an increasingly multiracial and multicultural society. To do so, we had to revise the story the curriculum told about identity and rewrite the characters who were central in that story, particularly who "we and they," "self and other," "regular and left over" were.

One incident from my course on literature for children, which I have taught in various iterations for more than twenty years, provides an example of the ways I tried consciously to alter the assumed definition of self and other, we and they, in my courses. What I wanted to do was to construct discussions where "we and they" shifted *away from* "we White people who are trying to learn to teach those other people — those people of color" *and toward* "we educators who are trying to be sensitive to, and learn to teach, all students — both those who are different from us and those who are like us in race, class, and culture." I began to use Lynne Reid Banks's *The Indian in the Cupboard* (1981) as one of the six or eight novels my students read in common for the literature course.[9] My course had for years included many children's books that were highly regarded for their portrayals of the perspectives of African American, Asian, and Hispanic family and childhood experiences (Harris, 1993), and the course had for years focused on the politics of children's literature (Taxel, 1993). The point of adding *The Indian in the Cupboard* was *not* to add "the Native American experience" to the list of cultures represented in the course. Rather, the point was to create an opportunity to prompt an altered conception of self and other, an altered sense of who "we" were as teachers.

Published in 1981, when the *New York Times* called it "the best novel of the year," *The Indian in the Cupboard* continues to be highly acclaimed and widely used as a whole-class text in upper elementary and middle schools, and its popularity has increased since it was made into a Disney motion picture. A fantasy about Omri, a British boy who receives as a present a collector's cupboard, the book revolves around a plastic Indian figure who comes to life (but remains three inches high) when the boy casually places him inside the cupboard and closes the door. A toy cowboy and soldier eventually come to life too and interact with the Indian and the boy. The book is charming in many ways, well written and pivoting on premises that are extremely appealing to children — being bigger than adults, having toys come to life, and keeping a powerful secret. But in addition to positive reviews about the popularity of the book and the high quality of its writing, the book has also been criticized as racist, perpetuating stereotypes about Native Americans at the same time that it charms and appeals. The first year I used the book, all of my students were prospective teachers, many of whom were just completing a year of student teaching in urban schools where the population was primarily African American, Asian, and/or Puerto Rican. I asked the class to read the novel and jot down their responses and then read the critical commentary I had assigned.

In an excoriating critique of images of Native Americans in children's books, MacCann (1993) argues that the vast majority of children's books with Native American characters or themes are written from a non-Native perspective. With few exceptions, they portray Native American cultures as futile and obsolete and turn on the "persistent generalization" that American society has been "shaped by the pull of a vacant continent drawing population westward" and available to any enterprising European (p. 139). About *The Indian in the Cupboard* specifically, MacCann writes:

> Even in the fantasy genre the displacement of American Indian societies can be an underlying theme, as in *The Indian in the Cupboard* [Banks, 1981] and its sequel *The Return of the Indian* [Banks, 1986]. These narratives are set in modern times . . . but the cultural content is rooted in the image of the Indian as presented in Hollywood westerns and dime novels. Little Bear is a plastic toy Indian who comes to life in the boy's magical cupboard, but remains just three inches in height. He grunts and snarls his way through the story, attacking the child, Omri, with a hunting knife, and later attacking a traditional enemy, a three-inch cowboy. At every turn of plot, Little Bear is either violent or childishly petulant until he finally tramples upon his ceremonial headdress as a sign of remorse. The historical culpability of the cowboy and others who invaded [Native American] territory is ignored. Native Americans are seen as the primary perpetrators of havoc, even as they defend their own borders. (p. 145)

In *Through Indian Eyes* (Slapin & Seale, 1992), a collection of articles written primarily by Native Americans, the review of *The Indian in the Cupboard* and its sequel is also wholly negative. It concludes:

> My heart aches for the Native child unfortunate enough to stumble across, and read, these books. How could she, reading this, fail to be damaged? How could a White child fail to believe that he is far superior to the bloodthirsty, sub-human monsters portrayed here? (p. 122)

My students read these critiques after they had read and responded to the novel and came to class prepared to discuss both.

Most of my students reported that they were completely engrossed in the unfolding story, and some were shocked by the negative critiques and even embarrassed that they had not noticed the racist overtones (and undertones) until after they finished the book. Many were uncertain about what to think. The discussion was intense and animated:[10]

> The book is full of stereotypes. If a book has stereotypes, does that mean you just shouldn't use it in your classroom?

> There are lots of stereotypes about Indians, but there are also stereotypes about cowboys and soldiers — doesn't this make the book sort of balanced?

> The very idea of an American Indian adult as the possession (and a miniature possession at that) of a White English child is totally offensive and off-putting — does it really matter what else the book does or doesn't do?

> Since the boy's wrong assumptions about Indians are for the most part pointed out and corrected by the narrator as the story goes along, doesn't it actually sort of "teach" some correct facts?

> In the final analysis, isn't what really matters how engaging the story is for kids and what the quality of the writing is?

> How can we evaluate the realism of the characters in a story that is obviously fantasy rather than history or biography?

> Since none of us had any Native American children in the classes we student taught this year, does that make the issue of potentially hurting a Native child reader irrelevant?

Students were divided about what they thought of the book. Many saw it as more or less harmless, assuming that those who considered the book racist were self-interested extremists, interested only in what was "politically correct," or manufacturing problems where there were none. Others strongly disagreed, assessing the book as promoting shallow stereotypes with little redeeming social value. At some point in this very intense discussion, I inserted, "What if it were *The* Jew *in the Cupboard* or *The* Black *in the Cupboard?* Would that be all right?" For a few minutes there was dead silence. The looks on the faces of my students, many of whom were Jewish, African American, or Hispanic, indicated that it would decidedly *not* be all right to have a children's book with those titles or those story lines. Why then, I asked, was it all right for elementary and middle school teachers each year to teach to the whole class a children's book that had an Indian in the cupboard?

This was a turning point in the course, one that prompted some of the best discussion of the semester. Several students, African American and Hispanic, talked about how this opened their eyes to racism in a different way. They admitted that they had never worried too much about "Redskins" and tomahawks as symbols for sports teams, or grotesque caricatures and cigar-store Indians as icons for margarine, sports utility vehicles, and blue jeans. The discussion about race and racism changed that day. For a while everybody seemed to have new questions, and nobody seemed as sure as they had been about the answers. I believe this was because in this discussion there was a different underlying construction of identity and difference, an altered perspective on what was assumed to be the standard from which we defined "regular and different," "self and other." When "other" was Native American and "self" everyone else in the room, there were new opportunities for students to interrogate their assumptions, new opportunities to struggle with the issue of what it means to teach those who are different from and the same as our multiple selves.

Telling the story of what happened when I added *The Indian in the Cupboard* to my course is in no way intended to suggest that all we have to do in teacher education is figure out who is "not in the room" and then construct that person as the "other," that all we have to do is be certain to include in the curriculum fictional or research literature about racial or cultural groups that are not actually represented in a given teacher education program. That is not at all the point here. Nor is the point to claim that this kind of "inclusion" would be desirable or even possible. The point I do wish to make is that it is critically important to scrutinize the often very subtle messages about identity and difference that float between the lines of the curriculum and consciously work to construct opportunities in which all the members of the community are able to interrogate their constructions of self and other. As I have argued already, however, these opportunities must always be connected to larger understandings of the histories of oppression and privilege and must always be couched in understandings of institutional and organizational racism.

CONCLUSION: LESSONS LEARNED AND UNLEARNED

What are the lessons learned here about unlearning racism? One has to do with the power of narrative *in* teacher education and, as importantly, the power of teacher education *as* narrative. As I have tried to show throughout this article, both the personal and the fictional stories about race and racism that we invite participants to read and write can break down the barriers of distanced, academic discourse and make possible revelations about participants' positions, identity, and standpoint. Stories can serve as touchstones for shared experience and commitment. As one primary way we understand and construct our professional lives and our multiple identities, stories can help us scrutinize our own work and theorize our own experience. But stories can also be extremely negative, particularly when the stories of some groups are used — unintentionally or not — in the service of others' desire to learn and/or when powerful emotions are unleashed and participants are then left to fend for themselves in the aftermath. Stories can be negative if they prompt a false sense of sameness and personal empathy that is unconnected to historical and institutional racism, to schools as sites for power struggles, or to ownership of the roles privilege and oppression play in everyday life. It may also be the case that there are some stories that individuals should not be coaxed to share in mixed racial groups and some that group leaders should not attempt to solicit. Finally, it must be understood that the narratives we use as tools and texts in the teacher education curriculum confound and are confounded by larger and more deeply embedded messages, messages that are revealed only when the curriculum is interrogated, or consciously read as racial text.

The second lesson is connected to the title of this article, which implies two contradictions: blind vision, a phrase that suggests simultaneous seeing and not seeing; and "*un*learning," a word that signifies both growth and the undoing or reversing of that growth. These contradictions are intentional, chosen not only to signal the enormous complexities inherent in the ways race and culture are implicated in teaching and teacher education, but also to caution that blindness is an inevitable aspect of trying to act on a vision about including racism in the teacher education curriculum, that failing is an inherent aspect of unlearning racism. I am completely convinced that "reading the curriculum as racial text," in the sense that I have described it in this article, is critical to a vision for preservice education. But I am also convinced that this is a slow and stumbling journey and that along the way difficulty, pain, self-exposure, and disappointment are inevitable. To teach lessons about race and racism in teacher education is to struggle to unlearn racism itself — to interrogate the assumptions that are deeply embedded in the curriculum, to own our own complicity in maintaining existing systems of privilege and oppression, and to grapple with our own failure.

Nikki Giovanni's "A Journey" (1983, p. 47) eloquently conjures up the image of blind vision that I wish to connect to the idea of unlearning racism. I conclude this article with her poem:

A Journey*

It's a journey . . . that I propose . . . I am not the guide . . . nor
technical assistant . . . I will be your fellow passenger . . .

Though the rail has been ridden . . . winter clouds cover . . .
autumn's exuberant guilt . . . we must provide our own guideposts . . .
I have heard . . . from previous visitors . . . the road washes out
sometimes . . . and passengers are compelled . . . to continue
groping . . . or turn back . . . I am not afraid . . .

I am not afraid of rough spots . . . or lonely times . . . I don't
fear . . . the success of this endeavor . . .
I promise you nothing . . . I accept your promise . . . of the
same we are simply riding . . . a wave . . . that may carry or crash . . .
It's a journey . . . and I want . . . to go . . .

* "A Journey" from *Those Who Ride the Night Winds* by Nikki Giovanni. Copyright © 1983 by Nikki Giovanni. Reprinted by permission of HarperCollins Publishers, Inc.

NOTES

1. I have outlined the ways this program addressed issues of race, class, and culture in a number of articles, particularly an earlier *Harvard Educational Review* piece (Cochran-Smith, 1995b).
2. This narrative was constructed based on my own and a colleague's notes about the seminar sessions, my own written reflections shortly following the event, notes on conversations with students and with other teacher educators prior to and following the sessions, written communications from students, and other program documents that described the structure and context of

the program. Excerpts from written communications and students' comments and papers are used with permission of the authors.

3. The idea of "reading teacher education as racial text" emerges from a number of sources, as described in the following section. The term itself draws from Castenell and Pinar's (1993) concept of "understanding curriculum as racial text," which is also the title of their edited collection of articles about identity and difference in education, particularly how these are represented in curriculum.

4. The analysis I offer here is based on multiple curriculum and teaching documents, as well as experiences captured in my own reflections over a six-year period at the University of Pennsylvania. These include syllabi and assignments for courses that I taught each year during that time period; program handbooks and advertising literature; my own and others' writing about the program (both formal papers and more personal reflections), detailed notes from meetings of student teachers, university-based supervisors, and whole-community meetings that included school-based cooperating teachers; letters and personal notes sent to me by program participants; two student group papers about racism and teaching that were written and presented in public forums during this time; and analytic descriptions of several key events and critical incidents that occurred.

5. These members of the teacher education community shared their personal accounts with the larger group by presenting orally, including their pieces in the course reading packet and in-house booklets, and facilitating small-group discussions.

6. These were some of the readings regularly used.

7. This is in no way intended to suggest that whole language proponents are unaware of the political and ideological aspects of language instruction, nor is it intended to suggest that they do not address issues of culture. Many whole language theorists locate their work and the debates about whole language perspectives squarely within a cultural and political context (Dudley-Marling, 1997; Edelsky, 1986, 1990; Edelsky, Altwerger, & Flores, 1991; Goodman, 1988; Shannon, 1988). Indeed, Carol Edelsky, arguably one of the best known and most articulate spokespersons and theorists for the whole language movement, gives explicit attention to the politics of pedagogy and to whole language as a theory of practice aimed at social justice and democracy (Edelsky, 1990; Edelsky et al., 1991). Edelsky's work on bilingual education is also explicitly connected to cultural contexts. The popular media debates about whole language and phonics, however, rarely frame these issues as cultural and political questions, and some of those who advocate whole language ignore cultural and political issues altogether and speak as if teaching from a whole language perspective were merely a matter of using certain materials and approaches to teaching.

8. The questions my students posed, the interpretations they constructed, and the pedagogies they developed when their readings and discussions included these new additions are part of a larger analysis I am currently completing.

9. I have used this example in a different way in a discussion about the politics of children's literature and the responsibility of teachers as agents for social change (see Cochran-Smith, 1999).

10. These excerpts represent a range of comments made by students in class discussions and/or in brief written responses to the book. This is not a direct transcription of the actual discussion that unfolded, but is rather a set of excerpts from written and oral comments.

REFERENCES

Apple, M. (1996). *Cultural politics in education*. New York: Teachers College Press.

Asante, M. (1991). The Afro-centric idea in education. *Journal of Negro Education, 62,* 170–180.

Au, K., & Kawakami, A. (1994). Cultural congruence in instruction. In E. Hollins, J. King, & W. Hayman (Eds.), *Teaching diverse population: Formulating a knowledge base* (pp. 5–23). Albany: State University of New York Press.

Ballenger, C. (1992). Because you like us: The language of control. *Harvard Educational Review, 62,* 199–208.

Banks, L. (1981). *The Indian in the cupboard*. Garden City, NY: Doubleday.

Banks, L. (1986). *The return of the Indian*. Garden City, NY: Doubleday.

Berthoff, A. (1987). The teacher as researcher. In D. Goswami & P. R. Stillman (Eds.), *Reclaiming the classroom: Teacher research as an agency for change* (pp. 28–48). Upper Montclair, NJ: Boynton/Cook.

Britton, J. (1987). A quiet form of research. In D. Goswami & P. Stillman (Eds.), *Reclaiming the classroom: Teacher research as an agency for change* (pp. 13–19). Upper Montclair, NJ: Boynton/Cook.

Britzman, D. (1991). *Practice makes practice: A critical study of learning to teach*. Albany: State University of New York Press.

Calkins, L. (1991). *Living between the lines*. Portsmouth, NH: Heinemann.

Calkins, L. (1994). *The art of teaching writing*. Portsmouth, NH: Heinemann.

Carini, P. (1986). *Prospect's documentary process*. Bennington, VT: Prospect School Center.

Castenell, L., & Pinar, W. (Eds.). (1993). *Understanding curriculum as racial text: Representations of identity and difference in education*. Albany: State University of New York Press.

Cochran-Smith, M. (1991). Learning to teach against the grain. *Harvard Educational Review, 51*, 279–310.

Cochran-Smith, M. (1995a). Color blindness and basket making are not the answers: Confronting the dilemmas of race, culture, and language diversity in teacher education. *American Educational Research Journal, 32*, 493–522.

Cochran-Smith, M. (1995b). Uncertain allies: Understanding the boundaries of race and teaching. *Harvard Educational Review, 65*, 541–570.

Cochran-Smith, M. (1999). Learning to teach for social justice. In G. Griffin (Ed.), *98th yearbook of NSSE: Teacher education for a new century: Emerging perspectives, promising practices, and future possibilities*. Chicago: University of Chicago Press.

Cochran-Smith, M., Dimattia, P., Dudley-Marling, C., Freedman, S., Friedman, A., Jackson, J., Jackson, R., Loftus, F., Mooney, J., Neisler, O., Peck, A., Pelletier, C., Pine, G., Scanlon, D., & Zollers, N. (1999, April). *Seeking social justice: A teacher education faculty's self study, year III*. Paper presented at the Annual Meeting of the American Educational Research Association, Montreal.

Cochran-Smith, M., & Lytle, S. (1992). Communities for teacher research: Fringe or forefront. *American Journal of Education, 100*, 298–323.

Cochran-Smith, M., & Lytle, S. (1993). *Inside/outside: Teacher research and knowledge*. New York: Teachers College Press.

Cochran-Smith, M., & Lytle, S. (1998). Teacher research: The question that persists. *International Journal of Leadership in Education, 1*(1), 19–36.

Cochran-Smith, M., & Lytle, S. (1999). Relationships of knowledge and practice: Teacher learning in communities. In A. Iran-Nejad & C. D. Pearson (Eds.), *Review of research in education* (vol. 24, pp. 251–307). Washington, DC: American Educational Research Association.

Cole, A., & Knowles, J. (1998). The self-study of teacher education practices and the reform of teacher education. In M. L. Hamilton (Ed.), *Reconceptualizing teaching practice: Self-study in teacher education* (pp. 224–234). London: Falmer Press.

Comer, J. (1989). Racism and the education of young children. *Teachers College Record, 90*, 352–361.

Delpit, L. (1986). Skills and other dilemmas of a progressive Black educator. *Harvard Educational Review, 56*, 379–385.

Delpit, L. (1988). The silenced dialogue: Power and pedagogy in educating other people's children. *Harvard Educational Review, 58*, 280–298.

Delpit, L. (1995). *Other people's children: Cultural conflict in the classroom*. New York: New Press.

Dewey, J. (1916). *Democracy and education: An introduction to the philosophy of education*. New York: Free Press.

Dudley-Marling, C. (1997). *Living with uncertainty: The messy reality of classroom practice*. Portsmouth, NH: Heinemann.

Dyson, A. (1987). The value of "time off-task": Young children's spontaneous talk and deliberate text. *Harvard Educational Review, 57*, 396–420.

Edelsky, C. (1986). *Writing in a bilingual program*. Norwood, NJ: Ablex.

Edelsky, C. (1990). Whose agenda is this anyway? A response to McKenna, Robinson, and Miller. *Educational Researcher, 19* (8), 3–6.

Edelsky, C., Altwerger, B., & Flores, B. (1991). *Whole language: What's the difference?* Portsmouth, NH: Heinemann.

Fine, M. (Ed.). (1994). *Chartering urban school reform: Reflections on pubic high schools in the midst of change*. New York: Teachers College Press.

Foster, M. (1993). Educating for competence in community and culture: Exploring views of exemplary African-American teachers. *Urban Education, 27*, 370–394.

Foster, M. (1994). Effective Black teachers: A literature review. In E. Hollins, J. King, & W. Hayman (Eds.), *Teaching diverse populations: Formulating a knowledge base* (pp. 225–241). Albany: State University of New York Press.

Ginsberg, M., & Clift, R. (1990). The hidden curriculum of preservice teacher education. In R. W. Houston (Ed.), *Handbook of research on teacher education* (pp. 450–468). New York: MacWilliams.

Giovanni, N. (1983). A journey. In *Those who ride the night winds* (p. 47) New York: William Morrow.

Giroux, H. (1984). Rethinking the language of schooling. *Language Arts, 61*, 33–40.

Giroux, H. (1988). *Teachers as intellectuals: Toward a pedagogy of learning*. Westport, CT: Bergin & Garvey.

Gitlin, A. (Ed.). (1994). *Power and method: Political activism and educational research*. New York: Routledge.

Goodman, K. (1988). *Report card on basal readers*. New York: Richard C. Owen.

Goswami, P., & Stillman, P. (1987). *Reclaiming the classroom: Teacher research as an agency for change*. Upper Montclair, NJ: Boynton/Cook.

Graves, D. (1983). *Writing: Teachers and children at work*. Portsmouth, NH: Heinemann.

Hardy, B. (1978). Towards a poetics of fiction: An approach through narrative. In M. Meek & G. Barton (Eds.), *The cool web* (pp. 12–23). New York: Antheneum.

Harris, V. (Ed.). (1993). *Teaching multicultural literature in grades K-8*. Norwood, MA: Christopher-Gordon.

Heath, S. (1982a). Questioning at home and at school: A comparative study. In G. Spindler (Ed.), *Doing an ethnography of schooling* (pp. 103–131). New York: Holt, Rinehart & Winston.

Heath, S. (1982b). What no bedtime story means: Narrative skills at home and school. *Language in Society, 11*, 49–76.

Hollins, E., King, J., & Hayman, W. (Eds.). (1994). *Teaching diverse populations: Formulating a knowledge base*. Albany: State University of New York Press.

hooks, b. (1994). *Teaching to transgress: Education as the practice of freedom*. New York: Routledge.

Irvine, J. (1990). *Black students and school failure: Policies, practice and prescriptions*. New York: Greenwood Press.

Irvine, J., & York, D. (1995). Learning styles and culturally diverse students: A literature review. In J. A. Banks & C. A. M. Banks (Eds.), *Handbook of research on multicultural education*. (pp. 494–497). New York: Macmillan.

King, J. (1994). The purpose of schooling for African American children: Including cultural knowledge. In E. R. Hollins, J. E. King, & W. C. Hayman (Eds.), *Teaching diverse populations: Formulating a knowledge base* (pp. 25–56). Albany: State University of New York Press.

King, J., Hollins, E., & Hayman, W. (Eds.). (1997). *Preparing teachers for cultural diversity*. New York: Teachers College Press.

Kozol, J. (1991). *Savage inequalities: Children in America's schools*. New York: Crown.

Ladson-Billings, G. (1994). *The dreamkeepers: Successful teachers of African-American children*. San Francisco: Jossey Bass.

Ladson-Billings, G. (1995). Toward a theory of culturally relevant pedagogy. *American Educational Research Journal, 32*, 465–491.

Lawrence, S., & Tatum, B. (1997). Teachers in transition: The impact of antiracist professional development on classroom practice. *Teachers College Record, 99*, 162–178.

Leistyna, P., Woodrum, A., & Sherblom, S. A. (Eds.). (1996). *Breaking free: The transformative power of critical pedagogy*. Cambridge, MA: Harvard Educational Review.

Lytle, S., & Cochran-Smith, M. (1992). Teacher research as a way of knowing. *Harvard Educational Review, 62*, 447–474.

MacCann, D. (1993). Native Americans in books for the young. In V. Harris (Ed.), *Teaching multicultural literature in grades K-8* (pp. 137–170). Norwood, MA: Christopher-Gordon.

McCarthy, C. (1990). Multicultural education, minorities, identities, textbooks, and the challenge of curriculum reform. *Journal of Education, 172*, 118–129.

McCarthy, C. (1993). Multicultural approaches to racial inequality in the United States. In L. A. Castenell & W. F. Pinar (Eds.), *Understanding curriculum as racial text*, (pp. 245–246). Albany: State University of New York Press.

McDonald, J. (1992). *Teaching: Making sense of an uncertain craft*. New York: Teachers College Press.

McIntosh, P. (1989). White privilege: Unpacking the invisible knapsack. *Peace and Freedom, 49*(4), 10–12.

Metzger, D. (1986). Circles of stories. *Parabola, 4*(4), 1–4.

Mishler, E. (1986). *Research interviewing: Context and marriage*. Cambridge, MA: Harvard University Press.

Moll, L., Amanti, C., Neff, D., Gonzalez, N. (1992). Funds of knowledge for teaching: Using a qualitative approach to connect homes and classrooms. *Theory Into Practice, 31*, 32–41.

National Education Goals Panel. (1997). *National education goals report*. Washington, DC: Author.

Nieto, S. (1999). *The light in their eyes: Creating multicultural learning communities*. New York: Teachers College Press.

Noffke, S. (1997). Professional, personal, and political dimensions of action research. In M. Apple (Ed.), *Review of research in education* (pp. 305–343). Washington, DC: American Educational Research Association.

Ogbu, J. (1978). *Minority education and caste*. New York: Academic Press.

Paley, V. (1979). *White teacher*. Cambridge, MA: Harvard University Press.

Philadelphia Teachers Learning Cooperative. (1984). On becoming teacher experts: Buying time. *Language Arts, 6*, 731–735.

Pincus, M. (1993). Following the paper trail. In M. Cochran-Smith & S. Lytle, *Inside/outside: Teacher research and knowledge* (pp. 249–255). New York: Teachers College Press.

Quality Education for Minorities Project. (1990). *Education that works: An action plan for the education of minorities*. Cambridge, MA: Author.

Rodriguez, A. (1998). What is (should be) the researcher's role in terms of agency? A question for the 21st century. *Journal of Research in Science Teaching, 35*, 963–965.

Rose, M. (1989). *Lives on the boundary*. New York: Penguin.

Rosenberg, P. (1997). Underground discourses: Exploring Whiteness in teacher education. In M. Fine, L. Weis, L. Powell, & L. Wong (Eds.), *Off-white: readings on race and power in society* (pp. 79–86). New York: Routledge.

Rosenblatt, L. (1976). *Literature as exploration*. New York: Noble & Noble.

Shannon, P. (1988). *Merging literacy: Reading instruction in 20th century America*. South Hadley, MA: Bergin & Garvey.

Sleeter, C. (1992). Restructuring schools for multicultural education. *Journal of Teacher Education, 43*, 141–148.

Sleeter, C., & Grant, C. (1987). An analysis of multicultural education in the United States. *Harvard Educational Review, 57*, 421–444.

Slapin, B., & Seale, B. (1992). *Through Indian eyes: The native experience in books for children*. Philadelphia: New Society.

Strieb, L. (1985). *A (Philadelphia) teacher's journal*. Grand Forks: North Dakota Study Group Center for Teaching and Learning.

Tatum, B. (1992). Talking about race, learning about racism: The applications of racial identity development theory. *Harvard Educational Review, 62*, 1–24.

Tatum, B. (1994). Teaching White students about racism: The search for White allies and the restoration of hope. *Teachers College Record, 95,* 462–476.

Tatum, B. (1997). *"Why are all the Black kids sitting together in the cafeteria?" and other conversations about the development of racial identity.* New York: Basic Books.

Taxel, J. (1993) The politics of children's literature: Reflections on multiculturalism and Christopher Columbus. In V. Harris (Ed.), *Teaching multicultural literature in grades K-8* (pp. 1–36). Norwood, MA: Christopher-Gordon.

Thompson, B., & Tyagi, S. (Eds.). (1996). *Names we call home: Autobiography on racial identity.* New York: Routledge.

Van Manen, M. (1990). *Researching lived experience: Human science for an action sensitive pedagogy.* Albany: State University of New York Press.

Villegas, A. (1991). *Culturally responsive pedagogy for the 1990s and beyond.* Princeton, NJ: Educational Testing Service.

Waff, D. (1994). Romance in the classroom: Inviting discourse on gender and power. *The Voice, 3*(1), 7–14.

Moving beyond Polite Correctness:
Practicing Mindfulness in the
Diverse Classroom

BARBARA VACARR

In a recent *Boston Globe* article, Harvard Professor Gary Orfield notes:

> Enrollment patterns since the late 1960's, when most school districts began court ordered desegregation remedies, show the trend toward resegregation is growing despite rising numbers of minority enrollments. According to a report . . . by the Civil Rights Project [at Harvard University,] . . . nearly 75 percent of Latino public school students go to schools that are predominantly minority. For black students, 69 percent attend predominantly minority schools while a majority of white students attend schools that are 80 percent or more white. (2000, p. A9)

Considering the reality of segregated schools, what prepares White teachers to enter the classroom and effectively deal with moments of difference that reveal racial, religious, ethnic, cultural, and class variations? What experiences can White teachers draw on in order to facilitate the necessary and predictable confrontations that lie at the heart of authentic encounters with the "Other"? What exists in the experience of privilege that prepares White teachers to risk themselves, and not merely to be bystanders in the very real world of the classroom? Certainly the world outside the classroom offers little preparation for moments of difference, given that most Americans live in homogeneous neighborhoods and most children attend schools with their ethnic and racial peers.

These difficult questions concern where and how White teachers, who themselves are often raised and trained in predominantly White schools, are prepared to examine the privileges they have as a result of being White. Such privileges often lie unspoken but threateningly close beneath the surface of our efforts to be culturally sensitive and inclusive of multiple perspectives. Janet Helms (1992) describes the challenge of confronting privilege as a process of "moral re-education" (p. 3). What prepares White

Harvard Educational Review   Vol. 71   No. 2   Summer 2001, 285–295

teachers to engage their White students in this process? Recently, in a challenging moment while I was teaching "Stories of the Holocaust" to a group of twenty-four students — twenty-three White students and one young African American woman — several questions surfaced regarding the preparation of White teachers to effectively address these moments of difference.

The moment occurred as the group was presenting its research on the complexities of the Holocaust, the culmination of a month's work. At that particular moment, a White student used the word *tolerance* during a discussion about people who rescued Jews during the Holocaust. The African American student expressed her dislike of the word while other students rolled their eyes as if to say, "Oh come on, don't make a big deal out of this. Do we really have to watch our every word?" The lone student courageously explained that it was painful to hear a White person use that word. She said, "When I hear you talk about tolerance, I hear you telling me that I am something to be put up with. That doesn't make me feel very good." In the silence that followed this moment I had the uncomfortable privilege of confronting myself as I struggled with the decision to address the differences in the room, and with trusting my ability to facilitate a safe and honest dialogue.

Remaining present in that struggle led me into a disturbingly vulnerable place where I was forced to confront my ineptitude. It is only in retrospect that I am grateful to the African American woman for taking a risk that brought me face to face with my own isolation, a place from which I could perceive her isolation as well as I stood facing the room of silent White students. In that moment, the silence of the room amplified the noise of my internal distress. Speaking felt risky — my words could leave me out there, exposed in much the same way that the student had exposed herself. Just as her declaration pierced the illusion of group unity and separated her from her classroom peers, my words could separate me from the White students or could further my distance from the African American student.

I sensed that several students wanted me to be their ally and to excuse our ignorance and our racism. And, in fact, I wanted to do just that; it would have been so much safer. It was a preciously frightening moment, laden with potential betrayal. Parker Palmer (1998) speaks about this as pathological fear, the kind that leads us to betray our students and ourselves: "It leads me to pander to students, to lose my dignity . . . so worried that the sloucher in the back row doesn't like me that I fail to teach him and everyone else in the room" (p. 49). In these moments, so much of who we are as human beings is at stake. Our integrity, our honesty, and our fundamental trustworthiness is jeopardized by our need to belong, our need for validation, and our need to feel in control.

It is easy to believe that the tension of this moment was related to the content of the Holocaust course, which examines the dangers of remaining silent in such instances. While it is true that the Holocaust material may heighten awareness of racial, ethnic, religious, and class differences, this awareness does not necessarily move people to speak out in the face of others' oppression. The stakes are high in such moments: bystanders are in grave danger of being betrayed, and of betraying, due to unspoken alliances with the oppressor; the illusion of safety can quickly evaporate, as the bystander in one moment becomes the target in the next. Bystanders' betrayal of others is not limited to those people for whom they do not speak. In their silent attempt to remove themselves from humanity's collective suffering, they betray their own humanity.

Like all of life's pivotal moments, the one in my classroom arrived unexpectedly. It was initiated by the use of the word *tolerance*, which danced provocatively around the room, inviting to the surface unspoken divisions — divisions that threatened our polite correctness and our membership in the group. A group's cohesiveness, particularly in the early stages of development, is contingent upon the agreeable interpersonal relationships of its members. In order to establish these relationships, members often unconsciously act as if cohesion requires the denial of their differences. As Irvin Yalom (1970) writes, "The search for similarities is common in early groups" (p. 302). In the development of group safety, the expression of individual differences may be perceived as divisive or confrontational.

The moment in my classroom demanded that we examine the not-so-hidden assumptions lurking in our language, and therein lies the divisiveness of the moment: to whom does "our" language belong? Certainly it belongs to whoever uses it, but spoken in different worlds, specific words mean different things. In his 1981 book, *The Primal Mind*, Jamake Highwater, a member of the Blackfoot and Cherokee tribes who grew up in an Anglo orphanage and attended public schools, relates his experiences of entering a world where his reality was turned upside-down because of the cultural lessons found in words. He was appalled to discover what is implied in the White man's language; for instance, when he first understood what White Americans meant by the word *wilderness*. For him a forest was not "wild" and in need of taming. In his cultural construction of reality, a city would more appropriately be termed a wilderness. He also became confused as he discovered that words such as *soil* and *dirt*, which for him describe the precious earth, are the same words that we use to describe uncleanness, as in *soiled* and *dirty*. Even the word *universe* presented tremendous complications, for "Indians do not believe in a universe but in a multi-verse" (Highwater, 1981, p. 5). What we understand when we use language to describe our reality is a preconception, a cultural package that we inherit as a result of our upbringing. We do not all inherit the same language and, thus, we do not all inherit the same truths. The cultural context of truth is denied when dominance and privilege are touted as universal truth.

For the African American student in my class, the idea of tolerance represented a painful reality, one that suggested the goodness of others willing to put up with her. In this case, these others were her peers — her liberal White classmates for whom tolerance was a desired attribute, something they believed was the "right" answer to moral and historical problems of prejudice and racism. Nobody wants to discover that his or her conception of rightness is just another form of oppression. It is embarrassing, and it shames liberal White Americans into an unfortunate silence in which dialogue and the possibility for healing and reconciliation become more and more remote. This silence is a place of refuge, of psychological withdrawal, where we attempt to protect ourselves from that which threatens to damage our subjective sense of self and our connections to one another. It is a place that, left alone, can dangerously widen the gaps that already exist between self and other. Before taking refuge and succumbing to that shameful silence, conscientious people often attempt to correct the "misconception."

In an attempt to shake off the embarrassment and bridge the gap that threatened the relationships in the classroom, one of the White students suggested that tolerance was actually a "good" word and that maybe she (the African American student) had misunderstood. This was THE moment. The sides were clearly and unevenly delineated, the advantage being with the majority. As I looked out and saw their faces — twenty-three White and one dark brown — they were all looking to me, the White authority. As the professor, I carry both the power of authority that is projected onto the role and the very real power of evaluation. In that moment I was the one with the power to decide guilt or innocence, terms I use intentionally. This was a moment when one has to either listen passively to racist slurs or to speak out and risk being ousted from the group (Helms, 1992). For human beings, for myself in that moment, the threat of being ousted from the group is not to be taken lightly. According to W. Goldschmidt:

> Man is by nature committed to social existence, and is therefore inevitably involved in the dilemma between serving his own interest and recognizing those of the group to which he belongs. . . . Need for positive affect means that each person craves response from his human environment. It may be viewed as a hunger not unlike that for food, but more generalized. (Goldschmidt, quoted in Yalom, 1970, p. 17)

I was aware of my own hunger in that moment. I felt deeply torn in my need for validation. I struggled to know how to respond, as it became very clear to me that the trappings of my role did not afford me a way to feel powerful. In fact, in that moment it felt paradoxically disempowering to appease my "hunger" by avoiding the very real challenge of risking my membership in the group.

Up until this moment, I might have described the incident simply as one of a lack of preparation: How was I, as a White teacher, prepared to be aware of the privilege that Whiteness affords me? While that is a true statement of the problem, it is simplistic and leads us to look for answers in places that may not foster our much-needed development as human beings. My experience living through the very real threat of the encounter suggested to me that preparation is primarily neither an intellectual understanding nor a developed social skill. Instead, it is a developmental leap sparked by a deep call to the soul to "re-member" our connections with one another and with the universe that we share. Educators require preparation that transcends pedagogical approaches and curriculum development. As Palmer (1998) describes, we need training that nurtures the development of self-consciousness:

> If I am willing to look in that mirror and not run from what I see, I have a chance to gain self-knowledge — and knowing myself is as crucial to good teaching as knowing my students and my subject. . . .When I do not know myself I cannot know who my students are . . . I cannot know my subject . . . not at the deepest level of embodied personal meaning. (p. 2)

There was so much at stake in that moment. A teacher wields a tremendous amount of power, and I did not want to abuse mine. There are two main ways I could have done so. First, to avoid the confrontation would have meant sanctioning the abandonment of a group member, potentially putting her survival in jeopardy, she who I suspect had already lived her short lifetime fighting wearying defensive battles. As I considered my options, I could feel that weariness. It was no longer just hers or mine. It lived in that space between us, the space that did not conform to the boundaries of our skin color. I anticipated the destructive power of the guilt that inevitably would fill the room if I named the offense of using a non-inclusive term such as tolerance. In essence, I would be acknowledging not only the White students' unconscious use of a word that was experienced by the lone African American student as a weapon, but also my own ignorance and culpability. I have lived in a world where, despite my subjective experience, I have had the privilege of being a "tolerator." Escaping from the moment provided one possible abuse of this privilege.

The second possible abuse was to separate myself from the group and disown my responsibility. In doing so, I would make the group responsible for causing pain, while I, the "Super Teacher," pontificated on the need for inclusive language. How many times have we found ourselves standing in front of a room full of students either encouraging the perception that we hold the key to knowing by making a lesson out of what we ourselves have yet to learn, or being led by our sense of helplessness to abandon the subject and the moment? Both of these options reflect an inability to stay in the pain of the present moment, and the possibility that we might betray ourselves, our students, and the potential that lives in these moments.

The unfortunate and inevitable price of either stance is the disempowerment of both teacher and students. The delicate balance of that paralyzing moment brought me a longing to know exactly what it is that heals. What is the ineffable something that would allow teachers and students to transform the polarization, to weave wholeness, and, in doing so, to create themselves anew? Toni Packer, a Zen Buddhist whose writings informed my doctoral studies in transpersonal psychology and whose thinking influences my practice as a teacher and a psychotherapist, describes a shift of consciousness that affects our self-relationships that can be accessed through meditative presence:

> The state that is reacting most of the time when we are talking to each other is the state of memory. Our language comes out of memory and we usually don't take the time to think about the way we say things, let alone look carefully at what we are saying. . . . So we're asking can there be talking and listening that are not governed solely by memory and habit. . . . Thinking "I know this" blocks listening and seeing. Seeing is never from memory. It has no memory, it is looking now. The total organism is involved in seeing. (1990, p. 2)

Our inner dialogue is also subject to the preconceived ideas and perceptions that are locked in memory. The dialogue is usually not the product of seeing "in the moment" but rather of our preconceptions, which can be quite distorting, as we tend to believe that what lives separate from us is a potential threat or enemy — that those who exist on the other side of the skin-color boundary line are the other. After all, the first boundary line that we create is the one that separates self from other. Thereafter, "every boundary line we construct is also a potential battle line" (Wilbur, 1979, p. 50). Certainly, the universe of the classroom contains many boundaries and many "others." It would seem that the deck is thus already stacked: How can a healing dialogue occur in a relationship that is based on a perceived fear of the other?

Within all of us there is a deep desire for others to see the true essence of who we are. Yet, I believe that in earliest childhood we construct a self that is a composite of all the messages we take in from the meaningful people in our lives. To answer the question "Who am I?" we shape our beings, progressively narrowing our field of self-perception to be congruent with how we believe others see us. In shame, we disown the parts of ourselves that do not fit, and in the process distance ourselves from authentic self-awareness. It is this shame that sometimes leads us, teachers and students alike, to distance ourselves from the issues so that the other ceases to pose a personal threat. Hence disempowerment shows up to teach the class, cloaked in the guise of the Super Teacher/pontificator or the helpless nice guy. What do we need in these moments to allow us (the "real" teachers), to remain in the room and not take silent refuge?

Seeing and being are intimately interconnected. Without permission to be who we are we become who we are seen to be. What others see in us is who we become, leaving large chunks of ourselves behind as we incorporate into ourselves others' perceptions. Locked within the discarded fragments of ourselves, the power and creativity of our wholeness remain inaccessible to us.

By what power can we overcome our experience of being incomplete? For example, in the 1939 Metro Goldwyn Meyer version of L. Frank Baum's *The Wizard of Oz*, how did the Scarecrow (who believed he had no brains), the Tinman (no heart), and the Cowardly Lion (no courage) move beyond their perceived deficiencies? For those of us who watched their journey on our television screens it was difficult to understand how they could have been so blind to themselves. The Tinman, after all, was the essence of heartfelt loving. Yet aren't we all well represented by this threesome, blind to our abilities, searching outside for the key to what is inside?

The act of confronting our perceived inadequacies invites us into the truth of our beings. For most of us there is no initiation into the truth of who we are. Lacking this, we create a self that is disconnected from the source of our wholeness, as well as from one another. Certainly, this disconnection is well represented by the teacher/pontificator. Lost in self-doubt, we often become paralyzed, unable to experience our ability to move, to love, and to act courageously. If we allow our paralysis to take hold, obsessed by our inadequacies, we lose our ability to be present and to see beyond our self. We respond by either creating a competent coping persona — the Super Teacher — or we end up seeing in ourselves and in our students a mirror of inadequacy. We create an unfortunate void in which there is no one to hold up the mirror to the vulnerable self, the truth-teller, the someone in us who extends beyond inadequacy and pretense.

In the world of Oz, the Wizard is helpful in facilitating the characters' self-seeing, although not in the way that the characters anticipated. How did he do it? What lessons does his behavior provide for those of us who attempt to do the same in our classrooms? The Great and Powerful Oz, the one to whom denizens of the Emerald City and its environs went in moments of need, existed as a larger than life, apparently omniscient "teacher." Initially we meet him as an imposing disembodied head, proclaiming his powers and authoritatively sending those who come to him out into the world to complete their assigned tasks, promising redemption as a reward. Both his appearance and his manner support our perception of his power.

By hiding behind the persona of the all-knowing, all-powerful Super Teacher, we lose our humanity as we leave moments of tension and potential discovery in order to maintain our elevated and exalted position. It is this position that keeps our students at a distance, unable to *know us*, unable to truly *see each other*, and unable to *connect with the source of their own knowing*. Only by becoming vulnerable do we gain access to our real power — the ability to know our true self and thus enable our students to know *their* truths and realize *their* power.

The Wizard's unveiling is an event for which the characters are unprepared. In the heat of the confrontation between the Wizard and those who came seeking his help, the Great and Powerful Oz is revealed to be merely the pretense of a small and vulnerable man. The Wizard's exposure is the moment in which he becomes embodied and provides the possibility of moving beyond pretense and helplessness — for all of us. The lesson is that the Great and Powerful Oz is actually a lost soul — a man stranded in Oz who, unable to find his way home, allowed himself to become what others needed him to be. As he discloses this truth, he names it not only for himself, but also for all of us who allow ourselves to be defined by how others see us.

In the diverse classroom, many of us are unprepared for the discoveries that await us. It is our willingness to step out of the role of the Super Teacher, to reveal our own ignorance, and to engage our students in exploring transformative possibilities that invites the students to do the same.

The moment in my classroom required that I, as the teacher in the room, be willing to hear a student's pain and respond as a curious and vulnerable human being, rather than as a truth-teller who already knew about the power of language. In that moment, I had no plan. The only thing I had was myself, the present moment, and the desire not to sacrifice my own humanity. I live in a world that has been neither woman friendly nor Jew friendly. As a White Jewish woman, I am vulnerable to both the role of oppressor and oppressed. In the classroom, the authority of my role combined with my White privilege makes me a potential oppressor, whereas being Jewish and a woman places me as a member of oppressed groups. The tension I felt at that moment was due to the fact that I needed to be aware of both positions but to identify with neither. That moment offered an invitation to step out and reveal my vulnerable self. I turned to the twenty-four faces in the room, walked over to the lone African American student, and said, "Let me see if I understand. You want me to know that it is hurtful to you, as a person of color, to have me, a White person, be willing to 'tolerate' or 'put up' with you. And, it is even worse [for you] to be told that it is my willingness to do so that makes me a good person. I guess I don't want to feel tolerated either. It makes me angry and resentful, and I would have to wonder who are *you* to be putting up with me? How might we want to change the word *tolerance*? What would you want me to use in its place? Does anyone have any ideas?"

The student began to speak about the difference between tolerance and respect. During the interaction, I was acutely aware of the dialectic, wanting to be seen as a "good" person and at the same time not wanting to be seen at all, fearful that I would be found lacking. I was also aware of the moment's irony; not trying to control the outcome of this encounter enabled me to be present in the moment of its happening. As she spoke about respect, she offered the group an alternative — a way to get off the hook. There was a release of tension, almost as if the group took a collective breath. The students remained silent; it was a contemplative silence, one in which we were digesting the revelations of the moment. At the end of that class session, the African American student caught up with me in the hallway. She said, "I'm sure you know that in the past four years of taking classes, this wasn't my first time being the 'only one.' But this time felt different because, while I was the only one, I did not feel all alone." Her words were reassuring. They suggested that she understood that I had joined her in the risky business of being "the only one." It was clear to me that she had experienced my intervention in the classroom as one of solidarity. More importantly, she offered me the experience of being seen in much the same way that I had seen her.

Given this experience and the risky nature of these interactions, how then do we prepare teachers to make themselves vulnerable in the real moments of the classroom? As a transpersonal psychologist, I am aware of how much I draw upon my professional training in order to be mindfully present while teaching in difficult moments of difference. The cultivation of mindful presence, which was central to my training, also has much to offer teachers in developing the ability to respond fully to the tension and vulnerability that often accompany moments of crisis, or "teachable moments." Mindful presence is a form of meditation — a way of being. It is the conscious focus of attention on the present moment:

> Mindfulness practice . . . does not have specific goals, but is open ended. It could easily be practiced for a whole lifetime, for broadening and deepening awareness has no limit. Meditation does not have the aim of solving problems or making us feel better; rather, it provides a space in which we can let ourselves be, just as we are, and thus discover our basic nature. (Welwood, 1983, p. 48)

The practice of mindfulness enhances and enlarges our capacity for empathy. It cultivates a sense of open curiosity toward each emerging moment, and it strengthens our ability to sustain a nonjudgmental stance both toward ourselves and in relation to the full range of our students' experiences. This ability allows us to make important connections between the experiences of self and other.

The marriage of training that focuses on the dynamics of an empathetic presence in inter- and intrapersonal relationships with training that centers on pedagogical models provides a way out of our protected positions. Bringing the experience of empathy, "the capacity to think and feel oneself into the inner life of another person" (Kohut, 1984, p. 82), into the classroom is central to creating an environment that invites taking the risk of sharing many different perspectives. But it is not all that is needed. In his article, "Nowness in the Helping Relationship," David Brandon (1983) describes a reverential kind of listening, "a form of meditation wherein the speaker becomes the object of concentration rather than the breathing or a mantra. The focus of the concentration is the sound of the speaker's voice and the possible meaning of his words" (p. 142). Listening in this way actually helps us to be present, and is a prerequisite for entering into the inner life of meaning-making. It is a form of conscious listening, unlike our ordinary way of listening and perceiving, that provides a path into the "meaningworld" of the other. Given the growing numbers of diverse students in our classrooms, it is essential that we learn to listen, to be vulnerable, and to willingly enter the predictable confrontations that emerge in this work.

Within the range of human experience there are numerous events that catalyze transformation and growth. These moments happen daily in our classrooms. Often we don't know how to enter into them fully and vulnerably. Yet this is exactly what is required of us if we truly want to teach diversity and bridge the gaps that divide us. The potential for this work resides inside of us. It lives in our fear of being seen, and in our conflicting desire to also (somehow) be fully seen. I believe that the same is true for our students. Transformation of boundaries from dividing lines that separate us into lines that connect us more deeply is contingent upon our willingness to experience the fear of being seen and known. It is in our ability to enter this experience that we will be able to enter the classroom, the moment, and our own transformation more fully.

As scholarship in the field of diversity and multiculturalism grows and expands, a bridge must be built between our intellectual understanding of difference, power, fear, domination, shame, oppression, isolation, and connection and our capacity to enter into these human experiences vulnerably and fully. Only then might we perhaps realize a self that is not limited by the distortions of its own perceptions. We are at the very beginning of our journey across that bridge. I owe thanks to my students and to my clients who lead the way for me to cross it. The courage to face the fear of their truths is what inspires me to continue to discover my own humanity. In order to achieve this goal, however, it is imperative that teachers open themselves to criticism and conversation, and engage in sincere self-reflection. We must begin to embody our role in society consciously as a vehicle for personal and communal transformation.

REFERENCES

Brandon, D. (1983). Nowness in the helping relationship. In J. Welwood (Ed.), *Awakening the heart* (pp. 140–147). Boston: Shambhala.

Helms, J. (1992). *A race is a nice thing to have.* Topeka, KS: Content Communications.

Highwater, J. (1981). *The primal mind: Vision and reality in Indian America.* Toronto: Harper & Row.

Kohut, H. (1984). *How does analysis cure?* New York: International Universities Press.

Orfield, G. (2000, May 19). Racial divide is widening in American schools, say educators. *Boston Globe*, p. A9.

Packer, T. (1990). *The work of this moment.* Boston: Shambhala.

Palmer, P. (1998). *The courage to teach.* San Francisco: Jossey Bass.

Wilbur, K. (1979). *No boundary: Eastern and Western approaches to personal growth.* Boston: Shambhala.

Yalom, I. (1970). *The theory and practice of group psychotherapy.* New York: Basic Books.

Welwood, J. (1983). On psychotherapy and meditation. In J. Welwood (Ed.), *Awakening the heart* (pp. 43–54). Boston: Shambhala.

Talking about Race, Learning about Racism: The Application of Racial Identity Development Theory in the Classroom

BEVERLY DANIEL TATUM

s many educational institutions struggle to become more multicultural in terms of their students, faculty, and staff, they also begin to examine issues of cultural representation within their curriculum. This examination has evoked a growing number of courses that give specific consideration to the effect of variables such as race, class, and gender on human experience — an important trend that is reflected and supported by the increasing availability of resource manuals for the modification of course content (Bronstein & Quina, 1988; Hull, Scott, & Smith, 1982; Schuster & Van Dyne, 1985).

Unfortunately, less attention has been given to the issues of process that inevitably emerge in the classroom when attention is focused on race, class, and/or gender. It is very difficult to talk about these concepts in a meaningful way without also talking and learning about racism, classism, and sexism.[1] The introduction of these issues of oppression often generates powerful emotional responses in students that range from guilt and shame to anger and despair. If not addressed, these emotional responses can result in student resistance to oppression-related content areas. Such resistance can ultimately interfere with the cognitive understanding and mastery of the material. This resistance and potential interference is particularly common when specifically addressing issues of race and racism. Yet, when students are given the opportunity to explore race-related material in a classroom where both their affective and intellectual responses are acknowledged and addressed, their level of understanding is greatly enhanced.

This article seeks to provide a framework for understanding students' psychological responses to race-related content and the student resistance that can result, as well as some strategies for overcoming this resistance. It is informed by more than a decade of experience as an African American engaged in teaching an undergraduate course on the psychology of racism, by thematic analyses of student journals and essays written for the racism class, and by an understanding and application of racial identity development theory (Helms, 1990).

Harvard Educational Review   Vol. 62   No. 2   Summer 1992, 1–24

SETTING THE CONTEXT

As a clinical psychologist with a research interest in racial identity development among African American youth raised in predominantly White communities, I began teaching about racism quite fortuitously. In 1980, while I was a part-time lecturer in the Black Studies department of a large public university, I was invited to teach a course called Group Exploration of Racism (Black Studies 2). A requirement for Black Studies majors, the course had to be offered, yet the instructor who regularly taught the course was no longer affiliated with the institution. Armed with a folder full of handouts, old syllabi that the previous instructor left behind, a copy of *White Awareness: Handbook for Anti-racism Training* (Katz, 1978), and my own clinical skills as a group facilitator, I constructed a course that seemed to meet the goals already outlined in the course catalogue. Designed "to provide students with an understanding of the psychological causes and emotional reality of racism as it appears in everyday life," the course incorporated the use of lectures, readings, simulation exercises, group research projects, and extensive class discussion to help students explore the psychological impact of racism on both the oppressor and the oppressed.

Though my first efforts were tentative, the results were powerful. The students in my class, most of whom were White, repeatedly described the course in their evaluations as one of the most valuable educational experiences of their college careers. I was convinced that helping students understand the ways in which racism operates in their own lives, and what they could do about it, was a social responsibility that I should accept. The freedom to institute the course in the curriculum of the psychology departments in which I would eventually teach became a personal condition of employment. I have successfully introduced the course in each new educational setting I have been in since leaving that university.

Since 1980, I have taught the course (now called the Psychology of Racism) eighteen times, at three different institutions. Although each of these schools is very different — a large public university, a small state college, and a private, elite women's college — the challenges of teaching about racism in each setting have been more similar than different.

In all of the settings, class size has been limited to thirty students (averaging twenty-four). Though typically predominantly White and female (even in coeducational settings), the class make-up has always been mixed in terms of both race and gender. The students of color who have taken the course include Asians and Latinos/as, but most frequently the students of color have been Black. Though most students have described themselves as middle class, all socioeconomic backgrounds (ranging from very poor to very wealthy) have been represented over the years.

The course has necessarily evolved in response to my own deepening awareness of the psychological legacy of racism and my expanding awareness of other forms of oppression, although the basic format has remained the same. Our weekly three-hour class meeting is held in a room with movable chairs, arranged in a circle. The physical structure communicates an important premise of the course — that I expect the students to speak with each other as well as with me.

My other expectations (timely completion of assignments, regular class attendance) are clearly communicated in our first class meeting, along with the assumptions and guidelines for discussion that I rely upon to guide our work together. Because the assumptions and guidelines are so central to the process of talking and learning about racism, it may be useful to outline them here.

Working Assumptions

1. Racism, defined as a "system of advantage based on race" (see Wellman, 1977), is a pervasive aspect of U.S. socialization. It is virtually impossible to live in U.S. contemporary society and not be exposed to some aspect of the personal, cultural, and/or institutional manifestations of racism in our society. It is also assumed that, as a result, all of us have received some misinformation about those groups disadvantaged by racism.

2. Prejudice, defined as a "preconceived judgment or opinion, often based on limited information," is clearly distinguished from racism (see Katz, 1978). I assume that all of us may have prejudices as a result of the various cultural stereotypes to which we have been exposed. Even when these preconceived ideas have positive associations (such as "Asian students are good in math"), they have negative effects because they deny a person's individuality. These attitudes may influence the individual behaviors of people of color as well as of Whites, and may affect intergroup as well as intragroup interaction. However, a distinction must be made between the negative racial attitudes held by individuals of color and White individuals, because it is only the attitudes of Whites that routinely carry with them the social power inherent in the systematic cultural reinforcement and institutionalization of those racial prejudices. To distinguish the prejudices of students of color from the racism of White students is *not* to say that the former is acceptable and the latter is not; both are clearly problematic. The distinction is important, however, to identify the power differential between members of dominant and subordinate groups.

3. In the context of U.S. society, the system of advantage clearly operates to benefit Whites as a group. However, it is assumed that racism, like other forms of oppression, hurts members of the privileged group as well as those targeted by racism. While the impact of racism on Whites is clearly different from its impact on people of color, racism has negative ramifications for everyone. For example, some White students might remember the pain of having lost important relationships because Black friends were not allowed to visit their homes. Others may express sadness at having been denied access to a broad range of experiences because of social segregation. These individuals often attribute the discomfort or fear they now experience in racially mixed settings to the cultural limitations of their youth.

4. Because of the prejudice and racism inherent in our environments when we were children, I assume that we cannot be blamed for learning what we were taught (intentionally or unintentionally). Yet as adults, we have a responsibility to try to identify and interrupt the cycle of oppression. When we recognize that we have been misin-

formed, we have a responsibility to seek out more accurate information and to adjust our behavior accordingly.

5. It is assumed that change, both individual and institutional, is possible. Understanding and unlearning prejudice and racism is a lifelong process that may have begun prior to enrolling in this class, and which will surely continue after the course is over. Each of us may be at a different point in that process, and I assume that we will have mutual respect for each other, regardless of where we perceive one another to be.

To facilitate further our work together, I ask students to honor the following guidelines for our discussion. Specifically, I ask students to demonstrate their respect for one another by honoring the confidentiality of the group. So that students may feel free to ask potentially awkward or embarrassing questions, or share race-related experiences, I ask that students refrain from making personal attributions when discussing the course content with their friends. I also discourage the use of "zaps," overt or covert put-downs often used as comic relief when someone is feeling anxious about the content of the discussion. Finally, students are asked to speak from their own experience, to say, for example, "I think . . ." or "In my experience, I have found . . ." rather than generalizing their experience to others, as in "People say . . ."

Many students are reassured by the climate of safety that is created by these guidelines and find comfort in the nonblaming assumptions I outline for the class. Nevertheless, my experience has been that most students, regardless of their class and ethnic background, still find racism a difficult topic to discuss, as is revealed by these journal comments written after the first class meeting (all names are pseudonyms):

> The class is called Psychology of Racism, the atmosphere is friendly and open, yet I feel very closed in. I feel guilt and doubt well up inside of me. (Tiffany, a White woman)
>
> Class has started on a good note thus far. The class seems rather large and disturbs me. In a class of this nature, I expect there will be many painful and emotional moments. (Linda, an Asian woman)
>
> I am a little nervous that as one of the few students of color in the class people are going to be looking at me for answers, or whatever other reasons. The thought of this inhibits me a great deal. (Louise, an African American woman)
>
> I had never thought about my social position as being totally dominant. There wasn't one area in which I wasn't in the dominant group. . . . I first felt embarrassed. . . . Through association alone I felt in many ways responsible for the unequal condition existing in the world. This made me feel like shrinking in a hole in a class where I was surrounded by 27 women and 2 men, one of whom was Black and the other was Jewish. I felt that all these people would be justified in venting their anger upon me. After a short period, I realized that no one in the room was attacking or even blaming me for the conditions that exist. (Carl, a White man)

Even though most of my students voluntarily enroll in the course as an elective, their anxiety and subsequent resistance to learning about racism quickly emerge.

SOURCES OF RESISTANCE

In predominantly White college classrooms, I have experienced at least three major sources of student resistance to talking and learning about race and racism. They can be readily identified as the following:

1. Race is considered a taboo topic for discussion, especially in racially mixed settings.
2. Many students, regardless of racial-group membership, have been socialized to think of the United States as a just society.
3. Many students, particularly White students, initially deny any personal prejudice, recognizing the impact of racism on other people's lives, but failing to acknowledge its impact on their own.

Race as Taboo Topic

The first source of resistance, race as a taboo topic, is an essential obstacle to overcome if class discussion is to begin at all. Although many students are interested in the topic, they are often most interested in hearing other people talk about it, afraid to break the taboo themselves.

One source of this self-consciousness can be seen in the early childhood experiences of many students. It is known that children as young as three notice racial differences (see Phinney & Rotheram, 1987). Certainly preschoolers talk about what they see. Unfortunately, they often do so in ways that make adults uncomfortable. Imagine the following scenario: A White child in a public place points to a dark-skinned African American child and says loudly, "Why is that boy Black?" The embarrassed parent quickly responds, "Sh! Don't say that." The child is only attempting to make sense of a new observation (Derman-Sparks, Higa, & Sparks, 1980), yet the parent's attempt to silence the perplexed child sends a message that this observation is not okay to talk about. White children quickly become aware that their questions about race raise adult anxiety, and as a result, they learn not to ask questions.

When asked to reflect on their earliest race-related memories and the feelings associated with them, both White students and students of color often report feelings of confusion, anxiety, and/or fear. Students of color often have early memories of name-calling or other negative interactions with other children, and sometimes with adults. They also report having had questions that went both unasked and unanswered. In addition, many students have had uncomfortable interchanges around race-related topics as adults. When asked at the beginning of the semester, "How many of you have had difficult, perhaps heated conversations with someone on a race-related topic?", routinely almost everyone in the class raises his or her hand. It should come as no surprise then that students often approach the topic of race and/or racism with both curiosity and trepidation.

The Myth of the Meritocracy

The second source of student resistance to be discussed here is rooted in students' belief that the United States is a just society, a meritocracy where individual efforts are fairly rewarded. While some students (particularly students of color) may already have become disillusioned with that notion of the United States, the majority of my students who have experienced at least the personal success of college acceptance still have faith in this notion. To the extent that these students acknowledge that racism exists, they tend to view it as an individual phenomenon, rooted in the attitudes of the "Archie Bunkers" of the world or located only in particular parts of the country.

After several class meetings, Karen, a White woman, acknowledged this attitude in her journal:

> At one point in my life — the beginning of this class — I actually perceived America to be a relatively racist free society. I thought that the people who were racist or subjected to racist stereotypes were found only in small pockets of the U.S., such as the South. As I've come to realize, racism (or at least racially orientated stereotypes) is rampant.

An understanding of racism as a system of advantage presents a serious challenge to the notion of the United States as a just society where rewards are based solely on one's merit. Such a challenge often creates discomfort in students. The old adage "ignorance is bliss" seems to hold true in this case; students are not necessarily eager to recognize the painful reality of racism.

One common response to the discomfort is to engage in denial of what they are learning. White students in particular may question the accuracy or currency of statistical information regarding the prevalence of discrimination (housing, employment, access to health care, and so on). More qualitative data, such as autobiographical accounts of experiences with racism, may be challenged on the basis of their subjectivity.

It should be pointed out that the basic assumption that the United States is a just society for all is only one of many basic assumptions that might be challenged in the learning process. Another example can be seen in an interchange between two White students following a discussion about cultural racism, in which the omission or distortion of historical information about people of color was offered as an example of the cultural transmission of racism.

"Yeah, I just found out that Cleopatra was actually a Black woman."

"What?"

The first student went on to explain her newly learned information. Finally, the second student exclaimed in disbelief, "That can't be true. Cleopatra was beautiful!" This new information and her own deeply ingrained assumptions about who is beautiful and who is not were too incongruous to allow her to assimilate the information at that moment.

If outright denial of information is not possible, then withdrawal may be. Physical withdrawal in the form of absenteeism is one possible result; it is for precisely this reason that class attendance is mandatory. The reduction in the completion of reading and/or written assignments is another form of withdrawal. I have found this response to be so common that I now alert students to this possibility at the beginning of the semester. Knowing that this response is a common one seems to help students stay engaged, even when they experience the desire to withdraw.

Following an absence in the fifth week of the semester, one White student wrote, "I think I've hit the point you talked about, the point where you don't want to hear any more about racism. I sometimes begin to get the feeling we are all hypersensitive." (Two weeks later she wrote, "Class is getting better. I think I am beginning to get over my hump.")

Perhaps not surprisingly, this response can be found in both White students and students of color. Students of color often enter a discussion of racism with some awareness of the issue, based on personal experiences. However, even these students find that they did not have a full understanding of the widespread impact of racism in our society. For students who are targeted by racism, an increased awareness of the impact in and on their lives is painful, and often generates anger.

Four weeks into the semester, Louise, an African American woman, wrote in her journal about her own heightened sensitivity:

Many times in class I feel uncomfortable when White students use the term Black because even if they aren't aware of it they say it with all or at least a lot of the negative connotations they've been taught goes along with Black. Sometimes it just causes a stinging feeling inside of me. Sometimes I get real tired of hearing White people talk about the conditions of Black people. I think it's an important thing for them to talk about, but still I don't always like being around when they do it. I also get tired of hearing them talk about how hard it is for them, though I understand it, and most times I am very willing to listen and be open, but sometimes I can't. Right now I can't.

For White students, advantaged by racism, a heightened awareness of it often generates painful feelings of guilt. The following responses are typical:

After reading the article about privilege, I felt very guilty. (Rachel, a White woman)
    Questions of racism are so full of anger and pain. When I think of all the pain White people have caused people of color, I get a feeling of guilt. How could someone like myself care so much about the color of someone's skin that they would do them harm? (Terri, a White woman)

White students also sometimes express a sense of betrayal when they realize the gaps in their own education about racism. After seeing the first episode of the documentary series *Eyes on the Prize*, Chris, a White man, wrote:

I never knew it was really that bad just 35 years ago. Why didn't I learn this in elementary or high school? Could it be that the White people of America want to forget this injustice? . . . I will never forget that movie for as long as I live. It was like a big slap in the face.

Barbara, a White woman, also felt anger and embarrassment in response to her own previous lack of information about the internment of Japanese Americans during World War II. She wrote:

> I feel so stupid because I never even knew that these existed. I never knew that the Japanese were treated so poorly. I am becoming angry and upset about all of the things that I do not know. I have been so sheltered. My parents never wanted to let me know about the bad things that have happened in the world. After I saw the movie (*Mitsuye and Nellie*), I even called them up to ask them why they never told me this. . . . I am angry at them too for not teaching me and exposing me to the complete picture of my country.

Avoiding the subject matter is one way to avoid these uncomfortable feelings.

"I'm Not Racist, But . . ."

A third source of student resistance (particularly among White students) is the initial denial of any personal connection to racism. When asked why they have decided to enroll in a course on racism, White students typically explain their interest in the topic with such disclaimers as, "I'm not racist myself, but I know people who are, and I want to understand them better."

Because of their position as the targets of racism, students of color do not typically focus on their own prejudices or lack of them. Instead they usually express a desire to understand why racism exists, and how they have been affected by it.

However, as all students gain a better grasp of what racism is and its many manifestations in U.S. society, they inevitably start to recognize its legacy within themselves. Beliefs, attitudes, and actions based on racial stereotypes begin to be remembered and are newly observed by White students. Students of color as well often recognize negative attitudes they may have internalized about their own racial group or that they have believed about others. Those who previously thought themselves immune to the effects of growing up in a racist society often find themselves reliving uncomfortable feelings of guilt or anger.

After taping her own responses to a questionnaire on racial attitudes, Barbara, a White woman previously quoted, wrote:

> I always want to think of myself as open to all races. Yet when I did the interview to myself, I found that I did respond differently to the same question about different races. No one could ever have told me that I would have. I would have denied it. But I found that I did respond differently even though I didn't want to. This really upset me. I was angry with myself because I thought I was not prejudiced and yet the stereotypes that I had created had an impact on the answers that I gave even though I didn't want it to happen.

The new self-awareness, represented here by Barbara's journal entry, changes the classroom dynamic. One common result is that some White students, once perhaps active participants in class discussion, now hesitate to continue their participation for fear that their newly recognized racism will be revealed to others.

Today I did feel guilty, and like I had to watch what I was saying (make it good enough), I guess to prove I'm really *not* prejudiced. From the conversations the first day, I guess this is a normal enough reaction, but I certainly never expected it in me. (Joanne, a White woman)

This withdrawal on the part of White students is often paralleled by an increase in participation by students of color who are seeking an outlet for what are often feelings of anger. The withdrawal of some previously vocal White students from the classroom exchange, however, is sometimes interpreted by students of color as indifference. This perceived indifference often serves to fuel the anger and frustration that many students of color experience, as awareness of their own oppression is heightened. For example, Robert, an African American man, wrote:

I really wish the White students would talk more. When I read these articles, it makes me so mad and I really want to know what the White kids think. Don't they care?

Sonia, a Latina, described the classroom tension from another perspective:

I would like to comment that at many points in the discussions I have felt uncomfortable and sometimes even angry with people. I guess I am at the stage where I am tired of listening to Whites feel guilty and watch their eyes fill up with tears. I do understand that everyone is at their own stage of development and I even tell myself every Tuesday that these people have come to this class by choice. Some days I am just more tolerant than others. . . . It takes courage to say things in that room with so many women of color present. It also takes courage for the women of color to say things about Whites.

What seems to be happening in the classroom at such moments is a collision of developmental processes that can be inherently useful for the racial identity development of the individuals involved. Nevertheless, the interaction may be perceived as problematic to instructors and students who are unfamiliar with the process. Although space does not allow for an exhaustive discussion of racial identity development theory, a brief explication of it here will provide additional clarity regarding the classroom dynamics when issues of race are discussed. It will also provide a theoretical framework for the strategies for dealing with student resistance that will be discussed at the conclusion of this article.

STAGES OF RACIAL IDENTITY DEVELOPMENT

Racial identity and racial identity development theory are defined by Janet Helms (1990) as

a sense of group or collective identity based on one's *perception* that he or she shares a common racial heritage with a particular racial group . . . racial identity development theory concerns the psychological implications of racial-group membership, that is belief systems that evolve in reaction to perceived differential racial-group membership. (p. 3)

It is assumed that in a society where racial-group membership is emphasized, the development of a racial identity will occur in some form in everyone. Given the dominant/subordinate relationship of Whites and people of color in this society, however, it is not surprising that this developmental process will unfold in different ways. For purposes of this discussion, William Cross's (1971, 1978) model of Black identity development will be described along with Helms's (1990) model of White racial identity development theory. While the identity development of other students (Asian Latino/ a, Native American) is not included in this particular theoretical formulation, there is evidence to suggest that the process for these oppressed groups is similar to that described for African Americans (Highlen, et al., 1988; Phinney, 1990).[2] In each case, it is assumed that a positive sense of one's self as a member of one's group (which is not based on any assumed superiority) is important for psychological health.

Black Racial Identity Development

According to Cross's (1971, 1978, 1991) model of Black racial identity development, there are five stages in the process, identified as Preencounter, Encounter, Immersion/ Emersion, Internalization, and Internalization- Commitment. In the first stage of Preencounter, the African American has absorbed many of the beliefs and values of the dominant White culture, including the notion that "White is right" and "Black is wrong." Though the internalization of negative Black stereotypes may be outside of his or her conscious awareness, the individual seeks to assimilate and be accepted by Whites, and actively or passively distances him/herself from other Blacks.[3]

Louise, an African American woman previously quoted, captured the essence of this stage in the following description of herself at an earlier time:

> For a long time it seemed as if I didn't remember my background, and I guess in some ways I didn't. I was never taught to be proud of my African heritage. Like we talked about in class, I went through a very long stage of identifying with my oppressors. Wanting to be like, live like, and be accepted by them. Even to the point of hating my own race and myself for being a part of it. Now I am ashamed that I ever was ashamed. I lost so much of myself in my denial of and refusal to accept my people.

In order to maintain psychological comfort at this stage of development, Helms writes:

> The person must maintain the fiction that race and racial indoctrination have nothing to do with how he or she lives life. It is probably the case that the Preencounter person is bombarded on a regular basis with information that he or she cannot really be a member of the "in" racial group, but relies on denial to selectively screen such information from awareness. (1990, p. 23)

This de-emphasis on one's racial-group membership may allow the individual to think that race has not been or will not be a relevant factor in one's own achievement, and may contribute to the belief in a U.S. meritocracy that is often a part of a Preencounter worldview.

Movement into the Encounter phase is typically precipitated by an event or series of events that forces the individual to acknowledge the impact of racism in one's life. For example, instances of social rejection by White friends or colleagues (or reading new personally relevant information about racism) may lead the individual to the conclusion that many Whites will not view him or her as an equal. Faced with the reality that he or she cannot truly be White, the individual is forced to focus on his or her identity as a member of a group targeted by racism.

Brenda, a Korean American student, described her own experience of this process as a result of her participation in the racism course:

> I feel that because of this class, I have become much more aware of racism that exists around. Because of my awareness of racism, I am now bothered by acts and behaviors that might not have bothered me in the past. Before when racial comments were said around me I would somehow ignore it and pretend that nothing was said. By ignoring comments such as these, I was protecting myself. It became sort of a defense mechanism. I never realized I did this, until I was confronted with stories that were found in our reading, by other people of color, who also ignored comments that bothered them. In realizing that there is racism out in the world and that there are comments concerning race that are directed towards me, I feel as if I have reached the first step. I also think I have reached the second step, because I am now bothered and irritated by such comments. I no longer ignore them, but now confront them.

The Immersion/Emersion stage is characterized by the simultaneous desire to surround oneself with visible symbols of one's racial identity and an active avoidance of symbols of Whiteness. As Thomas Parham describes, "At this stage, everything of value in life must be Black or relevant to Blackness. This stage is also characterized by a tendency to denigrate White people, simultaneously glorifying Black people. . . ." (1989, p. 190). The previously described anger that emerges in class among African American students and other students of color in the process of learning about racism may be seen as part of the transition through these stages.

As individuals enter the Immersion stage, they actively seek out opportunities to explore aspects of their own history and culture with the support of peers from their own racial background. Typically, White-focused anger dissipates during this phase because so much of the person's energy is directed toward his or her own group- and self-exploration. The result of this exploration is an emerging security in a newly defined and affirmed sense of self.

Sharon, another African American woman, described herself at the beginning of the semester as angry, seemingly in the Encounter stage of development. She wrote after our class meeting:

> Another point that I must put down is that before I entered class today I was angry about the way Black people have been treated in this country. I don't think I will easily overcome that and I basically feel justified in my feelings.

At the end of the semester, Sharon had joined with two other Black students in the class to work on their final class project. She observed that the three of them had planned their project to focus on Black people specifically, suggesting movement into the Immersion stage of racial identity development. She wrote:

> We are concerned about the well-being of our own people. They cannot be well if they have this pinned-up hatred for their own people. This internalized racism is something that we all felt, at various times, needed to be talked about. This semester it has really been important to me, and I believe Gordon [a Black classmate], too.

The emergence from this stage marks the beginning of Internalization. Secure in one's own sense of racial identity, there is less need to assert the "Blacker than thou" attitude often characteristic of the Immersion stage (Parham, 1989). In general, "pro-Black attitudes become more expansive, open, and less defensive" (Cross, 1971, p. 24). While still maintaining his or her connections with Black peers, the internalized individual is willing to establish meaningful relationships with Whites who acknowledge and are respectful of his or her self-definition. The individual is also ready to build coalitions with members of other oppressed groups. At the end of the semester, Brenda, a Korean American, concluded that she had in fact internalized a positive sense of racial identity. The process she described parallels the stages described by Cross:

> I have been aware for a long time that I am Korean. But through this class I am beginning to really become aware of my race. I am beginning to find out that White people can be accepting of me and at the same time accept me as a Korean.
>
> I grew up wanting to be accepted and ended up almost denying my race and culture. I don't think I did this consciously, but the denial did occur. As I grew older, I realized that I was different. I became for the first time, friends with other Koreans. I realized I had much in common with them. This was when I went through my "Korean friend" stage. I began to enjoy being friends with Koreans more than I did with Caucasians.
>
> Well, ultimately, through many years of growing up, I am pretty much in focus about who I am and who my friends are. I knew before I took this class that there were people not of color that were understanding of my differences. In our class, I feel that everyone is trying to sincerely find the answer of abolishing racism. I knew people like this existed, but it's nice to meet with them weekly.

Cross suggests that there are few psychological differences between the fourth stage, Internalization, and the fifth stage, Internalization-Commitment. However, those at the fifth stage have found ways to translate their "personal sense of Blackness into a plan of action or a general sense of commitment" to the concerns of Blacks as a group, which is sustained over time (Cross, 1991, p. 220). Whether at the fourth or fifth stage, the process of Internalization allows the individual, anchored in a positive sense of racial identity, both to proactively perceive and transcend race. Blackness becomes "the point of departure for discovering the universe of ideas, cultures and experiences beyond blackness in place of mistaking blackness as the universe itself" (Cross, Parham, & Helms, 1991, p. 330).

Though the process of racial identity development has been presented here in linear form, in fact it is probably more accurate to think of it in a spiral form. Often a person may move from one stage to the next, only to revisit an earlier stage as the result of new encounter experiences (Parham, 1989), though the later experience of the stage may be different from the original experience. The image that students often find helpful in understanding this concept of recycling through the stages is that of a spiral staircase. As a person ascends a spiral staircase, she may stop and look down at a spot below. When she reaches the next level, she may look down and see the same spot, but the vantage point has changed.[4]

WHITE RACIAL IDENTITY DEVELOPMENT

The transformations experienced by those targeted by racism are often paralleled by those of White students. Helms (1990) describes the evolution of a positive White racial identity as involving both the abandonment of racism and the development of a nonracist White identity. In order to do the latter,

> he or she must accept his or her own Whiteness, the cultural implications of being White, and define a view of Self as a racial being that does not depend on the perceived superiority of one racial group over another. (p. 49)

She identifies six stages in her model of White racial identity development: Contact, Disintegration, Reintegration, Pseudo-Independent, Immersion/ Emersion, and Autonomy.

The Contact stage is characterized by a lack of awareness of cultural and institutional racism, and of one's own White privilege. Peggy McIntosh (1989) writes eloquently about her own experience of this state of being:

> As a white person, I realized I had been taught about racism as something which puts others at a disadvantage, but had been taught not to see one of its corollary aspects, white privilege, which puts me at an advantage. . . . I was taught to see racism only in individual acts of meanness, not in invisible systems conferring dominance on my group. (p. 10)

In addition, the Contact stage often includes naive curiosity about or fear of people of color, based on stereotypes learned from friends, family, or the media. These stereotypes represent the framework in use when a person at this stage of development makes a comment such as, "You don't act like a Black person" (Helms, 1990, p. 57).

Those Whites whose lives are structured so as to limit their interaction with people of color, as well as their awareness of racial issues, may remain at this stage indefinitely. However, certain kinds of experiences (increased interaction with people of color or exposure to new information about racism) may lead to a new understanding that cultural and institutional racism exist. This new understanding marks the beginning of the Disintegration stage.

At this stage, the bliss of ignorance or lack of awareness is replaced by the discomfort of guilt, shame, and sometimes anger at the recognition of one's own advantage because of being White and the acknowledgment of the role of Whites in the maintenance of a racist system. Attempts to reduce discomfort may include denial (convincing oneself that racism doesn't really exist, or if it does, it is the fault of its victims).

For example, Tom, a White male student, responded with some frustration in his journal to a classmate's observation that the fact that she had never read any books by Black authors in any of her high school or college English classes was an example of cultural racism. He wrote, "It's not my fault that Blacks don't write books."

After viewing a film in which a psychologist used examples of Black children's drawings to illustrate the potentially damaging effect of negative cultural messages on a Black child's developing self-esteem, David, another White male student, wrote:

> I found it interesting the way Black children drew themselves without arms. The psychologist said this is saying that the child feels unable to control his environment. It can't be because the child has notions and beliefs already about being Black. It must be built in or hereditary due to the past history of the Blacks. I don't believe it's cognitive but more biological due to a long past history of repression and being put down.

Though Tom's and David's explanations seem quite problematic, they can be understood in the context of racial identity development theory as a way of reducing their cognitive dissonance upon learning this new race-related information. As was discussed earlier, withdrawal (accomplished by avoiding contact with people of color and the topic of racism) is another strategy for dealing with the discomfort experienced at this stage. Many of the previously described responses of White students to race-related content are characteristic of the transition from the Contact to the Disintegration stage of development.

Helms (1990) describes another response to the discomfort of Disintegration, which involves attempts to change significant others' attitudes toward African Americans and other people of color. However, as she points out,

> due to the racial naivete with which this approach may be undertaken and the person's ambivalent racial identification, this dissonance-reducing strategy is likely to be met with rejection by Whites as well as Blacks. (p. 59)

In fact, this response is also frequently observed among White students who have an opportunity to talk with friends and family during holiday visits. Suddenly they are noticing the racist content of jokes or comments of their friends and relatives and will try to confront them, often only to find that their efforts are, at best, ignored or dismissed as a "phase," or, at worst, greeted with open hostility.

Carl, a White male previously quoted, wrote at length about this dilemma:

> I realized that it was possible to simply go through life totally oblivious to the entire situation or, even if one realizes it, one can totally repress it. It is easy to fade into the woodwork, run with the rest of society, and never have to deal with these problems. So many people I know from home are like this. They have simply accepted what society has taught them with little, if any, question. My father is a prime example of this. . . . It has caused much friction in our relationship, and he often tells me as a father he has failed in raising me correctly. Most of my high school friends will never deal with these issues and propagate them on to their own children. It's easy to see how the cycle continues. I don't think I could ever justify within myself simply turning my back on the problem. I finally realized that my position in all of these domi-

nant groups gives me power to make change occur. . . . It is an unfortunate result often though that I feel alienated from friends and family. It's often played off as a mere stage that I'm going through. I obviously can't tell if it's merely a stage, but I know that they say this to take the attention off of the truth of what I'm saying. By belittling me, they take the power out of my argument. It's very depressing that being compassionate and considerate are seen as only phases that people go through. I don't want it to be a phase for me, but as obvious as this may sound, I look at my environment and often wonder how it will not be.

The societal pressure to accept the status quo may lead the individual from Disintegration to Reintegration. At this point the desire to be accepted by one's own racial group, in which the overt or covert belief in White superiority is so prevalent, may lead to a reshaping of the person's belief system to be more congruent with an acceptance of racism. The guilt and anxiety associated with Disintegration may be redirected in the form of fear and anger directed toward people of color (particularly Blacks), who are now blamed as the source of discomfort.

Connie, a White woman of Italian ancestry, in many ways exemplified the progression from the Contact stage to Reintegration, a process she herself described seven weeks into the semester. After reading about the stages of White identity development, she wrote:

I think mostly I can find myself in the disintegration stage of development. . . . There was a time when I never considered myself a color. I never described myself as a "White, Italian female" until I got to college and noticed that people of color always described themselves by their color/race. While taking this class, I have begun to understand that being White makes a difference. I never thought about it before but there are many privileges to being White. In my personal life, I cannot say that I have ever felt that I have had the advantage over a Black person, but I am aware that my race has the advantage.

I am feeling really guilty lately about that. I find myself thinking: "I didn't mean to be White, I really didn't mean it." I am starting to feel angry towards my race for ever using this advantage towards personal gains. But at the same time I resent the minority groups. I mean, it's not our fault that society has deemed us "superior." I don't feel any better than a Black person. But it really doesn't matter because I am a member of the dominant race. . . . I can't help it . . . and I sometimes get angry and feel like I'm being attacked.

I guess my anger toward a minority group would enter me into the next stage of Reintegration, where I am once again starting to blame the victim. This is all very trying for me and it has been on my mind a lot. I really would like to be able to reach the last stage, autonomy, where I can accept being White without hostility and anger. That is really hard to do.

Helms (1990) suggests that it is relatively easy for Whites to become stuck at the Reintegration stage of development, particularly if avoidance of people of color is possible. However, if there is a catalyst for continued self- examination, the person "begins to question her or his previous definition of Whiteness and the justifiability of racism in any of its forms . . ." (p. 61). In my experience, continued participation in a course on racism provides the catalyst for this deeper self-examination.

This process was again exemplified by Connie. At the end of the semester, she listened to her own taped interview of her racial attitudes that she had recorded at the beginning of the semester. She wrote:

> Oh wow! I could not believe some of the things that I said. I was obviously in different stages of the White identity development. As I listened and got more and more disgusted with myself when I was at the Reintegration stage, I tried to remind myself that these are stages that all (most) White people go through when dealing with notions of racism. I can remember clearly the resentment I had for people of color. I feel the one thing I enjoyed from listening to my interview was noticing how much I have changed. I think I am finally out of the Reintegration stage. I am beginning to make a conscious effort to seek out information about people of color and accept their criticism. . . . I still feel guilty about the feeling I had about people of color and I always feel bad about being privileged as a result of racism. But I am glad that I have reached what I feel is the Pseudo-Independent stage of White identity development.

The information-seeking that Connie describes often marks the onset of the Pseudo-Independent stage. At this stage, the individual is abandoning beliefs in White superiority, but may still behave in ways that unintentionally perpetuate the system. Looking to those targeted by racism to help him or her understand racism, the White person often tries to disavow his or her own Whiteness through active affiliation with Blacks, for example. The individual experiences a sense of alienation from other Whites who have not yet begun to examine their own racism, yet may also experience rejection from Blacks or other people of color who are suspicious of his or her motives. Students of color moving from the Encounter to the Immersion phase of their own racial identity development may be particularly unreceptive to the White person's attempts to connect with them.

Uncomfortable with his or her own Whiteness, yet unable to be truly anything else, the individual may begin searching for a new, more comfortable way to be White. This search is characteristic of the Immersion/Emersion stage of development. Just as the Black student seeks to redefine positively what it means to be of African ancestry in the United States through immersion in accurate information about one's culture and history, the White individual seeks to replace racially related myths and stereotypes with accurate information about what it means and has meant to be White in U.S. society (Helms, 1990). Learning about Whites who have been antiracist allies to people of color is a very important part of this process.

After reading articles written by antiracist activists describing their own process of unlearning racism, White students often comment on how helpful it is to know that others have experienced similar feelings and have found ways to resist the racism in their environments.[5] For example, Joanne, a White woman who initially experienced a lot of guilt, wrote:

> This article helped me out in many ways. I've been feeling helpless and frustrated. I know there are all these terrible things going on and I want to be able to do something. . . . Anyway this article helped me realize, again, that others feel this way, and gave me some positive ideas to resolve my dominant class guilt and shame.

Finally, reading the biographies and autobiographies of White individuals who have embarked on a similar process of identity development (such as Barnard, 1985/1987) provides White students with important models for change.

Learning about White antiracists can also provide students of color with a sense of hope that they can have White allies. After hearing a White antiracist activist address the class, Sonia, a Latina who had written about her impatience with expressions of White guilt, wrote:

> I don't know when I have been more impressed by anyone. She filled me with hope for the future. She made me believe that there are good people in the world and that Whites suffer too and want to change things.

For White students, the internalization of a newly defined sense of oneself as White is the primary task of the Autonomy stage. The positive feelings associated with this redefinition energize the person's efforts to confront racism and oppression in his or her daily life. Alliances with people of color can be more easily forged at this stage of development than previously because the person's antiracist behaviors and attitudes will be more consistently expressed. While Autonomy might be described as "racial self-actualization, . . . it is best to think of it as an ongoing process . . . wherein the person is continually open to new information and new ways of thinking about racial and cultural variables" (Helms, 1990, p. 66).

Annette, a White woman, described herself in the Autonomy stage, but talked at length about the circular process she felt she had been engaged in during the semester:

> If people as racist as C. P. Ellis (a former Klansman) can change, I think anyone can change. If that makes me idealistic, fine. I do not think my expecting society to change is naive anymore because I now *know* exactly what I want. To be naive means a lack of knowledge that allows me to accept myself both as a White person and as an idealist. This class showed me that these two are not mutually exclusive but are an integral part of me that I cannot deny. I realize now that through most of this class I was trying to deny both of them.
>
> While I was not accepting society's racism, I was accepting society's telling me as a White person, there was nothing I could do to change racism. So, I told myself I was being naive and tried to suppress my desire to change society. This is what made me so frustrated — while I saw society's racism through examples in the readings and the media, I kept telling myself there was nothing I could do. Listening to my tape, I think I was already in the Autonomy stage when I started this class. I then seemed to decide that being White, I also had to be racist which is when I became frustrated and went back to the Disintegration stage. I was frustrated because I was not only telling myself there was nothing I could do but I also was assuming society's racism was my own which made me feel like I did not want to be White. Actually, it was not being White that I was disavowing but being racist. I think I have now returned to the Autonomy stage and am much more secure in my position there. I accept my Whiteness now as just a part of me as is my idealism. I will no longer disavow these characteristics as I have realized I can be proud of both of them. In turn, I can now truly accept other people for their unique characteristics and not by the labels society has given them as I can accept myself that way.

While I thought the main ideas that I learned in this class were that White people need to be educated to end racism and everyone should be treated as human beings, I really had already incorporated these ideas into my thoughts. What I learned from this class is being White does not mean being racist and being idealistic does not mean being naive. I really did not have to form new ideas about people of color; I had to form them about myself — and I did.

IMPLICATIONS FOR CLASSROOM TEACHING

Although movement through all the stages of racial identity development will not necessarily occur for each student within the course of a semester (or even four years of college), it is certainly common to witness beginning transformations in classes with race-related content. An awareness of the existence of this process has helped me to implement strategies to facilitate positive student development, as well as to improve interracial dialogue within the classroom.

Four strategies for reducing student resistance and promoting student development that I have found useful are the following:

1. the creation of a safe classroom atmosphere by establishing clear guidelines for discussion;
2. the creation of opportunities for self-generated knowledge;
3. the provision of an appropriate developmental model that students can use as a framework for understanding their own process;
4. the exploration of strategies to empower students as change agents.

Creating a Safe Climate

As was discussed earlier, making the classroom a safe space for discussion is essential for overcoming students' fears about breaking the race taboo, and will also reduce later anxieties about exposing one's own internalized racism. Establishing the guidelines of confidentiality, mutual respect, "no zaps," and speaking from one's own experience on the first day of class is a necessary step in the process.

Students respond very positively to these ground rules, and do try to honor them. While the rules do not totally eliminate anxiety, they clearly communicate to students that there is a safety net for the discussion. Students are also encouraged to direct their comments and questions to each other rather than always focusing their attention on me as the instructor, and to learn each other's names rather than referring to each other as "he," "she," or "the person in the red sweater" when responding to each other.[6]

The Power of Self-Generated Knowledge

The creation of opportunities for self-generated knowledge on the part of students is a powerful tool for reducing the initial stage of denial that many students experience. While it may seem easy for some students to challenge the validity of what they read or what the instructor says, it is harder to deny what they have seen with their own eyes. Students can be given hands-on assignments outside of class to facilitate this process.

For example, after reading *Portraits of White Racism* (Wellman, 1977), some students expressed the belief that the attitudes expressed by the White interviewees in the book were no longer commonly held attitudes. Students were then asked to use the same interview protocol used in the book (with some revision) to interview a White adult of their choice. When students reported on these interviews in class, their own observation of the similarity between those they had interviewed and those they had read about was more convincing than anything I might have said.

After doing her interview, Patty, a usually quiet White student, wrote:

> I think I learned a lot from it and that I'm finally getting a better grip on the idea of racism. I think that was why I participated so much in class. I really felt like I knew what I was talking about.

Other examples of creating opportunities for self-generated knowledge include assigning students the task of visiting grocery stores in neighborhoods of differing racial composition to compare the cost and quality of goods and services available at the two locations, and to observe the interactions between the shoppers and the store personnel. For White students, one of the most powerful assignments of this type has been to go apartment hunting with an African American student and to experience housing discrimination firsthand. While one concern with such an assignment is the effect it will have on the student(s) of color involved, I have found that those Black students who choose this assignment rather than another are typically eager to have their White classmates experience the reality of racism, and thus participate quite willingly in the process.

Naming the Problem

The emotional responses that students have to talking and learning about racism are quite predictable and related to their own racial identity development. Unfortunately, students typically do not know this; thus they consider their own guilt, shame, embarrassment, or anger an uncomfortable experience that they alone are having. Informing students at the beginning of the semester that these feelings may be part of the learning process is ethically necessary (in the sense of informed consent), and helps to normalize the students' experience. Knowing in advance that a desire to withdraw from classroom discussion or not to complete assignments is a common response helps students to remain engaged when they reach that point. As Alice, a White woman, wrote at the end of the semester:

> You were so right in saying in the beginning how we would grow tired of racism (I did in October) but then it would get so good! I have *loved* the class once I passed that point.

In addition, sharing the model of racial identity development with students gives them a useful framework for understanding each other's processes as well as their own. This cognitive framework does not necessarily prevent the collision of developmental processes previously described, but it does allow students to be less frightened by it when it occurs. If, for example, White students understand the stages of racial identity development of students of color, they are less likely to personalize or feel threatened by an African American student's anger.

Connie, a White student who initially expressed a lot of resentment at the way students of color tended to congregate in the college cafeteria, was much more understanding of this behavior after she learned about racial identity development theory. She wrote:

> I learned a lot from reading the article about the stages of development in the model of oppressed people. As a White person going through my stages of identity development, I do not take time to think about the struggle people of color go through to reach a stage of complete understanding. I am glad that I know about the stages because now I can understand people of color's behavior in certain situations. For example, when people of color stay to themselves and appear to be in a clique, it is not because they are being rude as I originally thought. Rather they are engaged perhaps in the Immersion stage.

Mary, another White student, wrote:

> I found the entire Cross model of racial identity development very enlightening. I knew that there were stages of racial identity development before I entered this class. I did not know what they were, or what they really entailed. After reading through this article I found myself saying, "Oh. That explains why she reacted this way to this incident instead of how she would have a year ago." Clearly this person has entered a different stage and is working through different problems from a new viewpoint. Thankfully, the model provides a degree of hope that people will not always be angry, and will not always be separatists, etc. Although I'm not really sure about that.

Conversely, when students of color understand the stages of White racial identity development, they can be more tolerant or appreciative of a White student's struggle with guilt, for example. After reading about the stages of White identity development, Sonia, a Latina previously quoted, wrote:

> This article was the one that made me feel that my own prejudices were showing. I never knew that Whites went through an identity development of their own.

She later told me outside of class that she found it much easier to listen to some of the things White students said because she could understand their potentially offensive comments as part of a developmental stage.

Sharon, an African American woman, also found that an understanding of the respective stages of racial identity development helped her to understand some of the interactions she had had with White students since coming to college. She wrote:

> There is a lot of clash that occurs between Black and White people at college which is best explained by their respective stages of development. Unfortunately schools have not helped to alleviate these problems earlier in life.

In a course on the psychology of racism, it is easy to build in the provision of this information as part of the course content. For instructors teaching courses with race-related content in other fields, it may seem less natural to do so. However, the inclusion of articles on racial identity development and/or class discussion of these issues in conjunction with the other strategies that have been suggested can improve student receptivity to the course content in important ways, making it a very useful investment of class time. Because the stages describe kinds of behavior that many people have commonly observed in themselves, as well as in their own intraracial and interracial interactions, my experience has been that most students grasp the basic conceptual framework fairly easily, even if they do not have a background in psychology.

Empowering Students as Change Agents

Heightening students' awareness of racism without also developing an awareness of the possibility of change is a prescription for despair. I consider it unethical to do one without the other. Exploring strategies to empower students as change agents is thus a necessary part of the process of talking about race and learning about racism. As was previously mentioned, students find it very helpful to read about and hear from individuals who have been effective change agents. Newspaper and magazine articles, as well as biographical or autobiographical essays or book excerpts, are often important sources for this information.

I also ask students to work in small groups to develop an action plan of their own for interrupting racism. While I do not consider it appropriate to require students to engage in antiracist activity (since I believe this should be a personal choice the student makes for him/herself), students are required to think about the possibility. Guidelines are provided (see Katz, 1978), and the plans that they develop over several weeks are presented at the end of the semester. Students are generally impressed with each other's good ideas; and, in fact, they often do go on to implement their projects.

Joanne, a White student who initially struggled with feelings of guilt, wrote:

> I thought that hearing others' ideas for action plans was interesting and informative. It really helps me realize (reminds me) the many choices and avenues there are once I decided to be an ally. Not only did I develop my own concrete way to be an ally, I have found many other ways that I, as a college student, can be an active anti-racist. It was really empowering.

Another way all students can be empowered is by offering them the opportunity to consciously observe their own development. The taped exercise to which some of the previously quoted students have referred is an example of one way to provide this opportunity. At the beginning of the semester, students are given an interview guide with many open-ended questions concerning racial attitudes and opinions. They are asked to interview themselves on tape as a way of recording their own ideas for future reference. Though the tapes are collected, students are assured that no one (including me) will listen to them. The tapes are returned near the end of the semester, and students are asked to listen to their own tapes and use their understanding of racial identity development to discuss it in essay form.

The resulting essays are often remarkable and underscore the psychological importance of giving students the chance to examine racial issues in the classroom. The following was written by Elaine, a White woman:

> Another common theme that was apparent in the tape was that, for the most part, I was aware of my own ignorance and was embarrassed because of it. I wanted to know more about the oppression of people in the country so that I could do something about it. Since I have been here, I have begun to be actively resistant to racism. I have been able to confront my grandparents and some old friends from high school when they make racist comments. Taking this psychology of racism class is another step toward active resistance to racism. I am trying to educate myself so that I have a knowledge base to work from.
>
> When the tape was made, I was just beginning to be active and just beginning to be educated. I think I am now starting to move into the redefinition stage. I am starting to feel ok about being White. Some of my guilt is dissipating, and I do not feel as ignorant as I used to be. I think I have an understanding of racism; how it effects [*sic*] myself, and how it effects this country. Because of this I think I can be more active in doing something about it.

In the words of Louise, a Black female student:

> One of the greatest things I learned from this semester in general is that the world is not only Black and White, nor is the United States. I learned a lot about my own erasure of many American ethnic groups. . . . I am in the (immersion) stage of my identity development. I think I am also dangling a little in the (encounter) stage. I say this because a lot of my energies are still directed toward White people. I began writing a poem two days ago and it was directed to White racism. However, I have also become more Black-identified. I am reaching to the strength in Afro-American heritage. I am learning more about the heritage and history of Afro-American culture. Knowledge = strength and strength = power.

While some students are clearly more self-reflective and articulate about their own process than others, most students experience the opportunity to talk and learn about these issues as a transforming process. In my experience, even those students who are frustrated by aspects of the course find themselves changed by it. One such student wrote in her final journal entry:

> What I felt to be a major hindrance to me was the amount of people. Despite the philosophy, I really never felt at ease enough to speak openly about the feelings I have and kind of watched the class pull farther and farther apart as the semester went on. . . . I think that it was your attitude that kept me intrigued by the topics we were studying despite my frustrations with the class time. I really feel as though I made some significant moves in my understanding of other people's positions in our world as well as of my feelings of racism, and I feel very good about them. I feel like this class has moved me in the right direction. I'm on a roll I think, because I've been introduced to so much.

Facilitating student development in this way is a challenging and complex task, but the results are clearly worth the effort.

IMPLICATIONS FOR THE INSTITUTION

What are the institutional implications for an understanding of racial identity development theory beyond the classroom? How can this framework be used to address the pressing issues of increasing diversity and decreasing racial tensions on college campuses? How can providing opportunities in the curriculum to talk about race and learn about racism affect the recruitment and retention of students of color specifically, especially when the majority of the students enrolled are White?

The fact is, educating White students about race and racism changes attitudes in ways that go beyond the classroom boundaries. As White students move through their own stages of identity development, they take their friends with them by engaging them in dialogue. They share the articles they have read with roommates, and involve them in their projects. An example of this involvement can be seen in the following journal entry, written by Larry, a White man:

> Here it is our fifth week of class and more and more I am becoming aware of the racism around me. Our second project made things clearer, because while watching T.V. I picked up many kinds of discrimination and stereotyping. Since the project was over, I still find myself watching these shows and picking up bits and pieces every show I watch. Even my friends will be watching a show and they will say, "Hey, Larry, put that in your paper." Since they know I am taking this class, they are looking out for these things. They are also watching what they say around me for fear that I will use them as an example. For example, one of my friends has this fascination with making fun of Jewish people. Before I would listen to his comments and take them in stride, but now I confront him about his comments.

The heightened awareness of the White students enrolled in the class has a ripple effect in their peer group, which helps to create a climate in which students of color and other targeted groups (Jewish students, for example) might feel more comfortable. It is likely that White students who have had the opportunity to learn about racism in a supportive atmosphere will be better able to be allies to students of color in extracurricular settings, like student government meetings and other organizational settings, where students of color often feel isolated and unheard.

At the same time, students of color who have had the opportunity to examine the ways in which racism may have affected their own lives are able to give voice to their own experience, and to validate it rather than be demoralized by it. An understanding of internalized oppression can help students of color recognize the ways in which they may have unknowingly participated in their own victimization, or the victimization of others. They may be able to move beyond victimization to empowerment, and share their learning with others, as Sharon, a previously quoted Black woman, planned to do.

Campus communities with an understanding of racial identity development could become more supportive of special-interest groups, such as the Black Student Union or the Asian Student Alliance, because they would recognize them not as "separatist" but as important outlets for students of color who may be at the Encounter or Immersion stage of racial identity development. Not only could speakers of color be sought out to add diversity to campus programming, but Whites who had made a commitment to unlearning their own racism could be offered as models to those White students looking for new ways to understand their own Whiteness, and to students of color looking for allies.

It has become painfully clear on many college campuses across the United States that we cannot have successfully multiracial campuses without talking about race and learning about racism. Providing a forum where this discussion can take place safely over a semester, a time period that allows personal and group development to unfold in ways that day-long or weekend programs do not, may be among the most proactive learning opportunities an institution can provide.

NOTES

1. A similar point could be made about other issues of oppression, such as anti-Semitism, homophobia and heterosexism, ageism, and so on.
2. While similar models of racial identity development exist, Cross and Helms are referenced here because they are among the most frequently cited writers on Black racial identity development and on White racial identity development, respectively. For a discussion of the commonalities between these and other identity development models, see Phinney (1989, 1990) and Helms (1990).
3. Both Parham (1989) and Phinney (1989) suggest that a preference for the dominant group is not always a characteristic of this stage. For example, children raised in households and communities with explicitly positive Afrocentric attitudes may absorb a pro-Black perspective, which then serves as the starting point for their own exploration of racial identity.
4. After being introduced to this model and Helms's model of White identity development, students are encouraged to think about how the models might apply to their own experience or the experiences of people they know. As is reflected in the cited journal entries, some students resonate to the theories quite readily, easily seeing their own process of growth reflected in them. Other students are sometimes puzzled because they feel as though their own process varies from these models, and may ask if it is possible to "skip" a particular stage, for example. Such questions provide a useful departure point for discussing the limitations of stage theories in general, and the potential variations in experience that make questions of racial identity development so complex.
5. Examples of useful articles include essays by McIntosh (1988), Lester (1987), and Braden (1987). Each of these combines autobiographical material, as well as a conceptual framework for understanding some aspect of racism that students find very helpful. Bowser and Hunt's (1981) edited book, *Impacts of Racism on Whites*, though less autobiographical in nature, is also a valuable resource.
6. Class size has a direct bearing on my ability to create safety in the classroom. Dividing the class into pairs or small groups of five or six students to discuss initial reactions to a particular article or film helps to increase participation, both in the small groups and later in the large group discussions.

REFERENCES

Barnard, H. F. (Ed.). (1987). *Outside the magic circle: The autobiography of Virginia Foster Durr*. New York: Simon & Schuster. (Original work published 1985)

Bowser, B. P., & Hunt, R. G. (1981). *Impacts of racism on Whites*. Beverly Hills: Sage.

Braden, P. A., & Quina, K. (Eds.). (1988). *Teaching a psychology of people: Resources for gender and sociocultural awareness*. Washington, DC: American Psychological Association.

Cross, W. E., Jr. (1971). The Negro to Black conversion experience: Toward a psychology of black liberation. *Black World, 20*(9), 13–27.

Cross, W. E., Jr. (1978). The Cross and Thomas models of psychological nigrescence. *Journal of Black Psychology, 5*(1), 13–19.

Cross, W. E., Jr. (1991). *Shades of Black: Diversity in African-American identity.* Philadelphia: Temple University Press.

Cross, W. E., Jr., Parham, T. A., & Helms, J. E. (1991). The stages of black identity development: Nigrescence models. In R. Jones (Ed.), *Black psychology* (3rd ed., pp. 319–338). San Francisco: Cobb and Henry.

Derman-Sparks, L., Higa, C. T., & Sparks, B. (1980). Children, race and racism: How race awareness develops. *Interracial Books for Children Bulletin, 11*(3/4), 3–15.

Helms, J. E. (Ed.). (1990). *Black and White racial identity: Theory, research and practice.* Westport, CT: Greenwood Press.

Highlen, P. S., Reynolds, A. L., Adams, E. M., Hanley, T. C., Myers, L. J., Cox, C., and Speight, S. (1988, August 13). *Self-identity development model of oppressed people: Inclusive model for all?* Paper presented at the American Psychological Association Convention, Atlanta, GA.

Hull, G. T., Scott, P. B., & Smith, B. (Eds.). (1982). *All the women are White, all the Blacks are men, but some of us are brave: Black women's studies.* Old Westbury, NY: Feminist Press.

Katz, J. H. (1978). *White awareness: Handbook for anti-racism training.* Norman: University of Oklahoma Press.

Lester, J. (1987). *What happens to the mythmakers when the myths are found to be untrue?* Unpublished paper, Equity Institute, Emeryville, CA.

McIntosh, P. (1988). *White privilege and male privilege: A personal a account of coming to see correspondences through work in women's studies.* Working paper, Wellesley College Center for Research on Women, Wellesley, MA.

McIntosh, P. (1989, July/August). White privilege: Unpacking the invisible knapsack. *Peace and Freedom,* pp. 10–12.

Parham, T. A. (1989). Cycles of psychological nigrescence. *Counseling Psychologist, 17*(2), 187–226.

Phinney, J. (1989). Stages of ethnic identity in minority group adolescents. *Journal of Early Adolescence, 9,* 34–39.

Phinney, J. (1990). Ethnic identity in adolescents and adults: Review of research. *Psychological Bulletin, 108*(3), 499–514.

Phinney, J. S., & Rotheram, M. J. (Eds.). (1987). *Children's ethnic socialization: Pluralism and development.* Newbury Park, CA: Sage.

Schuster, M. R., & Van Dyne, S. R. (Eds.). (1985). *Women's place in the academy: Transforming the liberal arts curriculum.* Totowa, NJ: Towman & Allanheld.

Wellman, D. (1977). *Portraits of White racism.* New York: Cambridge University Press.

Teaching and Practice

SONDRA PERL

> We live our lives through texts. They may be read, or chanted, or . . . come to us, like the murmurings of our mothers, telling us what conventions demand. Whatever their form or medium, these stories have formed us all; they are what we must use to make new fictions, new narratives. (Heilbrun, 1988, p. 37)

Stories have mythic powers. To know this, as Carolyn Heilbrun suggests, is to know the shaping power of the tale. But how, I wonder, do we see beyond the boundaries of a familiar story and envision a new one? What, in other words, are the connections between the texts we read and the lives we live, between composing our stories and composing ourselves?

These questions come to me after teaching composition and literature at the City University of New York for over twenty years. They come to me after spending many years observing and describing the ways others teach and write.[1] And they come to me as I turn my gaze on my own practice with the understanding that one's own classroom can be an entry point for inquiry into the nature of teaching and learning.

This article, then, presents an approach to teaching in philosophy and practice that has grown over two decades and has its roots in several sources: composition studies, feminism, reader-response theory, and critical pedagogy. Each of these perspectives bears on my work. My thinking has been influenced by a host of scholars, among them John Dewey, Peter Elbow, Paulo Freire, Carol Gilligan, and Louise Rosenblatt. As important as the various theoretical frames, however, are the stories my work leads me to tell: stories of students, their writing and speaking, and what happens to them as they enter into an engagement with texts. It is also a story of teaching, of my teaching life, of the questions I bring to my work and the way they shift and change as I, too, write my way through a semester.

Above all, though, this article is an attempt to pay tribute to the power of composing. For in every class I conduct, it is composing — the act of discovering, constructing, and shaping meaning — that gives life and form to what my students and I do. Composing, in the broadest sense, enables all of us to use the gifts we are given to shape ideas, to call into being what does not yet exist, to inspire, and to touch others. In composition and literature classrooms, composing enables students and teachers

Harvard Educational Review Vol. 64 No. 4 Winter 1994, 427–449

to use language in the most exciting and powerful ways: to enable students to shape themselves, and in the shaping to discover both the limits that have been imposed on them and the possibilities for challenge and change. And, when teachers compose along with their students, reading and writing about their teaching as students read and write about texts, a new classroom story is also called into being.[2]

COMPOSING A TEACHER'S LIFE

"Ah wants tuh utilize mahself all over." So confides Janie Crawford to her friend Pheoby in Zora Neale Hurston's *Their Eyes Were Watching God* (1937/1978, p. 169). In many ways, Janie and I couldn't be more different. Black and working class, she was raised by a grandmother who pinched in the horizon until Janie nearly strangled. White and privileged, I was raised by parents, the children of immigrants, whose material success spoke of dreams fulfilled and horizons full of promise. But despite our differences, Janie's words speak to me. For in that one line, spoken unselfconsciously by Janie to Pheoby, my teaching life stands revealed.

Teaching allows me to utilize myself. An act that is, to me, at once profoundly serious and deeply pleasurable, teaching enables me to think, to shape, to compose both the class and myself. On the playful side, I want to liken it to fishing, where I cast out a line and see, first of all, if it stays poised on the surface or if it sinks. Is there a bite? Does someone have something to say? Then comes the reeling in, when someone grabs hold, sometimes two people or more, wrestling, thrashing. Landing the fish is never my job alone, but the job of the entire class. And, when a point emerges or an insight is shared, the joy is shared too, because we have worked at it together.

But what is the hook? What grabs my students? In large part, I think, it is the interest I evince, coming toward them from someone they assume "already knows." In fact, I don't "already know," but I do really want to find out how they regard what we are reading, to learn about their responses to the texts, and discover what these texts say to them. In this sense, then, the texts become the bait. And what I'm fishing for is what the texts bring to light: the students, their responses, and their lives as they see them. And as the students see that I am serious, that I truly do want to hear from them, they come to class more frequently with their own hooks baited. They initiate the discussion; they throw out their own lines, and we all, so to speak, fish together.

The metaphor of fishing is lighthearted, meant to call up images of both great effort and great fun. But beneath my frivolity is a more sober side. Throughout any given semester, I often question myself uneasily: What am I doing? What is my agenda? What matters most as I construct a lesson? Am I being true to what I believe about the ways people learn? In essence, have I evolved a practice consistent with my theories about students and teaching? What am I not yet seeing or hearing? And what might I learn when I approach teaching openly and write about what it is teaching me?

Looking back over two decades, I notice that my work revolves around three key features: a willingness, even a desire, to have my plans altered or disrupted by the issues and questions students bring to class; an interest in listening to and for students' voices, both oral and written; and an abiding love of stories.

The first feature, letting the ideas and the agenda I bring to class be shaped by what students bring, gives students an entry point and grants their ideas and questions a formative role in the curriculum I have constructed. Since no two students ever present the same questions and responses, on any given night, I am, if I am listening well, always faced with the creative act of gathering together their questions and responses so that we can use them to direct our learning.

The second feature, listening to and for my students' voices, is linked to the first. Many students, and certainly many of the adults I teach, will not risk raising questions or responding honestly if they suspect that their doubts or concerns will be ridiculed, ignored, or rejected. So, quite consciously, I attempt to create a classroom environment in which I invite students' voices to be heard and in which they are respected. In fact, I want our meetings to draw out their voices and to welcome the kind of speaking out that encourages dialogue.[3]

A third key feature is my own love of stories, both those read in literature and those told in response to that literature. Nothing instructs as well as a story. Nor do we learn so much about ourselves as when we delve into our own stories to discover how they have shaped us. Carol Witherall and Nel Noddings (1991), writing about education, recognize this power of the tale:

> Stories and narratives, whether personal or fictional, provide meaning and belonging in our lives. They attach us to others and to our own histories by providing a tapestry rich with threads of time, place, character, and even advice on what we might do with our lives. The story fabric offers us images, myths, and metaphors that are morally resonant and contribute both to our knowing and our being known. (p. 1)

Such stories, as they have been conceived by Witherall and Noddings, consist of what has already been told. But how, I wonder, harkening back to the Heilbrun epigram with which I began, do we use an old story to create a new one? Out of what do we create new narratives in which to live?

I propose that when we examine the stories we've been told, and when we consider the way we cast ourselves in the stories we tell, we can identify boundaries already set for us to which we may have unwittingly acquiesced. In fact, one way to uncover the inadvertent in our own lives is to enter literature and let the grounds for new tales and tellings be called out by the stories of others. Rubbing up against those stories creates an edge in us, one we can use to sharpen our understanding — of the tale already told or of the new one waiting to be written.

But to create a new narrative, a new fiction in which to live, we must risk even more: for by staying on that edge we may lose our bearings — and we risk losing our way. And so, to write what hasn't been written before, we must gather our energy, muster our courage, go to that edge, and follow it into the unknown and untold.

Negotiating edges, which is essential to composing, has two features that I want to understand. First, the struggles and surprises along the way are so intimate that we often assume that composing is a solitary affair. But, when we compose, we are never entirely alone. For who we are and what we write is often in response to, and in dialogue with, the larger world that also lives within us. Second, this interplay between individual experience and larger social and historical contexts only becomes composing when we give voice to what was formerly inchoate. And, it is by gaining access to and drawing upon the "never before said" that we are able to create a new story, a new version of ourselves.

To understand composing in this way is to lay the groundwork for a theory of pedagogy in which teaching, too, is seen as an act of composing. For it is not just creating new texts and revised versions of people's lives that matters here. The very settings for such tellings and retellings are ours to create as well. I am proposing, then, that we revise not only the traditional classroom story, in which the lecture is the dominant trope, but also the more recent revisions, in which students play an increasingly important role. The story evolving here is of classrooms that are created not only collaboratively, but also anew at each meeting, as we and our students author our coming together at the edges of our understanding. Composing teaching in this way calls us to be composers in the broadest sense — of the texts we read and write and of the lives we shall go on to live.

COMPOSING A SETTING AND A SYLLABUS

This story begins in the Bronx, in a literature class taught to students enrolled in the Adult Degree Program at Lehman College, City University of New York, a program for adults whose work and family lives have prevented them from attending college. Most are entering the university for the first time. Some are parents of young children; others, having already raised children, are fulfilling a lifelong dream of pursuing their own education.

My course, entitled "Goddesses, Temptresses, Wives and Others: Images of Women in Literature," is a two-hour seminar that attracts as many entering students as returning ones, as many first-year students as seniors. A few read widely; many express fear and uncertainty when faced with "literary" texts. Most register for the course out of an interest in women's issues; a handful just need the credit.[4]

From the course description, the students know that they will read works written by both men and women and examine how women have been portrayed in literature throughout the ages. When we meet, they will discover that the focus of the course is also on them. In that respect, my teaching is learner-centered. But I also hold to the more traditional idea that it is my responsibility to decide what we will read.[5] The works I use are those that illustrate a theme I want to pursue in the course: namely, that there are myths that have contributed to a generic idea of "woman," tales that have so molded Western consciousness that they live within us without our noticing it. I look for such illustrative texts and for others in which women's roles can be subjected to critique. The texts are also ones I care for personally, that I find beautiful, rich, and evocative, so that reading them stretches me, and has the potential to immerse us all in language I consider worth our time and attention.[6]

We start with reading Sophocles' *Antigone* (1986) and Euripides's *Medea* (1988). We then move back in time and read creation stories in Genesis, followed by feminist literature on the development of matriarchal societies and goddess worship. After several weeks of often heated debate over the impact of religion on women's lives, we read Charlotte Perkins Gilman's ironic utopian novel *Herland* (1915/1979), in which Gilman depicts a world governed by women, not unlike the idealized image students envision after reading about goddesses. To examine how women's lives have been stifled and suppressed, we read Henrik Ibsen's *A Doll's House* (1879/1966) and selected excerpts from Tillie Olsen's *Silences* (1978). Moving into more recent twentieth-century fiction, we read Buchi Emecheta's *Second-Class Citizen* (1987) and Hurston's *Their Eyes Were Watching God* (1978). To complete the term, I select stories that suggest new possibilities for women, such as Toni Morrison's *Sula* (1975) and Barbara Kingsolver's *The Bean Trees* (1989). Both of these offer images of women who are inventing new ways to be, Sula in a lonely, singular style, Taylor Greer in a more communal, politically conscious way.

The general syllabus, excluding supplementary handouts, presents a course already composed, already structured by choices I make. What is not yet composed, and can never fully be, is what comes into play when I invite the students to read, to write, and to talk together.

COMPOSING THE CLASS

It is the 1993–1994 fall term. I meet my students for the first time in a room I have never seen before. It is a science lab with large rectangular wooden tables set in three rows, facing front. We all recognize "the front" because there is one extra table, pulled out from all the others, standing alone. On one side of this table, posters of primates are tacked to the wall; on the other, there is a large sink.

My class consists of thirty-six women and one man, ages twenty-five to sixty-five, of whom one is Asian, eleven African American, ten Hispanic, eleven White, and four are from the Caribbean. Twenty-nine were born in the United States; a few came as children from Puerto Rico. Others recently arrived from the South, the Caribbean, Ireland, and Italy. Twelve are single, fifteen married, and nine divorced; one is a widow. Twenty-seven have children, and three are grandparents.

I drop my papers on the table and say, "Good evening," wondering how we will ever work intimately in this space. I assume we are placed here, in a science lab, because we are a large class. I like the tables, but not the long rows. Quickly, I tell the students what I'm after: a way for all of us to be able to see and talk to one another. After some discussion, we decide to rearrange the tables into a large square. It's not lost on most of us that we have already engaged in two subversive acts: by changing the seating, we have consciously altered the way conversations usually occur in class; by moving heavy pieces of furniture ourselves, we laughingly note that we have momentarily dispensed with the stereotype of the helpless female.

That first night, I invite students to write down their associations to the phrase "women in literature" and then to list the goals they want to set for themselves in the course. As a way of introduction, I invite each student to do what we will do repeatedly throughout the term — that is, to read aloud to the entire class a bit of what they have written. Some voices are shaky. Not everyone expects to speak in class, especially on the first night. But I am pleased when everyone contributes and the room begins to fill with their ideas and their dreams. A bit of what we all hear that night:

> Women have been conditioned to think that they are lesser than men.

> I graduated high school in 1959. As I think back, I can only remember names like Julius Caesar and the one female who said, "Out damn spot!"

> One thing I would like to get out of this course is to improve my self-esteem and confidence as a woman.

> My goal? Learn more about women in literature. I'm excited by the whole prospect of it.

Later that night, I write briefly in my journal:

> Once I'm here, in my classroom, all else in life recedes. The students come in, seemingly tired, with leather bags and large sweaters, at first shy and uncertain, then, slowly, more open, willing, interested. I look out and they are there, waiting, expectant. A few familiar faces — Irma who mentions the diaries of Anais Nin; Eileen who is reading Antonia Fraser and Emily Dickinson. And then so many . . . those whose only reading appears to be the Bible and those whose expressed desire is to improve the quality of their lives. Underneath their interest in reading literature is, I think, a deeper concern: how to take from this class a more satisfying view of women and of themselves. This suits me just fine.

For the second meeting of the course, I assign *Antigone* and ask students to record their responses to the reading in what many teachers call "literature logs."[7] I encourage them to respond in their logs as honestly as they can to what they are reading — raising questions, expressing doubt or confusion, quoting from specific passages, noting what touches, angers, or delights them, and writing their own stories in response. For most, this writing is done at home; others report that they are reading and writing at work; a few say they are starting to carry their logs everywhere and describe themselves writing furiously on the subway.

We begin this second night, then, with what they bring to class. Suzanne starts us off with a laugh. "The real Greek tragedy," she remarks, "is my pronunciation of the names." As I invite students to open their logs and read aloud, the talk turns serious. Students raise questions about characters, motivation, language, and poetry. Most of what I would want to come out in class is raised by them in their writing.

Irma, in her mid-forties, married, with two daughters, a paraprofessional who works with autistic children, writes:

> As I began reading *Antigone*, I thought to myself — Oh damn! Can I read this classical type story, let alone understand what the author was trying to say? . . . [But] as I was reading, I was struck by how much easier it is to read than I thought. The words flow and are almost rhyming like. A long poem is what came to my mind.

In her mid-thirties, Valerie is a single parent of one son. She starts off:

I've only read the first three pages and I can feel Antigone's passion, her loyalty, and deep desire to do what is right by those she holds dear. . . . I am having trouble understanding the Chorus. I guess it's because the form of speech is different from the story itself. I would like to strangle Creon with my bare hands.

A single parent of two children, Evelyn is in her mid-twenties and works for an insurance company. She writes:

It seems funny to me how indirectly men seem to be the reason for the disagreement between Antigone and Ismene. . . . At a time when they should be as one, Antigone lives by the laws of the gods whereas Ismene fears retribution from an earthbound god, Creon. I can understand both their turmoil. We've all been in situations where it's come down to follow your head or your heart.

Just turning fifty, Sarah, a grandmother who lives alone and works as a customer service director at a bank, responds:

The language is beautiful. I was struck by Creon's "But greed of gain has often made men fools" and the sentry's "So I've come scurrying at a snail's pace by the long shortcut." Somehow it reminds me of the phraseology of my African-American race. . . . This sentry is such a wuss but then so is Creon for both fail to see strength in a woman but are not so blind as to realize that by Antigone's strength all can see their weakness. I tremble both in fear and awe when I see Antigone's defiance.

And after commenting on Antigone's courage in standing up to Creon, Betty, a married, sixty-five-year-old woman who suffered a mild heart attack toward the end of the term, admits: "I see myself in Ismene. Afraid to do something on her own."
After the second class meeting, I write too:

I walk in at 6 PM and the students have already rearranged the tables into a large, open square, accommodating almost all 37 of us. We begin to talk about the reading. . . . Going over specific lines, hearing the poetry, describing Greek drama and theories of tragedy. . . .

But what is happening here? Everyone is engaged, but why? Is it that my questions are invitations to look and see what they think and feel — not challenges to trip them up? Or that Sarah can say, "It's just like this today: if a woman speaks up at work, they'll want to kill her" and many nod? . . .

What nags at me now is Mark, the only man in the class. . . . I've been ignoring rather than addressing his flip humor. I find it hard to accept or bring dignity to someone who, when asked for a way to describe Antigone chuckles, "dead." A good question: how to find what's dignified in Mark? Is his need to quip a cover for his own discomfort among all these women?

Mark, in fact, poses an interesting problem for me. If I want all of my students to speak honestly and openly, to assume that their perceptions are of value, what do I do with Mark? His comments are often funny, but to my hearing at least, they also come across as defensive, as if he is keeping himself distant from the work and ridiculing anyone else who chooses to take it seriously. Since I am not interested in silencing him and would prefer for him to join us in a more serious tone, I proceed on the hunch that by continuing to include him in the conversation, by smiling when I do find his comments funny but otherwise not indulging, excusing, or condemning his behavior, he might discover that there are other ways to act in class. I also suspect that the seriousness of other students' responses, the care they devote to their reading, and the honesty with which they speak might draw him in. This is precisely what happens.

After the first few weeks, the students, including Mark, become accustomed to writing in their logs and reading from them either to the whole class or in smaller groups. Reading and writing, followed by talking and reflecting, build their own momentum. Students, I notice, gravitate to particular groups. Often there is laughter. When I ask students in each group to report back to the entire class on their conversations, most seem eager to recount what went on. A few students approach me after class. Some want further instruction on ways of keeping lit-logs. Others want to check in, establishing fuller contact with me. A few want me to know how proud they are to have read Greek dramas and understood them. Mark comments aloud at the end of the evening, "I come to class tired and crabby, and I leave here exhilarated." As many nod in agreement, it dawns on me that he speaks for most of us.

But, I suspect, the community that is beginning to form among us, temporary though it may be, is not only a function of collaborative work. I am convinced that the practice of writing responses to texts, reading these responses in class, and then writing additional responses during our meetings has a unique power for drawing people out and bringing them together.

In composing their responses — tentative, angry, confused, celebratory, reflective — students are often able to place themselves in relation to each text and to discover what they think about it.[8] Having written, many initially look for support, sympathy, and encouragement from their peers. They talk of identifying with characters and vent anger at the treatment of such figures as Antigone and Medea. At times they also reveal hesitantly some of what they have suffered. For example, after reading *A Doll's House*, Betty writes:

> Torvald may have been domineering but this is the kind of man I was used to. The men in my childhood were my father and grandfather. Screaming was an everyday occurrence. Once, they both spanked me at the same time. Deep down, I've always been afraid of men.

Then, as students read and talk together, as they place their own thinking alongside the thinking of their peers, they often step back and think more critically. Again, Betty writes:

> I am looking at this play with a new eye. In some situations, a woman's life today is not too much different than it was in Norway in 1879. . . . My mother always asked me, "What do you want?" A marriage was good to her if a man didn't beat you, drink, go out with other women. If he handed his pay check to you, he was a good man. What more could you ask for?

Reminded by Nora's story of how she, too, was denied a loan in her own name, Betty describes her chagrin and, later on, her own manipulative behavior, which was not unlike Nora's:

I know what it is to cajole my husband into getting something I want. Sometimes to get what you want, you have to act "cutesy-poo." The sad thing was that I had internalized the situation to the point that I didn't see how degrading it was to behave like that.

While the students sort out their reactions to the plays we are reading, I use my journal to sort out my reactions to the way the course is developing and find myself composing a fresh understanding of the way I teach:

> I'm trying to figure out — where am I in all of this? I welcome the students each week, get things going, ask questions, read to them from the text, change the pace, invite questions, ask for responses, challenge them to go further, write their responses on the board, smile, encourage, say back to them what I've heard them say, contextualize, historicize, modernize.
>
> It's true, I do know where I want us to go but at the same time I build it from them — so that the creative moment comes when I can fashion something new to say from what they've given me — I can never predict what it will be that will get me to say something — but there is an unknown edge I'm pursuing and to get there I need what they offer me — but I also think that what they give me may be related to the kind of welcome I give them. . . .
>
> This seems to be a process way of talking about teaching — I don't know how to document what this moment feels like or looks like — what's the substance? Can it be shown? Is teaching at the edge of not-knowing a bit like writing "at the point of utterance?" (Britton, 1982, p. 139)

As I continue to write about my classroom and reflect on teaching, the semester, too, continues. We begin our study of the Bible, creation myths, poems that revere such goddesses as Ishtar, Isis, and Mami Aruru, and the emerging literature on matriarchal cultures.[9] These texts draw out students' thoughts on religion, women's roles, and their own places in the world, eliciting a mix of resistance, wonder, delight, and fear. At this time I write:

> This piece of the course always scares me and excites me. The readings are so affirming of women and spirituality. And yet, I am always fearful of offending someone. I try hard to make the distinction that we are reading the Bible with a critical eye just as we read *Antigone* and *Medea*. But for some even raising questions about the role of women in the Bible is a threat; treating the Bible as a literary text, a sacrilege.
>
> What am I trying to do here? . . . Not disparage their faith. What I'm after is to track down where some of our ideas about women have come from, encourage the students to rethink their beliefs and positions, reclaim, if it's been lost, a sense of their own dignity, and at the same time, teach respect for the differences among us.
>
> I try to build a frame here — about the importance of feminism as a way to challenge patriarchal notions, as a way to raise questions as we live and raise kids — and about our responsibility to care for the earth, not only to take from it because it's there, as if it were some acquiescent, helpless woman.

Student responses vary widely. In her lit-log, Valerie writes:

I just read *When God Was a Woman.* My reaction is this woman is an atheist. She's looking to blame someone for the troubles of the world, especially feminine problems. So why not blame God. . . . But man has caused his own oppression from the beginning of time, and has oppressed his fellow man, so how could women escape? . . . Merlin Stone needs to read the Bible more carefully.

I have many feelings concerning this literature. . . . I know there was a time in human history when the female was worshipped. I know this. The Bible does not dispute this. . . . I, too, have imagined, dreamed, fantasized and found I wasn't the first nor will I be the last, to imagine a world ruled by women which worshipped the female image. Why? Because in earthly form she was closer to having His abilities than man.

But I've grown up. I no longer need to imagine. I am in relationship with the Holy of Holies who far outshines man's abilities or should I say women's abilities.

In her first semester at college, Kristine, single, in her mid-twenties, provides another view:

I found Merlin Stone's writing very interesting. I did not know that in prehistoric and early historic periods people worshipped their creator as female. Her questions really put into light the idea of how and when men gained their right of power over women. It reinforces my questions about Adam and Eve, of who wrote this? Where did it come from? Her questioning makes me realize how I take for granted the story of Eve without thinking about its consequences on present day society's view of women. . . .

My doubts about religion and its teachings still linger even with the insights given by a fellow student who studies the Bible. I don't understand how one can put faith into something that oppresses groups of people. I find it particularly difficult to understand how women can believe. With the little I know of the Bible I get the view that women are looked down upon, are considered property and can be killed under "proper circumstances." How can we have faith in something that in a way glorifies these ideas, especially in the name of God?

Betty's lit-log shows a change in her thinking, a willingness to step back and reconsider all she had been taught and accepted as truth:

I am a Protestant. I have been going to church since I was four years old. Some of these stories and poems go against all I have been raised to believe. . . .

It is difficult for me to admit, but I suppose if I were alive during the popular times of the goddesses, I would be worshipping a goddess. I seem to be what I was raised. . . .

This is shocking stuff. A child is told something and it's the truth according to the child. . . . I told Mrs. Webber in church about this article. She bowed her head for a few seconds, picked it up, and said, "Don't take my faith away from me." . . .

Things will probably never go back to a peaceful existence as in a matriarchal society but *I* will never be the same.

While a few students, like Valerie, speak movingly of their faith and resist any challenges to their reading of the Bible, others, like Kristine, begin to see how deeply the traditional image of woman (as helpmate to her man, as property, as sexually taboo or unclean) has been embedded in Western consciousness. Some, like Betty, begin to consider that what they have always assumed to be true about women, religion, and reality is a version of a story someone told them — and that all stories can be reread, reinterpreted, and told in different ways.

Half-way through the term, I ask students to stop and reread all they have written in their literature logs. By this time, the logs have taken on lives of their own as companions for students as they chart the journey of their own readings. Each log has become, in effect, another primary text to be read and responded to, a text whose boundaries can also be revised and enlarged. So, I ask students to write me a letter reflecting on the person they see emerging in the log, almost as if the one writing the log were a character in a story she or he is now reading. These letters provide a way for students to step back and reflect, to look again at the paths they are traveling, to see more clearly the outlines of stories they now realize have governed them and the beginnings of new tales that are waiting to be told. Below is an abbreviated version of the letter written by Margaret, a mother of three, in her third year of college:

> Dear Professor,
>
> This is the fifth attempt I have made in writing to you. . . . The goddess literature . . . gives me a taste of peace and love. . . . Herland and Crete, two places, centuries apart, one fact, one fiction, both peaceful. I wonder what pushed Gilman to write *Herland.* . . . I thought back on my conversations with other women and all of them expressed this same desire, "All I want is some peace in my life. Is that too much to ask for?" Is this our connection with the past and the goddess literature? Are we all looking for our Crete, our Herland?
>
> I kept going back over my lit-log looking for something that would help explain why this literature had such a profound effect on me. What had I written about? I kept turning it over and all of a sudden I saw it: Herstory. Not his story but our story. We have a past. . . . Women have to make sure it is passed on and never let it be buried again.
>
> One other thought kept coming to my mind. Would I have been so receptive to this literature seven or eight years ago? . . . Five years ago my mother committed suicide. The loss was so great and the reality of how she ended her existence shook my very being. Questions? I was plagued with them. . . . My mother was a beautiful, intelligent woman. She had her dreams but destiny led her away from them. She was brought up to serve her father, brothers, husband and then her family. She put her desires and wants to the side like the women described in Olsen's *Silences.* She became depressed. Her doctor told her to do her work and take care of her family. . . . The pain of life and unfulfilled dreams were too much to bear. . . .
>
> I was so like my mother. Putting everyone before me and pushing my wants to the side. My mom's death made me face the realities of my life. I didn't like what I saw. A year after her death, I enrolled at Lehman College. I began to fulfill a lifelong dream. . . . I know that I am growing.

Margaret's letter is poignant and revealing. Like Margaret, most students tell of new and compelling questions, about having to listen harder and rethink where they stand in their lives. In responding to what I hear as their emerging voices, I make another attempt to place their thinking at the center of the course.

Reading through the letters, I choose widely divergent excerpts from different papers and create a handout to serve as another text for the class, one that speaks for (as well as to) the distinct voices beginning to speak up. This piece often runs to three pages. A few excerpts follow:

> A feminist is emerging from my lit-log. I am in many ways the silenced feminist, a product of my generation. . . . These readings are prompting me to examine more closely my role as woman, wife, mother, and the writer I want to be. . . . I am afraid for the future of women. There are more and more violent crimes against women each day.

> I have doubts now as to God's gender. Is he really a man? Are Genesis and the rest of the Bible accurate?

> I consider myself a religious person and find it hard to accept that the Bible has anything to do with negative images of women.

> As I read through my lit-log, from *Antigone* to *A Doll's House,* my emotions rise and fall like the chest of a marathon runner at the finish line. . . . I sit here with my bags packed ready to move to Herland . . . since I just can't wait any longer to be appreciated for what I am, nothing more, nothing less.

> In my opinion, Minoan Crete would be more of a utopia than Herland; partnership with men more perfect than no man at all.

> There is a lot of confusion in my mind because of this course — old ideas being beaten down by new ones. . . .
>   My constant question has been "Why?" Why are we still so fearful of becoming empowered?

Silence falls in our usually noisy room as students read their own words next to those of their classmates. We are all asking "Why?" or "What's going on here?" and writing our way into the midst of our questions. I write in my journal:

> They are reading their own words with the same quiet attention they give to published work — actually, I think, with even more attention. I love how this feels — Is it that I'm feeling more settled and connected too or is it just that things have clicked? Or that the material we are reading is so compelling to them. I don't know, but I do wonder what impact all of this will ultimately have. . . . What will they take away? Will they be encouraged to speak up more for themselves? Will the text of their lives change at all?

During the second half of the semester, we read twentieth-century women writers: Emecheta, Hurston, Kingsolver, Morrison. Excerpts from Olsen's *Silences* frame the questions we now raise concerning racism and sexism, the ways characters in the novels define themselves, and the choices and options available to women. Increasingly, our discussions become more personal and the writing in the lit-logs more filled with detail from lived experience. Irma, for instance, recounts two formative events, stories that have formed her:

Tillie Olsen has touched my soul. She has been able to put down on paper what I've felt for a lifetime. . . . Why is it women are told that they are unable to "create"? I remember when I was a child being told by my own mother that I should stop being a "tomboy" and behave more like a girl or else I would never get a boy to marry me. My mother loved me. But in her own ignorance she believed what had been told to her.

Two sentences from the beginning of *Second-Class Citizen* catch my attention: "She was a girl who had arrived when everyone was expecting and predicting a boy" and "She was so insignificant." . . . I thought about why these two sentences stuck in my mind and then I remembered that when I had my first child, Bianca, my father, who had left my mother when I was four years old and would pop up here and there, came to see me at the hospital. Instead of being happy with his grandchild, he called her *chancletta*, Spanish slang for house slippers — a word used to describe a woman, a second-choice, an insignificant person.

Evelyn is reminded of the small ways people can assert their independence or challenge restrictions:

During our class discussion I had a memory of an event of a few years ago. The passage [from *Silences*] dealt with the uncleanliness of women. It was discussed how orthodox Jews (Hasidics) are not allowed to touch women [other than their wives]. I was on the subway on the way to work and as usual standing room only. I stood near the door and hung on to a strap. At the Marcy Ave. stop three Hasidics got onto the train. Two older gentlemen and one young man (red hair with vivid blue eyes). They were having a discussion in Hebrew and before I knew it the young man was holding onto the same strap I was and our fingers were touching. What's the big deal? you may ask. But having grown up in Brooklyn and hearing how Hasidic men didn't even touch Hasidic women, I was very surprised. I was pleased for some reason that he had made this sign of independence outside the norm. Just as I am pleased to be coming outside of my own.

Mark, too, experiences revelations, insights showing how much he has let the material of the course speak to him and how willing he has become to grapple with difficult issues on a personal level. Still humorous during discussions, he also now reveals a more thoughtful side. At first, he talks only to his small group. Later on, he reads from his lit-log to the entire class:

Silence as oppression. How many great ideas have been smothered? Women as trophies for their men. As a mirror for their men. . . .

When you are told during your life that what you have to say is worthless, then why would you ever want to write it down?

Where am I now? Frankly disgusted that so much potential has been wasted. Worse than wasting talent is a *conspiracy* to oppress a whole group of people with so much to contribute. . . .

Women of course are not the only group to be oppressed. I feel genuine rage when this, the most obscene of all injustice, takes place. My part in the continuing oppression of others is something I am attempting to understand and remedy.

I am the product of years of misinformation and bias. Only as I enter my late twenties do I realize I am carrying a social disease with me. An attitude that does not foster growth or friendship with others. This condition also smothers my growth as a man and my ability to build strong relationships with women and others.

Kristine reflects upon the many messages she is now hearing, raising questions that are not easily answered:

> I never realized how the expectations of women can cause such sacrifice. No that's not correct; I knew it existed. I just didn't want to see it, believe it. It's very frightening, discouraging, intimidating. . . .
>
> As women, we are not brought up to believe in ourselves, to have strength, courage, determination, goals. We are to be considerate, concerned, fair, understanding, flexible. However, that strength as a person, I believe, allows one to trust themselves as a person, to have faith, which to me is the basis of creativity. Creativity is an inner power. Now that I think about it, maybe that is why it frightens many. Power is power; in whatever form it is intimidating. . . .
>
> When we speak of society oppressing women, I think we forget that there are women contributing to this oppression. . . .
>
> Why is it every piece of literature about a woman's road to independence, to self-fulfillment is one filled with sacrifice, hardship and pain? Is it ever easy? And for every one who does make it, how many have failed in the process? One, Twenty, a Hundred, a Thousand?

Students bring these insights to class. They offer their questions, stories, responses, and perspectives. On a given night, I cannot know what will emerge, who will speak, which direction we will follow, which points I will make, what I might miss because I'm paying attention to something else. But I am aware of keeping track of certain things: the feel of the class, checking in to see where people are — individually, in their own lives and with the reading, and as a whole, in their groups; the structure, setting up each evening so that students know whether they are going to work in groups in the beginning or the middle or not at all; the development, asking for responses or questions from them to help us get going, taking each person's comment seriously, and often, stopping after group work or an animated discussion to ask people to write, right then, what they are thinking. Finally, towards the end of each evening, I draw us together, to discover what points are emerging and to determine what doesn't fit, what needs to remain unanswered, and what new questions now need to be asked.

But however structured and controlled I may appear as I guide the class, teaching in such an open-ended fashion raises many questions for me, ones I inquire into by writing. Often I will write about the class to record what has occurred. But soon after, I find myself looking beneath the classroom descriptions to uncover what else they may reveal. For example, after an evening discussing responses to Emecheta's *Second-Class Citizen*, after two hours of examining the challenges that come with immigration and the impact of culture on our values and behavior, I write both to record what happened and to discover the questions writing will reveal to me:

> Tonight we went back and forth. What is the message given to us by American culture? Can we "have it all"? Should we pursue happiness at all costs? Lorna thinks yes. She is sad she didn't know this when she was much younger. Marsha thinks it

makes it much harder. We work, then we come home and take care of everything, and feel guilty when it's not perfect. . . . We get to the notion of risk and entitlement. I tie it back to the idea in *SCC* that one of the effects of racism is a lack of feeling entitled to anything — no rights, certainly no right to pursue happiness — and raise the question: when is it time for risks to be taken? . . .

And we go back and forth. Vicky, who has come here from Jamaica and is in the middle of a divorce, argues strongly for "making changes." Sarah, as strongly, replies, "You think you can walk away from your own culture? No way. Culture is inside of us. You can't get away." Both ideas are alive for us — here in the room.

But still I wonder:

What am I doing here? Am I teaching critical thinking? I rephrase, elaborate, make room for different views, pose differences as issues, try to get underneath. I don't just say "Yes, that's interesting," and affirm any opinion. I do correct blatant inaccuracies. I try, I think, to show the complexity, try to help them locate themselves in the issues and see how they arrived at their opinions. I try to hold up one idea against another and see what the two suggest. One of my guiding ideas here is that I don't give them answers but hope to help them see their own questions — Is that really enough? What is critical in critical thinking? Is the thinking we're doing critical enough?

Discussions in my classroom concerning, for example, women and religion or freedom and cultural constraints are often charged with emotion. This seems fitting to me, for thinking and feeling are deeply connected and both arise from and express deeply held values. When it seems, however, as if a particular classroom exploration might become too difficult or even explosive, I move in one of two directions. I focus the students back on the text we are studying so that we can continue to frame our discussion within the boundaries of an already existing text. Or I ask them to open their lit-logs and write. I say, for example, "Let's stop talking for a while. Open your logs and ask yourself, `What's going on with me right now? What am I thinking and feeling?' See if there's a way that writing can help you collect your thoughts right now."

Often, I put my head down and write as well, noticing peripherally how all of us seem to settle into the quiet in order to record whatever has been brewing as a result of the story we have been discussing or the issues we have raised. I find that writing at these times often diffuses the heat of the debate. Thinking then settles and ideas clarify. If time remains, I invite students to read a line or two of what they have written. Sometimes I read what I have written. In these situations, I have seen providing people first with time to compose their thoughts and then with opportunities to hear the nuances and differences among them draws out and legitimates the diversity of views present in the room. More effective than any other approach I have used for restoring balance and composure and for assessing where the students and I each stand in relation to a compelling question or issue, composing in this way enables us to recompose our classroom.

With several weeks remaining in the semester, there is always much left to do. We discuss Hurston's *Their Eyes Were Watching God*. Most students are, not surprisingly, caught up in the power of Hurston's language, in Janie's tale, and in the many issues raised in the novel. In her log, Valerie focuses on the effects of racism:

I wonder if there are white people who hate white people like some blacks who hate blacks. What is that called? I do know where it comes from. But how do you change hundreds of years of conditioning, brainwashing? This self-hate is so ugly. It hurts and it's sad.

I just finished reading *[Their Eyes Were Watching God]*. I cried for Janie's loss, for the injustice in our courts and for a hope of equality in the human race that seems to be lost. I wondered if Janie would have been freed if her skin was dark brown and her hair short and so curly it looked like wool. Would the jurors [still] be able to see the situation as an accident, a series of events that no one had any control over? Would they see a dark skinned woman with the ability to love deeply? Or were some of them like Mrs. Turner who hated black skin and just couldn't understand why Janie as white-looking as she was . . . was loving a man as dark as Teacake. . . .

This is a mighty powerful story. . . . Janie's many sacrifices for her husband remind me of Nora when she said that women sacrifice their honor for their men all the time. It's true. They sacrifice more than that.

Right now I am in the same place with Pheoby when she said, "Ah don growed ten feet higher from jus listenin to you, Janie." How could you not grow, not learn, not change?

The students are equally caught up in the life of Taylor Greer, the protagonist of Kingsolver's *The Bean Trees*. For Taylor, they rightly recognize, represents the first woman character we've studied whose story begins when she goes off to discover life on her own terms and concludes when she experiences personal triumphs. Raised by a mother who cares for her, willing to risk her life for what she considers honorable, Taylor begins to tell a new story to my students: a story that speaks of hope and possibility — in spite of abuse, alongside injustice, and in defiance of despair. Irma's writing speaks for many:

So finally we read a book where the main character is not married, not involved and not running away from a man. Here's a woman who is happy with herself and doesn't hate her mother. She's a woman who heads out in a car she purchased herself with her mother's blessing. She's not only driving alone but she has no definite destination. . . . Kingsolver shows us that life isn't all clean and smooth running — that children are sexually abused, people are killed or forced to run away in order to survive and that at some time, we must take a stand and fight for what we believe.

Writing about these novels brings students to raise complex issues in class: the impact of racism and sexism, the question of happiness and entitlement, the relationship of risk to isolation, and of friendship to support, the need to take a stand and speak out against injustice to children, to others, to themselves — and what is at stake if one does. And underneath all of these, we discuss the options open to women to create more satisfying lives as well as what stands in their way.

During the next to the last class of the term, I ask students to reflect, in writing, on what they have learned. After working quietly for about an hour, we move leisurely around the room, reading excerpts aloud and talking about the course. Vicky tells us that she's organized a curriculum for her friends and that they, too, will read what we have read this term, but in reversed order. She says to me, "You'll have students all over the place." Lorna, about to graduate, comments that she's "learned so much and feel[s] so much better" about herself, but she's angry it has taken her until her last class at Lehman to have this experience. Tina writes that she is no longer afraid of "literature." And Suzanne tells us that now she is recommending books to people on the subway.

Eileen brings up the word "feminist." Many students remark that the word has changed for them, that it no longer seems so negative, which prompts Irma to tell a story. Describing our course to some other students, she was asked, "Professor Perl? She's that feminist teacher, isn't she? But she can't really be a feminist. She has a husband and a couple of kids, right?"

Irma smiles and as I look around the room I see that others are smiling too. I have the momentary insight that having shared such a rich world for one term, we can now all recognize how much more complicated the notion of feminism has become. I sense that this is a territory we have arrived at and claimed together. I do not know whether my students would say this or whether they would just say it differently, but for me this territory opens up and expands my understanding of feminism. It says that feminism is rooted in issues of worth, value, dignity, and commitment, and that these issues will play themselves out in the stands my students and I take, in the relationships we create, in the voices in which we speak, and in the stories we tell.

Some of these stories are captured now in writing, in students' logs. Others have been spoken aloud, in small groups, in the presence of others. Many students confirm what matters most to them in the writing they do this night — writing that invites them to reflect on the journey they have taken and where they have arrived, to put into print their own understanding of the course. While I provide only a few excerpts here, the themes are repeated in journal after journal. Looking at the ways women have been portrayed in literature has brought many students to look more closely at the ways they see themselves and how they might want to construct new ways, new narratives, as Heilbrun suggests, in which to live. A few excerpts follow:

Faye: "Ah was born back due in slavery so it wasn't for me to fulfill my dreams of what a woman oughta be and to do." Nanny speaks these words to Janie as Janie embarks on her journey toward womanhood [in *Their Eyes Were Watching God.*] I found myself asking questions too. What ought a woman be and do? Have the readings this semester enlightened me further as to what it means to be a woman? A profound "yes." Many of my notions were reinforced as I conversed with Antigone, Sula, Janie, and Adah, just to mention a few. Our experiences, though different, bonded us together and made us stronger as we faced obstacles and hurdles that were placed in our paths. The readings this semester have allowed me to discover, ponder and analyze the ways in which I have been silenced. This makes it more critical for me to acquire the kind of education that will push me out of the darkness of silence into the brightness of freedom.

Vicky: From the Bible onward, we see that it is a common belief that women came into the world as "gifts" to men. Being a gift she becomes his possession. He is therefore convinced that he has the power to use her whichever way he pleases. He conjures up expectations of her and punishes her for deviating from his rules. . . . As women become more educated, they no longer suffer in silence or take revenge by some devious act. Definitely some still do. However, over the years laws have been written to condemn institutionalized abuse of women. Women can now use these laws to their own advantage even though men can still carry out their abuse with more subtlety. . . .

Attending college at age 44, I ask myself many times, why bother? I guess at times like these the little weakness in me is trying to overtake my thoughts by focusing on negative stereotypes of women over 40. Forced back to consciousness by the experiences of the female characters I met in class, I tell myself that at 44 I am just in time.

Mark: This course has allowed me to grow in so many ways I'm not sure where to start. What stands out most is the lack of self-esteem which has affected the women in the readings as well as the class. I never realized how women viewed themselves. . . . [But] I have learned that I lack self-esteem too . . . that I have a lot of baggage I am carrying around, misinformation about women, stereotypes about everyone from whites through blacks. I realized how tainted my views are. . . . It is exciting to see [us] benefit from reading and talking about women.

Louise: The tragedy is not that things are broken. The tragedy is that they are not mended. The tragedy is not that we have failed. The tragedy is that we do not have the courage to begin again. The tragedy is not that we speak and falter. The tragedy is that we are never really whole persons when we remain silent.

The final class is reserved for reading aloud a more formal piece of writing, which students have been working on for several weeks. Having emphasized throughout the term an appreciation for multiple voices and views, I want this last piece to allow for the same sort of openness. A form that readily accommodates disparate voices is dialogue, which allows students to talk to and with the different texts and to place the texts alongside one another to see what such interplay suggests. To conclude the course, I assign the writing of a dialogue using the student's voice and at least five others from among the authors and characters we have read.

The work in the course leads, then, not to any final word but to the creation of another open-ended conversation, arising first out of receptivity to texts and then critical reflection upon them. Space is too limited here to present a full dialogue, but I have included a highly abbreviated one written by Alice, who describes herself as a "mother, student, and wife":

In a comfortable country style dining room . . . Medea, Ellador, Janie and Nora come together to celebrate Alice's fortieth birthday. Their conversation is animated.

Alice: I'm so happy we could be together to celebrate my birthday. All of you have taught me so much.

Nora: I know you are aware of my experience with Torvald. I was forced to examine my life. I left home, my husband and children in order to find myself. It was the most difficult thing I ever had to do. In my time, there was no other way.

Alice: But Nora, wasn't it selfish to sacrifice everyone's happiness in order to find yourself?

Nora: How could I continue to be a wife to Torvald once I saw the lie I was living? Would my children have been happy with an emotionally absent mother?

Ellador: Where I come from, children are our most precious possessions. They are raised not only by their mothers but by the whole community. Perhaps that is why the women of Herland are so content. We do not have to sacrifice ourselves or give up our dreams when we bear a child.

Alice: I wish it were more like that in our culture. . . . When we become wives and mothers, many times we lose ourselves. . . . We become overly attached to our husbands and live through them instead of with them. . . . And the worst part of all is that we become strangers to ourselves. "Our creativity has been silenced, sacrificed to satisfy the needs of others."

Medea [angrily]: "Surely of all creatures that have life, we women are the most wretched. When for an extravagant sum we have bought a husband, we must then accept him as possessor of our body." After all I did for Jason, he repaid me with his infidelity. . . .

Ellador: Medea, I can't pretend to like you. The hideous murder of your sons sickens me. But I am intrigued by your strong will and your ambitious pursuit of living.

Medea: Ellador, don't forget that I was the creation of a man, and therefore it was necessary to turn a strong willed woman into something evil, in this case a murderer of her children. This is a message to all women who might have an urge to become their own person. Women who want equality and fairness in their lives can look at me and see how strong ambitions and autonomy corrupt the mind.

Nora: The thing that most of us have in common is that at some time in our lives we have needed a man to define ourselves.

Janie: Ah telz y'awl, when ah met Teacake ah waz alive fer de fust time. "Mah soul crawled out of its hiding place." Ah just love dat man. . . . He wazn't lak de oder menz. Togedda wez thought new thoughts and new words. "He taught me de maiden language all over."

Ellador: The women of Herland could not define themselves by men because there were none until Van and his friends arrived. We were able to develop ourselves fully because of this.

Alice: The only other woman I've met in this course who did not define herself through a man was Sula.

Ellador: Yes, but she was punished because of it. People in the Bottom hated and feared her. . . . I feel so lucky. Van is such an understanding, compassionate man. The only crime of which he is guilty is trying too hard to understand me and my homeland. He is my friend and companion. . . .

Medea: In our world, excuse me, in my world — I keep forgetting that my life takes place almost two thousand years before you were born — women were not equal to men. Women were told to accept their fate. . . . I orchestrated many of Jason's successes in life, yet he never acknowledged it.

Nora: Medea, my life takes place in the late nineteenth century and things haven't changed much. Women still have few privileges. Society tries to keep us uneducated. When we expose our intelligence, our sexuality is devalued.

Alice: Nora, that certainly hasn't changed in the late twentieth century.

Janie: In mah time de wimmen wuz no better den beasts of burden. Ah grew up spectin better treatment but Ah din't get it til Ah met Teacake. . . . In mah time, "de nigger woman was de mule uh de world."

Alice: Well, friends, women are in a very difficult situation. We are told by society that we can have it all yet no one gives us a clue as to how this is possible. Women who have children very often work eighteen hours a day. Exhausted, too tired to be creative and unable to find an outlet for their frustration, they wither away. . . . I have coped during periods of frustration by engaging in frantic activity in order not to think, but there is so much to think about.

On this last night, students assemble in groups, read their dialogues to one another, often to laughter and applause, and then each group selects one dialogue to read to the entire class. We do not finish on time, but no one leaves. When we do finally end, it is with the words of writers, ourselves included, in our ears.

NOTES

1. My early work in composition studies focused on the composing processes of underprepared college students (Perl, 1979). Later on, as a director of the New York City Writing Project, I spent many years in teachers' classrooms, documenting the ways they engaged in their work (Perl, 1983; Perl & Wilson, 1986). More recently, as I have taught teacher-research courses to graduate students, it dawned on me that my researcher's eye might usefully be turned upon my own work, making my own teaching the subject for inquiry and reflection.

2. With regard to method, the inquiry here proceeds by taking the act of teaching and all that occurs in the classroom as meaningful gestures, as "texts" that can be "read." What is involved here is a way of "looking into" teaching as a phenomenon and coming to understand it not by remaining outside, but rather by positioning oneself more fully within it. Attempting to "read" teaching in this way is an interpretive act (as any reading of any text may be), grounded in careful observation and documentation. The primary sources and the early outlines of the unfolding story include what students say and write, what the teacher says and writes, and how the class as a whole reflects on the journey it has taken. "Reading teaching" in this way leads one to draw out a new understanding of the classroom based on direct experience. This article is my attempt to "read" my own teaching and write about it in this manner. Others reading my story might, obviously, read it differently or hear in it stories I have yet to tell.

3. To speak of voice is controversial. Giroux (1990) emphasizes that teachers can no longer afford the naive conceit that people simply have a voice or are a voice, as if their voices are fixed, secure entities that stand apart from history, culture, gender, class, and race. While mindful that proclaiming the value of voice can be considered naive, I ask, how do students and teachers articulate and come to understand the conditions, constraints, and contradictions that bind them, if not by raising their voices? As a teacher of language and literature, I can do no less. For by calling on and calling out the voices of my students, I mean to speak for a pedagogy in which students and teacher alike may turn to shaping of their own, making the conditions they inherit the grounds on which to become authors in their own right, rather than merely being at the mercy of forces that shape them.

4. I have taught this course eight times and spent several years working on different versions of this article. The student writing I include comes from two different semesters; the classroom descriptions and dialogue come from the 1993–1994 fall semester, when I also kept a teaching journal to document the way the course was developing. All the students gave me permission to use their writing and at my request wrote brief descriptions of themselves to be used in this article. Other than standardizing the spelling for the sake of readability and selecting the excerpts, I did not alter their writing. The reading list varies slightly from year to year.

5. In composition courses, I continue to experiment with what Paulo Freire and Ira Shor (1987) call a "liberatory" stance toward curriculum, in which students and teacher create the materials of study together. In this setting, however, where most students have not read widely and the class time is limited to two hours a week, I choose to use our time for the discussion of texts rather than a debate, no matter how valuable, over reading selections. Of course, what we create together is our understanding and interpretation of texts.

6. It would be misleading to think that I create this syllabus entirely on my own. At Lehman's Institute for Literacy Studies, which houses the New York Writing Project and other school reform efforts, many colleagues and I consider the shaping of a syllabus to be a collaborative act. We spend many hours discussing books and approaches, students and classroom practice. The syllabus and the course described here represent one way work at the Institute continues to inform my teaching.

7. I first discovered literature logs, or "lit-logs," in 1981 in the classroom of Audre Allison, an eleventh-grade teacher in the Shoreham-Wading River school district in Shoreham, New York. Her classroom is described in Perl and Wilson (1986). Since that time, many teachers have invited students to write about their responses to readings and described their practices, providing teachers at all levels with a rich and growing literature, among them Kathleen Andrasick (1990), Nancie Atwell (1991), and Tom Newkirk (1984). Theories upon which such practices are based can be found in the work of David Bleich (1975), Norman Holland (1975, 1989), and Louise Rosenblatt (1938/1968, 1978, 1985). Two recent volumes also develop the concept of the transactional nature of reading: John Clifford (1991) and Edmund Farrell and James Squire (1990).

8. The lit-log samples are chosen to illustrate the range and depth of responses in the class. I have also chosen to focus on a few students whose names and writing can become recognizable to readers. I have collected hundreds of pages of such writing; the samples included here are quite typical and represent the kind of writing my students regularly produce in response to literature. I arrived at my descriptors for this writing (i.e., "tentative, angry, confused, celebratory, reflective") after reading lit-logs for many years and out of what might be called a teacher's intuitive knowledge of what students write. Above all, in selecting these samples, I have tried to illustrate how engaged students become with the readings and the different ways they allow the literature to open up perspectives on their lives.

9. Specifically, we read the following: excerpts from two books by Merlin Stone, *When God Was a Woman* (1976) and *Ancient Mirrors of Womanhood* (1991); chapter seven of Riane Eisler's *The Chalice and the Blade* (1987); chapter one of Christine Downing's *The Goddess: Mythological Issues of the Feminine* (1990); the final chapter of Eleanor Gadon's *The Once and Future Goddess* (1989); and chapter one of Starhawk's *The Spiral Dance* (1979). I also hand out a number of articles from a variety of journals.

REFERENCES

Andrasick, K. (1990). *Opening texts: Using writing to teach literature*. Portsmouth, NH: Heinemann.

Atwell, N. (1991). *Side by side: Essays on teaching to learn*. Portsmouth, NH: Heinemann.

Bleich, D. (1975). *Readings and feelings: An introduction to subjective criticism*. Urbana, IL: National Council of Teachers of English.

Britton, J. (1982). Shaping at the point of utterance. In G. Pradl (Ed.), *Prospect and restrospect: Selected essays of James Britton* (pp. 139–148). Portsmouth, NH: Boynton/Cook.

Clifford, J. (Ed.). (1991). *The experience of reading: Louise Rosenblatt and reader-response theory*. Portsmouth, NH: Boynton/Cook.

Downing, C. (1990). *The goddess: Mythological images of the feminine*. New York: Crossroad.

Eisler, R. (1987). *The chalice and the blade*. New York: Harper & Row.

Emecheta, B. (1987). *Second-class citizen*. New York: George Brazillier.

Euripides. (1988). Medea (P. Vellacott, Trans.). In *Medea and other plays* (pp. 17–61). New York: Penguin Books.

Farrell, E. J., & Squire, J. R. (Eds.). (1990). *Transactions with literature: A fifty-year perspective*. Urbana, IL: National Council of Teachers of English.

Freire, P., & Shor, I. (1987). *A pedagogy for liberation: Dialogues on transforming education*. South Hadley, MA: Bergin & Garvey.

Gadon, E. (1989). *The once and future goddess: A symbol for our time*. New York: Harper & Row.

Gilman, C. P. (1979). *Herland*. New York: Pantheon Books. (Original work published 1915)

Giroux, H. (1990). *Curriculum discourse as postmodernist critical practice*. Geelong, Australia: Deakin University Press.

Heilbrun, C. (1988). *Writing a woman's life*. New York: W. W. Norton.

Holland, N. N. (1975). *Five readers reading*. New Haven: Yale University Press.

Holland, N. N. (1989). *Poems in persons: An introduction to the psychoanalysis of literature*. New York: Columbia University Press.

Hurston, Z. N. (1978). *Their eyes were watching god*. Chicago: University of Illinois Press. (Original work published 1937)

Ibsen, H. (1966). A doll's house (M. Meyer, Trans.). In *Ghosts and three other plays* (pp. 1–102). New York: Anchor Books. (Original work published 1879)

Kingsolver, B. (1989). *The bean trees*. New York: Harper & Row.

Morrison, T. (1975). *Sula*. New York: Bantam.

Newkirk, T. (1984). Looking for trouble: A way to unmask our readings. *College English, 46*, 756–766.

Olsen, T. (1978). *Silences*. New York: Delacorte.

Perl, S. (1979). The composing processes of unskilled college writers. *Research in the Teaching of English, 4*, 317–336.

Perl, S. (1983). How teachers teach the writing process: Overview of an ethnographic research project. *Elementary School Journal, 84*, 19–24.

Perl, S., & Wilson, N. (1986). *Through teachers' eyes: Portraits of writing teachers at work*. Portsmouth, NH: Heineman.

Rosenblatt, L. (1968). *Literature as exploration*. New York: Noble & Noble. (Original work published 1938)

Rosenblatt, L. (1978). *The reader, the text, the poem: The transactional theory of the literary text*. Carbondale: Southern Illinois University Press.

Rosenblatt, L. (1985). Viewpoints: Transaction vs. interaction — A terminological rescue operation. *Research in the Teaching of English, 19*(1), 96–107.

Sophocles. (1986). Antigone (P. Roche, Trans.). In *The Oedipus plays of Sophocles* (pp. 161–210). New York: New American Library/Mentor.

Starhawk. (1979). *The spiral dance: A rebirth of the ancient religion of the great goddess*. New York: Harper & Row.

Stone, M. (1976). *When god was a woman*. New York: Harcourt Brace Jovanovich.

Stone, M. (1991). *Ancient mirrors of womanhood: A treasury of goddess and heroine lore from around the world*. Boston: Beacon Press.

Witherall, C., & Noddings, N. (Eds.). (1991). *Stories lives tell: Narrative and dialogue in education*. New York: Teachers College Press.

Composing, for me, occurs within a community of lively, challenging, and supportive voices. Those I thank for contributing to this article include my students in the Adult Degree Program at Lehman College, who graciously allowed me to use their writing; my colleagues in Lehman's Institute for Literacy Studies 1993–1994 Inquiry Group, who gave time and attention to an early draft of this article, especially Elaine Avidon and Cecelia Traugh; and Nancy Wilson and Richard Perl, who each read drafts with care and insight. Finally, I thank Arthur Egendorf, who collaborates with me on all of our life's work, from the reading and writing we do to the raising of our three children.

PART THREE

Theorizing about a
More Inclusive Pedagogy

A Dialogue:
Culture, Language, and Race

PAULO FREIRE
DONALDO P. MACEDO

The following is part of a dialogue that Donaldo Macedo and Paulo Freire had for over a decade. As it attempts to address criticisms of Freire's work along the the lines of gender and race, this dialogue not only challenges the frequent misinterpretations of his leading philosophical ideas by conservative and some liberal educators, but also embraces contemporary educational issues and discusses what it means to educate for critical citizenry in the ever-increasing multiracial and multicultural world of the twenty-first century.

MACEDO: In their attempt to cut the chains of oppressive educational practices, many North American educators blindly advocate the dialogical model, creating, in turn, a new form of methodological rigidity laced with benevolent oppression — all done under the guise of democracy with the sole excuse that it is for the students' own good. As educators, many of us have witnessed pedagogical contexts in which we are implicitly or explicitly required to speak, to talk about our experiences, as an act of liberation. We all have been at conferences where speakers have been chastised because they failed to locate themselves in history. In other words, the speakers failed to give primacy to their experiences in addressing issues of critical democracy. It does not matter that the speakers had important and insightful things to say. This is tantamount to dismissing Marx because he did not entrance us with his personal, lived experiences. Another form of rigidity manifested in these educational practices modeled on your leading ideas is the process in which teachers relinquish their authority to become what is called a facilitator. Becoming a facilitator signals, in the view of many educators, a democratization of power in the classroom. Can you speak about these issues and perhaps clarify them?

FREIRE: Donaldo, let me begin responding by categorically saying that I consider myself a teacher and always a teacher. I have never pretended to be a facilitator. What I

Harvard Educational Review   Vol. 65   No. 3   Fall 1995, 377–402

want to make clear also is in being a teacher, I always teach to facilitate. I cannot accept the notion of a facilitator who facilitates so as not to teach.

The true comprehension of dialogue must differentiate the role that only facilitates from the role that teaches. When teachers call themselves facilitators and not teachers, they become involved in a distortion of reality. To begin with, in de-emphasizing the teacher's power by claiming to be a facilitator, one is being less than truthful to the extent that the teacher turned facilitator maintains the power institutionally created in the position. That is, while facilitators may veil their power, at any moment they can exercise power as they wish. The facilitator still grades, still has certain control over the curriculum, and to deny these facts is to be disingenuous. I think what creates this need to be a facilitator is the confusion between authoritarianism and authority. What one cannot do in trying to divest of authoritarianism is relinquish one's authority as teacher. In fact, this does not really happen. Teachers maintain a certain level of authority through the depth and breadth of knowledge of the subject matter that they teach. The teacher who claims to be a facilitator and not a teacher is renouncing, for reasons unbeknownst to us, the task of teaching and, hence, the task of dialogue.

Another point worth making is the risk of perceiving facilitators as non-directive. I find this to be a deceitful discourse; that is, a discourse from the perspective of the dominant class. Only in this deceitful discourse can educators talk about a lack of direction in teaching. I do not think that there is real education without direction. To the extent that all educational practice brings with it its own transcendence, it presupposes an objective to be reached. Therefore, practice cannot be nondirective. There is no educational practice that does not point to an objective; this proves that the nature of educational practice has direction. The facilitator who claims that "since I respect students I cannot be directive, and since they are individuals deserving respect, they should determine their own direction," does not deny the directive nature of education that is independent of his own subjectivity. Rather, this facilitator denies himself or herself the pedagogical, political, and epistemological task of assuming the role of a subject of that directive practice. This facilitator refuses to convince his or her learners of what he or she thinks is just. This educator, then, ends up helping the power structure. To avoid reproducing the values of the power structure, the educator must always combat a laissez-faire pedagogy, no matter how progressive it may appear to be.

Authoritarian educators are correct, even though they are not always theoretically explicit, when they say that there is no education that is non-directive. I would not disagree with these educators; but, I would say that to claim to be a facilitator is authoritarian to the extent that the facilitators make their own objectives and dreams the directives that they give to learners in their educational practice. Facilitators are authoritarian because, as subjects of the educational practice, they reduce learners to objects of the directives they impose.

While educators divest of an authoritarian educational practice, they should avoid falling prey to a laissez-faire practice under the pretext of facilitating. On the contrary, a better way to proceed is to assume the authority as a teacher whose direction of education includes helping learners get involved in planning education, helping them create the critical capacity to consider and participate in the direction and dreams of education, rather than merely following blindly. The role of an educator who is pedagogically and critically radical is to avoid being indifferent, a characteristic of the facilitator who promotes a laissez-faire education. The radical educator has to be an active presence in educational practice. But, educators should never allow their active and curious presence to transform the learners' presence into a shadow of the educator's presence. Nor can educators be a shadow of their learners. The educator who dares to teach has to stimulate learners to live a critically conscious presence in the pedagogical and historical process.

MACEDO: I believe that to renounce the task of teaching under the guise of facilitating is part and parcel of a paternalistic ideology.

FREIRE: Exactly. The true issue behind the act of facilitating remains veiled because of its ideological nature. In the end, the facilitator is renouncing his or her duty to teach — which is a dialogical duty. In truth, the teacher turned facilitator rejects the fantastic work of placing an object as a mediator between him or her and the students. That is, the facilitator fails to assume his or her role as a dialogical educator who can illustrate the object of study. As a teacher, I have the responsibility to teach, and in order to teach, I always try to facilitate. In the first place, I am convinced that when we speak of dialogue and education, we are speaking, above all, about practices that enable us to approach the object of knowledge. In order to begin to understand the meaning of a dialogical practice, we have to put aside the simplistic understanding of dialogue as a mere technique. Dialogue does not represent a somewhat false path that I attempt to elaborate on and realize in the sense of involving the ingenuity of the other. On the contrary, dialogue characterizes an epistemological relationship. Thus, in this sense, dialogue is a way of knowing and should never be viewed as a mere tactic to involve students in a particular task. We have to make this point very clear. I engage in dialogue not necessarily because I like the other person. I engage in dialogue because I recognize the social and not merely the individualistic character of the process of knowing. In this sense, dialogue presents itself as an indispensable component of the process of both learning and knowing.

MACEDO: I could not agree with you more. I am reminded of how educators who embrace your notion of dialogue mechanistically reduce the epistemological relationship of dialogue to a vacuous, feel-good comfort zone. For instance, in a graduate class I taught last semester in which we discussed extensively an anti-racist pedagogy, many White teachers felt uncomfortable when the non-White students made connections between the assigned theoretical readings and their own lived experience with racism. In discussing her feelings of discomfort, a White teacher remarked that "we should spend at least three weeks getting to know each other so as to become friends before taking on sensitive issues such as racism." In other words, this White teacher failed to recognize her privileged position that enabled her to assume she can negotiate the terms under which classmates from oppressed groups can state their grievances. It is as if in order to be able to speak the truth about racism or to denounce racist structures, non-Whites must first befriend their White classmates. The inability of this White teacher to acknowledge her privileged position in demanding to negotiate her comfort zone before grievances against racism are made makes her unable to realize that, in most instances, certain groups such as African Americans are born and live always without any comfort zone, much less the privilege to assume they can negotiate the appropriate comfort zone within a graduate course.

FREIRE: All of this leads us to consider another dimension that is implicit, but not always clear, in relation to the concept of dialogue. That is to say, the dialogue about which we are now speaking, the dialogue that educators speak about, is not the same as the dialogue about a walk up the street, for example, which becomes no more than the object of mere conversation with friends in a bar. In this case, people are not necessarily engaged in a search for the delimitation of a knowable object. Here I am speaking with respect to dialogue in a strictly epistemological perspective. What then does dialogue require as a sine qua non condition?

MACEDO: If in this sense the object of knowledge is the fundamental goal, the dialogue as conversation about individuals' lived experiences does not truly constitute dialogue. In other words, the appropriation of the notion of dialogical teaching as a process of sharing experiences creates a situation in which teaching is reduced to a form of group therapy that focuses on the psychology of the individual. Although some educators may claim that this process creates a pedagogical comfort zone, in my view it does little beyond making the oppressed feel good about their own sense of victimization. Simply put, I do not think that the sharing of experiences should be understood in psychological terms only. It invariably requires a political and ideological analysis as well. That is, the sharing of experiences must always be understood within a social praxis that entails both reflection and political action. In short, dialogue as a process of learning and knowing must always involve a political project with the objective of dismantling oppressive structures and mechanisms prevalent both in education and society.

Part of the reason why many teachers who claim to be Freire-inspired end up promoting a laissez-faire, feel-good pedagogy is because many are only exposed to, or interpret, your leading ideas at the level of cliché. By this I mean that many professors who claim to be Freire-inspired present to their students a watered-down translation of your philosophical positions in the form of a lock-step methodology. Seldom do these professors require their students to read your work as a primary source and, in cases where they do read, let's say, *Pedagogy of the Oppressed,* they often have very little knowledge of other books that you have published. For example, I have been in many educational contexts throughout the country where students ask me, "Why is it that my professors are always talking about Freire and the dialogical method and yet they never ask us to read Freire?" This point was made poignant some time ago in a workshop when a teacher began the presentation of her project by saying, "My project is Freirean inspired. I'll be talking about Freire even though I haven't read his books yet." Assigning students secondary or tertiary sources is very common within education programs in the United States. The end result is that professors become translators of the primary source's leading ideas. In so doing, they elevate their status by introducing translated materials that students almost blindly consume as innovative and progressive and, in some instances, also begin to identify these translated ideas with the professor-translator and not with the original author. This occurs because students have been cut off from the primary source. On the other hand, the professor-translator assumes falsely that the primary source is too difficult for students, which points to the paternalistic notion that future teachers are not capable of engaging with complex, theoretical readings. This false assumption leads, unfortunately, to the total deskilling of teachers in that it kills epistemological curiosity.

FREIRE: You are absolutely correct. I think that your posture indicates clearly that you understand very well the difference between dialogue as a process of learning and knowing and dialogue as conversation that mechanically focuses on the individual's lived experience, which remains strictly within the psychological sphere.

MACEDO: In the United States, even many educators who like your work mistakenly transform your notion of dialogue into a method, thus losing sight of the fact that the fundamental goal of dialogical teaching is to create a process of learning and knowing that invariably involves theorizing about the experiences shared in the dialogue process. Unfortunately, some strands of critical pedagogy engage in an overdose of experiential celebration that offers a reductionist view of identity, leading Henry Giroux to point out that such pedagogy leaves identity and experience removed from the problematics of power, agency, and history. By overindulging in the legacy and importance of their respective voices and experiences, these educators often fail to move beyond a notion of difference structured in polarizing binarisms and uncritical appeals to the discourse of experience. I believe that it is for this reason that some of these educators invoke a romantic pedagogical mode that exoticizes discussing lived experiences as a process of coming to voice. At the same time, educators who misinterpret your notion of dialogical teaching also refuse to link experiences to the politics of culture and critical democracy, thus reducing their pedagogy to a form of middle-class narcissism. This creates, on the one hand, the transformation of dialogical teaching into a method invoking conversation that provides participants with a group therapy space for stating their grievances. On the other hand, it offers the teacher as facilitator a safe pedagogical zone to deal with his or her class guilt. It is a process that bell hooks characterizes as nauseating in that it brooks no dissent.

FREIRE: Yes, yes. In the end, what these educators are calling dialogical is a process that hides the true nature of dialogue as a process of learning and knowing. What you have described can provide certain dialogical moments, but, in general, it is a mere conversation overly focused on the individual and removed from the object of knowledge. Understanding dialogue as a process of learning and knowing establishes a previous requirement that always involves an epistemological curiosity about the very elements of the dialogue.

MACEDO: I agree; there has to be a curiosity about the object of knowledge. Otherwise, you end up with dialogue as conversation, where individual lived experiences are given primacy. I have been in many contexts where the over-celebration of one's own location and history often eclipses the possibility of engaging the object of knowledge by refusing to struggle directly, for instance, with the readings, particularly if these readings involve theory.

FREIRE: Yes. Curiosity about the object of knowledge and the willingness and openness to engage theoretical readings and discussions is fundamental. However, I am not suggesting an over-celebration of theory. We must not negate practice for the sake of theory. To do so would reduce theory to pure verbalism or intellectualism. By the same token, to negate theory for the sake of practice, as in the use of dialogue as conversation, is to run the risk of losing oneself in the disconnectedness of practice. It is for this reason that I never advocate either a theoretic elitism or a practice ungrounded in theory, but the unity between theory and practice. In order to achieve this unity, one must have an epistemological curiosity — a curiosity that is often missing in dialogue as conversation.

Returning to my original point, I would like to reiterate that human beings are, by nature, curious beings. They are ontologically curious. In order to be more rigorous, I would venture to say that curiosity is not a phenomenon exclusively human, but exclusively vital. That is, life is curious, without which life cannot survive. Curiosity is as fundamental to our survival as is pain. Without the ability to feel pain, and I am here referring to physical pain and not moral pain, we could possibly jump from a fourth-floor apartment without anticipating the consequences. The same would be true if we put our hands in fire. Pain represents one of the physical limitations on our practices. Thus, dialogue, as a process of learning and knowing, presupposes curiosity. It implies curiosity.

Teachers who engage in an educational practice without curiosity, allowing their students to avoid engagement with critical readings, are not involved in dialogue as a process of learning and knowing. They are involved, instead, in a conversation without the ability to turn the shared experiences and stories into knowledge. What I call epistemological curiosity is the readiness and eagerness of a conscious body that is open to the task of engaging an object of knowledge.

The other curiosity without which we could not live is what I call spontaneous curiosity. That is, along the lines of aesthetics, I may find myself before a beautiful tall building and I spontaneously exclaim its beauty. This curiosity does not have as its fundamental objective the apprehension and the understanding of the raison d'etre of this beauty. In this case, I am gratuitously curious.

As you pointed out earlier, Donaldo, one of the difficulties often confronted by an educator in assuming an epistemologically curious posture is that, at certain moments, the educator falls prey to the bureaucratization of the mind, becoming a pure methodologist. The bureaucratized educator is the one who assigns time slots for students to take turns speaking in a bureaucratized, if not vulgarized, democracy without any connection with the object of knowledge. In this case, the educator turned facilitator becomes mechanical, mechanizing the entire dialogue as a process of learning and knowing so as to make it a mechanical dialogue as conversation. In a bureaucratized dialogue as conversation, both students and teacher speak and speak, all convinced that they are engaged in a substantive educational practice just because they are all participating in an unknown bureaucratized discourse that is not connected to an object of knowledge. This pattern is not dialogical because you cannot have dialogue without a posture that is epistemologically curious. The educator who wants to be dialogical cannot relinquish his or her authority as a teacher, which requires epistemological curiosity, to become a facilitator who merely orchestrates the participation of students in pure verbalism.

MACEDO: This bureaucratized dialogical process orchestrated by the facilitator who falsely relinquishes his or her authority as teacher ends up being a process that gives rise to politics without content.

FREIRE: In my view, each class is a class through which both students and teachers engage in a search for the knowledge already obtained so they can adopt a dialogical posture as a response to their epistemological inquietude that forces the revision of what is already known so they can know it better. At the same time, it is not easy to be a dialogical teacher because it entails a lot of work. What is easy is to be a pure descriptivist.

MACEDO: You can also have the other extreme: A descriptive dialogue.

FREIRE: Of course you can.

MACEDO: This is what happens a lot with those teachers who relinquish their authority in order to become facilitators and, in the process, impose their bureaucratized dialogical method in a rigid manner that may require, for example, that all students must speak even if they choose not to do so. This rigidity transforms dialogical teaching, not into a search for the object of knowledge, but into a superficial form of democracy in which all students must forcefully participate in a turn-taking task of "blah-blah-blah." I have had the experience of students suggesting to me that I should monitor the length of time students talk in class in order to insure equal participation for all students. In most instances, these suggestions are raised without any concern that the turn-at-talk be related to the assigned readings. In fact, in many cases, students go through great lengths to over-emphasize the process of turn-taking while de-emphasizing the critical apprehension of the object of knowledge. In the end, their concerns attempt to reduce dialogue to a pure technique. I want to make it clear that in criticizing the mechanization of turn-at-talk I do not intend to ignore the voices that have been silenced by the inflexible, traditional method of lecturing. What is important to keep in mind is not to develop a context whereby the assignment of turn-taking to give voice to students results in a new form of rigid imposition. Instead, it is important to create pedagogical structures that foster critical engagement as the only way for the students to come to voice. The uncritical license to take equal turns speaking in a rigid fashion gives rise to a "blah-blah-blah" dialogue resulting in a form of silencing while speaking. Critical educators should avoid at all costs the blind embracing of approaches that pay lip-service to democracy and should always be open to multiple and varied approaches that will enhance the possibility for epistemological curiosity with the object of knowledge. The facile and uncritical acceptance of any methodology regardless of its progressive promise can easily be transformed into a new form of methodological rigidity that constitutes, in my view, a form of methodological terrorism. A vacuous dialogue for conversation only is pernicious to the extent that it deskills students by not creating pedagogical spaces for epistemological curiosity, critical consciousness, and agency, which is the only way through which one can transcend valorized experience to embrace new knowledge in order to universalize one's own experience.

FREIRE: Exactly. This is where dialogical teaching ceases to be a true process of learning and knowing to become, instead, pure formalism; everything but dialogue. It represents a process to bureaucratize the mind. The educator who is really dialogical has a tiring task to the extent that he or she has to 1) remain epistemologically curious, and 2) practice in a way that involves epistemological curiosity that facilitates his or her process of learning and knowing. The problem lies in the fact that students often have not sufficiently developed such habits. It is for this reason that many students end up reading only mechanically and can easily spend an entire semester doing so because they were not able to transcend the spontaneity of curiosity you spoke of earlier so as to engage the epistemological curiosity that involves methodological rigor. Students today find it difficult to engage in this type of educational rigor precisely because they are often not challenged to engage in a rigorous process of learning and knowing. The end result is that they often remain at the periphery of the object of knowledge. Their curiosity has not yet been awakened in the epistemological sense. It is for this reason that we now witness more and more a disequilibrium between chronological age and epistemological curiosity. In many cases, epistemological curiosity remains truncated, giving rise to students who are intellectually immature.

What dialogical educators must do is to maintain, on the one hand, their epistemological curiosity and, on the other hand, always attempt to increase their critical reflection in the process of creating pedagogical spaces where students become apprentices in the rigors of exploration. Without an increased level of epistemological curiosity and the necessary apprenticeship in a new body of knowledge, students cannot truly be engaged in a dialogue.

MACEDO: I think this is a very important point that needs to be highlighted. That is, when students lack both the necessary epistemological curiosity and a certain conviviality with the object of knowledge under study, it is difficult to create conditions that increase their epistemological curiosity so as to develop the necessary intellectual tools that will enable them to apprehend and comprehend the object of knowledge. If students are not able to transform their lived experiences into knowledge and to use the already acquired knowledge as a process to unveil new knowledge, they will never be able to participate rigorously in a dialogue as a process of learning and knowing. In truth, how can you dialogue without any prior apprenticeship with the object of knowledge and without any epistemological curiosity? For example, how can you dialogue about linguistics if the teacher refuses to create the pedagogical conditions that will apprentice students into the new body of knowledge? By this I do not mean that the apprenticeship process should be reduced to the authoritarian tradition of lecturing without student input and discussion.

FREIRE: As you can see, Donaldo, my pedagogical posture always implies rigor, and never a laissez-faire dialogue as conversation orchestrated by facilitators. A mere appearance does not transform itself into the concreteness and substanticity of the actual object. Then, you cannot realistically have a dialogue by simply thinking that dialogue is a kind of verbal ping-pong about one's historical location and lived experiences.

MACEDO: Unfortunately, that is what happens too frequently.

FREIRE: The problem that is posed concerning the question of location is important. I do not think that anyone can seriously engage in a search for new knowledge without using his or her point of view and historical location as a point of departure. This does not mean, however, that I should remain frozen in that location, but, rather, that I should seek to universalize it. The task of epistemological curiosity is to help students gain a rigorous understanding of their historical location so they can turn this understanding into knowledge, thus transcending and universalizing it. If one remains stuck in his or her historical location, he or she runs the risk of fossilizing his or her world disconnected from other realities.

MACEDO: I agree. We need to avoid making our historical, locational experience into barriers that impede the universalization of the object of knowledge. This object of knowledge needs to be generalizable.

Paulo, let me turn to criticism of your pedagogical proposals. You are criticized not only by conservative educators for what they characterize as your "radical ties," but some liberals also feel uncomfortable with your critical perspectives. For example, Gregory Jay and Gerald Graff have argued that your proposal, in *Pedagogy of the Oppressed,* to move students toward "a critical perception of the world" — which "implies a correct method of approaching reality" so they can get "a comprehension of total reality" — assumes that you already know the identity of the oppressed. As Jay and Graff point out, "Freire assumes that we know from the outset the identity of the `oppressed' and their `oppressors.' Who the oppressors and the oppressed are is conceived not as an open question that teachers and students might disagree about, but as a given of Freirean pedagogy."[1] Can you address these criticisms?

FREIRE: Over the years I have been the object of much criticism concerning my pedagogical proposals. The criticism that you just mentioned was made more frequently during the seventies than today. However, as you have attested, the same criticism appears and reappears every so often. In my recent book, *Pedagogy of Hope,* published in 1994, I address these criticisms by making my pedagogical position very clear so as to leave less room for individuals like Gerald Graff not only to misread and misinterpret my philosophical ideas concerning a pedagogy of the oppressed, but also to reflect critically on some of the concrete pedagogical proposals I have been making over the years. The problem with some of these individuals is that they have read my work fragmentally. That is, they continually refer to my book, *Pedagogy of the Oppressed,* which I published over twenty years ago, without making any reference to my later works, including *Reading the Word and the World,* which I coauthored with you, *The Politics of Education,* and *Pedagogy of Hope,* among others. Critics often treat my work as if I had only published *Pedagogy of the Oppressed* and that I have not done anything for the past twenty years.

MACEDO: I agree with you. Even many progressive educators who have embraced and been inspired by your work have only read it fragmentally. Thus, they also, sometimes, fall prey to misinterpretations of your ideas.

FREIRE: But, Donaldo, I am surprised that someone like Gerald Graff, who I think considers himself an honest intellectual, would have difficulty identifying oppressive conditions and fall prey to a form of misguided relativism. I do not think it is difficult to identify the thirty-three million people in my country who are in constant danger of dying of hunger as belonging to the oppressed group. Even in the very rich United States, as my good friend Jonathan Kozol so succinctly shows in his book *Savage Inequalities,* it is not very difficult to identify oppressed people. For example, would Graff have difficulty identifying the oppressive conditions in East St. Louis, as documented by my friend Kozol?

> East St. Louis . . . has some of the sickest children in America. Of 66 cities in Illinois, East St. Louis ranks first in fetal death, first in premature birth, and third in infant death. Among negative factors listed by the city's health directory are the sewage running in the streets, air that has been fouled by the local plants, the high lead levels noted in the soil, poverty, lack of education, crime, dilapidated housing, insufficient health care, unemployment.[2]

If Graff has difficulty identifying the oppressive conditions described above, he fits very well within the framework presented in your new book, *Literacies of Power: What Americans Are Not Allowed to Know,* which characterizes intellectuals who engage in the social construction of not seeing. As you point out, if you cannot see it, you cannot name it, which results in what you have categorized as a "discourse of not naming it," proving the old proverb, "The eyes do not see; they only record while the mind sees."

MACEDO: This is the real issue. To the extent that the mind can be ideologically controlled, it filters in order to transform what the eyes record, as is perhaps the case with Gerald Graff's reluctance to identify the oppressed and their oppressors. Graff's relativistic posture concerning the identity of the oppressed versus the oppressor eclipses the possibility for students to critically understand "the multiple experiences of identity by both historicizing it and revealing its partiality and incompleteness [and that] its limits are realized in the material nature of experience as it marks the body through the specificity of place, space and history."[3] This is very much in line with John Fiske's notion that "there is a material experience of homelessness that is of a different order from the cultural meanings of homelessness . . . but the boundary between the two cannot be drawn sharply. Material conditions are inescapably saturated with culture and, equally, cultural conditions are inescapably experienced as material."[4] As suggested by Fiske, the ideological and material conditions that produce oppression cannot be hidden blindly by the refusal to name the oppressor. The existence of oppression does not depend on the refusal or willingness to simply name it. Such oppression instead must be seen as part of the politics of representation that engages a particular project, and for you, Paulo, is defined by the ongoing struggle to promote and expand democratic social relations. The virtue of a radical democratic project is that it provides an ethical referent both for engaging in a critique of its own authority and as part of a wider expression of authority. In my view, what needs to be pedagogically engaged is not merely who is really oppressed, but the social, economic, and cultural conditions that lead to the creation of savage inequalities in East St. Louis and in the human misery of ghetto life, where African Americans and other oppressed groups materially experience the loss of their dignity, the denial of human citizenship, and, in many cases, outright violent and criminal acts committed by those institutions responsible for implementing the law, as we vividly witnessed in the beating of Rodney King by members of the Los Angeles police force. Those who materially experience oppression have little difficulty identifying their oppressors. The adoption of a relativistic posture concerning the oppressed and the oppressor not only points to Graff's privileged position that enables him to intellectualize oppression so as to make it abstract, but is also not unlike those individuals who attempt to rewrite the history of oppression as mere narratives. I believe that to be suspicious of one's own politics should not be an excuse to attempt to understand and address how power can work to oppress and exploit.

FREIRE: The issues that you just raised, Donaldo, are at the heart of the critical posture I call for in my educational proposals. As you can see, the criticism that my work proposes to know a priori what the oppressed peasants should know and what is best for them indicates that the individuals who critique me were, at best, able to read *Pedagogy of the Oppressed* mechanistically, thus superficially, and, at worst, they misread my book. Let me try to address some of the issues that they have raised, even though I may repeat what I clearly discussed in the *Pedagogy of Hope*.

As usual, I never deal with themes directly. I always do what I have been referring to as an epistemological approximation to the object of knowledge. I sometimes leave the linearity of my inquiry, so as to develop a global grasp of the object of knowledge in order to apprehend the total essence before I can learn it. Now, for example, in attempting to put myself critically in front of Graff's critique of my work, I would begin by saying that as men and women we are cultural beings endowed with the option to choose. We are also cultural beings who can make our own decisions and, for this reason, we are cultural beings endowed with the ability to rupture. It is impossible to decide without rupturing. It is not possible to opt without choosing one over the other.

Then, we can conclude that we are innately programmed to choose, to make decisions, and to take positions in the world. We are born programmed to learn. Thus, we are programmed to learn, to teach, and, in doing so, our human agency cannot be reduced to any form of determinism. Because we are programmed to learn, to know, and to teach, we are born also with an undefined curiosity. It is for this reason that I consider the death of curiosity that sometimes happens in schools, a form of ontological violence, because curiosity is part of human ontology.

If what I have just said is true, why should the educator hide his or her option, including his or her political position? On the other hand, it is not the role of the educator to impose his or her position. This is what has been said of my work. I have never advanced any pedagogical proposal that called for teachers to impose their political perspective. On the contrary, I have always fought against any form of imposition, any form of anti-democratic practice, and any form of social injustice. However, in doing so, I have never had the need to hide or the fear of hiding my political beliefs. Making my beliefs bare does not constitute, in my view, a form of imposition.

MACEDO: I agree. I think the courage to make your beliefs known, particularly your political ideals, does not point to any form of imposition. In my view, it is plain honesty. Unfortunately, we are living in a culture, particularly an academic culture, that requires courage in order to speak the truth. Our conviviality with the lie is not only rewarded, but is astutely vieled under the guise of objectivity, a form of lie in itself. What we need to understand is that the very claim of objectivity necessarily involves a dimension of subjectivity. Thus, it is dialectical.

FREIRE: Certainly. I think what constitutes an imposition is to engage with the oppressed educationally without providing them with the critical tools to understand their world, the tools that they were denied by not giving them access to education, to literacy, so they can read the word as well as the world. The educator who pretends to be objective and, in doing so, denies the oppressed the pedagogical space to develop a critical posture towards the world, particularly the world that has reduced them to a half-human object, exploited and dehumanized, is an educator who is complicit with the ideology of the oppressor. If objectivity means omission of historical truths that may prevent the oppressed from critically exercising their innate ability to opt, to decide, then objectivity and non-directivity in education is, in some real sense, a form of imposition. In other words, by not engaging the oppressed critically so they can understand the veiled ideology that continually dehumanizes them, the educator is in complicity with the oppressor. To do so is to be indifferent towards the plight of the oppressed who have been violated in terms of their capacity to opt and to decide. In the face of the denial to educate the oppressed and the ever-present violence perpetrated against their humanity, to not create pedagogical structures where the educator can make it feasible for the oppressed to retake what has been denied them, including the ability to think critically and the option to act on their world as subjects of history and not objects, constitutes a veiled imposition of the oppressive conditions that have been responsible for their subordinated status to begin with. For example, illiteracy is not something that the peasants in Brazil created for themselves. It was imposed on them so as to deny them the ability to understand their historical conditions. This imposed illiteracy is, in my view, a violence against the peasants' human rights. To work with peasants in order to put an end to this violence and crime against humanity is not an imposition, but an act of courage that should lead to liberation.

If we are cultural beings with the capacity to learn and to opt, to discover knowledge, then we create because we discover, since, for human beings, to discover is to create. If all of this is true, the education of human beings should never be restricted to a true intellectual training that limits itself to merely exposing students to what Graff calls a pedagogy of conflict — as if all existed on an equal basis — without creating conditions that will enable students to understand the nature of the ideologies that created the conflicts in the first place. But, even if education were merely an intellectual training, it would have to exert itself so as to enable people to become conscious beings, conscious of their world and, for this reason, it could never remain at a pure technical posture. Even if education were purely technical intellectual training it would eventually transcend the pure training and respond to our innate programming to learn and to know and to be curious. What technical training sometimes does, and with some success, is to constrain our human nature as knowing beings. Thus, education involves a globalizing practice. It is a practice that does not only involve technical knowledge, but also world knowledge. Therefore, the oppressed need to develop the necessary critical tools that will enable them to read their world so they can apprehend the globality of their reality and choose what world they want for themselves.

MACEDO: This is precisely what some of your critics claim, that you propose to know what world the oppressed want to be in. What if the oppressed do not want the world that you may have in mind for them?

FREIRE: I think that those who say this about me and my pedagogical proposals have totally misunderstood my work. In the first place, I cannot propose to the oppressed the world that I believe would be best for them. Obviously I can't. On the other hand, I cannot hide from the oppressed what I think about their situation as oppressed people nor refuse to talk with them about ways in which their lives could be improved. I have, as an educator, the right to think and dream about a world that is less oppressive and more humane toward the oppressed, just as the poet has the right to write and to dream about a utopian world. This does not mean that I am going to incarnate Picasso's art, but he had all the right to see the world the way he saw it. I would be imposing if I had the power to tell the oppressed the following: you either opt for liberation or be killed. What I do in my pedagogical proposal is to present them with possibilities to opt for an alternative. Should they reject the choice to opt for an alternative, then there is little that I can do as an educator. Imposition is when one willfully refuses to present alternatives and multiple points of reference.

MACEDO: That is what the conservative right does, in fact, by denying students opportunities to juxtapose historical events and facts so as to relate these events in order to have a global reading of reality.

FREIRE: Exactly. Conservative educators have the right to propose their view of the world. And as a student, I also have the right to reject this conservative position. What educators cannot do is to impose their view. What educators must do is to never fail to debate various positions without imposing any. Then, any pedagogical proposal is to challenge students around various hypotheses. However, these proposals must be dealt with from a concrete reality. Without anchoring these hypotheses in a concrete reality, the educator runs the risk of erasing the framework within which the tools for critical understanding of reality can be developed. For example, how can I teach peasants in Brazil without helping them understand the reasons why thirty-three million of them are dying of hunger? What I would have to tell these thirty-three million peasants is that to die from hunger is not a predetermined destiny. I would have to share with them that to die from hunger is a social anomaly. It is not a biological issue. It is a crime that is practiced by the capitalist economy of Brazil against thirty-three million peasants. I need to also share with them that the Brazilian economy is not an autonomous entity. It is a social production, a social production that is amoral and diabolical and should be considered a crime against humanity. What I cannot do as a teacher is to tell them not to discuss hunger but to think of it only as a phenomenon. I think teaching peasants how to read the word hunger and to look it up in the dictionary is not sufficient. They also need to know the reasons behind their experience of hunger. It is not sufficient only to discuss hunger. The peasants need also to understand those ideological elements that generate and maintain the hunger that is killing them and their children daily. As they study and discuss the raison d'etre of hunger, they will begin to see the asymmetrical social and economic distribution of wealth that contributes to their misery.

MACEDO: If you don't mind, let me interrupt you. What if these peasants do not want to know the reasons behind hunger and the asymmetrical distribution of wealth? Your insistence on this form of analysis may be viewed as an imposition.

FREIRE: I think that the issue is not purely pedagogical. It requires an ethical posture. I would ask the educator who criticizes my pedagogy as a form of imposition the following: If one day after class a student waits and, after all the other students leave, approaches the teacher and says, "I am thinking of committing suicide right here in front of you. I think I am going to kill myself now," does the teacher allow the student to kill himself because it is his wish to do so, or does he try to intervene ethically to try to prevent a tragedy? As you see, Donaldo, by not intervening so as not to impose, the teacher commits an ethical error. I think it is an ethical duty for educators to intervene in challenging students to critically engage with their world so they can act upon it and on it. I do not accept the present philosophical posture in which truth is relative and lies and truths are merely narratives. They have the right to say so. They also have the right to say, as some thinkers have been saying, that with the fall of communism we have reached the end of history. They have all the right to propose what they want to propose, as I also have the right to reject their proposals. I would have to point out that history continues, and I cannot remain silent before an error. By the same token, if a student wants to kill himself in front of me in my class,

I cannot remain neutral. I must intervene, as I must intervene in teaching the peasants that their hunger is socially constructed and work with them to help identify those responsible for this social construction, which is, in my view, a crime against humanity.

MACEDO: I agree with the need to intervene, not only pedagogically but also ethically. However, before any intervention, an educator must have political clarity — a posture that makes many liberals like Graff very uncomfortable to the degree that he considers "Radical educational theorists like [you], Henry Giroux, and Stanley Aronowitz . . . [as having a] tunnel-vision style of . . . writing . . . which speaks of but never to those who oppose its premises."[5] The assumption that you, Giroux, and Aronowitz engage in a "tunnel-vision style of . . . writing" is not only false, but also points to a distorted notion that there is an a priori agreed upon style of writing that is monolithic, available to all, and "free of jargon." This blind and facile call for writing clarity represents a pernicious mechanism used by academic liberals who suffocate discourses different from their own. Such a call often ignores how language is being used to make social inequality invisible. It also assumes that the only way to deconstruct ideologies of oppression is through a discourse that involves what these academics characterize as a language of clarity.

When I was working with you on the book *Literacy: Reading the Word and the World,* I asked a colleague who I considered to be politically progressive and to have a keen understanding of your work to read the manuscript. Yet, during a discussion we had of our book, she asked me, a bit irritably, "Why do you and Paulo insist on using this Marxist jargon? Many readers who may enjoy reading Paulo may be put off by the jargon." I was at first taken aback, but proceeded to explain calmly to her that the equation of Marxism with jargon did not fully capture the richness of your analysis. In fact, I reminded her that your language was the only means through which you could have done justice to the complexity of the various concepts dealing with oppression. For one thing, I reminded her, "Imagine that instead of writing the *Pedagogy of the Oppressed* you had written the *Pedagogy of the Disenfranchised.*" The first title utilized a discourse that names the oppressor, whereas the second fails to do so. If you have "oppressed," you must have "oppressor." What would be the counterpart of disenfranchised? The *Pedagogy of the Disenfranchised* dislodges the agent of the action while leaving in doubt who bears the responsibility for such action. This leaves the ground wide open for blaming the victim of disenfranchisement for his or her own disenfranchisement. This example is a clear case in which the object of oppression can also be understood as the subject of oppression. Language such as this distorts reality.

And yet, mainstream academics like Graff seldom object to these linguistic distortions that disfigure reality. I seldom hear academics on a crusade for "language clarity" equate mainstream terms such as "disenfranchised" or "ethnic cleansing," for example, to jargon status. On the one hand, they readily accept "ethnic cleansing," a euphemism for genocide, while, on the other hand, they will, with certain automatism, point to the jargon quality of terms such as "oppression," "subordination," and "praxis." If we were to deconstruct the term "ethnic cleansing" we would see that it prevents us from becoming horrified by Serbian brutality and horrendous crimes against Bosnian Muslims. The mass killing of women, children, and the elderly and the rape of women and girls as young as five years old take on the positive attribute of "cleansing," which leads us to conjure a reality of "purification" of the ethnic "filth" ascribed to Bosnian Muslims, in particular, and to Muslims the world over, in general.

I also seldom heard any real protest from these same academics who want "language clarity" when, during the Gulf War, the horrific blood bath of the battlefield became a "theater of operation," and the violent killing of over one hundred thousand Iraqis, including innocent women, children, and the elderly by our "smart bombs," was sanitized into a technical term, "collateral damage." I can go on and on giving such examples to point out how academics who argue for language clarity not only seldom object to language that obfuscates reality, but often use the same language as part of the general acceptance that the "standard" discourse is a given and should remain unproblematic. Although these academics accept the dominant standard discourse, they aggressively object to any discourse that both fractures the dominant language and bares the veiled reality in order to name it. Thus, a discourse that names it becomes, in their view, imprecise and unclear, and wholesale euphemisms such as "disadvantaged," "disenfranchised," "educational mortality," "theater of operation," "collateral damage," and "ethnic cleansing" remain unchallenged since they are part of the dominant social construction of images that are treated as unproblematic and clear.

I am often amazed to hear academics complain about the complexity of a particular discourse because of its alleged lack of clarity. It is as if they have assumed that there is a monodiscourse that is characterized by its clarity and is also equally available to all. If one begins to probe the issue of clarity, we soon realize that it is class specific, thus favoring those of that class in the meaning-making process.

The following two examples will bring the point home: Henry Giroux and I gave a speech at Massassoit Community College in Massachusetts to approximately three hundred unwed mothers who were part of a GED program. The director of this program later informed us that most of the students were considered functionally illiterate. After Henry's speech, during the question and answer period, a woman got up and eloquently said, "Professor Giroux, all my life I have felt the things you talked about. I just didn't have a language to express what I have felt. Today I have come to realize that I do have a language. Thank you." And you, Paulo, told me this story of what happened to you at the time you were preparing the English translation of *Pedagogy of the Oppressed*. Remember, you gave an African American student at Harvard a chapter of the book to read to see how she would receive it. A few days later, when you asked the woman if she had read it, she enthusiastically responded, "Yes. Not only did I read it, but I gave it to my sixteen-year-old son to read. He read the whole chapter that night and in the morning said, `I want to meet the man who wrote this. He is talking about me.'" The question that I have for all those "highly literate" academics who find Giroux's and your discourse so difficult to understand is, Why is it that a sixteen-year-old boy and a poor, "semiliterate" woman could so easily understand and connect with the complexity of both Giroux's and your language and ideas, and the academics, who are the most literate, find the language incomprehensible?

I believe that the answer has little to do with language and everything to do with ideology. That is, people often identify with representations that they are either comfortable with or that help deepen their understanding of themselves. The call for language clarity is an ideological issue, not merely a linguistic one. The sixteen-year-old and the semiliterate poor woman could readily connect with your ideology, whereas the highly literate academics are "put off" by some dimensions of the same ideology. It is, perhaps, for this reason that a university professor I know failed to include your work in a graduate course on literacy she taught. When I raised the issue with her, she explained that students often find your writing too difficult and cumbersome. It could also be the reason why although the Divinity School at Harvard University offers a course entitled "Education for Liberation," where students study you and James Cone extensively, no such opportunities are available at Harvard's School of Education.

For me, the mundane call for language simplicity and clarity represents yet another mechanism to dismiss the complexity of theoretical issues, particularly if these theoretical constructs interrogate the prevailing dominant ideology. It is for this very reason that Gayatri Spivak correctly pointed out that the call for "plain prose cheats." I would go a step further and say, "The call for plain prose not only cheats, it also bleaches."

For me, it is not only plain prose that bleaches. Graff's pedagogy of "teaching the conflict" also bleaches to the extent that it robs students of the opportunity to access the critical discourses that will enable them not only to deconstruct the colonial and hegemonic paradigms, but will also help them realize that one cannot teach the conflict as if, all of a sudden, it fell from the sky. The conflict must be anchored in those competing histories and ideologies that generated the conflict in the first place. David Goldberg captures this problem when he argues that Graff's suggestion

> presupposes that educators — even the humanists of Graff's address — occupy a neutral position, or at least can suspend their prejudices, in presenting the conflicts, and that the conflicts are fixed and immobile. One cannot teach the conflicts (or anything else, for that matter) by assuming this neutral "view from nowhere," for it is no view at all. In other words, the Assumption of a View from Nowhere is the projection of local values as neutrally universal ones, the globalizing of ethnocentric values, as Stam and Shohat put it.[6]

The problem with the teaching of the conflict is that the only referent for engaging authority is a methodological one. As a result, Graff demeans the ability of oppressed people to name their oppression as a pedagogical necessity and, at the same time, he dismisses the politics of pedagogy that "could empower `minorities' and build on privileged students' minimal experience of otherization to help them imagine alternative subject positions and divergent social designs."[7]

FREIRE: As you can see, Donaldo, in criticizing my educational proposal as being too directive, these educators are also directive. There is no neutral education. All education is directive.

MACEDO: Paulo, if you don't mind, I would like to turn at this point to what I believe to be one of the most pressing educational challenges we face as we approach the end of this century. I would like to turn to the issue of multiculturalism. You mentioned to me a talk you gave in Jamaica where you stressed the need to find unity in diversity. How do you propose to achieve this noble goal when multicultural conflicts are intensifying everywhere?

FREIRE: A very first step is to understand the nature of multicultural coexistence so as to minimize the glaring ignorance of the cultural other. Part of this understanding implies a thorough understanding of the history that engenders these cultural differences. We need to understand that: a) there are intercultural differences that exist due to the presence of such factors as class, race, and gender and, as an extension of these, you have national differences; and b) these differences generate ideologies that, on the one hand, support discriminatory practices and, on the other hand, create resistance.

The culture that is discriminated against does not generate the discriminatory ideology. Discrimination is generally generated by the hegemonic culture. The discriminated culture may give rise to an ideology of resistance that, as a function of its experience with struggle, adopts cultural behavior patterns that are more or less pacifist. In other instances, resistance is manifested in rebellious forms that are more or less indiscriminately violent. However, sometimes resistance emerges as a critical reflection leading toward the re-creation of the world. There is an important point that needs to be underlined: to the extent that these relations between these ideologies are dialectical, they interpenetrate each other. These relations do not take place in pure form and they can change from person to person. For example, I can be a man as I am and not necessarily be a *machista.* I can be Black, but in defending my economic interests, I might become complicit with White discrimination.

MACEDO: This is absolutely correct: Clarence Thomas, President Bush's Supreme Court appointee, represents an example of the interface between class and race ideologies par excellence. In his case, race is not a guarantee that the interests of millions of oppressed African Americans who have not yet broken loose from the yoke of White racism will be protected. Clarence Thomas's class interests override his race position. Thus, we cannot lump the many factors that cut across cultural difference into one monolithic cultural entity.

FREIRE: It is impossible to understand these differences without an analysis of ideologies and their relations between power and lack of power. These ideologies, whether discriminatory or resistant, embody themselves in special forms of social or individual behavior that vary from context to context. These ideologies express themselves in language — in the syntax and the semantics — and also in concrete forms of acting, of choosing, of valuing, of dressing, and even in the way one says hello on the street. These relations are dialectical. The level of these relations, their contents, their maximum dose of power revealed in the superior air one demonstrates, the distance, the coldness with which those in power treat those without power, the greater or lesser degree of accommodation or rebellion with which the dominated people respond to oppression — all of these are fundamental in the sense of overcoming the discriminatory ideologies so we can live in utopia; no more discrimination, no more rebelliousness or accommodation, but Unity in Diversity.

It is impossible to think, however, of overcoming oppression, discrimination, passivity, or pure rebellion without first acquiring a critical comprehension of history in which these intercultural relations take place in a dialectical form. Thus, they are contradictory and part of a historical process. Second, we cannot think of overcoming oppression without political pedagogical projects that point to the transformation or the reinvention of the world.

Let's speak a little about the first question, the comprehension of the history that we have. As historical beings, our actions are not merely historical, but also are historically conditioned. Sometimes, without wanting to, in acting we are consciously clear with respect to the conception of history that defines us. Hence, I recognize the importance of discussions in courses of teacher preparation concerning the different ways we comprehend history that makes us as we make it.

Let's talk succinctly of some different ways we reflect on our presence in the world and in which we find ourselves. One way of seeing ourselves is as spiritual beings, endowed with reason and the ability to make judgements, capable of distinguishing between good and bad, marked by original sin, thus needing to avoid at all costs falling into sin. From this perspective, falling into sin is viewed as always being preceded by strong temptations and the search for the road to salvation. Here sin and its negation become such that the former signals absolute weakness and the latter a facile cry of victory, in which human existence, reduced to this struggle, ends up almost losing itself in the fear of freedom or in the Puritanical hypocrisy that is a form of staying with the ugliness and rejecting the beauty of purity. History, in truth, is the history of the search for the beauty of purity, the salvation of the soul through the escape from sin. The prayers, the penitences, and promises are the principal arms and fundamental methods of action for those who idealistically experiment with this conception of history. Liberation theology signifies a radical rupture with this magical-mystical religiosity discussed above and, by putting its roots in the concrete context of experiences of women and men, God's people, it speaks of another comprehension of history that is, in reality, made by us. According to this interpretation of history, God is a presence. However, his presence does not prevent people from making their own history. On the contrary, God pushes people not only to make history, but to do so without negating the rights of others just because they are different from us.

With relation to the future, I would like to highlight two other comprehensions of history. Both are immobilizing and deterministic. The first has in the future a mere repetition of the present. In general, this is how the dominant class thinks. The tomorrow for them is always their present, as dominance is reproduced only with adverbial alterations. There is no place in this historical conception for a substantive overcoming of racial, sexual, linguistic, and cultural discrimination.

Blacks continue to be considered inferior, but now they can sit anywhere on the bus. . . . Latin Americans are good people, but they are not practical. . . . Maria is an excellent young woman; she is Black *but* she is intelligent. . . . In the three examples, the adversative co-function *but* is impregnated with ideology that is authoritarianly racist and discriminatory.

Another conception of history is, just as much as the others, at very least conditioned by practices regardless of the area. The cultural, educational, and economic relations among nations, and the environmental, scientific, technological, artistic, and communication areas reduce the tomorrow to a given fact. The future is predetermined, a type of fate, of destiny. The future is not problematic. On the contrary, it is unyielding. The dialectic that this vision of history reclaims, and has its origin in a certain Marxist dogmatism, is the domesticated dialectics. We know synthesis before we experience the dialectical collision between thesis and antithesis.

Another way of understanding history is to submit it to the caprice of individual will. The individual, from whom the social is dependent, is the subject of history. His or her conscience is the arbitrary maker of history. For this reason, the better education shapes individuals, that much better are their hearts, that much more will they who are full of beauty make the ugly world become beautiful. According to this vision of history, the role of women and men in the world is to take care of their hearts, leaving out, untouched, the social structures.

I see history exactly as do the liberation theologians, among whom I feel very good, and am in total disagreement with the other comprehensions of history I have discussed. For me, history represents a time of possibilities and not determinism. And if it is a time of possibilities, the first consequence that comes to the fore is that history does not only exist, but also requires freedom. To struggle for freedom is possible when we insert ourselves in history so as to make ourselves equally possible. Instead of being the constant persecutor of sin in order to be saved, we need to view history as possibility so we can both liberate and save ourselves. This is possible only through a historical perspective in which men and women are capable of assuming themselves, as both objects and subjects of history, capable of reinventing the world in an ethical and aesthetic mold beyond the cultural patterns that exist. This makes sense when we discuss communication as a new phase of continuous change and innovation. This, then, necessitates the recognition of the political nature of this struggle.

To think of history as possibility is to recognize education as possibility. It is to recognize that if education cannot do everything, it can achieve some things. Its strength, as I usually say, resides in its weakness. One of our challenges as educators is to discover what historically is possible in the sense of contributing toward the transformation of the world, giving rise to a world that is rounder, less angular, more humane, and in which one prepares the materialization of the great Utopia: Unity in Diversity.

MACEDO: After your public lecture at Harvard University in November of 1994, an African American woman talked impatiently to me inquiring why it is that your work on liberation struggles does not ever address the race issue in general, and the African American plight in particular. Can you address this criticism and attempt to clarify how your pedagogy takes on the role of race in liberation struggles?

FREIRE: In the first place, when I wrote the *Pedagogy of the Oppressed,* I tried to understand and analyze the phenomenon of oppression with respect to its social, existential, and individual tendencies. In doing so, I did not focus specifically on oppression marked by specificities such as color, gender, race, and so forth. I was extremely more preoccupied with the oppressed as a social class. But this, in my view, does not at all mean that I was ignoring the racial oppression that I have denounced always and struggled against even as a child. My mother used to tell me that when I was a child, I used to react aggressively, not physically, but linguistically, against any manifestation of racial discrimination. Throughout my life, I have worked against all forms of racial oppression, which is in keeping with my desire and need to maintain coherence with my political posture. I could not write on the defense of the oppressed while being a racist, just as I could not be a *machista* either.

In the second place, I would like to point out that today I have spoken and written a great deal about the question of race in my deep quest to fight against any form of discrimination. You need to keep in mind that my work is not limited to the *Pedagogy of the Oppressed,* and that all my writings are not available in English. It is exactly because of my growing awareness over the years concerning the specificities of oppression along the lines of language, race, gender, and ethnicity that I have been defending the fundamental thesis of Unity in Diversity, so that the various oppressed groups can become more effective in their collective struggle against all forms of oppression. To the extent that each specificity of oppression contains itself within its historical location and accepts the profile that was created by the oppressor, it becomes that much more difficult to launch an effective fight that will lead to victory. For example, when the oppressors speak of the minorities, in this process they hide the basic element of oppression. The label "minority" distorts and falsifies the reality if we keep in mind that the so-called minorities actually constitute the majority, while the oppressors generally represent the dominant ideology of a minority.

MACEDO: This is how language is used to distort reality so as to make social discrimination invisible. The same ideological mechanisms operate with the label *people of color,* which has even been embraced by many racial and ethnic groups to designate themselves. By calling non-White racial and ethnic groups "people of color," one is proposing that white is not a color, even though colorless white as a proposition is a semantic impossibility. Ideologically, "people of color" functions as a mechanism to make "White" as an ideological category invisible. However, it is precisely through this invisibility that the dominant White supremacy makes the ideological distinction against which all non-White groups are measured so as to be devalued and denigrated. This process facilitates the continued dance with bigotry without having to take responsibility for the poisonous effects of racism.

FREIRE: You are absolutely right. That is why I argue that the oppressed groups cannot and should not accept the dominant class's categorization of them as "minority" and, in the process, remain divided along race, class, gender, language, and ethnicity lines. Such divisions may lead not only to a form of essentialism, but also make it more difficult for these groups to dismantle the oppressive structures that rob them of their humanity. By noting this, I do not want to minimize the specific historical location of oppression. In fact, it is only through one's historical location that one is able to develop the critical tools to understand the globality of oppression. What I want to make very clear to all oppressed groups, including racial, gender, linguistic, and ethnic groups, is that I maintain a great solidarity with their struggles against their oppressive conditions and that I have been expressing this more and more explicitly in my work.

MACEDO: You and I have talked extensively about the racial issue in other discussions we have had. Without wanting to press you on this question, I think it is important to address each aspect of the criticism leveled against your work concerning race. Therefore, I think it is important to clarify your position even if you have to repeat yourself.

Some educators in North America also point out that your theory of oppression does not speak directly to the issue of race. They argue that you have failed to assign the appropriate weight to race as a fundamental factor of oppression. In their view, your class analysis oversimplifies the role of race and its historical location of oppression. Can you discuss your views on this issue?

FREIRE: I became keenly aware during the decade of the twenties of the cruel symbolic and material violence perpetrated against Blacks in my country, even though some Brazilians like to think that there is no racism in Brazil. Even our own language contradicts this ignorant but never innocent position, given the verbal violence that Blacks endure in their day-to-day struggle for survival. Like the issue of gender, race as an ideological category did not feature predominantly, as I mentioned before in this discussion, in my early work, particularly in *Pedagogy of the Oppressed*. However, once again as mentioned earlier, my critics should not use *Pedagogy of the Oppressed* as the only measure to evaluate my solidarity with subordinate racial groups, particularly Africans and African Americans.

My involvement with literacy campaigns in various African countries, particularly Guinea-Bissau and São Tomé and Principe, speak of my commitment and my fight against all racial oppression and my admiration for the courage of Black people in Africa in throwing out the colonizers. Obviously, the race situation in Africa is somewhat different than that of the United States and we should — and I am becoming more and more aware of this — always take into consideration both the historical specificity and the different forms of oppression. In other words, in Africa, the vast majority of the population is Black, while the White colonizers represented only a small minority. The challenge for me in Africa, as I pointed out in *Letters to Guinea-Bissau: Pedagogy in Process*, was to be cautious always and aware of my role as an outsider who had been invited to provide some help with the transformation of the inherited colonial educational structure. In many discussions, as well as in many letters I wrote to my colleagues in Guinea-Bissau, I always stressed the importance of a thorough analysis of culture in the development of a liberatory educational plan. In fact, the importance of culture was not my idea, since their leader Amilcar Cabral understood extremely well the role of culture in the struggle for liberation. As I have said to you in our many discussions, Donaldo, I learned immense amounts from Cabral's insights, particularly from his analysis of culture.

The issue of race in Guinea-Bissau, as well as in other African countries where I worked, is different, in my view, from that of the United States. The challenge for the liberators and educators was to understand how race as an ideological category served to legitimize the colonizers' exploitation and domination. When colonizers used the pretext of racial inferiority to dehumanize Africans, relegating them to subhuman status, as I said before, almost animal-like creatures, the anti-colonialist struggle had to take race as a determinant factor in their condemnation of colonialism. At least, in my denunciation of colonialism, I always felt revolted by the raw racism of the colonialist ideology. My collaboration in the fight against colonialism invariably involved a fight against racism. All anti-colonialist leaders and intellectuals fighting to break their countries from the yoke of colonialism were very clear about the colonizers' violent racism. From Amilcar Cabral to Franz Fanon you find brilliant analyses of the cruel and tragic history of racist imperialism.

MACEDO: Albert Memmi's work is a prime example of a penetrating analysis of racism as the mainstay of colonialism. For Memmi, "it is significant that racism is part of colonialism throughout the world: and it is not coincidence. Racism sums up and symbolizes the fundamental relation which unites colonialists and colonized."[8] Paulo, we need however, to understand what has happened to the role of race once the colonialists were defeated and expelled from the colonized countries.

FREIRE: Yes. Here is where we need to understand how culture is cut across by race, gender, class, ethnicity, and languages. In the post-independence reconstruction of these African nations, where the population is all Black, other factors may play a more significant role. For example, take Guinea-Bissau with its multiple cultural, linguistic, and ethnic groups. The challenge during post-independence is to understand how to reconcile the historical specificities of these differences and successfully achieve national unity. In this complex analysis, we cannot underestimate the role of class.

MACEDO: This is an important factor. The understanding of class as an ideological category becomes important so as to prevent the generalization that reduces all analysis to race. For instance, the petit bourgeois class of African functionaries who assimilated to the colonial cultural values is part of the same racial entity, but has a very different ideological orientation and aspiration for the new nation. I think what we need to avoid is a framework of analysis that collapses all of these factors into one monolithic entity of race. The same is true, to a degree, of African Americans in the United States. It would be a big mistake to view all African Americans as one monolithic cultural group without marked differences. Although U.S. Supreme Court Justice Clarence Thomas is Black, there is a tremendous gulf between him and, let us say, our friend bell hooks, even though they share the same race and class positions. They differ, however, significantly in their ideological orientations and on gender issues. Similar gulfs exist between the vast mass of African Americans who remain subordinated and reduced to ghettoes and middle-class African Americans who, in some sense, have also partly abandoned the subordinated mass of African Americans. I am reminded of a discussion I had with a personal friend of Martin Luther King Jr., who had joined him in the important struggle to end Black segregation and oppression during the sixties. During our discussion, King's friend remarked, "Donaldo, you are right. We are using unreflexively the dominant discourse based on euphemisms such as `economically marginal' and avoid more pointed terms such as `oppression.' I confess that I often feel uneasy when I am invited to discuss at institutions issues pertaining to the community. In reality, I haven't been there in over twenty years." Having achieved great personal success and having moved to a middle-class reality, this African American gentleman began to experience a distance from other African Americans who remain abandoned in ghettoes.

In a recent discussion with a group of students, a young African American man who attends an Ivy League university told me that his parents usually vote with the White middle-class, even if, in the long run, their vote is detrimental to Black people. Thus we see again that race, itself, is not necessarily a unifying force.

FREIRE: You see, Donaldo, things have not changed much with respect to those who work for anti-racist and anti-sexist movements, but oppose the presence of class in a comprehensive social analysis. You remember the discussion we had in Boston with my wife Nita and an African American friend who is a college professor who refused to accept class as a significant factor in social analysis of the African American reality. You remember that we tried to point out to her that while one cannot reduce the analysis of racism to social class, we cannot understand racism fully without a class analysis, for to do one at the expense of the other is to fall into a sectarianist position, which is as despicable as the racism that we need to reject.

MACEDO: Paulo, we also need to keep in mind that the level of violent racism in the United States gives primacy to race in most contexts. For instance, a recent discussion I had with a taxi driver in Washington, DC, highlights this point. During our conversation, the taxi driver told me that he was from Ghana and he showed me pictures of his wife and his son who were still there. I asked him if they were going to join him in the United States, and he quickly responded, "Oh, no! I don't want to expose my son to the racism I have to deal with. You see, I got a master's degree in business administration five years ago and the only job I was able to get is driving this taxi. Back home, I am somebody; here, I'm just a nigger."

I think what is important is to approach race analysis through a convergent framework where race is cut across by such factors as class, gender, culture, language, and ethnicity. The brilliant work of bell hooks that unmasks African American male sexist orientation brings home the point that these historical specificities, even within the same race, give rise to multiple identities that should never be collapsed into one monolithic entity. However, it would also be a major mistake to give class primacy so as to diminish the urgency of analyses concerning racism. This would be a mechanism that would play to the White supremacists, who prefer to keep the ideological structure of racism unexamined. We have to always bear in mind that in a society that is so violently racist, a movement into a middle-class reality does little for African Americans when they are outside their professional contexts. They are still followed in stores, not because they are being rendered great service, but because they are Black. Being a renowned intellectual did little for Cornel West, who watched nine taxis go by, all refusing to pick him up as a passenger in the streets of New York just because of the color of his skin. Henry Louis Gates Jr.'s prominence as a scholar did not lessen the racism he had to face at Duke University. bell hooks's eminence as a major feminist scholar does not lessen the pain of racism coupled with sexism that she endures. Having written eight highly acclaimed feminist books still does not provide her access to the media and magazines, as enjoyed by many White feminists such as Naomi Wolf. bell hooks recently noted:

> I have written eight feminist books. None of the magazines that have talked about your book, Naomi, have ever talked about my books at all. Now, that's not because there aren't ideas in my books that have universal appeal. It's because the issue that you raised in *The Beauty Myth* is still about beauty. We have to acknowledge that all of us do not have equal access.[9]

For me, the real issue is never to fall into a false dichotomy between race and class. The fundamental challenge is to accept Derrick Bell's "continuing quest for new directions in our struggle for racial justice, a struggle we must continue even if . . . racism is an integral, permanent, and indestructible component of this society."[10]

FREIRE: Absolutely. It is the work of African Americans, such as our friends bell hooks, Toni Morrison, Cornel West, Manning Marable, and Derrick Bell, among many others, that will help point us to a pedagogy of hope, born from the painful experiences of dehumanizing racism.

NOTES

1. Gregory Jay and Gerald Graff, "A Critique of Critical Pedagogy," in *Higher Education Under Fire*, ed. Michael Berube and Gary Nelson (New York: Routledge, 1995), p. 203.
2. Jonathan Kozol, *Savage Inequalities: Children in America's Schools* (New York: Crown, 1991), p. 20.
3. Henry Giroux, "Transgression of Difference," Series introduction to *Culture and Difference: Critical Perspectives on Bicultural Experience* (Westport, CT: Bergin & Garvey, in press).
4. John Fiske, *Power Plays, Power Works* (London: Verso Press, 1994), p. 13.
5. Gerald Graff, "Academic Writing and the Uses of Bad Publicity," in *Eloquent Obsessions*, ed. Mariana Torgornick (Durham, NC: Duke University Press, 1994), p. 215.
6. David Theo Goldberg, "Introduction," in *Multiculturalism: A Critical Reader*, ed. David Theo Goldberg (Oxford, Eng.: Blackwell, 1994), p. 19.
7. Robert Stam and Ella Shohat, "Contested Histories: Eurocentrism, Multiculturalism, and the Media," in *Multiculturalism: A Critical Reader*, ed. David Theo Goldberg (Oxford, Eng.: Blackwell, 1994), p. 320.

8. Albert Menni, *The Colonizer and the Colonized* (Boston: Beacon Press, 1991), pp. 69–70.

9. bell hooks, Gloria Steinem, Uruashi Vaid, and Naomi Wolf, "Get Real about Feminism: The Myths, the Backlash, the Movement," *Ms. Magazine,* September/October 1993, p. 41.

10. Derrick Bell, *Faces at the Bottom of the Well: The Permanance of Racism* (New York: Basic Books, 1992), p. xiii.

Freire and a Feminist Pedagogy
of Difference

KATHLEEN WEILER

e are living in a period of profound challenges to traditional Western epistemology and political theory. These challenges, couched in the language of postmodernist theory and in postcolonialist critiques, reflect the rapid transformation of the economic and political structure of the world order: the impact of transnational capital; the ever more comprehensive integration of resources, labor, and markets; the pervasiveness of media and consumer images. This interdependent world system is based on the exploitation of oppressed groups, but the system at the same time calls forth oppositional cultural forms that give voice to the conditions of these groups. White male bourgeois dominance is being challenged by people of color, women, and other oppressed groups, who assert the validity of their own knowledge and demand social justice and equality in numerous political and cultural struggles. In the intellectual sphere, this shifting world system has led to a shattering of Western metanarratives and to the variety of stances of postmodernist and cultural-identity theory. A major theoretical challenge to traditional Western knowledge systems is emerging from feminist theory, which has been increasingly influenced by postmodernist and cultural-identity theory. Feminist theory, like other contemporary approaches, validates difference, challenges universal claims to truth, and seeks to create social transformation in a world of shifting and uncertain meanings.

In education, these profound shifts are evident on two levels: first, at the level of practice, as excluded and formerly silenced groups challenge dominant approaches to learning and to definitions of knowledge; and second, at the level of theory, as modernist claims to universal truth are called into question.[1] These challenges to accepted truths have been raised not only to the institutions and theories that defend the status quo, but also to the critical or liberatory pedagogies that emerged in the 1960s and 1970s. Feminist educational critics, like other theorists influenced by postmodernism and theories of difference, want to retain the vision of social justice and transformation that underlies liberatory pedagogies, but they find that their claims to universal truths and their assumptions of a collective experience of oppression do not adequately address the realities of their own confusing and often tension-

Harvard Educational Review Vol. 61 No. 4 Winter 1991, 449–474

filled classrooms. This consciousness of the inadequacy of classical liberatory pedagogies has been particularly true for feminist educators, who are acutely aware of the continuing force of sexism and patriarchal structures and of the power of race, sexual preference, physical ability, and age to divide teachers from students and students from one another.

Paulo Freire is without question the most influential theorist of critical or liberatory education. His theories have profoundly influenced literacy programs throughout the world and what has come to be called critical pedagogy in the United States. His theoretical works, particularly *Pedagogy of the Oppressed*, provide classic statements of liberatory or critical pedagogy based on universal claims of truth.[2] Feminist pedagogy as it has developed in the United States provides a historically situated example of a critical pedagogy in practice. Feminist conceptions of education are similar to Freire's pedagogy in a variety of ways, and feminist educators often cite Freire as the educational theorist who comes closest to the approach and goals of feminist pedagogy.[3] Both feminist pedagogy as it is usually defined and Freirean pedagogy rest upon visions of social transformation; underlying both are certain common assumptions concerning oppression, consciousness, and historical change. Both pedagogies assert the existence of oppression in people's material conditions of existence and as a part of consciousness; both rest on a view of consciousness as more than a sum of dominating discourses, but as containing within it a critical capacity — what Antonio Gramsci called "good sense"; and both thus see human beings as subjects and actors in history and hold a strong commitment to justice and a vision of a better world and of the potential for liberation.[4] These ideals have powerfully influenced teachers and students in a wide range of educational settings, both formal and informal.

But in action, the goals of liberation or opposition to oppression have not always been easy to understand or achieve. As universal goals, these ideals do not address the specificity of people's lives; they do not directly analyze the contradictions between conflicting oppressed groups or the ways in which a single individual can experience oppression in one sphere while being privileged or oppressive in another. Feminist and Freirean teachers are in many ways engaged in what Teresa de Lauretis has called "shifting the ground of signs," challenging accepted meanings and relationships that occur at what she calls "political or more often micropolitical" levels, groupings that "produce no texts as such, but by shifting the `ground' of a given sign . . . effectively intervene upon codes of perception as well as ideological codes."[5] But in attempting to challenge dominant values and to "shift the ground of signs," feminist and Freirean teachers raise conflicts for themselves and for their students, who also are historically situated and whose own subjectivities are often contradictory and in process. These conflicts have become increasingly clear as both Freirean and feminist pedagogies are put into practice. Attempting to implement these pedagogies without acknowledging the conflict not only of divided consciousness — what Audre Lorde calls "the oppressor within us" — but also the conflicts among groups trying to work together to name and struggle against oppression — among teachers and students in classrooms, or among political groups working for change in very specific areas — can lead to anger, frustration, and a retreat to safer or more traditional approaches.[6] The numerous accounts of the tensions of trying to put liberatory pedagogies into practice demonstrate the need to reexamine the assumptions of the classic texts of liberatory pedagogy and to consider the various issues that have arisen in attempts at critical and liberatory classroom practice.[7]

As a White feminist writing and teaching from the traditions of both critical pedagogy and feminist theory, these issues are of particular concern to me. In this article, I examine and critique the classic liberatory pedagogy of Paulo Freire, particularly as it is presented in *Pedagogy of the Oppressed*, his most famous and influential text. I then examine the development and practice of feminist pedagogy, which emerged in a particular historical and political moment in the United States, and which, as a situated pedagogy, provides an example of some of the difficulties of putting these ideals into practice and suggests at the same time some possible theoretical and practical directions for liberatory pedagogies in general. I argue that an exploration of the conflicts and concerns that have arisen for feminist teachers attempting to put into practice their versions of a feminist pedagogy can help enrich and re-envision Freirean goals of liberation and social progress. This emerging pedagogy does not reject the goals of justice — the end of oppression, and liberation — but frames them more specifically in the context of historically defined struggles and calls for the articulation of interests and identity on the part of teacher and theorist as well as student. This approach questions whether the oppressed cannot act also as oppressors and challenges the idea of a commonality of oppression. It raises questions about common experience as a source of knowledge, the pedagogical authority of the teacher, and the nature of political and pedagogical struggle.

THE PEDAGOGY OF PAULO FREIRE

Freire's pedagogy developed in particular historical and political circumstances of neocolonialism and imperialism. As is well known, Freire's methods developed originally from his work with peasants in Brazil and later in Chile and Guinea-Bissau.[8] Freire's thought thus needs to be understood in the context of the political and economic situation of the developing world. In Freire's initial formulation, oppression was conceived in class terms and education was viewed in the context of peasants' and working people's revolutionary struggles. Equally influential in Freire's thought and pedagogy were the influence of radical Christian thought and the revolutionary role of liberation theology in Latin America. As is true for other radical Christians in Latin America, Freire's personal knowledge of extreme poverty and suffering challenged his deeply felt Christian faith grounded in the ethical teachings of Jesus in the Gospels. Freire's pedagogy is thus founded on a moral imperative to side with the oppressed that emerges from both his Christian faith and his knowledge and experience of suffering in the society in which he grew up and lived. Freire has repeatedly stated that his pedagogical method cannot simply be transferred to other settings, but that each historical site requires the development of a pedagogy appropriate to that setting. In his most recent work, he has also addressed sexism and racism as systems of oppression that must be considered as seriously as class oppression.[9] Nonetheless, Freire is frequently read without consideration for the context of the specific settings in which his work developed and without these qualifications in mind. His most commonly read text still is his first book to be published in English, *Pedagogy of the Oppressed*. In this classic text, Freire presents the epistemological basis for his pedagogy and discusses the concepts of oppression, conscientization, and dialogue that are at the heart of his pedagogical project, but as he enacted it in settings in the developing world and as it has been appropriated by radical teachers in other settings.

Freire organizes his approach to liberatory pedagogy in terms of a dualism between the oppressed and the oppressors and between humanization and dehumanization. This organization of thoughts in terms of opposing forces reflects Freire's own experiences of literacy work with the poor in Brazil, a situation in which the lines between oppressor and oppressed were clear. For Freire, humanization is the goal of liberation; it has not yet been achieved, nor can it be achieved so long as the oppressors oppress the oppressed. That is, liberation and humanization will not occur if the roles of oppressor and oppressed are simply reversed. If humanization is to be realized, new relationships among human beings must be created:

> Because it is a distortion of being more fully human, sooner or later being less human leads the oppressed to struggle against those who made them so. In order for this struggle to have meaning, the oppressed must not, in seeking to regain their humanity (which is a way to create it), become in turn oppressors of the oppressors, but rather restorers of the humanity of both.[10]

The struggle against oppression leading to humanization is thus utopian and visionary. As Freire says elsewhere, "To be utopian is not to be merely idealistic or impractical but rather to engage in denunciation and annunciation."[11] By denunciation, Freire refers to the naming and analysis of existing structures of oppression; by annunciation, he means the creation of new forms of relationships and being in the world as a result of mutual struggle against oppression. Thus Freire presents a theoretical justification for a pedagogy that aims to critique existing forms of oppression and to transform the world, thereby creating new ways of being, or humanization.

Radical educators throughout the world have used *Pedagogy of the Oppressed* as the theoretical justification for their work. As an eloquent and impassioned statement of the need for and possibility of change through reading the world and the word, there is no comparable contemporary text.[12] But when we look at *Pedagogy of the Oppressed* from the perspective of recent feminist theory and pedagogy, certain problems arise that may reflect the difficulties that have sometimes arisen when Freire's ideas are enacted in specific settings. The challenges of recent feminist theory do not imply the rejection of Freire's goals for what he calls a pedagogy for liberation; feminists certainly share Freire's emphasis on seeing human beings as the subjects and not the objects of history. A critical feminist rereading of Freire, however, points to ways in which the project of Freirean pedagogy, like that of feminist pedagogy, may be enriched and re-envisioned.

From a feminist perspective, *Pedagogy of the Oppressed* is striking in its use of the male referent, a usage that was universal when the book was written in the 1960s.[13] Much more troublesome, however, is the abstract quality of terms such as humanization, which do not address the particular meanings imbued by men and women,

Black and White, or other groups. The assumption of *Pedagogy of the Oppressed* is that in struggling against oppression, the oppressed will move toward true humanity. But this leaves unaddressed the forms of oppression experienced by different actors, the possibility of struggles among people oppressed differently by different groups — what Cameron McCarthy calls "nonsynchrony of oppression."[14] This assumption also presents humanization as a universal, without considering the various definitions this term may bring forth from people of different groups. When Freire speaks of the oppressed needing to fight the tendency to become "sub-oppressors," he means that the oppressed have only the pattern of oppression before them as a way of being in a position other than the one they are in. As Freire writes, "Their ideal is to be men; but for them, to be men is to be oppressors. This is their model of humanity."[15] What is troubling here is not that "men" is used for human beings, but that the model of oppressor implied here is based on the immediate oppressor of men — in this case, bosses over peasants or workers. What is not addressed is the possibility of simultaneous contradictory positions of oppression and dominance: the man oppressed by his boss could at the same time oppress his wife, for example, or the White woman oppressed by sexism could exploit the Black woman. By framing this discussion in such abstract terms, Freire slides over the contradictions and tensions within social settings in which overlapping forms of oppression exist.

This usage of "the oppressed" in the abstract also raises difficulties in Freire's use of experience as the means of acquiring a radical literacy, "reading the world and the word." At the heart of Freire's pedagogy is the insistence that all people are subjects and knowers of the world. Their political literacy will emerge from their reading of the world — that is, their own experience. This reading will lead to collective knowledge and action. But what if that experience is divided? What if different truths are discovered in reading the world from different positions? For Freire, education as the practice of freedom "denies that men are abstract, isolated, independent, and unattached to the world. . . . Authentic reflection considers neither abstract man nor the world without men, but men in their relations with the world."[16] But implicit in this vision is the assumption that, when the oppressed perceive themselves in relation to the world, they will act together collectively to transform the world and to move toward their own humanization. The nature of their perception of the world and their oppression is implicitly assumed to be uniform for all the oppressed. The possibility of a contradictory experience of oppression among the oppressed is absent. As Freire says:

> Accordingly, the point of departure must always be with men in the "here and now," which constitutes the situation within which they are submerged, from which they emerge, and in which they intervene. Only by starting from this situation — which determines their perception of it — can they begin to move.[17]

The assumption again is that the oppressed, these men, are submerged in a common situation of oppression, and that their shared knowledge of that oppression will lead them to collective action.

Central to Freire's pedagogy is the practice of conscientization; that is, coming to a consciousness of oppression and a commitment to end that oppression. Conscientization is based on this common experience of oppression. Through this reading of the world, the oppressed will come to knowledge. The role of the teacher in this process is to instigate a dialogue between teacher and student, based on their common ability to know the world and to act as subjects in the world. But the question of the authority and power of the teacher, particularly those forms of power based on the teacher's subject position as raced, classed, gendered, and so on, is not addressed by Freire. There is, again, the assumption that the teacher is "on the same side" as the oppressed, and that as teachers and students engage together in a dialogue about the world, they will uncover together the same reality, the same oppression, and the same liberation. In *Pedagogy of the Oppressed*, the teacher is presented as a generic man whose interests will be with the oppressed as they mutually discover the mechanisms of oppression. The subjectivity of the Freirean teacher is, in this sense, what Gayatri Chakravorty Spivak refers to as "transparent."[18] In fact, of course, teachers are not abstract; they are women or men of particular races, classes, ages, abilities, and so on. The teacher will be seen and heard by students not as an abstraction, but as a particular person with a certain defined history and relationship to the world. In a later book, Freire argues that the teacher has to assume authority, but must do so without becoming authoritarian. In this recognition of the teacher's authority, Freire acknowledges the difference between teacher and students:

> The educator continues to be different from the students, but, and now for me this is the central question, the difference between them, if the teacher is democratic, if his or her political dream is a *liberating* one, is that he or she cannot permit the necessary difference between the teacher and the students to become "antagonistic."[19]

In this passage, Freire acknowledges the power of the teacher by virtue of the structural role of "teacher" within a hierarchical institution and, under the best of circumstances, by virtue of the teacher's greater experience and knowledge. But Freire does not go on to investigate what the other sources of "antagonism" in the classroom might be. However much he provides a valuable guide to the use of authority by the liberatory teacher, he never addresses the question of other forms of power held by the teacher by virtue of race, gender, or class that may lead to antagonisms. Without naming these sources of tension, it is difficult to address or build upon them to challenge existing structures of power and subjectivities. Without recognizing more clearly the implicit power and limitations of the position of teacher, calls for a collective liberation or for opposition to oppression slide over the surface of the tensions that may emerge among teachers and students as subjects with conflicting interests and histories and with different kinds of knowledge and power. A number of questions are thus left unaddressed in *Pedagogy of the Oppressed:* How are we to situate ourselves in relation to the struggle of others? How are we to address our own contradictory positions as oppressors and oppressed? Where are we to look for liberation when our collective "reading of the world" reveals contradictory and conflicting experiences and struggles? The Freirean vision of the oppressed as undifferentiated and as the source of unitary political action, the transparency of the subjectivity of the Freirean teacher, and the claims of universal goals of liberation and social transformation fail to provide the answers to these questions.

Calling into question the universal and abstract claims of *Pedagogy of the Oppressed* is certainly not to argue that Freire's pedagogy should be rejected or discarded. The ethical stance of Freire in terms of praxis and his articulation of people's worth and ability to know and change the world are an essential basis for radical pedagogies in opposition to oppression. Freire's thought illuminates the central question of political action in a world increasingly without universals. Freire, like liberation theologians such as Sharon Welch, positions himself on the side of the oppressed; he claims the moral imperative to act in the world. As Peter McLaren has commented in reference to Freire's political stand, "The task of liberating others from their suffering may not emerge from some transcendental fiat, yet it nevertheless compels us to affirm our humanity in solidarity with victims."[20] But in order better to seek the affirmation of our own humanity and to seek to end suffering and oppression, I am arguing for a more situated theory of oppression and subjectivity, and for the need to consider the contradictions of such universal claims of truth or process.

In the next section of this chapter, I explore feminist pedagogy as an example of a situated pedagogy of liberation. Like Freirean pedagogy, feminist pedagogy is based on assumptions of the power of consciousness raising, the existence of oppression and the possibility of ending it, and the desire for social transformation. But in its historical development, feminist pedagogy has revealed the shortcomings that emerge in the attempt to enact a pedagogy that assumes a universal experience and abstract goals. In the attempt of feminist pedagogy to address these issues, a more complex vision of a liberatory pedagogy is being developed and explored.

FEMINIST PEDAGOGY, CONSCIOUSNESS RAISING, AND WOMEN'S LIBERATION

Feminist pedagogy in colleges and universities has developed in conjunction with the growth of women's studies and what is inclusively called "the new scholarship on women." These developments within universities — the institutionalization of women's studies as programs and departments and the challenge to existing canons and disciplines by the new scholarship on women and by feminist theory — are reflected in the classroom teaching methods that have come to be loosely termed feminist pedagogy. Defining exactly what feminist pedagogy means in practice, however, is difficult. It is easier to describe the various methods used in specific women's studies courses and included by feminist teachers claiming the term feminist pedagogy than it is to provide a coherent definition.[21] But common to the claims of feminist teachers is the goal of providing students with the skills to continue political work as feminists after they have left the university. Nancy Schniedewind makes a similar claim for what she calls "feminist process," which she characterizes as "both a feminist vision of equalitarian personal relations and societal forms and the confidence and skills to make their knowledge and vision functional in the world."[22]

The pedagogy of feminist teachers is based on certain assumptions about knowledge, power, and political action that can be traced beyond the academy to the political activism of the women's movement in the 1960s. This same commitment to social change through the transformative potential of education underlay Freire's pedagogy in Brazil during the same period. Women's studies at the university level have since come to encompass a wide variety of political stances and theoretical approaches. Socialist feminism, liberal feminism, radical feminism, and postmodern feminism all view issues from their different perspectives. Nonetheless, feminist pedagogy continues to echo the struggles of its origins and to retain a vision of social activism. Virtually all women's studies courses and programs at least partially reflect this critical, oppositional, and activist stance, even within programs now established and integrated into the bureaucratic structures of university life. As Linda Gordon points out:

> Women's studies did not arise accidentally, as the product of someone's good idea, but was created by a social movement for women's liberation with a sharp critique of the whole structure of society. By its very existence, women's studies constitutes a critique of the university and the body of knowledge it imparts.[23]

Despite tensions and splits within feminism at a theoretical level and in the context of women's studies programs in universities, the political commitment of women's liberation that Gordon refers to continues to shape feminist pedagogy. Thus, like Freirean pedagogy, feminist pedagogy is grounded in a vision of social change. And, like Freirean pedagogy, feminist pedagogy rests on truth claims of the primacy of experience and consciousness that are grounded in historically situated social change movements. Key to understanding the methods and epistemological claims of feminist pedagogy is an understanding of its origins in more grassroots political activity, particularly in the consciousness-raising groups of the women's liberation movement of the late 1960s and early 1970s.

Women's consciousness-raising groups began to form more or less spontaneously in northeastern and western U.S. cities in late 1967 among White women who had been active in the civil rights and new left movements.[24] In a fascinating parallel to the rise of the women's suffrage movement out of the abolitionist movement in the mid-nineteenth century, these activist and politically committed women came to apply the universal demands for equality and justice of the civil rights movement to their own situation as women.[25] While public actions such as the Miss America protest of 1968, mass meetings, and conferences were organized in this early period, the unique organizational basis for the women's liberation movement was grounded in the small groups of women who came together for what came to be known as consciousness raising. Early consciousness-raising groups, based on friendship and common political commitment, focused on the discussion of shared experiences of sexuality, work, family, and participation in the male-dominated left political movement. Consciousness raising focused on collective political change rather than on individual therapy. The groups were unstructured and local — they could be formed anywhere and did not follow formal guidelines — but they used the same sorts of methods because these methods addressed common problems. One woman remembers the first meeting of what became her consciousness-raising group:

The flood broke loose gradually and then more swiftly. We talked about our families, our mothers, our fathers, our siblings; we talked about our men; we talked about school; we talked about "the movement" (which meant new left men). For hours we talked and unburdened our souls and left feeling high and planning to meet again the following week.[26]

Perhaps the clearest summary of consciousness raising from this period can be found in Kathie Sarachild's essay, "Consciousness Raising: A Radical Weapon."[27] In this article, Sarachild, a veteran of the civil rights movement in the South and a member of Redstockings, one of the earliest and most influential women's groups, presents an account that is both descriptive and proscriptive.[28] She makes it clear that consciousness raising arose spontaneously among small groups of women and that she is describing and summarizing a collective process that can be used by other groups of women. Fundamental to Sarachild's description of consciousness raising is its grounding in the need for political action. She describes the emergence of the method of consciousness raising among a group of women who considered themselves radicals in the sense of demanding fundamental changes in society. As Sarachild comments:

> We were interested in getting to the roots of problems in society. You might say we wanted to pull up weeds in the garden by their roots, not just pick off the leaves at the top to make things look good momentarily. Women's liberation was started by women who considered themselves radicals in this sense.[29]

A second fundamental aspect of consciousness raising is the reliance on experience and feeling. According to Sarachild, the focus on examining women's own experience came from a profound distrust of accepted authority and truth. These claims about what was valuable and true tended to be accepting of existing assumptions about women's "inherent nature" and "proper place." In order to call those truths into question (truths we might now call hegemonic and that Foucault, for example, would tie to structures of power), women had nowhere to turn except to their own experience. Sarachild describes the process in her group:

> In the end the group decided to raise its consciousness by studying women's lives by topics like childhood, jobs, motherhood, etc. We'd do any outside reading we wanted to and thought was important. But our starting point for discussion, as well as our test of the accuracy of what any of the books said, would be the actual experience we had in these areas.[30]

The last aspect of consciousness raising was a common sharing of experience in a collective, leaderless group. As Michele Russell points out, this sharing is similar to the practice of "testifying" in the Black church, and depends upon openness and trust in the group.[31] The assumption underlying this sharing of stories was the existence of commonality among women; as Sarachild puts it, "we made the assumption, an assumption basic to consciousness raising, that most women were like ourselves — not different."[32]

The model for consciousness raising among the Redstockings, as with other early groups, came from the experiences of many of the women as organizers in the civil rights movement in the South. Sarachild, for instance, cites the example of the Student Nonviolent Coordinating Committee, and quotes Stokely Carmichael when she argues for the need for people to organize in order to understand their own conditions of existence and to fight their own struggles. Other sources cited by Sarachild include the nineteenth-century suffragist Ernestine Rose, Mao Zedong, Malcolm X, and the practice of "speaking bitterness" in the Chinese revolution described by William Hinton in *Fanshen*.[33] Both the example of the civil rights movement and the revolutionary tradition of the male writers that provided the model for early consciousness raising supported women's commitment to political action and social change.[34] As Sarachild comments:

> We would be the first to dare to say and do the undareable, what women really felt and wanted. The first job now was to raise awareness and understanding, our own and others — awareness that would prompt people to organize and to act on a mass scale.[35]

Thus consciousness raising shared the assumptions of earlier revolutionary traditions: that understanding and theoretical analysis were the first steps to revolutionary change, and that neither was adequate alone; theory and practice were intertwined as praxis. As Sarachild puts it, "Consciousness raising was seen as both a method for arriving at the truth and a means for action and organizing."[36] What was original in consciousness raising, however, was its emphasis on experience and feeling as the guide to theoretical understanding, an approach that reflected the realities of women's socially defined subjectivities and the conditions of their lives. Irene Peslikis, another member of Redstockings, wrote, "When we think of what it is that politicizes people it is not so much books or ideas but experience."[37]

While Sarachild and other early feminists influenced by a left political tradition explored the creation of theory grounded in women's feelings and experiences, they never lost the commitment to social transformation.[38] In their subsequent history, however, consciousness raising and feminist pedagogy did not always retain this political commitment to action. As the women's movement expanded to reach wider groups of women, consciousness raising tended to lose its commitment to revolutionary change. This trend seems to have been particularly true as the women's movement affected women with a less radical perspective and with little previous political involvement. Without a vision of collective action and social transformation, consciousness raising held the possibility of what Berenice Fisher calls "a diversion of energies into an exploration of feelings and `private' concerns to the detriment of political activism."[39] The lack of structure and the local natures of consciousness-raising groups only reinforced these tendencies toward a focus on individual rather than collective change. The one site in which the tradition of consciousness raising did find institutional expression was in academia, in the growth of women's studies courses and programs stimulated by the new scholarship on women. The founders of these early courses and programs tended to be politically committed feminists who themselves had experienced consciousness raising and who, like Freire, assumed that education could and should be a means of social change.

The first women's studies courses, reflecting the growth of the women's move-ment in what has come to be called the second wave of feminism, were taught in the late 1960s.[40] In 1970, Paul Lauter and Florence Howe founded The Feminist Press, an important outlet for publishing early feminist scholarship and recovering lost texts by women writers.[41] In 1977, the founding of the National Women's Studies Association provided a national organization, a journal, and yearly conferences that gave femi-nists inside and outside of academia a forum to exchange ideas and experiences. By the late 1980s, respected journals such as *Signs* and *Feminist Studies* were well estab-lished, and women's studies programs and courses were widespread (if not always en-thusiastically supported by administrations) in colleges and universities.[42] At the same time, feminist research and theory — what has come to be called "the new scholarship on women" — put forth a profound challenge to traditional disciplines.[43] The growth of women's studies programs and feminist scholarship thus provided an institutional framework and theoretical underpinning for feminist pedagogy, the at-tempt to express feminist values and goals in the classroom. But while feminist schol-arship has presented fundamental challenges to traditional androcentric knowledge, the attempt to create a new pedagogy modeled on consciousness raising has not been as successful or coherent a project. Serious challenges to the goal of political transfor-mation through the experience of feminist learning have been raised in the attempt to create a feminist pedagogy in the academy. The difficulties and contradictions that have emerged in the attempt to create a feminist pedagogy in traditional institutions like universities raise serious questions for all liberatory pedagogies and echo some of the problems raised by the unitary and universal approach of *Pedagogy of the Op-pressed.* But in engaging these questions, feminist pedagogy suggests new directions that can enrich Freirean pedagogies of liberation.

Feminist pedagogy has raised three areas of concern that are particularly useful in considering the ways in which Freirean and other liberatory pedagogies can be en-riched and expanded. The first of these concerns the role and authority of the teacher; the second addresses the epistemological question of the source of the claims for knowledge and truth in personal experience and feeling; the last, emerging from chal-lenges by women of color and postmodernist feminist theorists, raises the question of difference. Their challenges have led to a shattering of the unproblematic and unitary category "woman," as well as of an assumption of the inevitable unity of "women." Instead, feminist theorists have increasingly emphasized the importance of recogniz-ing difference as a central category of feminist pedagogy. The unstated assumption of a universal experience of "being a woman" was exploded by the critiques of post-modern feminists and by the growing assertion of lesbians and women of color that the universal category "woman" in fact meant "White, heterosexual, middle-class woman," even when used by White, heterosexual, socialist feminists, or women vet-erans of the civil rights movement who were committed to class or race struggles.[44] These theoretical challenges to the unity of both "woman" and "women" have in turn called into question the authority of women as teachers and students in the class-room, the epistemological value of both feeling and experience, and the nature of political strategies for enacting feminist goals of social change. I turn next to an exploration of these key issues of authority, experience, feeling, and difference within feminist pedagogy and theory.

The Role and Authority of the Teacher

In many respects, the feminist vision of the teacher's authority echoes that Freirean image of the teacher who is a joint learner with students and who holds authority by virtue of greater knowledge and experience. But as we have seen, Freire fails to address the various forms of power held by teachers depending on their race, gender, and the historical and institutional settings in which they work. In the Freirean account, they are in this sense "transparent." In the actual practice of feminist pedagogy, the central issues of difference, positionality, and the need to recognize the implications of subjectivity or identity for teachers and students have become central. Moreover, the question of authority in institutional settings makes problematic the possibility of achieving the collective and nonhierarchical vision of early consciousness-raising groups within university classrooms. The basic elements of early consciousness-raising groups — an emphasis on feeling, experience, and sharing, and a suspicion of hierarchy and authority — continue to influence feminist pedagogy in academic settings. But the institutionalized nature of women's studies in the hierarchical and bureaucratic structure of academia creates tensions that run counter to the original commitment to praxis in consciousness-raising groups. Early consciousness-raising groups were homogeneous, antagonistic to authority, and had a commitment to political change that had directly emerged from the civil rights and new left movements. Feminist pedagogy within academic classrooms addresses heterogeneous groups of students within a competitive and individualistic culture in which the teacher holds institutional power and responsibility (even if she may want to reject that power).[45] As bell hooks comments, "The academic setting, the academic discourse [we] work in, is not a known site for truthtelling."[46] The very success of feminist scholarship has meant the development of a rich theoretical tradition with deep divisions and opposing goals and methods.[47] Thus the source of the teacher's authority as a "woman" who can call upon a "common woman's knowledge" is called into question; at the same time the feminist teacher is "given" authority by virtue of her role within the hierarchical structure of the university.

The question of authority in feminist pedagogy seems to be centered around two different conceptions. The first refers to the institutionally imposed authority of the teacher within a hierarchical university structure. The teacher in this role must give grades, is evaluated by administrators and colleagues in terms of expertise in a body of knowledge, and is expected to take responsibility for meeting the goals of an academic course as it is understood within the wider university. This hierarchical structure is clearly in opposition to the collective goals of a common women's movement and is miles from the early structureless consciousness-raising groups in which each woman was an expert on her own life. Not only does the university structure impose this model of institutional authority, but students themselves expect it. As Barbara Hillyer Davis comments: "The institutional pressure to [impart knowledge] is reinforced by the students' well-socialized behavior. If I will tell them `what I want,' they will deliver it. They are exasperated with my efforts to depart from the role of dispenser of wisdom."[48] Feminist educators have attempted to address this tension between their ideals of collective education and the demands of the university by a variety of expedients: group assignments and grades, contracts for grades, pass/fail courses, and such techniques as self-revelation and the articulation of the dynamics of the classroom.[49]

Another aspect of institutionalized authority, however, is the need for women to *claim* authority in a society that denies it to them. As Culley and Portuges have pointed out, the authority and power of the woman feminist teacher is already in question from many of her students precisely because she is a woman:

> As women, our own position is precarious, and the power we are supposed to exercise is given grudgingly, if at all. For our own students, for ourselves, and for our superiors, we are not clearly "us" or "them." The facts of class, of race, of ethnicity, of sexual preference — as well as gender — may cut across the neat divisions of teacher/student.[50]

Thus the issue of institutional authority raises the contradictions of trying to achieve a democratic and collective ideal in a hierarchical institution, but it also raises the question of the meaning of authority for feminist teachers, whose right to speak or to hold power is itself under attack in a patriarchal (and racist, homophobic, classist, and so on) society. The question of asserting authority and power is a central concern to feminists precisely because as women they have been taught that taking power is inappropriate. From this perspective, the feminist teacher's acceptance of authority becomes in itself liberating to her and to her students. It becomes a claim to authority in terms of her own value as a scholar and a teacher in a patriarchal society that structurally denies or questions that authority as it is manifest in the organization and bureaucracy of the university. Women students, after all, are socialized to be deferential, and both men and women students are taught to accept male authority. It is instructive for students to see women assert authority. But this use of authority will lead to positive social change only if those teachers are working also to empower students in a Freirean sense.[51] As Susan Stanford Friedman argues:

> What I and other women have needed is a theory of feminist pedagogy consistent with our needs as women operating at the fringes of patriarchal space. As we attempt to move on to academic turf culturally defined as male, we need a theory that first recognizes the androcentric denial of *all* authority to women and, second, points out a way for us to speak with an authentic voice not based on tyranny.[52]

These concerns lead to a conception of authority and power in a positive sense, both in terms of women asserting authority as women, and in terms of valuing intellectual work and the creation of theory as a means of understanding and, thus, of changing the world.

The authority of the intellectual raises issues for feminists in the academy that are similar to those faced by other democratic and collective political movements, such as those described by Freire. There is a contradiction between the idea of a women's movement including all women and a group of what Berenice Fisher calls "advanced women."[53] Feminists who question the whole tradition of androcentric thought are deeply suspicious of women who take a position of "experts" who can translate and interpret other women's experiences. Fisher articulates these tensions well:

> Who are intellectuals in relation to the women's movement? . . . Are intellectuals sorts of leaders, sage guides, women who give voice to or clarify a broader urge toward social change? Is intellectual work essentially elitist, a matter of mere privilege to think, to write, to create? Is it simply a patriarchal mode of gaining and maintaining power, a way of negating women's everyday experience, a means of separating some women from the rest of the "community?"[54]

Fisher argues that feminist intellectuals are struggling with these questions in their scholarship, teaching, and roles within the universities and the wider women's movement. She does not reject the authority of the feminist intellectual, but she also does not deny the need to address and clarify these contradictions. She, like Charlotte Bunch, is an embodiment of this attempt to accept both the authority and responsibility of the feminist intellectual who is creating theory.

In terms of feminist pedagogy, the authority of the feminist teacher as intellectual and theorist finds expression in the goal of making students themselves theorists of their own lives by interrogating and analyzing their own experience. In an approach very similar to Freire's concept of conscientization, this strategy moves beyond the naming or sharing of experience to the creation of a critical understanding of the forces that have shaped that experience. This theorizing is antithetical to traditional views of women. As Bunch points out, traditionally

> women are supposed to worry about mundane survival problems, to brood about fate, and to fantasize in a personal manner. We are not meant to think analytically about society, to question the ways things are, to consider how things could be different. Such thinking involves an active, not a passive, relationship to the world.[55]

Thus feminist educators like Fisher and Bunch accept their authority as intellectuals and theorists, but they consciously attempt to construct their pedagogy to recognize and encourage the capacity of their students to theorize and to recognize their own power.[56] This is a conception of authority not in the institutional terms of a bureaucratized university system, but rather an attempt to claim the authority of theorist and guide for students who are themselves potential theorists.

Feminist concerns about the authority of the feminist teacher address questions of classroom practice and theory ignored by Freire — in his formulation of the teacher and student as two "knowers" of the world, and in his assertion that the liberatory teacher should acknowledge and claim authority but not authoritarianism. The feminist exploration of authority is much richer and addresses more directly the contradictions between goals of collectivity and hierarchies of knowledge. Feminist teachers are much more conscious of the power of various subject positions than is represented in Freire's "transparent" liberatory teacher. An acknowledgment of the realities of conflict and tensions based on contradictory political goals, as well as of the meaning of historically experienced oppression for both teachers and students, leads to a pedagogy that respects difference not just as significant for students, but for teachers as well.

Personal Experience as a Source of Knowledge and Truth

As feminists explore the relationship of authority, theory, and political action, they raise questions about the categories and claims for truth underlying both consciousness raising and feminist pedagogy. These claims rest on categories of experience and feeling as guides to theoretical understanding and political change. Basic to the Freirean method of conscientization is the belief in the ability of all people to be knowers and to read both the word and the world. In Freirean pedagogy, it is through the interrogation of their own experiences that the oppressed will come to an understanding of their own power as knowers and creators of the world; this knowledge will contribute to the transformation of their world. In consciousness-raising groups and in feminist pedagogy in the university, a similar reliance on experience and feeling has been fundamental to the development of a feminist knowledge of the world that can be the basis for social change. Underlying both Freirean and early feminist pedagogy is an assumption of a common experience as the basis for political analysis and action. Both experience and feeling were central to consciousness raising and remain central to feminist pedagogy in academia; they are claimed as a kind of "inner knowing," shaped by society but at the same time containing an oppositional quality. Feeling is looked to as a guide to a deeper truth than that of abstract rationality. Experience, which is interpreted through ideologically constructed categories, also can be the basis for an opposition to dominant schemes of truth if what is experienced runs counter to what is set forth and accepted as "true." Feminist educators, beginning with women in the early consciousness-raising groups, have explored both experience and feeling as sources of knowledge, and both deserve closer examination.

In many ways, feeling or emotion has been seen traditionally as a source of women's knowledge about the world. As we have seen, in the early consciousness-raising groups, feelings were looked to as the source of a "true" knowledge of the world for women living in a society that denied the value of their perceptions. Feelings or emotions were seen as a way of testing accepted claims of what is universally true about human nature or, specifically, about women. Claims such as Freud's theory of penis envy, for example, were challenged by women first because these theoretical descriptions of women's psychology did not match women's own feelings about their lives. As feminist pedagogy has developed, with a continued emphasis on the function of feelings as a guide to knowledge about the world, emotions have been seen as links between a kind of inner truth or inner self and the outer world — including ideology, culture, and other discourses of power.[57] However, as feminist educators have explored the uses of feeling or emotion as a source of knowledge, several difficulties have become clear. First of all, there is a danger that the expression of strong emotion can be simply cathartic and can deflect the need for action to address the underlying causes of that emotion. Moreover, it is not clear how to distinguish among a wide range of emotions as the source of political action. At a more theoretical level, there are contradictions involved in claiming that the emotions are a source for knowledge and at the same time arguing that they are manipulated and shaped by dominant discourses. Both consciousness-raising groups and feminist theorists have asserted the social construction of feelings and their manipulation by the dominant culture; at the same time, they look to feelings as a source of truth. Berenice Fisher points to the contradiction implicit in these claims:

> In theoretical terms, we cannot simultaneously claim that all feelings are socially conditioned and that some feelings are "true." We would be more consistent to acknowledge that society only partly shapes our emotions, leaving an opening where we can challenge and change the responses to which we have been socialized. That opening enables the consciousness-raising process to take place and gives us the space in which to reflect on the new emotional responses that our process evokes.[58]

In this formulation, Fisher seems to be arguing for a kind of Gramscian "good sense," a locus of knowing in the self that is grounded in feeling as a guide to theoretical understanding. Feelings thus are viewed as a kind of cognition — a source of knowledge.

Perhaps the most eloquent argument for feelings as a source of oppositional knowledge is found in the work of Audre Lorde. Lorde, a Black lesbian feminist theorist and poet, writes from the specificity of her own socially defined and shaped life. For her, feeling is the source of poetry, a means of knowing that challenges White, Western, androcentric epistemologies. She specifically ties her own feelings as a Black woman to a non-Western way of knowing. She writes:

> As we come more into touch with our own ancient, non-European consciousness of living as a situation to be experienced and interacted with, we learn more and more to cherish our feelings, to respect those hidden sources of power from where true knowledge and, therefore, lasting action comes.[59]

Lorde is acutely aware of the ways in which the dominant society shapes our sense of who we are and what we feel. As she points out, "Within living structures defined by profit, by linear power, by institutional dehumanization, our feelings were not meant to survive."[60] Moreover, Lorde is conscious of the oppressor within us: "For we have, built into all of us, old blueprints of expectation and response, old structures of oppression, and these must be altered at the same time as we alter the living conditions which are the result of those structures."[61] But although Lorde does not deny what she calls "the oppressor within," she retains a belief in the power of deeper feeling to challenge the dominant definitions of truth and to point the way to an analysis that can lead to an alternative vision:

> As we begin to recognize our deepest feelings, we begin to give up, of necessity, being satisfied with suffering and self-negation, and with the numbness which so often seems like their only alternative in society. Our acts against oppression become integral with self, motivated and empowered from within.[62]

For Lorde, then, feelings are a guide to analysis and to action. While they are shaped by society and are socially constructed in that sense, Lorde insists on a deeper reality of feeling closer in touch with what it means to be human. This formulation echoes the Freirean vision of humanization as a new way of being in the world other than as oppressor and oppressed. Both Freire and Lorde retain a Utopian faith in the possibility that human beings can create new ways of being in the world out of collective struggle and a human capacity to feel. Lorde terms this the power of the erotic; she speaks of the erotic as "a measure between the beginnings of our sense of self and the chaos of our strongest feelings," a resource "firmly rooted in the power of our unexpressed or unrecognized feeling."[63] Because the erotic can challenge the dominant, it has been denied as a source of power and knowledge. But for Lorde, the power of the erotic provides the basis for visionary social change.

In her exploration of feelings and of the erotic as a source of knowledge about the world, Lorde does not reject analysis and rationality. But she questions the depth of critical understanding of those forces that shape our lives that can be achieved using only the rational and abstract methods of analysis given to us by dominant ideology. In Foucault's terms, she is seeking a perspective from which to interrogate dominant regimes of truth; central to her argument is the claim that an analysis framed solely in the terms of accepted discourse cannot get to the root of structures of power. That is what her well-known phrase, "The Master's Tools Will Never Dismantle the Master's House," implies. As she argues:

> Rationality is not unnecessary. It serves the chaos of knowledge. It serves feeling. It serves to get from this place to that place. But if you don't honor those places, then the road is meaningless. Too often, that's what happens with the worship of rationality and that circular, academic analytic thinking. But ultimately, I don't see feel/think as a dichotomy. I see them as a choice of ways and combinations.[64]

Lorde's discussion of feeling and the erotic as a source of power and knowledge is based on the assumption that human beings have the capacity to feel and know, and can engage in self-critique; people are not completely shaped by dominant discourse. The oppressor may be within us, but Lorde insists that we also have the capacity to challenge our own ways of feeling and knowing. When tied to a recognition of positionality, this validation of feeling can be used to develop powerful sources of politically focused feminist education.

For Lorde and Fisher, this kind of knowing through an exploration of feeling and emotion requires collective inquiry and constant reevaluation. It is a contingent and positioned claim to truth. Similar complexities arise in the use of experience as the basis for feminist political action. Looking to experience as the source of knowledge and the focus of feminist learning is perhaps the most fundamental tenet of feminist pedagogy. This is similar to the Freirean call to "read the world" to seek the generative themes that codify power relationships and social structures. The sharing of women's experiences was the touchstone of early consciousness-raising groups and continues to be a fundamental method of feminist pedagogy. That women need to examine what they have experienced and lived in concrete ways, in their own bodies, is a materialistic conception of experience. In an early essay, Adrienne Rich pointed to this materiality of experience: "To think like a woman in a man's world means . . . remembering that every mind resides in a body; remaining accountable to the female bodies in which we live; constantly retesting given hypotheses against lived experience."[65] As became clear quite early in the women's movement, claims about experience as a source of women's knowledge rested on certain assumptions about commonalities in women's lives. Women were conceived of as a unitary and relatively undifferentiated group. Sarachild, for example, spoke of devising "new theories which . . . reflect the actual experience and feelings and necessities of women."[66] Underlying this approach was the assumption of a common woman's experience, one reflecting the world of the White, middle-class, heterosexual women of the early feminist movement. But as the critiques of lesbians, women of color, and postmodernist feminist theorists have made clear, there is no single woman's experience to be revealed. Both experience and feeling thus have been called into question as the source of an unproblematic knowledge of the world that will lead to praxis. As Diana Fuss comments: "`female experience' is never as unified, as knowable, as universal, and as stable as we presume it to be."[67]

Challenges to the concept of a unitary women's experience by both women of color and by postmodern critics has not meant the abandonment of experience as a source of knowledge for feminist teachers. Of course experience, like feeling, is socially constructed in the sense that we can only understand it and speak about it in ideas and terms that are part of an existing ideology and language. But in a stance similar to that of Lorde in her use of the erotic, feminist teachers have explored the ways in which women have experienced the material world through their bodies. This self-examination of lived experience is then used as a source of knowledge that can illuminate the social processes and ideology that shape us. As Fuss suggests, "Such a position permits the introduction of narratives of lived experience into the classroom while at the same time challenging us to examine collectively the central role social and historical practices play in shaping and producing these narratives."[68] One example of this approach is found in the work of Frigga Haug and the group of German feminists of which she is a part.[69] Haug and this group use what they call collective memory work to explore their feelings about their own bodies in order to uncover the social construction of their selves:

> Our collective empirical work set itself the high-flown task of identifying the ways in which individuals construct themselves into existing structures, and are thereby themselves formed; the way in which they reconstruct social structures; the points at which change is possible, the points where our chains chafe most, the point where accommodations have been made.[70]

This collective exploration of "the point where . . . chains chafe most" recalls the Freirean culture circles, in which peasants would take such examples as their personal experiences with the landlord as the starting point for their education or conscientization. Basic to their approach is a belief in reflection and a rejection of a view of people as "fixed, given, unchangeable." By working collectively on "memory work," a sharing and comparison of their own lives, Haug and her group hope to uncover the workings of hegemonic ideology in their own subjectivities. Another example of such collective work can be found in the Jamaican women's theater group, Sistren. Founded in 1977, Sistren is a collaborative theater group made up of working-class Jamaican women who create and write plays based on a collaborative exploration of their own experiences. The life histories of the women of Sistren have been collected in *Lionheart Girl: Life Stories of Jamaican Women*. In the compilation of this book, the Sistren collective used the same process of the collective sharing and analysis of experience that is the basis for their theater work. As the company's director Honor Ford-Smith writes:

> We began meeting collectively at first. Starting with our childhood, we made drawings of images based on such themes as where we had grown up, symbols of oppression in our lives, our relationships with men, our experience with race and the kind of work we had done.[71]

For Haug and her group, the Sistren collective, the early consciousness-raising groups, and the Freirean culture circles, collective sharing of experience is the source of knowledge of the forces that have shaped and continue to shape them. But their recognition of the shifting meaning of experience as it is explored through memory insists on the profoundly social and political nature of who we are.

The Question of Difference

Both women of color writing from a perspective of cultural feminism and postmodernist feminist theorists converge in their critique of the concept of a universal "women's experience." While the idea of a unitary and universal category "woman" has been challenged by women of color for its racist assumptions, it has also been challenged by recent analyses of feminist theorists influenced by postmodernism, who point to the social construction of subjectivity and who emphasize the "unstable" nature of the self. Postmodernist feminist critics such as Chris Weedon have argued that socially given identities such as "woman" are "precarious, contradictory, and in process, constantly being reconstituted in discourse each time we speak."[72] This kind of analysis considers the ways in which "the subject" is not an object; that is, not fixed in a static social structure, but constantly being created, actively creating the self, and struggling for new ways of being in the world through new forms of discourse or new forms of social relationships. Such analysis calls for a recognition of the positionality of each person in any discussion of what can be known from experience. This calling into question the permanence of subjectivities is what Jane Flax refers to as the "unstable self."[73] If we view individual selves as being constructed and negotiated, then we can begin to consider what exactly those forces are in which individuals shape themselves and by which they are shaped. The category of "woman" is itself challenged as it is seen more and more as a part of a symbolic system of ideology. Donna Haraway calls all such claims of identity into question:

> With the hard-won recognition of their social and historical constitution, gender, race, and class cannot provide the basis for belief in "essential" unity: There is nothing about being "female" that naturally binds women. There is not even such a state as "being" female, itself a highly complex category constructed in contested sexual discourses and other social practices. Gender, race, or class consciousness is an achievement forced on us by the terrible historical experience of the contradictory social realities of patriarchy, colonialism, and capitalism.[74]

These analyses support the challenges to assumptions of an essential and universal nature of women and women's experience that have come from lesbian critics and women of color.[75]

Both women of color and lesbian critics have pointed to the complexity of socially given identities. Black women and other women of color raise challenges to the assumption that the sharing of experience will create solidarity and a theoretical understanding based upon a common women's standpoint. Lesbian feminists, both White and of color, point to the destructive nature of homophobia and what Adrienne Rich has called compulsory heterosexuality. As is true of White, heterosexual, feminist educators, these theorists base their analysis upon their own experiences, but those experiences reveal not only the workings of sexism, but of racism, homophobia, and class oppression as well. This complex perspective underlies the Combahee River Collective Statement, a position paper written by a group of African-American feminists in Boston in the 1970s. This statement makes clear what a grounded theory of experience means for women whose value is denied by the dominant society in numerous ways. The women in the Combahee River Collective argue that "the most profound and potentially most radical politics come directly out of our own identity, as opposed to working to end somebody else's oppression."[76] For African-American women, an investigation of the shaping of their own identities reveals the ways in which sexism and racism are interlocking forms of oppression:

> As children we realized that we were different from boys and that we were treated differently. For example, we were told in the same breath to be quiet both for the sake of being "ladylike" and to make us less objectionable in the eyes of white people. As we grew older we became aware of the threat of physical and sexual abuse from men. However, we had no way of conceptualizing what was so apparent to us, what we *knew* was really happening.[77]

When African-American teachers like Michele Russell or Barbara Omolade describe their feminist pedagogy, they ground that pedagogy in an investigation of experience in material terms. As Russell describes her teaching of an introductory Black Studies class for women at Wayne County Community College in Detroit: "We have an hour together. . . . The first topic of conversation — among themselves and with me — is what they went through just to make it in the door, on time. That, in itself becomes a lesson."[78] And Omolade points out in her discussion of her teaching at Medgar Evers College in New York, a college whose students are largely African-American women:

> No one can teach students to "see," but an instructor is responsible for providing the coherent ordering of information and content. The classroom process is one of information-sharing in which students learn to generalize their particular life experiences within a community of fellow intellectuals.[79]

Thus the pedagogy of Russell and Omolade is grounded in experience as a source of knowledge in a particularly materialistic way; the knowledge generated reveals the overlapping forms of oppression lived by women of color in this society.

The investigation of the experiences of women of color, lesbian women, women whose very being challenges existing racial, sexual, heterosexual, and class dominance, leads to a knowledge of the world that both acknowledges differences and points to the need for an "integrated analysis and practice based upon the fact that the major systems of oppression are interlocking."[80] The turning to experience thus reveals not a universal and common women's essence, but, rather, deep divisions in what different women have experienced, and in the kinds of knowledge they discover when they examine their own experience. The recognition of the differences among women raises serious challenges to feminist pedagogy by calling into question the authority of the teacher/theorist, raising feelings of guilt and shame, and revealing tensions among students as well as between teacher and students. In classes of African-American women taught by African-American teachers, the sharing of experience can lead to the same sense of commonality and sharing that was true of early consciousness-raising groups. But in settings in which students come from different positions of privilege or oppression, the sharing of experience raises conflicts rather than building solidarity. In these circumstances, the collective exploration of experience leads not to a common knowledge and solidarity based on sameness, but to the tensions of an articulation of difference. Such exploration raises again the problems left unaddressed by Freirean pedagogy: the overlapping and multiple forms of oppression revealed in "reading the world" of experience.

CONCLUSION

Both Freirean and feminist pedagogies are based on political commitment and identification with subordinate and oppressed groups; both seek justice and empowerment. Freire sets out these goals of liberation and social and political transformation as universal claims, without exploring his own privileged position or existing conflicts among oppressed groups themselves. Writing from within a tradition of Western modernism, his theory rests on a belief of transcendent and universal truth. But feminist theory influenced by postmodernist thought and by the writings of women of color challenges the underlying assumptions of these universal claims. Feminist theorists in particular argue that it is essential to recognize, as Julie Mitchell comments, that we cannot "live as human subjects without in some sense taking on a history."[81] The recognition of our own histories means the necessity of articulating our own subjectivities and our own interests as we try to interpret and critique the social world. This stance rejects the universalizing tendency of much "malestream" thought, and insists on recognizing the power and privilege of who we are. As Biddy Martin and Chandra Mohanty comment:

> The claim to a lack of identity or positionality is itself based on privilege, on the refusal to accept responsibility for one's implication in actual historical or social relations, or a denial that positionalities exist or that they matter, the denial of one's own personal history and the claim to a total separation from it.[82]

Fundamental to recent feminist theory is a questioning of the concept of a coherent subject moving through history with a single essential identity. Instead, feminist theorists are developing a concept of the constant creation and negotiation of selves within structures of ideology and material constraints.[83] This line of theoretical analysis calls into question assumptions of the common interests of the oppressed, whether conceived of as women or peasants; it challenges the use of such universal terms as oppression and liberation without locating these claims in a concrete historical or social context. The challenges of recent feminist theory and, in particular, the writings of feminists of color point to the need to articulate and claim a particular historical and social identity, to locate ourselves, and to build coalitions from a recognition of the partial knowledges of our own constructed identities. Recognizing the standpoint of subjects as shaped by their experience of class, race, gender, or other socially defined identities has powerful implications for pedagogy, in that it emphasizes the need to make conscious the subject positions not only of students but of teachers as well. These lines of theoretical analysis have implications for the ways in which we can understand pedagogy as contested, as a site of discourse among subjects, teachers, and students whose identities are, as Weedon puts it, contradictory and in process. The theoretical formulation of the "unstable self," the complexity of subjectivities, what Giroux calls "multi-layered subjects," and the need to position ourselves in relation to our own histories raise important issues for liberatory pedagogies. If all people's identities are recognized in their full historical and social complexity as subject positions that are in process, based on knowledges that are partial and that reflect deep and conflicting differences, how can we theorize what a liberatory pedagogy actively struggling against different forms of oppression may look like? How can we build upon the rich and complex analysis of feminist theory and pedagogy to work toward a Freirean vision of social justice and liberation?

In the complexity of issues raised by feminist pedagogy, we can begin to acknowledge the reality of tensions that result from different histories, from privilege, oppression, and power as they are lived by teachers and students in classrooms. To recognize these tensions and differences does not mean abandonment of the goals of social justice and empowerment, but it does make clear the need to recognize contingent and situated claims and to acknowledge our own histories and selves in process. One significant area of feminist work has been grounded in the collective analysis of experience and emotion, as exemplified by the work of Haug and her group in Germany or by the Jamaican women's theater group, Sistren. In many respects, these projects look back to consciousness raising, but with a more developed theory of ideology and an acute consciousness of difference. As Berenice Fisher argues, a collective inquiry "requires the slow unfolding of layers of experience, both the contradictory experiences of a given woman and the conflicting experiences of different women."[84] Another approach builds on what Bernice Reagon calls the need for coalition building, a recognition and validation of difference. This is similar to what has come to be known as identity politics, exemplified in what Minnie Bruce Pratt is seeking in her discussion of trying to come to terms with her own identity as a privileged Southern White woman.[85] Martin and Mohanty speak of this as a sense of "home," a recognition of the difficulties of coming to terms with privilege or oppression, of the benefits of being an oppressor, or of the rage of being oppressed.[86] This is a validation of both difference and conflict, but also an attempt to build coalitions around common goals rather than a denial of differences.[87] It is clear that this kind of pedagogy and exploration of experiences in a society in which privilege and oppression are lived is risky and filled with pain. Such a pedagogy suggests a more complex realization of the Freirean vision of the collective conscientization and struggle against oppression, one which acknowledges difference and conflict, but which, like Freire's vision, rests on a belief in the human capacity to feel, to know, and to change.

NOTES

1. See as representative Henry Giroux, ed., *Postmodernism, Feminism and Cultural Politics* (Albany: State University of New York Press, 1991); Cleo Cherryholmes, *Power and Criticism: Poststructural Investigations in Education* (New York: Teachers College Press, 1988); Henry Giroux and Roger Simon, eds., *Popular Culture, Schooling and Everyday Life* (Westport, CT: Bergin & Garvey, 1989); Deborah Britzman, *Practice Makes Practice* (Albany: State University of New York Press, 1991); Patti Lather, *Getting Smart: Feminist Research and Pedagogy With/in the Postmodern* (New York: Routledge, 1991).

2. Paulo Freire, *Pedagogy of the Oppressed* (New York: Herder & Herder, 1971), p. 28.

3. Margo Culley and Catherine Portuges, "Introduction," in *Gendered Subjects* (Boston: Routledge & Kegan Paul, 1985). For comparisons of Freirean and feminist pedagogy, see also Frances Maher, "Classroom Pedagogy and the New Scholarship on Women," in *Gendered Subjects*, pp. 29–48, and "Toward a Richer Theory of Feminist Pedagogy: A Comparison of `Liberation' and `Gender' Models for Teaching and Learning," *Journal of Education, 169*, No. 3 (1987), 91–100.

4. Antonio Gramsci, *Selections from the Prison Notebooks* (New York: International Publishers, 1971).

5. Teresa de Lauretis, *Alice Doesn't: Feminism, Semiotics, Cinema* (Bloomington: Indiana University Press, 1984), p. 178.

6. Audre Lorde, *Sister Outsider* (Trumansburg, NY: The Crossing Press, 1984).

7. See, for example, Elizabeth Ellsworth, "Why Doesn't This Feel Empowering? Working through the Repressive Myths of Critical Pedagogy," *Harvard Educational Review, 59* (1989), 297–324; Ann Berlak, "Teaching for Outrage and Empathy in the Liberal Arts," *Educational Foundations, 3*, No. 2 (1989), 69–94; Deborah Britzman, "Decentering Discourses in Teacher Education: Or, the Unleashing of Unpopular Things," in *What Schools Can Do: Critical Pedagogy and Practice*, ed. Candace Mitchell and Kathleen Weiler (Albany: State University of New York Press, 1992).

8. Freire's method of codifications and generative themes have been discussed frequently. Perhaps the best introduction to these concrete methods can be found in Paulo Freire, *Education for Critical Consciousness* (New York: Seabury,1973).

9. See, for example, Paulo Freire, *The Politics of Education* (Westport, CT: Bergin & Garvey, 1985); Paulo Freire and Donaldo Macedo, *Literacy: Reading the Word and the World* (Westport, CT: Bergin & Garvey, 1987); Paulo Freire and Ira Shor, *A Pedagogy For Liberation* (London: Macmillan, 1987); Myles Horton and Paulo Freire, *We Make the Road by Walking: Conversations on Education and Social Change*, ed. Brenda Bell, John Gaventa, and John Peters (Philadelphia: Temple University Press, 1990).

10. Freire, *Pedagogy of the Oppressed*, p. 28.

11. Paulo Freire, "The Adult Literacy Process as Cultural Action for Freedom," in *The Politics of Education*, p. 57.

12. Freire and Macedo, *Literacy: Reading the Word and the World*.

13. See Simone de Beauvoir, *The Second Sex* (New York: Knopf, 1953), for a more striking use of the male referent.

14. Cameron McCarthy, "Rethinking Liberal and Radical Perspectives on Racial Inequality in Schooling: Making the Case for Nonsynchrony," *Harvard Educational Review, 58* (1988), 265–280.

15. Freire, *Pedagogy of the Oppressed*, p. 30.

16. Freire, *Pedagogy of the Oppressed*, p. 69.

17. Freire, *Pedagogy of the Oppressed*, p. 73.

18. Gayatri Chakravorty Spivak, "Can the Subaltern Speak?," in *Marxism and the Interpretation of Culture*, ed. Cary Nelson and Lawrence Grossberg (Urbana: University of Illinois Press, 1988), pp. 271–313.

19. Freire and Shor, *A Pedagogy for Liberation*, p. 93.

20. Peter McLaren, "Postmodernity and the Death of Politics: A Brazilian Reprieve," *Educational Theory*, 36 (1986), p. 399.

21. When definitions of feminist pedagogy are attempted, they sometimes tend toward generalization and such a broad inclusiveness as to be of dubious usefulness. For example, Carolyn Shrewsbury characterizes feminist pedagogy as follows:

    It does not automatically preclude any technique or approach. It does indicate the relationship that specific techniques have to educational goals. It is not limited to any specific subject matter but it does include a reflexive element that increases the feminist scholarship component involved in the teaching/learning of any subject matter. It has close ties with other liberatory pedagogies, but it cannot be subsumed under other pedagogical approaches. It is transformative, helping us revision the educational enterprise. But it can also be phased into a traditional teaching approach or another alternative pedagogical approach. (Shrewsbury, "What Is Feminist Pedagogy?," *Women's Studies Quarterly*, 15, Nos. 3–4 [1987], p. 12)

    Certain descriptions of feminist pedagogy show the influence of group dynamics and interactionist approaches. See, for example, Nancy Schniedewind, "Feminist Values: Guidelines for Teaching Methodology in Women's Studies," *Radical Teacher*, 18, 25–28. Methods used by feminist teachers include cooperation, shared leadership, and democratic process. Feminist teachers describe such techniques as keeping journals, soliciting students' responses to readings and to the classroom dynamics of a course, the use of role playing and theater games, the use of self-revelation on the part of the teacher, building leadership skills among students by requiring them to teach parts of a course, and contracting for grades. For accounts of classroom practice, see the articles in the special issue on feminist pedagogy of *Women's Studies Quarterly*, 15, Nos. 3–4 (1987); Culley and Portuges, *Gendered Subjects*; Charlotte Bunch and Sandra Pollack, eds., *Learning Our Way* (Trumansburg, NY: The Crossing Press, 1983); Gloria Hull, Patricia Bell Scott, and Barbara Smith, ed., *But Some of Us Are Brave* (Old Westbury, NY: The Feminist Press, 1982); and numerous articles in *Women's Studies Newsletter* and *Radical Teacher*.

22. Nancy Schniedewind, "Teaching Feminist Process," *Women's Studies Quarterly*, 15, Nos. 3–4 (1987), p. 29.

23. Linda Gordon, "A Socialist View of Women's Studies: A Reply to the Editorial, Volume 1, Number 1," *Signs*, 1 (1975), p. 559.

24. A discussion of the relationship of the early women's liberation movement to the civil rights movement and the new left can be found in Sara Evans, *Personal Politics* (New York: Vintage Press, 1980). Based on extensive interviews as well as pamphlets and private documents, Evans shows the origins of both political goals and methods in the earlier male-dominated movement, particularly the model of Black student organizers and the Black church in the South.

25. While mid-nineteenth-century suffragists developed their ideas of human equality and justice through the abolitionist movement, by the late nineteenth century, White suffragists often demonstrated racist attitudes and employed racist strategies in their campaigns for suffrage. This offers another instructive parallel to the White feminist movement of the 1960s. Here, once again, feminist claims emerged out of an anti-racist struggle for civil rights, but later too often took up the universalizing stance that the experiences and issues of White women represented the lives of all women. See bell hooks, *Ain't I a Woman?* (Boston: South End Press, 1981) and *Feminist Theory from Margin to Center* (Boston: South End Press, 1984) for powerful discussions of these issues.

26. Nancy Hawley as quoted in Evans, *Personal Politics*, p. 205.

27. Kathie Sarachild, "Consciousness Raising: A Radical Weapon," in *Feminist Revolution*, ed. Redstockings (New York: Random House, 1975).
28. Redstockings included a number of women who were influential in the women's movement; Shulamith Firestone, Rosalyn Baxandall, Ellen Willis, and Robin Morgan were among a number of other significant feminist writers and activists who participated.
29. Sarachild, "Consciousness Raising," p. 144.
30. Sarachild, "Consciousness Raising," p. 145.
31. Michele Russell, "Black-Eyed Blues Connection: From the Inside Out," in Bunch and Pollack, *Learning Our Way*, pp. 272–284.
32. Sarachild, "Consciousness Raising," p. 147.
33. William Hinton, *Fanshen* (New York: Vintage Books, 1966).
34. See Berenice Fisher, "Guilt and Shame in the Women's Movement: The Radical Ideal of Political Action and Its Meaning for Feminist Intellectuals," *Feminist Studies, 10* (1984), 185–212, for an extended discussion of the impact of the methods and goals of the civil rights movement on consciousness raising and the early women's liberation movement.
35. Sarachild, "Consciousness Raising," p. 145.
36. Sarachild, "Consciousness Raising," p. 147.
37. Irene Peslikis, "Resistances to Consciousness," in *Sisterhood Is Powerful*, ed. Robin Morgan (New York: Vintage Books, 1970), p. 339.
38. See, for example, Kathy McAfee and Myrna Wood, "Bread and Roses," in *Voices from Women's Liberation*, ed. Leslie Tanner (New York: New American Library, 1970) for an early socialist feminist analysis of the need to connect the women's movement with the class struggle.
39. Berenice Fisher, "What is Feminist Pedagogy?," *Radical Teacher, 18*, 20–25. See also bell hooks, "on self-recovery," in *talking back: thinking feminist, thinking black* (Boston: South End Press, 1989).
40. Marilyn Boxer, "For and about Women: The Theory and Practice of Women's Studies in the United States," in *Reconstructing the Academy: Women's Education and Women's Studies*, ed. Elizabeth Minnich, Jean O'Barr, and Rachel Rosenfeld (Chicago: University of Chicago Press, 1988), p. 71.
41. See Florence Howe, *Myths of Coeducation* (Bloomington: University of Indiana Press, 1984), for a collection of essays documenting this period.
42. Boxer estimates there were over 300 programs and 30,000 courses in women's studies given in 1982. See "For and about Women," p. 70.
43. The literature of feminist challenges to specific disciplines is by now immense. For general discussions of the impact of the new scholarship on women, see Ellen DuBois, Gail Kelly, Elizabeth Kennedy, Carolyn Korsmeyer, and Lillian Robinson, eds., *Feminist Scholarship: Kindling in the Groves of Academe* (Urbana: University of Illinois Press, 1985), and Christie Farnhum, ed., *The Impact of Feminist Research in the Academy* (Bloomington: Indiana University Press, 1987).
44. See, for example, Diana Fuss, *Essentially Speaking* (New York: Routledge, 1989); hooks, *talking back*; Britzman, *Practice Makes Practice*.
45. Susan Stanford Friedman, "Authority in the Feminist Classroom: A Contradiction in Terms?" in Culley and Portuges, *Gendered Subjects*, 203–208.
46. hooks, *talking back*, p. 29.
47. See Alison Jaggar, *Feminist Politics and Human Nature* (Sussex, Eng.: Harvester Press, 1983), for an excellent discussion of these perspectives.
48. Barbara Hillyer Davis, "Teaching the Feminist Minority," in Bunch and Pollack, *Learning Our Way*, p. 91.
49. See, for example, Evelyn Torton Beck, "Self-disclosure and the Commitment to Social Change," *Women's Studies International Forum, 6* (1983), 159–164.
50. Margo Culley and Catherine Portuges, "The Politics of Nurturance," in *Gendered Subjects*, p. 12. See also Margo Culley, "Anger and Authority in the Introductory Women's Studies Classroom," in *Gendered Subjects*, pp. 209–217.

51. See Davis, "Teaching the Feminist Minority," for a thoughtful discussion of the contradictory pressures on the feminist teacher both to nurture and challenge women students.

52. Friedman, "Authority in the Feminist Classroom," p. 207.

53. Fisher, "What is Feminist Pedagogy?" p. 22.

54. Fisher, "Guilt and Shame in the Women's Movement," p. 202.

55. Charlotte Bunch, "Not by Degrees: Feminist Theory and Education," in Bunch and Pollack, *Learning Our Way*, p. 156.

56. See Berenice Fisher, "Professing Feminism: Feminist Academics and the Women's Movement," *Psychology of Women Quarterly*, 7 (1982), 55–69, for a thoughtful discussion of the difficulties of retaining an activist stance for feminists in the academy.

57. See Arlie Russell Hochschild, *The Managed Heart* (Berkeley: University of California Press, 1983), for a discussion of the social construction of emotions in contemporary society. Hochschild argues that emotion is a "biologically given sense . . . and a means by which we know about our relation to the world" (p. 219). At the same time she investigates the ways in which the emotions themselves are manipulated and constructed.

58. Berenice Fisher, "The Heart Has Its Reasons: Feeling, Thinking, and Community Building in Feminist Education," *Women's Studies Quarterly*, 15, Nos. 3–4 (1987), 48.

59. Lorde, *Sister Outsider*, p. 37.

60. Lorde, *Sister Outsider*, p. 34.

61. Lorde, *Sister Outsider*, p. 123.

62. Lorde, *Sister Outsider*, p. 58.

63. Lorde, *Sister Outsider*, p. 53.

64. Lorde, *Sister Outsider*, p. 100.

65. Adrienne Rich, "Taking Women Students Seriously," in *On Lies, Secrets, and Silence*, ed. Adrienne Rich (New York: W. W. Norton, 1979), p. 243.

66. Sarachild, "Consciousness Raising," p. 148.

67. Fuss, *Essentially Speaking*, p. 114.

68. Fuss, *Essentially Speaking*, p. 118.

69. Frigga Haug, *Female Sexualization* (London: Verso Press, 1987).

70. Haug, *Female Sexualization*, p. 41.

71. Sistren Collective with Honor Ford-Smith, *Lionheart Girl: Life Stories of Jamaican Women* (London: Woman's Press, 1986), p. 15.

72. Chris Weedon, *Feminist Practice and Poststructuralist Theory* (Oxford: Basil Blackwell, 1987), p. 33.

73. Jane Flax, "Postmodernism and Gender Relations in Feminist Theory," *Signs*, 12 (1987), 621–643.

74. Donna Haraway, "A Manifesto for Cyborgs," *Socialist Review*, 80 (1985), 72.

75. As representative, see Johnella Butler, "Toward a Pedagogy of Everywoman's Studies," in Culley and Portuges, *Gendered Subjects*; hooks, *talking back*; Hull, Scott, and Smith, *But Some of Us Are Brave*; Gloria Joseph and Jill Lewis, *Common Differences: Conflicts in Black and White Perspectives* (New York: Anchor Books, 1981); Chierrie Moraga and Gloria Anzaldua, eds., *This Bridge Called My Back* (Watertown, MA: Persephone Press, 1981); Barbara Omolade, "A Black Feminist Pedagogy," *Women's Studies Quarterly*, 15, Nos. 3–4 (1987), 32–40; Russell, "Black-Eyed Blues Connection," pp. 272–284; Elizabeth Spellman, "Combatting the Marginalization of Black Women in the Classroom," in Culley and Portuges, *Gendered Subjects*, pp. 240–244.

76. Combahee River Collective, "Combahee River Collective River Statement," in *Home Girls*, ed. Barbara Smith (New York: Kitchen Table — Women of Color Press, 1983), p. 275.

77. Combahee River Collective, "Combahee River Collective Statement," p. 274.

78. Russell, "Black-Eyed Blues Connection," p. 155.

79. Omolade, "A Black Feminist Pedagogy," p. 39.

80. Combahee River Collective, "Combahee River Collective Statement," p. 272.

81. Juliet Mitchell, *Women: The Longest Revolution* (New York: Pantheon Books, 1984).

82. Biddy Martin and Chandra Mohanty, "Feminist Politics: What's Home Got to Do With It?" in *Feminist Studies/ Critical Studies,* ed. Teresa de Lauretis (Bloomington: University of Indiana Press, 1986), p. 208.

83. See, for example, Flax, "Postmodernism and Gender Relations in Feminist Theory"; Sandra Harding, *The Science Question in Feminism* (Ithaca: University of Cornell Press, 1986); Dorothy Smith, *The Everyday World as Problematic* (Boston: Northeastern University Press, 1987); Haraway, "A Manifesto for Cyborgs," *Socialist Review, 80* (1985), 64–107; Nancy Hartsock, *Money, Sex, and Power* (New York: Longman, 1983); Mary O'Brien, *The Politics of Reproduction* (Boston: Routledge & Kegan Paul, 1981); Irene Diamond and Lee Quinby, eds., *Feminism and Foucault* (Boston: Northeastern University Press, 1988); Linda Alcoff, "Cultural Feminism versus Post Structuralism: The Identity Crisis in Feminist Theory," *Signs, 13* (1988), 405–437; Special Issue on Feminism and Deconstruction, *Feminist Studies, 14,* No. 1 (1988); Judith Butler, *Gender Trouble* (New York: Routledge, 1990); Linda Nicholson, ed., *Feminism/Postmodernism* (New York: Routledge, 1990).

84. Fisher, "The Heart Has Its Reasons," p. 49.

85. Minnie Bruce Pratt, "Identity: Skin Blood Heart," in *Yours in Struggle,* ed. Elly Bulkin, Minnie Bruce Pratt, and Barbara Smith (Brooklyn, NY: Long Hand Press, 1984).

86. Martin and Mohanty, "What's Home Got to Do With It?"

87. Bernice Reagon, "Coalition Politics: Turning the Century," in Smith, *Home Girls,* pp. 356–369.

Afterword:
Realizing a More Inclusive Pedagogy

FRANK TUITT

In recent times, one of the most active debates in academia has been whether or not changes in curriculum and pedagogy should be made to meet the needs of an increasingly diverse student population.[1] Of growing concern is the possibility that the teaching practices of traditional academic culture do not serve today's racially diverse student body (Adams, 1992; Banks, 1991). The belief is that university and college faculty members, operating on the notion that one pedagogy fits all students, continue to use traditional modes of instruction that create hostile and potentially harmful learning environments (Feagin & Imani, 1993).[2]

In response to this dilemma, many theorists, including Antonia Darder (1996) and bell hooks (1994), have explored ways to create a hospitable and productive learning environment that addresses the needs of a racially diverse student population. This chapter is intended as a resource for educators who are seeking to improve their teaching in racially diverse college classrooms. The discussion is divided into three sections. In the first, I describe the theoretical and guiding principles behind pedagogical models that seek to create inclusive learning environments. In the next two sections, I outline the common characteristics of inclusive pedagogical models and present an analysis of the implications this approach has for teaching and learning in racially diverse college classrooms. It is my hope that this essay will contribute to the development of a more inclusive pedagogy for professors seeking to improve the manner in which they teach.

Inclusive pedagogy is a term I use to describe an emerging body of literature (Adams, 1992; Banks, 1991; Darder, 1996; Giroux & McLaren, 1996; hooks, 1994) that advocates teaching practices that embrace the whole student in the learning process. Unlike traditional modes of instruction, proponents of inclusive pedagogical models argue that students enter the classroom as personal, political, and intellectual beings (Reyes, Smith, Yazzie, Hussein, & Tuitt, 2001). These scholars propose a variety of pedagogical models that focus on the education of the whole individual — that is, the union of the mind, body, and soul of human beings. By viewing students as whole human beings with complex lives and experiences, inclusive pedagogy offers some insight into how college educators can create classrooms in which diversity is valued as a central component of the learning process.[3]

While the inclusive pedagogy literature offers a range of theoretical and pedagogical practices related to educating the whole student, limited research has been conducted on the impact of inclusive pedagogical practices in higher education (Baker, 1998; Zimmerman, 1991). However, the literature does provide some insight into the benefits and consequences of inclusive pedagogy on the educational experience of students in racially diverse college classrooms (Baker, 1998; Steele, 1999; Zimmerman, 1991). For instance, Zimmerman's study indicates that college teaching and learning can be improved through inclusive pedagogical practices. She identifies increased opportunities for student interaction during the learning process and the development of a genuine sense of community in the classroom as positive influences on the educational experience. Steele studies whether or not reducing the "stereotype threat" that Black students might experience improves academic performance.[4] Finally, Baker examines undergraduate African American students' perceptions of their classroom environment at a traditionally White institution.

Baker (1998) notes that while higher education classrooms are becoming increasingly diverse, existing pedagogical practices are not leading toward a healthy learning environment for these students. She identifies three components that, in theory, are central to creating a learning environment that is accessible to all students regardless of their race or ethnicity. These components — the synthesis of faculty-student relationships, issues of instructional design, and understanding perceptual barriers — serve as a functional link to theoretical arguments about inclusive pedagogy and provide the framework for this essay.

First, Baker (1998) argues that teaching is a process of social interaction in that the classroom climate is directly connected to the interpersonal relationships among professor and students. Like their White counterparts, African American students view their relationships with faculty members as important factors in achieving success within the academic environment (Dorsey & Jackson, 1995). Higher education scholarship has shown that the relationship between professor and student has a significant impact on the success of students of color in the classroom (Hurtado, Milem, Clayton-Pederson, & Allen, 2000). However, in traditional college classrooms, there is little teacher-student interaction because these college classes revolve around the activity and control of the professor. As Palmer (1993) states, "In many circumstances the lecturing is authoritarian, the listening is unengaged and the memorization is mechanical" (pp. 32–33). In contrast, inclusive pedagogical models value relationships between professors and students by challenging the notion that only the professor possesses knowledge. For example, Banks and McGee's "equity pedagogy" (1997) intentionally incorporates students in a process of knowledge construction and production that alters the traditional power relationship between teachers and students.

Baker (1998) also speaks to the need for faculty members to understand, improve, and apply methods of instruction that include the learner in the process. However, she notes that this transformation in instructional design rarely happens because college professors do not necessarily possess any formal training in instructional design, and they therefore tend to imitate the pedagogical strategies of their own former instructors (Baker, 1998; King, 1995). To create more inclusive learning environments, professors must reconfigure how they situate themselves in their classrooms by regarding each classroom as a distinct space where strategies must constantly be changed, reinvented, and reconceptualized to address each new teaching experience (hooks, 1994).

Lastly, empirical evidence suggests that students' perception of their professors' attitudes toward them have potentially negative consequences for their participation in the learning environment. Several studies (Allen, 1988; Baker, 1998; Feagin & Imani, 1993) indicate that African American students believe their faculty members had preconceived notions about their academic ability. These scholars conclude that such negative perceptions could lead students to withdraw from participating in the learning environment and consequently weaken their academic performance:

> There is extensive evidence that underrepresented minority students — including many academically well prepared individuals — tend to earn lower grades, on average, at historically white colleges and universities than do majority students with similar academic backgrounds, such as similar college admission test scores. (Gándara & Maxwell-Jolly, 1999, pp. vii–viii)

Steele (1999) found that when gifted Black students take a difficult exam "the extra apprehension they feel in comparison with whites is less about their own ability than it is about having to perform on a test in a situation that may be primed to treat them stereotypically" (p. 52). This suggests that talented Black students who perceive their learning environment to be racially unfair will not perform to their ability. To address these and other pedagogical issues in the classroom, an increasing number of scholars now call for new modes of teaching and learning to create a more inclusive learning environment (hooks, 1994; Karenga, 1995; Obiakor, 1994). Some of these inclusive pedagogical models are described in the next section.

INCLUSIVE PEDAGOGICAL MODELS

hooks (1994) argues that students today want a meaningful education, one in which their professors will not offer them information without addressing the connection between what they are learning and their overall life experiences. According to hooks, an engaging pedagogy that respects and cares for the souls of our students is essential if we are to provide conditions in which learning can deeply and intimately begin. Prince and Igbineweka (1995) suggest that professors need to go beyond the inclusion of new course material; they contend that professors also need to transform their consciousness in order to understand that the creation of knowledge must have a liberating purpose behind it.

Darder (1996) states that "prior to any engagement with instrumental questions of practice, educators must delve rigorously into those specific theoretical issues that are fundamental to the establishment of a culturally democratic foundation for a critical bicultural pedagogy in the classroom" (p. 2). Similarly, Banks and McGee (1997) define equity pedagogy as teaching strategies and classroom environments that allow students from diverse racial, ethnic, and cultural groups to obtain the knowledge, skills, and attitudes needed to function effectively within, and to help create and perpetuate, a just, humane, and democratic society.[5] Their definition suggests that it is not enough to help students learn to read and write in traditional classrooms without challenging assumptions, paradigms, and hegemonic characteristics embedded in the learning process. As they write, "helping students to become reflective and active citizens of a public, democratic society is at the essence of our conception of equity pedagogy" (pp. 78–79).

Inclusive pedagogical models seeking to transform higher education are not new to the academic arena. Since the development of women's studies in the late 1960s and early 1970s, efforts have been underway to transform the higher education curriculum and pedagogy. Sullivan (1995) contends that "the addition of women's studies in various forms as a part of higher education provides one significant marker for this change" (p. 5). Some consider the women's studies movement a successful example of how mainstream curriculum and pedagogy can be altered to become more inclusive in the extent to which they address the experiences of diverse students — in this case women.[6] Another major influence on the movement to transform higher education evolved from the work of Paulo Freire (1971). According to Weiler (1993), both feminist pedagogy and Freirean pedagogy rest on visions of social transformation:

> Both pedagogies assert the existence of oppression in people's material conditions of existence and as a part of consciousness; both rest on a view of consciousness as more than a sum of dominating discourse, but as containing within it a critical capacity; . . . and both thus see human beings as subjects and actors in history and hold a strong commitment to justice as a vision of a better world and a potential for liberation. (p. 450)

Friere's work was the genesis of critical pedagogy. According to Giroux and Simon (1988), critical pedagogy "takes into consideration how the symbolic and material transactions of the everyday provide the basis for rethinking how people give meaning and ethical substance to their experiences and voices" (p. 10). Critical pedagogy has spawned several variations. For example, Giroux's (1992) border pedagogy moves beyond the opening of diverse cultural and historical spaces by allowing students to explore the fragile nature of their identities, as students of color cross borderlands distinguished by different languages, voices, and experiences (Dlamini, 2002). Another extension of critical pedagogy is critical race pedagogy (Solorzano & Yosso, 1997). Lynn (1999) defines critical race pedagogy "as an analysis of racial, ethnic, and gender subordination in education that relies mostly on the perceptions, experiences, and counterhegemonic practices of educators of color" (p. 12). Other pedagogical models take into account the impact of race and ethnicity in their design.

Recognizing that Black students might perform better in learning environments that are socioculturally, cognitively, and linguistically compatible, several scholars advocate for pedagogy that is grounded in an African American culture (Murrel, 2002). For example, Karenga (1995) embraces the Afrocentric model, which challenges students to frame questions and projects from their own experience and for their own futures. Ladson-Billings (1994, 1995) promotes a pedagogical model that incorporates African and African American culture. She argues that a culturally relevant pedagogy will prepare students for their participation in a White-dominated world. Murrel (2002) engages in an African-centered pedagogy, which seeks to circumvent structures of inequality in schooling that compromise the education of African American students. Hill-Collins (1991) combines Afrocentricism with feminist pedagogy "to form a more integrated and holistic cultural critique . . . that is grounded in the history and struggles of African peoples" (cited in Lynn, 1999, p. 6). According to Henry (1992), African womanist pedagogy provides students with positive reinforcement, promotes collective responsibility and sharing, and teaches them to take ownership of their own learning. The common features of the aforementioned inclusive pedagogical models are outlined in the next section.

CHARACTERISTICS OF AN INCLUSIVE PEDAGOGY

Faculty-Student Interaction

Baker (1998) posits that the social interaction between faculty and students provides the foundation for a positive faculty-student relationship. She notes that students expect to be challenged, and admire professors who do this in a concerned manner. Baker argues that faculty who are knowledgeable, caring, enthusiastic, and available to students in and outside of the classroom have more positive social interactions with their students: "In order for students to feel comfortable in seeking help, the faculty must foster this relationship by creating an open welcoming environment" (p. 68). In essence, interpersonal relationships are most important to students who need to feel connected to the group, who are aware of being upset when their own voices are not heard, and who do not believe that the instructor is the sole source of knowledge (Zimmerman, 1991). One way inclusive pedagogical models attempt to debunk the notion that the professor is the only source of knowledge is by sharing power in the classroom.

Sharing Power

> Professors must genuinely value everyone's presence. There must be ongoing recognition that everyone influences the classroom dynamic. These contributions are resources. Used constructively they enhance the capacity of any class to create an open learning community. (hooks, 1994, p. 8)

Inclusive pedagogical models challenge the traditional notion that only the professor possesses knowledge, and instead propose that professors and students are equally responsible for constructing knowledge (Tuitt, 2000). According to hooks (1994), before the process of creating an inclusive learning environment can occur, "there has to be some deconstruction of the traditional notion that only the professor will always be responsible for classroom dynamics" (p. 8). Dlamini (2002) posits that in critical pedagogy the concept of power-sharing makes students responsible for their own learning. She writes, "When power is shared, voices are given equal opportunity of expression; different critical ways of knowing and learning are validated" (p. 58). Obidah (2000) contends that critical pedagogy, which begins with human agency, sees professors as transformative intellectuals who reject traditional notions of power and authority in the classroom and "allow intellectual and critical spaces to exist wherein students may make meaning and find power for themselves" (p. 7).

Feminist pedagogical models acknowledge that professors work with heterogeneous groups of students within a competitive and individualistic culture where the teacher holds institutional power and responsibility — even if she may want to reject that power (Weiler, 1993). The teacher gives grades, is evaluated by colleagues in terms of expertise in a specific discipline or body of knowledge, and is expected to take responsibility for meeting the goals of an academic course, as it is understood within the university. Weiler (1993) notes that "not only does the university structure impose this model of institutional authority, but students themselves expect it" (p. 460). She says that feminist educators address this tension between their ideals of collective education and the demands of the university by using a variety of pedagogical models that enhance their ability to theorize and to recognize their own power. This strategy views authority "not in the institutional terms of a bureaucratized university system, but rather as an attempt to claim the authority of theorist and guide students who are themselves potential theorists" (p. 462).

According to hooks (1994), professors' efforts to respect cultural diversity often lead them to confront the limitations of their own training and knowledge, and the potential loss of their authority. She writes that "many teachers are disturbed by the political implications of a multicultural education because they fear losing control in a classroom where there is no one way to approach a subject — only multiple ways and multiple references" (p. 36). As an alternative, hooks proposes that the central goal of transformative pedagogy is to make the classroom a democratic setting where everyone has the responsibility to contribute. Consequently, in an effort to alter power relationships in the learning environment, inclusive pedagogical models advocate for a dialogical relationship between professor and students.

Dialogical Professor-Student Interaction

According to Shor (1992), a dialogue is "a mutually created discourse which questions existing canons of knowledge and challenges power relations in the classroom and in society" (p. 87). He advocates for a dialogical process that values student voices as much as teacher expertise and knowledge.[7] Consequently, the dialogical process seeks to create respectful, challenging, and collaborative learning environments and to ensure that there is mutual professor-student participation. However, this work requires more time and effort from teachers and students and a willingness to trust and take risks with one another (hooks, 1994). Therefore, it is safer for professors, and perhaps more comfortable for some students, to choose safe, conventional techniques, such as the lecture mode (Zimmerman, 1991). Zimmerman notes that "when teachers deviate from lecture format there often is discomfort among their students, some of whom may feel that not lecturing is tantamount to a dereliction of duty. These instructors may be seen as stepping outside the traditional role and even accused of withholding knowledge" (p. 58). One strategy for creating a successful dialogical interaction between professor and student is the activation of student voices.

Activation of Student Voice

Another important element of inclusive pedagogical models is the acknowledgment that all students have a voice and that they should be encouraged to use it. Darder (1996) stresses that one of the most important goals of a critical pedagogy is to allow for diverse voices to make their way to the center of the dialogical process, rather than to remain forever silent or at the periphery of traditional classroom life. According to Giroux and McLaren (1996):

> The concept of voice is crucial to the development of a critical classroom pedagogy because it provides an important basis for constructing and demonstrating the fundamental imperatives of a strong democracy. Such a pedagogy attempts to organize classroom relationships so that students can draw upon and confirm those dimensions of their own histories and experiences which are deeply rooted in the surrounding community. (p. 324)

As a teacher, hooks "recognizes that students from marginalized groups enter the classrooms within institutions where their voices have been neither heard nor welcomed, whether these students discuss facts — those which any of us might know — or personal experience" (1994, p. 84). Her pedagogy is shaped to respond to the misuse of power by bringing to the classroom pedagogical practices that affirm students' presence and their right to speak in multiple ways on diverse subject matter. This type of pedagogical strategy is based on the assumption that everyone brings to the classroom experiential knowledge that can strengthen the learning environment. One approach to building community in the classroom is to acknowledge individual voice.[8] hooks accomplishes this by having her students keep journals and write paragraphs during class that they read to one another. She believes that "to hear each other is an exercise in recognition. It also ensures that no student remains invisible in the classroom" (p. 41).

Burbules and Rice (1993) posit that professors should be careful how they attempt to activate students' voices in the classroom so that they are sensitive to the various kinds of diversity that may exist. Traditional pedagogy often favors speech that is dispassionate and disembodied. It tends to demand a separation between mind and body, reason and emotion (Young, 1996). It falsely identifies objectivity with calm and unemotional expression. "Thus," writes Young, "expressions of anger, hurt, and passionate concern discount claims and reasons they accompany" (p. 124). To reduce this pattern, Burbules and Rice (1993) suggest that professors must ask questions such as:

- Who may feel unable to speak without explicit or implicit retribution?
- Who may want to speak, but feel so demoralized, or intimidated, by the circumstances that they are entirely silenced?

- What tacit rules of communication may be operating in schools and classrooms that rule certain areas of concern or modes of speech out of bounds by the very procedures the discussion takes for granted? (p. 5)

Finally, the activation of students' voices in diverse classrooms needs to be accompanied by a sense of the context and personal histories that inform the various outlooks that individuals in different positions have on the situation.

According to Giroux and McLaren (1996):

> When communities are ignored by teachers, students often find themselves trapped in institutions that not only deny them a voice, but also deprive them of a relational or contextual understanding of how the knowledge they acquire in the classroom can be used to influence and transform the public sphere. (p. 26)

The failure to create a space for voice appears to limit some students' ability to imagine how they can make a difference in the communities about which they care. By having a voice, students can bring into the classroom the world as they have experienced it.

Utilization of Personal Narratives

In inclusive pedagogical models, life experiences are a central part of the curriculum (Courts & McInerney, 1993). In this instructional strategy, professors encouraged students to personalize subject matter with examples from their own histories and to make connections between the ideas learned in the classroom and those learned through life experiences (Tuitt, 2000). This synthesis can be accomplished using personal narratives. For example, Obidah (2000) encourages students in her classes to integrate their life experiences as they discuss the required readings.

According to Adams (1992), teaching methods should involve a balance of subjective exploration of course material with objective presentation and an invitation for students to personalize the subject matter with examples from their experience. Weiler (1993) explains that "the self-examination of lived experience is then used as a source of knowledge that can illuminate the social processes and ideology that shape us" (p. 466). Fuss (1989) suggests that this initiative introduces narratives of life experience into the classroom and pushes students to explore collectively how these narratives are shaped socially and historically. The Afrocentric model advocates the creation of spaces where students can ascertain and articulate the truth and meaning of their own cultural experience. Critical race pedagogists use the experiences and life stories of students of color to build theories about the impact of race and racism in the United States (Solorzano, 1997).

Macedo declares that "if students are not able to transform their lived experiences into knowledge and to use the already acquired knowledge as a process to unveil new knowledge, they will never be able to participate rigorously in a dialogue process of learning and knowing" (Macedo & Freire, 1996, p. 208). In theory, students are successful in connecting their lived experiences to the content when they are getting the information from a caring, compassionate teacher (Baker, 1998). However, professors must be cautious when introducing life experiences into the classroom; in settings where students come from differing positions of privilege or oppression, the sharing of experiences may generate conflicts rather than build solidarity (Weiler, 1993). When weighing the benefits, inclusive pedagogy recognizes the teacher's responsibility to design instructional strategies that help students use the curriculum to make sense of their particular life experiences within a community of fellow intellectuals (Omolade, 1987).

INSTRUCTIONAL DESIGN ISSUES

Faculty members must understand, improve, and apply methods that include the learner in their instructional design. If professors hope to create inclusive learning environments, they must reconceptualize how they situate themselves in their classrooms.[9] Using theoretical frameworks is one way professors can address this challenge.

Utilization of Theoretical Frameworks

Inclusive pedagogical models employ a range of theoretical frameworks to guide classroom experiences and student learning. According to Severance (1993), "education often seems focused on what goes on in an individual's head; ethos, on the other hand, looks at what occurs in the community of learners and that contributes to the individual's experience of higher education" (p. 115). He argues that professors should move beyond just questioning how learning takes place in the classroom at any given time and place, and consider under what conditions students would like the learning to occur.

— Student Centered

Inclusive pedagogical models situate the student at the center of the learning process and focus on the effectiveness of the learning environment. For example, the ecosystem model (Moos, 1979) asserts that environments, like people, possess unique coherent characteristics. Just as we describe an individual's personality, it is possible to characterize an environment. Moos affirms that a student's comprehension of a classroom influences the way he or she behaves in that space. "Thus", he writes, "environments develop and shape potential as well as support or inhibit initiating and coping behavior" (p. 18). Zimmerman (1991) uses social construction theory as an emerging paradigm for understanding how knowledge is generated. In traditional paradigms, obtaining knowledge involves the student internalizing and reflecting on the ideas and beliefs of the teacher. Zimmerman notes that "this internalization stage is the beginning of an interpersonal process to construct knowledge through interaction and revision with peers" (p. 60).

— Collaboration

Zimmerman (1991) explores various theories of how learners benefit from interacting with and relating and connecting to each other in the classroom. She argues "that each of these theories directly or indirectly support the notion that effective learning is not an autonomous and individualistic act but rather an act of social interaction, of collaboration, and of personal connection" (p. 59).[10] Bruffee (1984) advocates for learners to have more opportunities to collaborate in "knowledge communities" (p. 642). Writing exercises that involve collaboration and class discussion are seen as effective ways to create these knowledge communities, which foster ways of learning together (Zimmerman, 1991).

According to Bruffee (1984), it is not enough to have students work together; it is also necessary to "create and maintain a demanding academic environment that makes collaboration — social engagement in intellectual pursuits — a genuine part of the students' educational environment" (p. 652). Zimmerman (1991) proposes that collaborative learning can have positive implications for students when educators realize that some college learners have a profound desire to feel a personal connection to their teachers, their peers, and their subject matter. She believes that "the ability to develop a sense of community within the structure of a single course could be a great asset to today's college educator" (pp. 220–221). In inclusive pedagogical models, collaborative frameworks are used to embrace the range of cultural differences in the learning environment.

— Cultural Fit

According to Bruner (1996), instructional theory should consider how culture influences learning and apply this knowledge to develop instructional designs that will enable and empower students. For example, Gilligan (1982; Gilligan, Lyons, & Hanmer, 1990) contends that male-generated theories tend to be grounded in ideas of autonomy, competitiveness, and rules — or the "ethic of justice" — while women's developmental theory was grounded in intimacy, cooperation, and caring — or the "ethic of care." Consequently, in inclusive pedagogical models there is recognition of greater diversity in the needs of learners and the awareness that for some students "opportunities for connectedness or relationships are valuable components of the learning process" (Zimmerman, 1991, pp. 73–74).

Baker (1998) believes that educators should engage in "learner analysis," a process that involves identifying the needs of learners in an effort to develop modes of instruction that promote an optimal learning environment. This approach suggests that theoretical frameworks should be developed to design instruction that accounts for cultural differences in the learning environment. For example, Afrocentric womanist pedagogy seeks to guide students' learning by focusing on their academic, intellectual, and cultural development. Similarly, de los Reyes et al. (2001) make their learning model (consisting of three theoretical lenses: the personal, the political, and the intellectual) explicit to their students. They encourage their students to reunite these different ways of understanding the world to engage in coherent, transparent, and effective social and political action. By focusing on the personal, intellectual, and political, students enter the learning environment as whole human beings.

Awareness of Different Learning Styles

Inclusive pedagogical models also take into consideration the fact that students may have different learning styles or different ways of knowing (Tuitt, 2000). Shaw (1996) defines learning style as the characteristics that students bring to a learning situation and that influence how they learn. Anderson and Adams (1992) explain that "a diverse student population means that there is greater variability in learning styles in the same classroom than typically exists with a (racially) homogeneous population of traditional college students" (p. 24). While there is no consensus within the research tradition to directly connect cultural ways of knowing based on race or ethnicity to classroom learning (Adams, 1992), there is adequate evidence to suggest that faculty members should give consideration to the various ways in which students acquire knowledge:

> Recent emphasis on social and cultural diversity in the college classroom reflects the recognition that groups of students enter college with variations in the following areas: (1) social relational skills, values, and characteristics, (2) information-processing orientation and skills, (3) communication patterns, (4) motivational styles, and (5) psychological characteristics. (Anderson & Adams, 1992, p. 20)

Anderson and Adams (1992) discerned that the research concerning learning styles tends to find that White females and African American, Native American, and Hispanic American males and females fall toward the relational end of the continuum, whereas Euro-American and Asian American males fall toward the analytical end of the spectrum. They write, "These differences have distinct implications for preferences in student instruction and teaching strategies. Correspondingly, one initial approach to a teaching change might be to develop a sense of the expectations of students and instructors as they simply interact with one another" (p. 23). Bell (1994) suggests that African American students have a preference for social, interactive learning. Learning environments that foster these characteristics will positively enforce African American students' problem-solving ability. Shade (1984) indicates that African American students analyze and organize information in a relational or holistic rather than an analytic manner. Additionally, Irvine and York (1995) identified three important areas discussed in learning-style research. They include "the cultural content of the teaching-learning process, the importance of affect in teaching culturally diverse students, and the recognition that teachers are accountable for designing instruction that meets individual learning needs" (p. 19). Paying attention to the various ways in which students might be most comfortable accessing the learning environment requires professors to be flexible in managing classrooms.

Fluid and Reflective Practice

> Professors must develop a variable, flexible repertoire of teaching strategies that allow them to match the cultural styles of students from targeted social groups in their college classes. . . . A mixed repertoire enables all students in a college classroom to experience an environment that equalizes cultural styles rather than requires minority cultural styles to give way and acculturate or adapt to the dominant mode, maintaining thereby the cultural edge of students from the dominant culture. (Adams, 1992, p. 15)

Inclusive pedagogical models include a great deal of fluidity in classroom instruction. Correspondingly, agendas are flexible and allow for spontaneous shifts in direction. For example, an engaged pedagogy (hooks, 1994) assumes that, to teach in diverse classrooms, professors must shift not only paradigms but also the way they think, write, and speak. hooks writes that "the engaged voice must never be fixed and absolute but always changing, always evolving in dialogue with a world beyond itself" (p. 11). Freire (1987) suggests that technical expertise and the mastery of content area and methodology is not enough to ensure effective instruction of subordinated cultures. He posits that teachers must have political clarity to effectively create, adopt, and modify teaching strategies that simultaneously respect and challenge learners from diverse cultural groups in a variety of learning environments.

Baker (1998) contends that flexible teaching is critical to the promotion of optimal learning. The students in her study felt that when professors employed multiple strategies, such as group process, lecture, and discussion, their ability to grasp the information improved. Engaging in flexible practice allows professors to adopt and modify their teaching to fit the needs of diverse students in the learning environment. But in order to make adjustments to their teaching, professors should take the time to reflect on their practice.

Professors who employ inclusive pedagogies must constantly interrogate the beliefs and assumptions that guide their practice and allow themselves to enter uncomfortable territory (Obidah, 2000). According to Obidah, this reflective practice protects faculty members from developing new forms of academic rigidity. De los Reyes (2000) states that, for professors to become compassionate and effective educators, they need to engage in the process of introspection, reflection, and action. She combines the concept of praxis (reflection and action) with the process of introspection, or the "systematic and careful linking of the personal, political, and intellectual in a system of beliefs and values" (p. 40). Essentially, professors need to invent and — through reflection — reinvent their teaching so that it is consistent with the goals set for the learning environment (de los Reyes et al., 2000). The aforementioned instructional design strategies take into consideration the fact that students enter the learning environment with their own set of expectations, perceptions, and beliefs that may or may not be in sync with those of the professor.

Perceptual Barriers

Inclusive pedagogical models recognize that students' perceptions of their professors' attitudes toward them may have negative consequences for their participation in the learning environment.[11] Steele (1999) observed that, when Black students' "stereotype threat" was removed, their level of performance increased to that of equally qualified Whites. This change occurred when the students in his study believed that they were participating in a racially fair environment. In Baker's (1998) study, students identified the professor's ability to be "unbiased" as being important to the establishment of an effective faculty-student relationship. She observed that "faculty members created a positive learning atmosphere by being open to the ideas of others, challenging students, and demonstrating concern and belief in the (academic) ability of students" (p. 58). In this context, openness did not just involve openness to students but openness to the ideas of others often excluded from the discourse as well. Both Steele's and Baker's findings suggest that "the success of Black students may depend less on expectations and motivations — things that are thought to drive academic performance — than on trust that stereotypes about their group will not have a limiting effect in their school world" (Steele, 1999, p. 51). In theory, where perceptual barriers may lead students to withdraw from the learning environment, positive faculty-student interaction can lead to higher levels of trust on the part of students.

Reexamination of Belief and Value Systems

To diagnose our students well we must diagnose ourselves. (Palmer, 1993, p. 11)

Inclusive pedagogical models mandate that faculty members examine basic issues as well as deep and unconsciously held beliefs (Prince & Igbineweka, 1995). For example, equity pedagogy requires professors to examine their understanding of the histories, modal characteristics, and intragroup differences of students of color (Banks & McGee, 1997). The majority of people who teach students of color in college are White, and these White teachers must invest time and energy in establishing critical dialogues with students of color if they wish to understand their communities better (Darder, 1996).[12] If professors want to effectively instruct in a racially diverse learning environment, "they must be well versed in the various cultural paradigms that serve to guide human behavior" (Adams, 1992, p. 11). It is not simply a matter of learning about the cultures and experiences of students of color; professors must also examine how their own experiences, values, and beliefs influence how they understand these diverse groups.

Weiler (1993) argues that professors need to name their particular historical and social identity, to locate themselves, and to build coalitions from an awareness of the partial knowledge of their own constructed identities. Understanding how students enter the learning environment — shaped by their experience of class, race, gender, or other socially defined identities — has powerful implications for pedagogy. "It emphasizes the need to make conscious the subject positions not only of students but of teachers as well" (pp. 469–470). Fundamentally, professors need to look inward to understand how their life experiences influence their behavior in the classroom.

Transparent and Self-Actualized Professors

According to hooks (1994), the vast majority of her professors lacked basic communication skills, were not self-actualized, and often used the classroom to enact rituals of control that were about domination and the unjust exercise of power. In contrast, inclusive pedagogical models ask that professors be willing to demonstrate their humanity by identifying weaknesses and sharing personal accounts. It is important for students to understand what experiences and philosophies shape the way their professors teach, for example, what ideology informs their practice. This approach seeks to alleviate perceptual barriers by asking professors to give students a sense of who they are as individuals when they enter the classroom. What lessons do they expect students to take away from their class? For example, Steele (1999) suggests that when professors hold high standards that are reflected in their direct feedback, students feel that they are not viewed stereotypically. According to Steele,

> high standards, at least in a relative sense, should be an inherent part of teaching, and critical feedback should be given in the belief that the recipient can reach those standards. These things go without saying for many students. But they have to be made explicit for students under the stereotype threat. (p. 53)

Steele's study shows that when professors make their expectations and standards explicit, the students trust and respond to the feedback they receive. In theory, increased levels of transparency give students a way of better understanding the intentions and ideas of their professors.

Clarity in Theoretical Objectives of the Course

Many students of color enter learning environments committed to transforming their lives and the communities from which they come. However, a mismatch often exists between faculty and student expectations that is potentially harmful to everyone involved in the learning process (Severance, 1993). hooks (1994) argues that when professors allow their pedagogy to be radically changed by their awareness of a multicultural world, they can provide students the education they desire and deserve. Professors are more explicit about the learning that is supposed to take place in their courses when they are clear about their theoretical objectives. This clarity helps students know what is expected of them. Faculty members must be transparent, and one way professors can accomplish this is to connect their own life experiences to the subject matter.

In theory, when students are allowed to bring life experiences into the learning environment, they are able to use personal narratives as a way of understanding the subject matter. However, professors who are unwilling to share their own personal narratives should not expect students to do so. Exercising power in this manner is coercive. hooks (1994) argues that when professors bring their personal narratives into the discussion it keeps them from functioning as all-knowing, silent interrogators. She advocates for professors to take the first risk by linking personal narratives to academic discussions to show how experience can illuminate and enhance our understanding of academic material. Furthermore, most inclusive pedagogical models invite the sharing of personal experience as a tool for liberatory or transformative agendas.

Transformative Intellectuals

Inclusive pedagogical models are transformative, meaning that the educational process seeks to empower students to change the worlds in which they live. For example, Macedo (Macedo & Freire, 1996) posits that the exchange of life experiences requires a political and ideological analysis and must always be understood within a social praxis that involves both reflection and political action: "A dialogue as a process of learning and knowing must always involve a political project with the objective of dismantling oppressive structures and mechanisms prevalent both in education and society" (p. 203). Accordingly, the Afrocentric pedagogical model encourages students to raise and seek to answer questions about the meaning, the quality, and the direction of their lives, not as abstracted individuals but as members of a community (Karenga, 1995). Therefore, their goal is not simply to make sense of the world they live in, but to change it. Professors need to be aware of this reality and find an effective balance between what they think is valuable learning and the intentions that students have for their education.

— Radical Educators

According to Ellsworth (1993), critical pedagogy emerged from the notion of the "radical" educator who helps students to identify and act against their own and others' oppression. Since the goal of critical pedagogy is to promote a critical democracy, individual freedom, social justice, and social action, these radical professors are willing to transform their own beliefs in response to the understanding of their students. Darder (1996) asserts that political commitment to a liberatory vision is fundamental to creating the conditions for cultural democracy. She argues that a critical bicultural pedagogy can only develop within a social context where teachers are committed to both individual and social empowerment. Similarly, under the Afrocentric pedagogical model, students focus on critical thinking and on challenging the given and plausible alternatives to the established order of things. Most important, this model assumes an integral relationship between knowledge and reflective action (Karenga, 1995). Finally, equity pedagogy creates an environment in which students can acquire, interrogate, and produce knowledge and envision new possibilities (Banks & McGee, 1997). In essence, inclusive pedagogical models call for professors to teach in a manner that transforms consciousness and creates a climate of free expression that is the essence of a truly liberatory education (hooks, 1994).

— Conscientization

According to Freire and Macedo (1987), the more investigative and less certain your pedagogy, the more critical and radical it becomes. Central to Freirean pedagogy is the practice of conscientization: "that is, coming to a consciousness of oppression and a commitment to end that oppression. . . . The role of the teacher in this process is to instigate a dialogue between the teacher and student, based on their common ability to know the world and to act as subjects in the world" (Weiler, 1993, p. 454). According to Freire (1987), dialogue is central to the process of conscientization, in that it leads to the naming of the world, and naming the world empowers the oppressed to act to change it. Feminist pedagogy is similarly grounded in a vision of social change. As Weiler (1993) observes, "it rests solely on truth claims of the primacy of experience and consciousness that are grounded in historically situated social movements" (p. 456). According to Weiler, underlying both Freirean and feminist pedagogy is an assumption of common experience as the basis for political analysis and action. In summary, inclusive pedagogical models require professors to assume the role of transformative intellectuals by treating students as critical agents, questioning how knowledge is produced and distributed, utilizing dialogue, and making knowledge meaningful, critical, and ultimately emancipatory (Giroux & McLaren, 1996).

While inclusive pedagogy has the potential to transform traditional classrooms, the students in them, and the worlds in which they live, its successful application depends on faculty and students' acceptance and implementation of teaching strategies, and consequently has implications for teachers and learners working to change their classroom culture. In the next section, I explore several of these implications in an effort to help professors seeking to create hospitable learning environments in which all students — regardless of their racial background — have a chance to succeed.

INCLUSIVE PEDAGOGY:
CHALLENGES AND IMPLICATIONS FOR TEACHING

Professors committed to engaging in an inclusive pedagogy face the challenge of designing a learning environment that is reflective of a multicultural society and of individual differences among our students. To successfully teach students to participate in a democratic and pluralistic society, educators must "respond to the needs of various groups within our classes as well as to individual students" (Knefelkamp, 1997, p. 11). According to Knefelkamp, the challenge of educating racially diverse students is no different from the very same challenges that an increasingly racially diverse society generates for this country. How can educators create classrooms in which all students, regardless of racial background, have a chance to succeed? If we can't succeed in the classroom, what hope do we have for the larger society? Inclusive pedagogy offers professors some guidance as to how they might reconsider their teaching practices in light of these challenges.

A Return to Excellent Teaching

> Effective teachers are those who involve all of their students in learning how to learn. (Anderson & Adams, 1992, p. 20)

According to Palmer (1993), excellent teaching comes from carefully woven connections among students, the subject, and the professor. Frederick (1995) believes that "good teaching for diverse classes, whether in biology, English, mathematics, or sociology, is good teaching, pure and simple, meaning classrooms with a degree of peer interactions, mutual respect, collaborative small groups, and other forms of active learning" (p. 84). hooks (1994) adds that it is especially important to acknowledge that the teaching approaches and styles (holistic, cooperative, connected, caring, interactive) that facilitate the learning of most students of color, women, and other nonmainstream students are also those that help *all* students learn.[13] Anderson and Adams (1992) agree: "There is an emerging consensus that the repertoires of teaching strategies most effective and responsive in a socially and culturally diverse college classroom are the very same strategies that were identified at an earlier time as the characteristics of teaching excellence for traditional students" (p. 30). To these scholars, excellent teaching is commonly defined in a manner that mirrors inclusive pedagogy as described in this chapter.[14] For example, being aware of multiple learning styles and taking into account what impact the institution and classroom climate have on the learning environment are common elements of inclusive pedagogy and effective teaching. Given the similarity between effective teaching and inclusive pedagogical practices, why hasn't college teaching improved?

In order for professors to place more importance on effective teaching, higher education institutions need to reexamine the ways teaching is valued in academe. Scapp (cited in hooks, 1994) declares that most professors are not inclined to see discussion of pedagogy as central to their academic work and intellectual growth, or the practice of teaching as work that enhances or enriches scholarship. Shulman (1992) insists on a strategy that makes teaching community — and therefore valued — property. He argues for reconnecting pedagogy to disciplines, because in the academy the communities that matter to faculty the most are strongly identified within the disciplines of scholarship:

> If pedagogy is to become an important part of scholarship, we have to provide it with this same kind of documentation and transformation. . . . If teaching is community property in the academy, we have an obligation to judge it. Peer reviews must be applied to teaching. (Shulman, 1993, p. 6)

Shulman (1993) proposes to make the review, examination, and support of teaching part of the responsibility of the disciplinary community. Palmer (1993) concurs; he posits that "no surgeon can do her work without being observed by others who know what she is doing, without participating in grand-round discussions of the patients she and her colleagues are treating" (p. 8). The current academic culture is not one that places a great deal of emphasis on teaching. Though institutional missions may state eloquently that teaching is important, rarely is it assessed on the same level as research and scholarship. While faculty searches may seek scholars who are skilled at both research and teaching, how often are candidates required to address the design of their course and how their pedagogy affords students the opportunity to engage in the intellectual and moral work of the discipline (Shulman, 1993)? While some faculty searches require job talks, teaching remains a relatively private enterprise. Consequently, professors often fail to recognize the importance of linking teaching and learning to their institutional context.

Understanding the Institution and Classroom Context

To Burbules and Rice (1993), universities are no freer from social and political conflict and patterns of domination than are any other institutions. They argue that institutional factors, and the presumptions that students bring intro the classroom, provide a context that often limits the degree of understanding that can be achieved in the learning environment:

> We should try to consider the elements of difference that might affect the communicative possibilities in a particular encounter from the point of view of the parties in-

volved. We should elicit and respect their self-identifications, and admit to ourselves the limits of our ability to identify with, or make inferences about, the subjectivity of others. (Burbules & Rice, 1993, pp. 15–16)

Equity pedagogy recognizes that peer relationships are an important part of the social context of the classroom and should be an important instructional consideration (Banks & McGee, 1997). Furthermore, this premise requires the dismantling of school structures that foster inequality. Banks and McGee (1997) warn that "teachers who try to implement equity pedagogy without attending to factors such as the physical arrangement of space in the classroom and the control inherent in certain types of physical conditions will rarely experience success" (p. 82). Correspondingly, Ellsworth (1993) states that her class does not debate whether or not racist structures and practices are operating at the university; rather, it investigates how they operate and with what effects and contradictions, and where they are vulnerable to political opposition. She argues that a vital interruption of existing power relations within the university consists of disrupting the business as usual — that is, prevailing social relations — in a university classroom. Essentially, inclusive pedagogy will not be effective in a social and political context where professors do not challenge racism, sexism, and other inequalities (Banks & McGee, 1997).

Confronting Racism When It Rears Its Ugly Head

According to Darder (1996), regardless of how committed a professor is to the notion of cultural diversity, it is impossible to create an inclusive environment for students if he or she is not capable of challenging incidences of racism when they surface in the classroom. As she explains, "When educators fail to criticize discriminatory attitudes and behaviors, they permit bicultural students to suffer needless humiliation and psychological violence that negatively reinforce feelings of disentitlement and marginalization in society" (p. 116). Tatum (1992) acknowledges that it is difficult to have meaningful conversations in the classroom without also talking and learning about racism, classism, and sexism. She found that students often had powerful emotional responses to the introduction of issues of oppression, ranging from guilt and shame to anger and despair. To facilitate dialogue involving race-related material, Tatum gives her students guidelines that are intended to structure their participation in the learning environment. However, the use of any set of guidelines cannot guarantee that lessons will go according to the plan.

In the spring of 1988, Ellsworth taught a class at a midwestern university, titled "Media and Anti-Racist Pedagogies." At the end of the semester, students acknowledged that commitment to rational discussion about racism in a classroom setting was not enough to make that setting a safe space for speaking out and talking back. They concluded that "a safe space required high levels of trust and personal commitment to individuals in the class, gained in part through social interaction outside of the class — potlucks, field trips, participation in rallies, and other gatherings" (Ellsworth, 1993, p. 60). Ellsworth learned that voices within the classroom do not and can not carry equal legitimacy, safety, and power in dialogue at any historical moment, and that there are times when the inequalities must be named and addressed by constructing alternative ground rules for communication.

Inevitably, inclusive pedagogical practices that explore experiences of privilege and oppression are risky and filled with pain (Weiler, 1993). However, Tatum (1992) found that when students were given the opportunity to explore race-related material in a classroom where both their affective and intellectual responses were acknowledged and addressed, their level of understanding was greatly enhanced. She identified the development of a safe classroom atmosphere as one strategy for facilitating student development. A safe classroom atmosphere is one in which students' ideas are respected and confidentiality is maintained. Finally, Tatum warns that if professors do not address these reactions, students will develop a resistance to oppression-related content areas. This resistance can ultimately interfere with the cognitive understanding and mastery of the subject matter.

Challenging Students' Resistance

hooks (1994) encountered many students who did not want to learn new pedagogical processes or be in a classroom that differed in anyway from the norm.[15] She attempted to redirect students' attention away from her voice to the voices of other students in the class. This strategy was most effective when students shared experiences in conjunction with academic subject matter. Tatum (1992) identified several sources of student resistance. First, her students typically considered race a taboo topic of discussion, especially in racially mixed settings. Second, many students, regardless of racial-group membership, have been socialized to think of the United States as a just society. She found that many students, particularly White students, initially deny any personal prejudice, recognizing the impact of racism on other people's lives but failing to acknowledge its impact on their own:

> One common result is that some white students, once perhaps active participants in class discussions, now hesitate to continue their participation for fear that their newly recognized racism will be revealed to others. . . . This withdrawal on the part of white students is often paralleled by an increase in participation by students of color who are seeking an outlet for what are often feelings of anger. (Tatum, 1992, p. 156)

Tatum (1992) notes that, when previously vocal White students withdraw from the classroom exchange, students of color often interpret this retrenchment as indifference and experience anger and frustration as their own oppression is heightened. She addresses students' resistance by familiarizing them with racial identity development theory, which attempts to explain how students of different racial backgrounds respond to exploring race-related issues in the classroom (Cross, 1991; Helms, 1990). Additionally, Tatum (1992), Adams (1992), and Frederick (1995) provide a set of strategies that seek to make the learning environment more conducive to student participation. However, even with the aid of instructional strategies, teaching in an inclusive manner is difficult.

Finding the Courage to Teach

In inclusive pedagogy, faculty members have the responsibility to adopt pedagogical approaches that help students learn how to engage in open, intercultural discussions about the multicultural nation and the world in which we live — first by supporting each other in dealing with their own fears (Frederick, 1995). Recognizing that teaching in an inclusive manner is hard work and risky, Darder (1996) argues that educators who strive for culturally democratic environments will need to call on their own courage and inner strength to challenge the tension and discomfort they experience when confronting issues of discrimination in the classroom. She observed that professors of color are generally more able to use their own learning experiences and cultural values to develop effective curricula that engage issues related to cultural diversity. In addition, through their awareness of community, these teachers find ways to integrate the students' multiple experiences into the learning process. They are also genuinely able to value and nurture the development of the bicultural voice, given their ability to engage with the lived conditions of cultural domination and resistance.

Finally, Weiler (1993) warns that attempting to engage in inclusive pedagogical practices without recognizing the conflict — not only of divided consciousness (what Audre Lorde calls "the oppressor" within us) but also among teachers and students attempting to work together to name and struggle against oppression — "can lead to anger, frustration, and a retreat to safer more traditional approaches" (p. 451). Professors must stay the course with the realization that some moments will be more successful than others. In that sense, engaging in inclusive pedagogy will require that professors find the courage to teach without falling back on the familiar and safe when lessons do not go as planned. In order to be successful, professors must envision themselves differently in the classroom. Inclusive pedagogy requires professors to step outside of their traditional roles and become more human in the classroom. As hooks (1994) might insist, the days of separating the mind, body, and spirit have outgrown their usefulness in extremely diverse classrooms.

CONCLUSION

> The academy is not paradise. But learning is a place where paradise can be created. The classroom, with all its limitations, remains a location of possibility. In that field of possibility we have the opportunity to labor for freedom, to demand of ourselves and our comrades, an openness of mind and heart that allows us to face reality even as we collectively imagine ways to move beyond boundaries, to transgress. This is education as the practice of freedom. (hooks, 1994, p. 207)

The characteristics of an inclusive pedagogy include but are not limited to faculty-student relationship issues such as sharing power, dialogical professor-student interaction, activation of student voices, and utilization of personal narratives. In theory, faculty members using inclusive pedagogical practices seek to achieve an optimal learning environment by ensuring that there is dialogical professor-student participation — both the professor and students engage in dialogue that affirms their presence and acknowledges their right to speak in multiple ways on diverse subject matter (Tuitt, 2000). In this kind of learning environment, students are encouraged to personalize subject matter with examples from their own history so that there is a connection between ideas learned in the classroom and those learned through life experiences. Classes are taught in a way that is neither teacher centered nor student centered but learning centered, where both professor and students are responsible for constructing knowledge.

Characteristics of inclusive pedagogy related to instructional design are the utilization of theoretical frameworks to inform all aspects of the course, awareness of different learning styles, and fluid and flexible classroom instruction. Professors in search of specific instructional design strategies that will fit a broad range of cultural characteristics may use a range of pedagogical practices that connect variability of individual learning styles to flexibility in the learning environment (Anderson & Adams, 1992). For example, Nelson (1996) identified small-group discussion and flexibility with deadlines as pedagogical practices that professors have successfully implemented for a diverse group of students within the college classroom. Additionally, Baker (1998) found that students favored group discussion over the lecture format because it allowed them to process the information with their peers and ask questions in a more comfortable setting. The students in her study expressed a need to have more interactive or pragmatic experience. Specifically, students identified instructional materials that provided visual examples, did not eliminate faculty interaction, and were accurate in relation to cultural content as most effective (Baker, 1998).

Finally, characteristics of inclusive pedagogy pertaining to perceptual barriers include a reexamination of beliefs and value systems, transparent and self-actualized professors, clarity in theoretical objectives of the course, and transformative intellectuals. To compensate for potential perceptual barriers, inclusive pedagogies dictate that faculty members examine basic issues and often deep and unconsciously held beliefs (Tuitt, 2000). According to Prince and Igbineweka (1995), "if faculty are to be part of the solution and not part of the problem, they must examine their own views and emotional roots" (p. 22). Another way that inclusive pedagogical models seek to alleviate the problems of perceptual barriers is by asking professors to give students a sense of who they are as individuals and what beliefs inform their practice when they enter the classroom. To reduce confusion, professors should be clear about the theory and pedagogy that informs their teaching. Steele (1999) discovered that when professors make explicit their expectations and standards, students trust and respond to the feedback they receive. This transparency can increase students' trust, comfort, and safety in a particular environment and lead to higher levels of class participation.

Overall, inclusive pedagogy requires professors to strive for excellence in their teaching, confront racism when it surfaces, challenge student resistance, and find the courage to teach. In order for traditionally White institutions to experience campuswide cultural transformation in the classroom that enables all students to engage the learning process, colleges and universities must make teaching as much — if not more — of a priority as academic scholarship. Unless higher education institutions meet this challenge, there will be no incentives for today's professors to acquire and implement a broad range of teaching skills that would allow them to create the little pockets of hope so many students are desperately seeking.

NOTES

1. For example, two national organizations, the Association of American Colleges and Universities (AAC&U) and the American Association for Higher Education (AAHE), have been concerned with teaching and learning in diverse classroom. Specifically, AAC&U created a multiproject initiative, American Commitments: Diversity, Democracy and Liberal Learning, to address fundamental questions about higher education in a diverse democracy (see http://www.aacu-edu.org/amcommit/index.cfm). AAHE sponsors similar initiatives that focus on inclusive teaching and learning and the importance of diversity issues in different disciplines (see http://www.aahe.org/diversityprogram.htm).

2. In this chapter, "traditional" refers to a style of teaching that has minimal professor-student interaction. In traditional teaching, only the professor is responsible for the learning that is to occur (Zimmerman, 1991). Traditional teaching requires that students be unemotional, detached, and apolitical (Adams, 1992).

3. In theory, when professors embrace students in the classroom as complete individuals with a range of personal, political, and intellectual experiences, the entire educational process is enriched because students are not forced to exclude central components of their identity.

4. Steele (1999) defines stereotype threat as "the threat of being viewed through the lens of a negative stereotype, or the fear of doing something that would inadvertently confirm that stereotype" (p. 46).

5. Equity pedagogy is a dynamic instructional process that focuses not only on the identification and use of effective instructional techniques and methods, but also on the context in which they are used (Banks & McGee, 1997).

6. Howe (1982) notes that women's studies aims "to develop a body of scholarship and a new curriculum about women and the issue of gender [and] to use this knowledge to transform mainstream curriculum" (Cited in Sullivan, 1995, p. 5).

7. Burbules and Rice (1993) assert "that there are three prospective kinds of benefits that can be derived from dialogue across differences: those related to the construction of identity along lines that are more flexible without becoming arbitrary; those related to broadening our understanding of ourselves; and those related to fostering more reasonable and sustainable communicative practices" (p. 12).

8. hooks (1994) argues that educators must enter the classroom with the assumption that they must build community in order to create a climate of openness and intellectual rigor. Rather than focusing on issues of safety, she believes that the feeling of community creates a sense that there is a shared commitment and a common good that binds students.

9. hooks (1994) asserts that exposing certain truths and biases in the classroom often creates chaos and confusion. The idea that the classroom should be a safe, harmonious place is challenged. Consequently, it is hard for individuals to fully grasp the idea that recognizing difference might also require a willingness to see the classroom change, to allow for shifts in relations between students.

10. Whipple (1987) writes: "Collaboration in undergraduate education is a pedagogical style that emphasizes cooperative efforts among students, faculty, and administrators. Rooted in the belief that learning is inherently social in nature, it stresses common inquiry as the basic learning process. Although academically and culturally challenging, it benefits participants by making them more active as learners, more interactive as teachers, more balanced as researchers, more effective as leaders, and more humane as individuals" (p. 3).

11. "Prior experiences may have created feelings of intimidation, resentment, and hurt; an imposition of silence, or the self-imposed habit of silence, may be ingrained in some of the participants. . . . One starting point in overcoming such barriers is eliciting and honoring the self-expressions of previously silenced partners" (Burbules & Rice, 1993, pp. 18–19).

12. In 1995, 73 percent of all faculty members were White (Wilds & Wilson, 1998, p. 15).

13. "This generative process of learning is most effective when instructors 1) affirm the presence and validity of diverse learning styles and 2) maximize the climate or conditions for learning in the classroom through the deliberate use of instructional design principles that take account of learning differences and increase the possibilities of success for all students" (Anderson & Adams, 1992, p. 20).

14. According to Anderson and Adams (1992), professors engage in excellent teaching if "They assess their own strengths and weaknesses. They tend to be student-centered. They posses a repertoire of alternate teaching strategies. They provide perspectives that reflect a respect for diverse views. They are well prepared and organized. They use techniques that encourage independent and critical thinking. They develop and utilize interpersonal skills that motivate students and facilitate learning" (p. 31).

15. hooks (1994) states that "there can be and usually is, some degree of pain involved in giving up old ways of thinking and knowing and learning new approaches. . . . They may recognize non-progressive thinking, racism, and so on, and it may hurt them that new ways of knowing may create estrangement where there was none" (p. 41).

REFERENCES

Adams, M. (1992). Cultural inclusion in the American college classroom. In N. V. N. Chism & L. L. B. Border (Eds.), *New directions for teaching and learning: Teaching for diversity* (vol. 49, pp. 5–17). San Francisco: Jossey-Bass.

Allen, W. (1988). The education of Black students on White college campuses: What quality the experience? In M. Nettles (Ed.), *Toward Black undergraduate student equality in American higher education* (pp. 57–86). New York: Greenwood Press.

Anderson, J., & Adams, M. (1992). Acknowledging the learning styles of diverse student populations: Implications for instructional design. In N. V. N. Chism & L. L. B. Border (Eds.), *New directions for teaching and learning: Teaching for diversity* (vol. 49, pp. 19–35). San Francisco: Jossey-Bass.

Baker, P. (1998). Students' perception of classroom factors that impact success for African-American students in higher education settings. Doctoral dissertation, Northern Illinois University, 1998. *DAI-A, 59*, p. 1434.

Banks, J. (1991). Multicultural literacy and curriculum reform. *Education Horizons Quarterly, 69*, 135–140.

Banks, J., & McGee, C. M. (1997). *Educating citizens in a multicultural society*. New York: Teachers College Press.

Bell, Y. (1994). A culturally sensitive analysis of Black learning styles: Research and teaching implications. *Journal of Black Psychology, 20*(1), 47–61.

Bruffee, K. A. (1984). Collaborative learning and the conversation of mankind. *College English, 46*, 635–640.

Bruner, J. (1996). *The culture of education*. Cambridge, MA: Harvard University Press.

Burbules, N., & Rice, S. (1993). Dialogue across difference: Continuing the conversation. In K. Geismar & G. Nicoleau (Eds.), *Teaching for change: Addressing issues of difference in the college classroom* (pp. 1–26). Cambridge, MA: Harvard Educational Review.

Courts, P. L., & McInerney, K. H. (1993). *Assessment in higher education: Politics, pedagogy, and portfolios*. Westport, CT: Praeger.

Cross, W. E., Jr., (1991). *Shades of Black: Diversity in African-American identity*. Philadelphia: Temple University Press.

Darder, A. (1996). Creating the condition for cultural democracy in the classroom. In C. Turner, M. Garcia, A. Nora, & L. I. Rendon (Eds.), *Racial and ethnic diversity in higher education* (pp. 134–149). Needham Heights, MA: Simon & Schuster.

de los Reyes, E., Smith, H., Yazzie, T., Hussein, Y., & Tuitt, F. (2001). *A democratic pedagogy for a democratic society: Education for social and political chance*. Unpublished manuscript, Harvard Graduate School of Education.

Dlamini, S. N. (2002). From the other side of the desk: Notes on teaching about race when racialized. *Race, Ethnicity, and Education, 5*(1), 51–66.

Dorsey, M., & Jackson, A. (1995). Afro-American students' perception of factors affecting academic performance at a predominantly White school. *Western Journal of Black Studies, 19*(8), 189–214.

Ellsworth, E. (1993). Why doesn't this feel empowering? Working through the repressive myths of critical pedagogy. In K. Geismar & G. Nicoleau (Eds.), *Teaching for change: Addressing issues of difference in the college classroom* (pp. 43–70). Cambridge, MA: Harvard Educational Review.

Feagin, J., & Imani, N. (1993). Black in a White world. In J. R. Feagin & M. P. Sikes, *Living with racism: The Black middle-class experience*. Boston: Beacon Press.

Frederick, P. (1995). Walking on eggs: Mastering the dreaded diversity discussions. *College Teaching, 43*(3), 83–92.

Freire, P. (1971). *Pedagogy of the oppressed*. New York: Seaview.

Freire, P. (1987). *Pedagogy of the oppressed*. New York: Continuum.

Freire, P., & Macedo, D. (1987). *Literacy: Teaching the word and the world*. Westport, CT: Bergin & Garvey.

Fuss, D. (1989). *Essentially speaking*. New York: Routledge.

Gándara, P., & Maxwell-Jolly, J. (1999). *Priming the pump: Strategies for increasing the achievement of underrepresented minority undergraduates*. New York: College Board.

Gilligan, C. (1982). *In a different voice: Psychological theory and women's development*. Cambridge, MA: Harvard University Press.

Gilligan, C., Lyons, N., & Hanmer, T. (1990). *Making connections*. Cambridge, MA: Harvard University Press.

Giroux, H., & McLaren, P. (Eds.). (1996). Teacher education and the politics of engagement: The case for democratic schooling. In P. Leistyna, A. Woodrum, & S. Sherblom (Eds.), *Breaking free: The transformative power of critical pedagogy* (pp. 301–332). Cambridge, MA: Harvard Educational Review.

Giroux, H. A. (1988). Postmodernism and the discourse of educational criticism. *Journal of Education, 170*(3), 5–30.

Giroux, H. A. (1992). *Border crossings: Cultural workers and the politics of education*. New York: Routledge.

Giroux, H. A., & Simon, R. (1988). Schooling, popular culture, and the pedagogy of possibility. *Journal of Education, 170*(1), 9–26.

Helms, J. E. (Ed.). (1990). *Black and White racial identity; Theory, research, and practice*. Westport, CT: Greenwood Press.

Henry, A. (1992). African, Canadian women teachers' activism: Recreating communities of caring and resistance. *Journal of Negro Education, 61*, 392–404.

Hill-Collins, P. (1990). *Black feminist thought: Knowledge, consciousness and pedagogy*. Boston: Unwin Hyman.

hooks, b. (1994). *Teaching to transgress: Education as the practice of freedom*. New York: Routledge.

Howe, K. G. (1985). Psychological impact of a woman's studies. *Women's Studies Quarterly, 13*, 23–24.

Hurtado, S., Milem, J., Clayton-Pederson, A., & Allen, W. (2000). *Enacting diverse learning environments: Improving the climate for racial/ethnic diversity in higher education*. Washington, DC: George Washington University Press.

Irvine, J., & York, D. (1995). Learning styles and culturally diverse students: A literature review. In C. Banks & J. Banks (Eds.), *Handbook of research on multicultural education* (pp. 484–497). New York: Macmillian.

Karenga, M. (1995). Afrocentricity and multicultural education: Concept, challenge, and contribution. In B. P. Bowser, T. Jones, & G. A. Young (Eds.), *Toward the multicultural university* (pp. 41–61). Westport, CT: Praeger.

King, W. M. (1995). The triumphs of tribalism: The modern American university as reflection of Eurocentric culture. In B. P. Bowser, T. Jones, & G. A. Young (Eds.), *Toward the multicultural university* (pp. 41–61). Westport, CT: Praeger.

Knefelkamp, L. (1997). Effective teaching for the multicultural. *Diversity Digest, 2*(1), 11–12.

Ladson-Billings, G. (1994). *The dreamkeepers: Successful teachers of African-American children.* San Francisco: Jossey-Bass.

Ladson-Billings, G. (1995). Toward a theory of culturally relevant teaching. *American Educational Research Journal, 32,* 465–491.

Lynn, M. (1999). Toward a critical race pedagogy: A research note. *Urban Education, 33,* 606–626.

Macedo, D., & Freire, P. (Eds.). (1996). A dialogue: culture, language, and race. In P. Leistnya, A. Woodrum, & S. Sherblom (Eds.), *Breaking free: The transformative power of critical pedagogy* (pp. 199–228). Cambridge, MA: Harvard Educational Review.

Moos, R. H. (1979). *Evaluating educational environments: Procedures, measures, findings, and policy implications.* San Francisco: Jossey-Bass.

Murrel, P. C. (2002) *African-centered pedagogy: Developing schools of achievement for African American children.* Albany: State University of New York Press.

Nelson, C. (1996). Student diversity requires different approaches to college teaching, even in math and science. *American Behavioral Scientist, 40,* 165–175.

Obiakor, F. E. (1994). *Multiculturalism in the university curriculum: Infusion for what?* Paper presented at the Regents Conference on Diversity and Multiculturalism in the University, Manhattan, Kansas.

Obidah, J. (2000). Mediating boundaries of race, class and professorial authority as a critical multiculturalist. *Teachers College Record, 102,* 1035–1061.

Omolade, B. (1987). A Black feminist pedagogy. *Women's Studies Quarterly, 15*(3/4), 32–40.

Palmer, P. J. (1993). Good talk about good teaching: Improving conversation through community. *Change, 25*(6), 8–13.

Prince, C. D. W., & Igbineweka, A. O. (1995). *The social and political dimensions of achieving a multicultural college curriculum.* Paper presented at the 25th Silver Anniversary Celebration of the Pennsylvania Black Conference on Higher Education, Philadelphia.

Severance, T. N. (1993). *Student and faculty perceptions of higher education: The ethos of culturally diverse learning environments (student perceptions).* Nashville, TN: Vanderbilt University Press.

Shade, B. (1984). *Afro-American patterns of cognition: A review of research.* Paper presented at the annual meeting of the American Educational Research Association, New Orleans.

Shaw, C. C.. (1996). Instructural pluralism: A means to realizing the dream of multicultural, social reconstructionist education. In C. Grant & M. Gomez (Eds.), *Making schooling multicultural: Campus and classroom* (pp. 55–76). Englewood Cliffs, NJ: Merrill.

Shor, I. (1992). *Empowering education: Critical teaching for social change.* Chicago: University of Chicago Press.

Shulman, L. S. (1993). Teaching as community property: Putting an end to pedagogical solitude. *Change, 25*(6), 8–9.

Sorlorzano, D., & Yosso, T. (1997). Toward a critical race theory of Chicana and Chicano education. In C. Tejada, C. Martinez, Z. Leonardo, & P. McLaren (Eds.), *Demarcating the border of Chicana(o)/Latina(o) education* (pp. 35–65). Cresskill, NJ: Hampton Press.

Steele, C. (1977). A threat in the air: How stereotypes shape intellectual identity and performance. *American Psychologist, 52,* 613–629.

Steele, C. M. (1999, August). Thin ice: "Stereotype threat" and Black college students. *Atlantic Monthly,* pp. 44–54.

Sullivan, A. V. S. (1995). Realizing the vision: Transforming the curriculum through women's studies. *Journal of General Education, 44*(1), 45–57.

Tatum, B. (1992). Talking about race, learning about racism: The application of racial identity development theory in the classroom. *Harvard Educational Review, 62*, 1–24.

Tuitt, F. A. (2000). *Towards a more inclusive pedagogy: Rethinking how we teach racially diverse college classrooms.* Unpublished qualifying paper, Harvard Graduate School of Education, Cambridge, MA.

Weiler, K. (1993). Freire and a feminist pedagogy of difference. *Harvard Educational Review, 61*, 449–474.

Whipple, W. R. (1987). Collaborative learning: Recognizing it when you see it. *AAHE Bulletin, 40*(2), 3–7.

Wilds, D., & Wilson, R. (1998). *Minorities in higher education, 15th Annual Status Report.* Washington, DC: American Council on Education.

Young, I. M. (1996). Communication and the other: Beyond deliberative democracy. In S. Benhabig (Ed.), *Democracy and difference: Contesting the boundaries of the political* (pp.120–136). Princeton, NJ: Princeton University Press.

Zimmerman, M. H. (1991). *Perspectives on the interpersonal relationships of learners in college learning communities.* Seattle: Seattle University Press.

ABOUT THE CONTRIBUTORS

Marilyn Cochran-Smith is a professor of education and director of the Doctoral Program in Curriculum and Instruction at Boston College. Her research and writing center around teacher education and teacher research, as well as issues of diversity in schools and universities. She is coauthor, with K. Fries, of "Sticks, Stones, and Ideology: The Discourse of Reform in Teacher Education" in *Educational Researcher* (2001) and, with S. Lytle, of "Relationships of Knowledge and Practice: Teacher Learning in Communities" in *Review of Research in Education* (edited by A. Iran-Nejad and C. D. Pearson, 1999). She is also editor of the *Journal of Teacher Education* and a cochair of the AERA National Consensus Panel on Teacher Education.

Eric L. Dey is executive associate dean and an associate professor at the University of Michigan School of Education in Ann Arbor. His research is concerned with the ways that colleges and universities shape the experiences and lives of students and faculty. He is coauthor, with J. F. Milem and J. B. Berger, of "Faculty Time Allocation: A Study of Change over Twenty Years" in the *Journal of Higher Education* (2000) and, with S. H. Taylor and K. M. Borland, of "Accountability Planning as a Strategic Tool for Change" in the *Journal of Career Planning and Employment* (2000).

Paulo Freire was a world-renowned educator who conducted literacy campaigns throughout the world, particularly in developing countries. Among the many books he wrote, he is best known for his classic work, *The Pedagogy of the Oppressed* (1970). Friere was exiled from Brazil for more than sixteen years for teaching peasants to read. He later served as Secretary of Education in São Paulo and was a professor of literacy and educational theory at Pontifícia Universidade Católica São Paulo. He died in 1997.

Gerald Gurin is a professor and research scientist emeritus at the University of Michigan in Ann Arbor. Since his retirement, he has continued to conduct research with the university's Office of Academic Multi-Cultural Initiatives. A major focus of his research and teaching is the impact of higher education on students and the increasing inclusion of racial/ethnic minorities in higher education. His publications include *Inner-City Negro Youth in a Job Training Project: A Study of Factors Related to Attrition and Job Success* (1968) and *Americans View Their Mental Health* (1957).

Patricia Gurin is a professor of psychology at the University of Michigan in Ann Arbor. Her professional interests include the social psychology of group identity, intergroup relations, and race and politics. She is the author of numerous books and articles, including the forthcoming *Defending Diversity: Michigan's Affirmative Action Cases*, with J. Lehman and E. Lewis, and "Preparation for Citizenship," with R. Nagda and G. Lopez, in *Journal of Social Issues*.

Annie Howell is a doctoral candidate at the Harvard Graduate School of Education, where she works as a teaching fellow and a facilitator for the Harvard Institute for School Leadership. She is also a doctoral fellow with the Change Leadership Group and a former cochair of the *Harvard Educational Review*. Her research centers on adult transformational learning.

Sylvia Hurtado is associate professor and director of the Center for the Study of Higher and Postsecondary Education at the University of Michigan in Ann Arbor. Her research centers on how colleges impact students' cognitive, social, and democratic skills to participate in a diverse society. She is coeditor, with D. Schoem, of *Intergroup Dialogue: Deliberative Democracy in School, College, Community, and Workplace* (2001), and coauthor, with J. Milem, A. Clayton-Pederson, and W. Allen, of *Enacting Diverse Learning Environments: Improving the Climate for Racial/Ethnic Diversity in Higher Education* (1999).

Kevin K. Kumashiro is director of the Center for Anti-Oppressive Education in El Cerrito, California. He has worked previously as a teacher and teacher educator in elementary and secondary schools and colleges. He is author of *Troubling Education: Queer Activism and Anti-Oppressive Pedagogy* (2002) and editor of *Troubling Intersections of Race and Sexuality: Queer Students of Color and Anti-Oppressive Education* (2001).

Donaldo P. Macedo is a distinguished professor of liberal arts and education and director of the Applied Linguistics Graduate Program at the University of Massachusetts Boston. His research interests are literacy, linguistics, language education, and critical pedagogy. He is coauthor of *Ideology Matters* (in press) and *Literacy: Reading the Word and the World* (1987), both with P. Freire, and editor of *Noam Chomsky on MisEducation* (2000).

Frances A. Maher is a professor in the Education Department of Wheaton College, located in Norton, Massachusetts. Her professional interests center around feminist pedagogy and women's studies. She is coauthor, with M. K. Tetreault, of *The Feminist Classroom: Dynamics of Gender, Race, and Privilege* (2nd ed., 2001) and author of *"Women's Ways of Knowing* in Women's Studies, Feminist Pedagogies, and Feminist Theory" in *Knowledge, Difference, and Power: Essays Inspired by* Women's Ways of Knowing (1996).

Sondra Perl is a professor of English and Urban Education at the City University of New York Graduate Center. She is interested in cross-cultural dialogue, teaching as a site of inquiry, and asking what it means to foster an ethics of education. Her latest book is *On Austrian Soil: Teaching Those I Was Taught to Hate* (in press).

Beverly Daniel Tatum is president of Spelman College in Atlanta, Georgia. She is the former dean and acting president of Mount Holyoke College, and a clinical psychologist. Her professional expertise includes Black families in White America, racial identity in teens, and race in the classroom. A fifth-anniversary edition of her book *Why Are All the Black Kids Sitting Together in the Cafeteria: And Other Conversations about Race* was released in January 2003. She is also the author of *Assimilation Blues: Black Families in a White Community* (1987).

Mary Kay Thompson Tetreault is provost and vice president for academic affairs at Portland State University in Oregon. Her research interests include feminist pedagogy, social constructions of Whiteness, and the epistemology of knowing and learning. She is coauthor, with F. Maher, of *The Feminist Classroom: Dynamics of Gender, Race, and Privilege* (2nd ed., 2001) and author of *"They Got the Paradigm and Painted It White: Higher Education Classrooms and Legal Discourse"* in the *Duke Journal of Gender Law and Policy* (1997).

Frank Tuitt is an advanced doctoral student at the Harvard Graduate School of Education and a research assistant for the National Campus Diversity Project. He is also a former cochair of the *Harvard Educational Review*. His dissertation, "Black Souls in an Ivory Tower: Understanding What It Means to Teach in a Manner That Respects and Cares for the Souls of African American Graduate Students," seeks to identify the pedagogical practices and learning conditions that African American graduate students identify as most beneficial to their learning. Tuitt is a 1987 graduate of Connecticut College.

Barbara Vacarr is an associate professor at Lesley University in Cambridge, Massachusetts. She is also a psychologist in private practice. Her areas of professional interest include adult learning and development, transformational education, and transpersonal psychology. She is author of "Power of Place, Power of Story: A Co-Transformational Journey" in *Challenges of Practice: Transformative Learning in Action* (2000) and "Stories of the Holocaust: Teaching the Hidden Narrative" in the *Journal of Power, Pedagogy, and Practice* (1997).

Kathleen Weiler is a professor of education at Tufts University in Medford, Massachusetts. Her professional interests center on women and education. She is editor of *Feminist Engagements* (2001), *Country Schoolwomen: Teaching in the California Countryside, 1850–1950* (1998), and *Women Teaching for Change* (1988).